THE
POLITICS AND PHILOSOPHY
OF ECONOMICS

Marxians, Keynesians and Austrians

T. W. HUTCHISON

NEW YORK UNIVERSITY PRESS
NEW YORK AND LONDON
1981

First published in 1981 by
New York University Press
Washington Square
New York, NY 10003

Library of Congress Card Catalog Number 81–11239

ISBN 0–8147–3416–2

Printed in Great Britain

Contents

Foreword   vi

Acknowledgements   ix

1   Friedrich Engels and Marxian Political
Economy   1

2   The Market Economy and the Franchise,
or 1867 and All That   23

3   The Philosophy and Politics of the
Cambridge School   46

4   Keynes *versus* the Keynesians   108

5   Walter Eucken and the German Social–Market
Economy   155

6   Carl Menger on Philosophy and Method   176

7   Austrians on Philosophy and Method
(since Menger)   203

8   The Limitations of General Theories
in Macroeconomics   233

9   On the Aims and Methods of Economic
Theorizing   266

Index   308

Foreword

About a hundred years ago 'Political Economy' became 'Economics'. This happened at a phase (briefly described in chapter 2) when the interconnections and interdependencies of economics and politics were at an all-time low – though still, it could be argued, of fundamental importance. The role of government in the economy was minute compared with today, just beginning its long, vast expansion. The political and social framework of the economy (as well as the monetary framework) seemed *comparatively* stable, though, with hindsight, the initial moves in a long revolution are discernible. During this period it was natural for economists to focus their interests, in theory and policy, primarily on what has come to be called 'microeconomics', that is, on processes and policies small enough to be examined on the assumption that their effects on the political and social order would be negligible.

Today, with such an extended role for government the outlook is very different. The political and social order is far from 'given' or stable. 'Macro' policies and theories dominate economic analysis. The interconnections and interdependencies between economics and politics are much more important and complex. But the subject is still called 'Economics', and in textbooks and academic departments, it is still presented as separate from 'Politics'. Nor, in these highly specialized times, can it be expected that people will emerge who can combine the treatment of economics with that of political theory and processes in the manner of such past masters as Hume, Smith, Mill and Sidgwick. Consequently, politics have come back into economics to a major extent, both normatively in respect of values and objectives, and positively regarding processes and institutions: but often inexplicitly or naively or crudely. Moreover, political issues are often vitally, if latently, involved in methodological debates, as we show in chapters 1, 7 and 9.

In this volume we examine some of the political, philosophical and epistemological presuppositions of three currently much discussed schools of thought, or types of economic theory, Marxian, Keynesian and Austrian. Other economists or schools figure more briefly in these pages, in particular Marshall and the pre-Keynesian (and pre-Marxian) Cambridge school, and Eucken and the Freiburg school. The last two chapters are concerned with general methodological or politico-philosophical issues, rather than with the ideas of particular economists or schools.

The table of contents indicates the mainly, but not strictly, chronological sequence of topics. Here, we would simply call attention to some of the themes which recur in different parts of the book.

One theme, which figures in chapters 1, 7 and 9, is concerned with the political significance of different methodological or epistemological doctrines: that is, with how an empirical, fallibilist epistemology is compatible with libertarian values in a way in which epistemological infallibilism is not. Such infallibilism, in the methodology of economics, has been based either – as with the Marxian school – on a nineteenth-century, dogmatic scientism, claiming the authority of certainty; or, as with Mises, and some of his Austrian followers, on a priorist claims to 'apodictic certainty' – though, as we observe in chapters 6 and 7, Austrians, ancient and modern, have been far from united on these methodological issues.

A second, normative and even, to some extent, political theme is that of the desirability of methodological distinctions, demarcations and discipline in economics (including, as far as possible, which is quite far, the normative-positive distinction) as against the rejection of distinctions and discipline and the proclamation and practice of 'Anything Goes'. Chapter 3 on the Cambridge School may be regarded as a kind of cautionary tale on this subject, while chapter 9 argues the case in general terms.

A third, less political, subject is that of excessive claims to generality on behalf of macroeconomic and politico-economic theories and models, in particular, those of the Marxians and Keynesians (see chapters 1, 4 and 8). Such excessive epistemological aims and claims regarding the generality of economic theories sometimes seem to stem from a failure fully to recognize vital differences between the material of economics and that of the natural sciences, and hence to take account of the obsolescence which afflicts many economic theories and models in the course of historical and institutional change. Such obsolescence tends to be met by *ad hoc* shifts and stratagems by those trying to cling to a kind of generality. In the nineteenth century, with a slower rate of change, this kind of obsolescence developed more gradually and there was more time for adaptation. But today an all-too-apparent phenomenon is the clinging to general theories rendered obsolete by historical-institutional change.

Finally, a recurring political theme deals with how political and historical changes shape and transform demands on economic policy, and place constraints on the acceptability of the answers which economists try to provide. In chapter 2 are traced the changes in demands on economic policy resulting from the successive extensions of the franchise in Britain in the nineteenth century. In chapter 5 it is shown how the sharply contrasting political and economic histories of Britain and Germany between 1914 and 1945 – in particular, regarding inflation and deflation, and the experience of central planning – shaped the expectations, fears and hopes of politicians and public, and placed differing constraints on the kind of policy ideas that were acceptable. It is, however, also shown that when, as in the German Federal Republic after World War II, the conjuncture of history, events and experience 'conspires' (as J. S. Mill put it) with the emergence of appropriate economic ideas, then these ideas are not slow in having the most powerful and beneficent results.

Birmingham, January 1981   T.W.H.

Acknowledgements

·

Six of these papers have appeared in print before. They have been more or less heavily revised for this volume. Three have not appeared before. Details are as follows.

'Friedrich Engels and Marxian Political Economy' appeared first as a review article of the two-volume *Life of Friedrich Engels* by W. O. Henderson (1977), in *The Journal of Political Economy*, 1978, vol. 86, no. 2, pt 1, pp. 303ff. A few quotations, together with a methodological conclusion, have been added, and an opening section has been removed.

'The Market Economy and the Franchise, or 1867 and All That' was published under a slightly different title as an Occasional Paper by the Institute of Economic Affairs in 1966. Some additions have been made and the final section has been removed and replaced by a briefer summary.

'The Philosophy and Politics of the Cambridge School' has been written in the summer of 1980 and, apart from a 600-word Comment on this subject in the first number of the *Journal of Economic Affairs* (Blackwell), has not appeared before.

'Keynes *versus* the Keynesians' was published (with comments by Professors Lord Kahn and E. A. G. Robinson) as a Hobart Paper by the IEA in 1977. A number of additions have been made arising out of the abundant subsequent literature on this subject. The original version was published in Italian in the journal *Bancaria*, nos 1, 2 and 3 of 1978, and as a separate booklet. The translation was provided by the Servizio Studi dell'Associazone Bancaria Italiana. A Spanish edition has also appeared, translated by F. Muñoz de Bustillo, with an introduction by José Antonio Aguirre (Espasa-Calpe S.A., Madrid, 1980).

'Walter Eucken and the German Social-Market Economy' was published under a slightly different title in the *Zeitschrift für die gesamte Staatswissenschaft* (vol. 135, no. 3, Sept. 1979, pp. 426ff) as part of a Symposium on Currency and Economic Reform in West Germany after World War II.

The paper on Carl Menger was first given at a Symposium held at Vienna in 1971 to celebrate the centenary of the publication of his *Grundsätze der Volkswirtschaftslehre*. It was subsequently published in 1973 in a volume, *Carl Menger and the Austrian School of Economics*, edited by J. R. Hicks and W. Weber (Oxford University Press). Considerable alterations and additions have been made arising out of the recent markedly growing literature on this subject.

The continuation of the preceding paper, on Austrians since Menger, has not been published before. It was, in part, delivered as a paper at the History of Economic Thought Conference at the University of Bath in September 1979. I am most grateful for the comments and criticisms at that meeting.

'The Limitations of General Theories in Macroeconomics' was first given as a paper at a Seminar of the American Enterprise Institute in Washington in October 1979 and has been published as a pamphlet by the Institute (1980). I am most grateful to Professors Gottfried Haberler and William J. Fellner for valuable advice. An expanded version of this paper was given as two lectures at the American University in Cairo in March 1980, and I am very grateful for the stimulating discussion, and for the generous hospitality of the AUC; and in particular to Dean Lamont, Professor Sullivan, and Professor Michael Harvey-Phillips.

'On the Aims and Methods of Economic Theorizing' has not been published before. This paper is an attempt to restate my views on a subject to which, at various times over the years, I have tried to contribute. It draws briefly on the Preface to the 1960 edition of *The Significance and Basic Postulates of Economic Theory*, and also on a paper entitled 'The Natural and the Social Sciences and the Development and Underdevelopment of Economics', which was published (in German translation by Gretl Albert) in the volume *Theorie und Erfahrung, Beiträge zur Grundlagenproblematik der Sozialwissenschaften*, edited by H. Albert and K. H. Stapf, 1979.

I am indebted to the editors and publishers mentioned above for permission, where necessary, to republish.

I wish to add my warm thanks to Diana Sheedy for her devoted work on the typescipt of this as on previous books of mine.

1

Friedrich Engels and
Marxian Political Economy

Engels's writings on political economy date from two periods, early and late, with a large 20–30-year blank in the middle. The early period consists mainly of the 1840s, when Engels (b. 1820) was in his 20s. His severely bourgeois, industrialist, Pietist and monarchist father intended a career in the family textile business for his eldest son. Engels, deeply attached to his mother, rebelled vehemently against his father at an early age and against all his political, social and religious beliefs, protesting that 'he would not make even the pettiest concession to a fanatical and tyrannical old man' (Carlton, 1965, p. 33).

After a reluctant apprenticeship in the family firm in Barmen, and then in a firm in Bremen (1837–41), Engels departed to do his military service in Berlin (1841–42), finding time there to join up with the Young Hegelians centred on the university and to imbibe their heady, radical ideas about religion, philosophy and politics. But the decisive influence in his conversion to communism was that of Moses Hess, 'the Communist rabbi', whom he met in Cologne (1842) as one of the editors of the *Rheinische Zeitung* (another being the youthful Marx).

However, in 1842, Engels's own burgeoning political interests happened to coincide with his father's business plans. His father wanted him in the Manchester branch of his firm. Engels himself, under the influence of Hess, saw Manchester as the centre of the English industrial revolution, which would soon, inevitably, be followed by a political revolution. Manchester, therefore, was the place where the politicoeconomic action was, or was soon going to be. In fact, it was in his first stay in Manchester (1842–44) that Engels wrote or gathered, the material for his seminal works, and that Marxian political economy may be said to have been conceived. After 20 months he broke away, and it was on his way home via Paris that the fateful meeting with Marx took place (August 1844) and the lifelong partnership was launched. Engels spent most of the rest of the decade as a roaming freelance journalist and revolutionary in Belgium, France, Germany and Switzerland.

By the end of 1849, however, with the revolutionary movement on the Continent in a state of collapse, Engels and the Marx family found themselves destitute refugees in England. Engels was a brilliant journalist and linguist and could probably have supported himself in much more congenial work. But to obtain financial security for himself and the Marx family, he returned for the next 20 years to the Manchester office of the family firm. He sacrificed the prime years of his life to support the rapidly growing Marx family and the writing of *Das Kapital*.

Eventually in 1869, reaching 50, Engels was able to sell out his share in the business and to retire as a wealthy man in considerable comfort, while continuing to support the Marx family with its largely bourgeois aspirations.[1] In fact, one of the few respects in which the family was not thoroughly and admirably bourgeois in its tastes and life-style (piano and drawing lessons for the daughters, balls, seaside holidays, cures at fashionable spas, etc.) was that the paterfamilias himself never accepted much financial responsibility for the support of his wife and numerous offspring (legitimate and illegitimate). At any rate, in addition to his vast and essential intellectual and financial contributions, Engels also rendered Marx another remarkable service by accepting paternity of Marx's illegitimate son Freddy Demuth (b. 1851), who, incidentally, was quite disgracefully treated by both Marx and (much more strangely) Engels. But Dr and Mrs Marx were thus enabled to 'keep up appearances', which meant so much to them. (No wonder a note of hysteria, exceptional even for Marx, is detectable in his references to Parson Malthus on population.)[2]

Active up to his death, much of Engels's energy after his retirement from business (1869–95) went into editing Marx's voluminous manuscripts. But in prefaces and articles, Engels managed to contribute, in this second, later period, several interesting insights qualifying or supplementing Marxist economic doctrines.

II

A review of Engels's economic writings must begin with his remarkable essay 'Outlines of a Critique of Political Economy', first published in 1844 (see Henderson, ed. 1967). Schumpeter dismisses this work as 'a distinctly weak performance' (1954, p. 386). By some standards this is so. The essay contains many crudities. But (1) it was written by a 23-year-old autodidact, without formal higher education, starting simply from his own voracious reading of Smith, Ricardo, McCulloch, Say, List, and others; (2) Engels's essay preceded all of Marx's economic writings and played a vital part in turning Marx's interests from philosophy to political economy; and (3) Engels announced here what were to become two or three of the most interesting and least invalid themes of Marxist political economy (recognized as such by Schumpeter).

Of the important ideas outlined by Engels there is, first, his emphasis on periodic crises. Engels sees economic activity in a constant state of oscillation and disequilibrium. There are forces on the side of bringing supply and demand into equilibrium, but, according to Engels, this is never attained and hardly even approached. Engels maintains that economists regard this equilibrating tendency as a 'law':

Economists regard this law as their chief glory. They cannot see enough of it and they study it in all possible and impossible applications. . . . Economists come along with this wonderful law of supply and demand and prove that 'one can never produce too much.' Practice replies with trade crises which reappear as regularly as the comets. . . . What are we to think of a law that can assert itself only through periodic slumps? (Henderson, ed., 1967, pp. 165–6)

Engels makes the prediction that these crises will get worse: 'Every new crisis must be more serious and more universal than the last. Every fresh slump must ruin more small capitalists and increase the workers who live only by their labour.' (Henderson, ed., 1967, p. 166)

Right or wrong, here is a central theme of Marxist political economy; and if Engels and Marx grossly exaggerated instability and disequilibrium, surely Smith, Ricardo and Mill erred somewhat in the opposite direction. Schumpeter himself stated regarding Marx's treatment of business fluctuations that 'the mere

perception of the existence of cyclical movements was a great
achievement of the time' (1962, p. 40). This perception, as far as
Marxian political economy is concerned, was largely due to the
23-year-old autodidact, Engels.

A second of Marx's major contributions, according to
Schumpeter (1962, p. 34), was his prediction regarding business
concentration: 'To predict the advent of big business was,
considering the conditions of Marx's day, an achievement in
itself.' This 'achievement' is to be found, well before Marx
developed the theme, outlined in Engels's youthful essay:

It is well known that large manufacturers and merchants enjoy great
advantages over their smaller rivals and that big landowners enjoy great
advantages over smallholders who are cultivating only a single acre. The
result is that under normal conditions, large capital and large landed
property swallow small capital and small landed property. This leads to
the concentration of property. When there are depressions in industry
and agriculture this process of concentration is greatly accelerated. . . .
The middle classes must increasingly disappear until the world is divided
into millionaires and paupers and into large landowners and poor farm
labourers. (Henderson, ed., 1967, p. 174)

Crude stuff perhaps, written before the development of the
joint-stock company, but an important element in the formation
of Marxist political economy. Henderson is well justified in
concluding regarding these ideas of Engels: 'He was one of the
first to discuss the trade cycle and the existence of a pool of
unemployed workers and to offer explanations for these phenomena. He saw the significance of the growth of big business at
the expense of small undertakings. These topics were later
discussed more thoroughly by Karl Marx, but to deal with them
all in 1845 was no mean achievement.' (p. 72)

Third, an emphasis on technological change and its implications
has been held to be one of the most significant contributions of
Marxist political economy, as contrasted with classical orthodoxy
(or what Jevons was to call the Ricardo-Mill economics). The
youthful Engels's ponderous sarcasm at the expense of the
orthodoxy of his time was not entirely unjustified: 'Economists
regard land, capital and labour as the conditions of wealth and that
is all. Science is no concern of the economists. What does it matter
to the economists that they have received the gifts of science
through the work of men like Berthollet, Davy, Liebig, Watt and

Cartwright? And have not the advances in Science greatly increased production?' (Henderson, ed., 1967, p. 159)

Engels proceeds to counter Malthus:

The amount of land is limited. That is agreed. The labour force which can be used on this land increases as the population grows. Let us even assume that the increase in the yield of crops brought about by the expansion of the labour force does not always rise in proportion to the increased labour force. Even so there is another factor to be considered. This is the advance of scientific knowledge. And this of course is ignored by the economists. The progress of scientific knowledge is as unceasing and at least as rapid as the growth of population. . . . Population grows in proportion to the size of the last generation. Scientific knowledge advances in proportion to the knowledge bequeathed to it by the previous generation. And this progress, under the most ordinary conditions, is also in geometrical progression. What is impossible to science? (Henderson, ed., 1967, p. 173)

However, as the last sentence indicates, Engels by no means confined himself to a valid and valuable emphasis on scientific and technological progress as a factor in economic development; he went on to indulge, as we shall see, in the wildest Utopian fantasies about how technological change would abolish scarcity and so lay the essential foundations for communism.

But Engels's interest in the economic roles of science and technology led him to what might have been a fruitful point about factors and the cost of production. Engels insists that there is a third separate factor in addition to land and labour (including capital as stored-up labour): 'There is a third element that economists ignore. That is the mental element of thought and invention *which is different from the physical element of sheer labour*' (Henderson, ed., 1967, p. 159, italics added). This distinction of Engels is certainly fatal to the fundamental Marxian concept of homogeneous labour power as the sole human source of value. It even suggests the idea of innovation as a vital agent earning remuneration. Of course such dangerous thoughts would have undermined from the start the whole development of the Marxian system. No wonder, decades later, in his last years, Engels refused permission for an English translation of his youthful 'Outline' as 'not only full of mistakes but actual howlers' (Carlton, 1965, p. 219).

This brings us to the centrepiece of Marxist economic theory to which, to his credit, Engels did not contribute. This is the

Marxian ideological pseudotheory of value and exploitation – described as 'incantations' even by so enthusiastic a Marxian as Professor Joan Robinson (1966, p. 22). In fact, perpetrating another 'howler', Engels pointed to the obvious inadequacy of the labour-cost theory: 'Imagine someone making an utterly useless article with great exertion and at great expense. And suppose that no one wants this article. Do production costs represent the "value" of such a commodity? "Of course not," says the economist. "Who will want to buy it?" So we suddenly have both Say's despised utility but (with the idea of buying) competition as well.' (Henderson, ed., 1967, p. 156)

Engels then goes for a Marshallian 'both blades of the scissors' approach, including both the elements (cost and utility) so exclusively stressed on the one hand by Ricardo and on the other by Say: 'The value of an article includes both the factors which contending economists have so rudely and so unsuccessfully attempted to separate' (Henderson, ed., 1967, p. 157). But again, from the standpoint of what was subsequently to emerge as dogmatic Marxian orthodoxy, these were dangerous thoughts, or 'howlers'.

III

The second of Engels's sociopolitico/economic works dating from this early period in the 1940s is his well-known book *The Condition of the Working Class in England* (1845). Again, Schumpeter's description of this work as 'a creditable piece of factual research' (1954, p. 386n) is uncharacteristically less than adequate. The leading German historical economist Bruno Hildebrand, though severely critical of Engels's interpretations of English statistics, concluded a 70-page review with the verdict that Engels was 'the most gifted and knowledgeable German writer on social problems' (quoted Henderson 1976, p. 64). After every appropriate reservation, this is not bad for a 24-year-old autodidact.

It was housing conditions in Manchester, aggravated by a large Irish immigration, that received young Engels's special attention. Here again, support is sought from the orthodox classicals. He cites Nassau Senior on housing, who recommended a considerable role for government with regard to housing, and according to whom the new industrial towns 'have been erected by small speculators with an utter disregard to everything except immediate profit' (Henderson, ed., 1967, p. 51). (Under 'everything', Senior was presumably including what have come to be called 'externalities'.) It was in his survey of housing in Manchester that Engels developed what was to become Marx's most effective, empirically based method, or source. Henderson observes:

A comparison between Engels's book and certain sections of the first volume of *Das Kapital* – for example Marx's discussion of the working day – shows how much Marx owed to his friend's book. It was from Engels that Marx learned how to make effective use of evidence collected by parliamentary commissions, by the Registrar General, and by factory inspectors to gain a real insight into the workings of the industrial economy. (p. 73)

It is from the broader aspects of the economic and political development of England that Engels's book derives much of its interest today.[3] When he first went to England, Engels at once found there what his preconceived ideas had told him he would find. These ideas were derived from Moses Hess, who had just published an article with the ominous title, 'On an Impending Catastrophe in England', in which he remarked:

England, where distress has reached frightful proportions, is heading for a catastrophe sooner than had been expected. And no one can foretell the consequences that this catastrophe will have not only for Great Britain but also for the Continent. . . . Industry has passed from the hands of the people to the machines of the capitalists. Commerce – formerly operated on a modest scale by many small merchants – is now concentrated more and more in the hands of capitalists and adventurers (i.e. swindlers). The land has fallen into the grasp of a few aristocratic families owing to the working of the laws of inheritance. In fact a few great families expand and control ever greater amounts of capital. . . . (Hess, 1842; as translated by Henderson, 1976, pp. 21, 39)

Certainly these seem exaggeratedly catastrophic forebodings, markedly proto-Marxist in tendency. A profound and perhaps much more accurate comment on the political setting of 'the industrial revolution' in England was supplied in a very interesting anonymous review article on Engels's work in the *Allgemeine Preussische Zeitung*, which Henderson has translated and appended among the documents (pp. 311ff). The Prussian reviewer, after remarking that 'the author appears to be a young man in a hurry', makes a fundamental point regarding the political conditions in which industrial development was taking place in England. The reviewer rejects Engels's argument that it was industrialism as such that was responsible for the condition of the working class in England, so violently denounced by Engéls (and Moses Hess) – it is the workers' lack of political power which is the vital element:

The industrial revolution has taken place within the framework of an aristocratic constitution. . .
. Why should industry plunge the workers into poverty and distress and turn them into a proletariat? Certainly not because industry, as such, brings distress in its wake. If that were true then industry would be an evil whereas in fact it benefits humanity. The unsatisfactory condition of the workers can be explained by the fact that when modern industry began to grow in England the impact of the new type of economy was felt by a society in which it was already inevitable that the workers should fall upon evil days. . .
A small group of wealthy persons have been able to gain control over all effective political power. It is most unfortunate that this autocratic power has not been checked in any way by the higher authority of the monarchy. In a country with such a constitution the worker is in an utterly helpless situation. (Henderson, 1976, pp. 312, 316, italics added)

Of course, as Adam Smith had observed, in labour markets there tended to be a strong element of monopsony, with trade unions prohibited. In fact, the reviewer goes on to observe how Engels:

shows how this situation conforms to the doctrines enunciated by the well-known economist Adam Smith. There is much that is new and interesting in Engels's discussion of the failure to establish a balance between the competition among the workers themselves and the competition (among the employers) to secure the services of workers. The first (competition among the workers) has always been stronger than the second (competition among employers for labour) and this has happened despite the continual expansion of industry and the ever increasing demand for labour. (p. 321)

It was only after the reform of 1867 (coincidentally, of course, the year of the publication of *Das Kapital*) that the political power of propertyless workers gradually began to develop, together with the removal, and in due course reversal, of the general imbalance in labour markets and the rise to power of trade unions. There was a wide difference, sometimes forgotten, between the political conditions and distribution of political power under which the market economy was developed in England, as contrasted with the United States. It has recently been observed regarding the United States:

At the beginning of the nineteenth century, the natural rights justification for property was entirely compatible with a decentralized market economy. Under these circumstances, it was still possible to believe that those who engaged in market transactions possessed relatively equal bargaining power and that the results of the market system would produce a reliable distribution of rewards according to the ability and energy of those who participated. Indeed, the market was thought to be the most powerful institutional expression of the ideal of equality of opportunity. (Horwitz, 1976, p. 629)

It was never easy to believe this as regards England for much of the earlier part of the nineteenth century, with the distribution of the franchise and political power as they then were. In Britain the market economy was imposed under a very restricted franchise, with strict property qualifications. This may have had serious and lasting results, as contrasted with countries where it was introduced under different political or electoral conditions.

IV

The third work of Engels from this early period, partly on political economy, is his essay entitled 'The Principles of Communism' (written in November 1847), of which Henderson supplies an English translation. Engels's essay, in the form of a catechism, can be described as a first draft of the *Communist Manifesto* (put together by Marx and Engels a few weeks later). But Engels's 'Principles' contains one highly significant theme, omitted from the *Manifesto*, regarding the organization of the future communist economy which will emerge after the rapidly approaching collapse of capitalism. Not that Engels is at all clear about the workings of the communist economy. He does not get beyond the airiest generalizations and gestures. But he is highly revealing regarding the underlying assumptions. Subsequently, Engels was to proclaim as 'the task of economic science', with the capitalist economy moving toward its collapse, 'to uncover amid the changes of the economic transition the elements of the future new organisation of production and exchange which will remove the previous malfunctioning [of the capitalist economy]' (Engels, 1878, p. 153).

This proclaimed 'task of economic science' was never seriously attempted by Marx. It never seemed irresponsible to Engels and Marx to seek not merely reforms but the total and violent destruction of an economic order (which they admitted was producing much economic growth and freedom) without giving more than the slightest serious thought as to how an alternative could or would be organized. It would be difficult to argue that Engels was notably less irresponsible than his comrades. But he had, as Wilhelm Liebknecht put it, 'a clear bright mind', and he was apt boyishly to blurt out that surely the king might be getting rather cold without any clothes on. Marx considered it more politic to keep quiet or to indulge in obfuscatory, abstract jargon. If, in fact, Marx was less optimistic or Utopian than Engels, he was never ready to face the problems of 'the future new organisation of production and exchange'.

At any rate, Engels, in 'The Principles of Communism', reveals the economic and technical assumption on which the communist economy must rest. This is no less than that of a degree of technological progress which has brought the abolition of scarcity and of the division of labour with its alienating effects:

Private property can be abolished only when the economy is capable of producing the volume of goods needed to satisfy everyone's require-ments. . . . *The new rate of industrial growth will produce enough goods to satisfy all the demands of society.* . . . Society will achieve an output sufficient for the needs of all members. . . The main results of the abolition of private property will be . . . *the ending of the system by which one man's requirements can be satisfied only at the expense of someone else.* (Henderson, 1976, pp. 372–6, italics added)

This technological progress will not be based on or require more specialized skills, but quite the opposite:

At present machinery has led to the division of labour and has turned one man into a peasant, a second into a shoemaker, a third into a factory worker, and a fourth into a speculator on the stock exchange. All this will be swept away. Education in the future will enable young people to appreciate the whole process of production and will give them the training necessary to exercise one skill after another according to the varying needs of society and their own inclinations. (p. 375)

This particular Utopian fantasy had been developed two years previously by Engels and Marx in an extraordinary passage in *The German Ideology*. There they explain how with private property and the division of labour:

Each man has a particular exclusive sphere of activity, which is forced upon him and from which he cannot escape. He is a hunter, a fisherman, a shepherd, or a critical critic, and must remain so if he does not want to lose his means of livelihood; while in a communist society, where nobody has one exclusive sphere of activity but each can become accomplished in any branch he wishes, society regulates the general production and thus makes it possible for me to do one thing today and another tomorrow, to hunt in the morning, fish in the afternoon, rear cattle in the evening, criticize after dinner, just as I have a mind, without ever becoming hunter, fisherman, shepherd, or critic. (Freedman, ed., 1962, p. 234)

With the complete removal of virtually all forms of scarcity, including the need for specialization and the division of labour, it is difficult to conceive what if any function would remain to be performed by any type of economic organization, either based on markets or on state controls. In such an economic and technological Utopia – established, as Engels and Marx insist, worldwide – the state indeed could and would 'wither away', and, of course, markets and prices would wither away also. But Engels felt bound to admit that the millennium would not be attainable 'immediately'. He felt that he had to insert at least the thin end of the 'transition' wedge – the abolition of all private property and simultaneously of scarcity could not be done 'with one blow': 'It would not be possible *immediately* to expand the existing forces of production to such an extent that enough goods could be made to satisfy all the needs of the community' (Henderson, 1976, p. 371, italics added). In the transition, at least, 'industry will have to be run by society as a whole for everybody's benefit. It must be operated by all members of society in accordance with a common plan. . . . Private property will also have to be abolished and it must be replaced by the sharing of all products in accordance with an agreed plan'. (pp. 369–70) These vacuous phrases are never filled out with any substance. On the other hand, the *Manifesto* insists quite bluntly that initially, or in the 'transition', the proletariat will proceed 'to centralise all instruments of production in the hands of the state'.

Never has there been a wider contrast or more extreme

contradiction between short-term, 'transitional' aims and methods requiring the creation of vast bureaucratic vested interests and, on the other hand, what was professed to be the long-term objective of the 'withering away' of the state. Here is the central moral and intellectual irresponsibility of Engels and Marx, a lineal intellectual descendant of which is the attack on both markets and bureaucracy by today's 'new left'.

It must be emphasized that the Utopian, millenarian fantasies regarding the wonders of technological progress and the disappearance of scarcity and of the alienation brought about by the division of labour were *essential* for the Engels-Marx ideology; they provided the emotional driving force. Much of the Engels-Marx theorizing might be more or less acceptable, or at least arguable in positive neutral terms, that is, regarded as an assessment of social and economic trends to be accepted, maybe with pessimistic resignation and regret, on the assumption that the costs of the vast historic process, as envisaged by Marx and Engels, were very probably going to exceed the benefits. (This, in fact, was to some extent Schumpeter's attitude.) But naive progressivism and the powerful charge of extreme Utopian and millenarian fantasy have been essential to Marxism as a mass political creed, and this was derived, though usually inexplicitly, from the underlying eschatological fantasies regarding the economic Utopia which was just around the next corner. The proximity of Utopia justified both the persecution and mass murder of those who continued to obstruct its arrival, together with the extreme harshness of what was claimed to be the short-term 'transition' (now, of course, 60 years long in Russia). Engels was later to claim as a forerunner the religious revolutionary Thomas Müntzer in the Peasants' War of the early sixteenth century. This parallel certainly possesses some validity, as Professor Norman Cohn has observed: 'Müntzer was a *propheta* obsessed by eschatological phantasies which he attempted to translate into reality by exploiting social discontent. Perhaps after all it is a sound instinct that has led Marxists to claim him for their own.' (1972, p. 251) Nowhere in Marxian literature is this obsession with 'eschatological phantasies' more frankly and clearly revealed than in Engels's draft, 'The Principles of Communism'. Moreover, for both Engels and Marx the day of judgement was very near at hand.

It must be emphasized that for Engels and Marx the replacement of 'capitalism', and a revolution in economic organization, were not some distant possibilities in the remote future. For

Engels and Marx the 'revolution' was constantly just around the next corner, with the next downturn in the economy.

Decade after decade, through the heyday of Victorian capitalism, Engels and Marx were predicting an early revolution. As Henderson observes (1976, p. 21), 'within a few days of Engels arriving in England', in the autumn of 1842: 'He asserted that a workers' revolution in England was inevitable. Events proved him to be wrong. For years Engels waited for the fulfilment of his gloomy prophecy and for years he waited in vain.'

In 1844 some strikes took place, with a certain amount of violence. For Engels: 'They prove conclusively that the decisive battle between the proletariat and the bourgeois is approaching' (Henderson, 1976, p. 59). Again, as Henderson tells us: 'In April 1848 Engels was so confident of the success of the Chartists, that he bet his brother-in-law "any sum" that the Chartist leader Harney would be Prime Minister in a couple of months' (p. 277).

Indeed, when Engels in 1850, in order to support himself and the Marx family, with the greatest reluctance and repugnance accepted a post in his father's Manchester office, it was in the lively expectation that at any moment he would be set free by the outbreak of 'the revolution'. In the crisis of 1857, with bank failures in New York:

Engels once more felt certain that the capitalist system was at last on the verge of collapse. But capitalism survived and there were no revolutions in England or on the Continent. Only a year later Engels had to recognise that in Manchester 'business is very good indeed.' Many years afterwards Engels admitted that in the 1850s and 1860s the British economy, far from being on the verge of collapse had been passing through a phase of 'unparalleled expansion'. Engels's gloomy but mistaken prophecies in the 1850s were shared by Marx who confidently anticipated a world wide economic collapse in 1851, 1852, 1853 and 1855. (Henderson, 1976, p. 200)

Similarly, in France, in 1851: 'Just as Marx and Engels expected that the next trade slump would herald the collapse of capitalism in England, so they were convinced that Napoleon III's next failure at home or abroad would see the building of the barricades in Paris' (Henderson, 1976, p. 465). It has, in fact, been estimated of Marx and Engels that 'in thirty years they foresaw forty revolutions, none of which took place' (Payne, 1968, p. 338).

Of course Engels and Marx never, until they were nearly 60, and scarcely then, made any revisions in their theories consequent upon the repeated empirical falsification of their predictions. It would also, naturally, be quite erroneous to suppose, because Engels and Marx for decades on end believed that the demise of capitalism, which they so desired, was only months away, that they therefore felt any intellectual or moral obligation to give some thought to the kind of economic organization which would, or could, follow. The Utopian vacuities blurted out by Engels are as far as they got. But Engels certainly reveals a great deal regarding their basic assumptions, which were, however, all cut out by Marx from the *Manifesto*, which ends with much haughty and sarcastic denunciation of Utopian socialism. More than a quarter of a century later Engels, in another denunciation of Utopian socialism, had some further penetrating insights to offer.

V

Of outstanding interest among Engels's intellectual contributions to political economy in the later period, after his retirement from business in 1869, is his preface to the first German edition (1884) of Marx's *The Poverty of Philosophy* (see also Hutchison, 1957). This is a document which should be (but never has been) given the most prominent place in the literature of Marxist political economy. On the lines, just noted, of the concluding paragraphs of *The Communist Manifesto*, Engels in his preface has the effrontery to attack, for Utopian naïveté, some of the socialist rivals of himself and Marx, such as Proudhon, John Gray and Rodbertus, especially the last named. In outlining how his socialist economy would work, Rodbertus had propounded a system of labour money which would be paid out to workers in accordance with the amount of labour they had contributed to production. Denouncing, witheringly, this 'childishly naïve' labour-money Utopia, Engels explains:

Since for every paper certificate a corresponding object of value has been delivered, and no object of value is given out except against a corresponding paper certificate, the sum total of paper certificates must always be covered by the sum total of objects of value. The calculation works out without any remainder, it agrees down to a second of labour time, and no *Regierungs-Hauptkassen-Rentamts-Kalkulator*, however grey in the service, could prove the slightest error in the reckoning. What more could one want? (1884/n.d., p. 19)

Engels then goes on to set out, with masterly insight, just what 'more' one could want, or what is required for the guidance of production. In doing so he recognizes the essential role of the competitive market mechanism.:

To desire in a society of producers who exchange their commodities, to establish the determination of value by labour time, *by forbidding competition to establish this determination of value through pressure on prices in the only way in which it can be established*, is therefore merely to prove that, at least in this sphere, one has adopted the usual Utopian disdain of economic laws.

Secondly, competition, by bringing into operation the laws of value of commodity production in a society of producers who exchange their commodities, precisely thereby brings about the only organization and arrangement of social production which is possible in the circumstances. *Only through the undervaluation and overvaluation of products is it forcibly brought home to the individual commodity producers what things and what quantity of them society requires or does not require.* But it is just this sole regulator that the Utopia in which Rodbertus also shares would abolish. And if we have to ask what guarantee we have that the necessary quantity and not more of each product will be produced, that we shall not go hungry in regard to corn and meat while we are choked in beet sugar and drowned in potato spirit, that we shall not lack trousers to cover our nakedness while trouser buttons flood us in millions[4] – Rodbertus triumphantly shows us his famous calculation, according to which the correct certificate has been handed out for every superfluous pound of sugar, for every unsold barrel of spirit, for every unusable trouser button, a calculation which 'works out' exactly, and according to which 'all claims will be satisfied and the liquidation correctly brought about.' And anyone who does not believe this can apply to the governmental chief revenue office accountant, X, in Pomerania, who has supervised the calculation and found it correct and who, as one who has never yet been found guilty of a mistake in his cash account, is thoroughly trustworthy. . . . *If now competition is to be forbidden to make the individual producers aware, by the rise or fall of prices, how the world market stands, then their eyes are completely blinded.* (pp. 21–2, italics added)

Mises and Hayek could hardly have made the point more forcefully. What is most extraordinary is the combination of penetrating critical insight regarding the vital function of the competitive price mechanism as applied to the Utopian notions of Rodbertus together with the totally uncritical, purblind complacency regarding his own and Marx's Utopian assumptions (as he himself had earlier revealed them in his 'Principles of

Communism' in such irresponsible vacuities as 'the joint and planned exploitation of the forces of production by society as a whole') (Henderson, 1976, p. 376). The hordes of infallible Prussian officials and 'the Prussian State Socialism', for relying on which Engels so castigates Rodbertus, would inevitably be required (and, of course, have been deployed) many times over for Engels's and Marx's own Utopian 'planning'. Surely no one in the whole of intellectual history can have looked a major, pressing intellectual and practical problem so clearly and piercingly in the face and then so blithely and confidently passed on without a word. But Marx, like most subsequent Marxists, never even looked the problem in the face. Similarly, never have what were first proclaimed as short-term, transitional measures – the centralization of all production in the hands of the state – been so diametrically at variance with, and contradictory of, the professed long-term goal: 'the withering away of the state'. Here lies the central intellectual and moral irresponsibility of Engels and Marx. Engels renders us the service, so far largely unrecognized, of revealing this irresponsibility in an especially crass form.

VI

Unlike Marx, Engels in his later years did make some references to Jevons and Menger and to the development of marginal utility analysis. Henderson (1976) quotes a letter of 1890 by Engels criticizing the Fabians and their belief in 'the rotten vulgarised economics of Jevons, which is so vulgarised that one can make anything out of it – even socialism' (pp. 681 and 742, n. 146).

If any meaning can be ascribed to 'vulgarised' here – apart from 'non-Marxist' – it can only be something like 'general', 'empirically empty', and/or 'politically neutral', implying that if the appropriate political assumptions regarding utility and egalitarianism are fed into the Jevonian analysis, appropriate political conclusions can be derived.

In his preface to volume 3 of *Capital*, Engels repeats that *the same conclusions as those reached by Marx regarding what he called the 'exploitation' of workers can be reached on the basis of the monopoly analysis developed by the neoclassicals.*

Engels recognized that the 'vulgar' (i e., non-Marxist) economist Wilhelm Lexis, by assuming monopolistic conditions in product markets and monopsony in labour markets, had reached what 'amounts in practice to the same thing as the Marxian theory of surplus value' (1894/1959, p. 10). In fact, 'this theory is merely a paraphrase of the Marxian', so that Lexis is really 'a Marxist disguised as a vulgar economist'. This somewhat grudging admission by Engels seems to refute the accusation, repeated with such parrot-like monotony by vulgar Marxist economists, that the 'neoclassical' analysis was inherently 'apologetic'. In fact, of course, 'neoclassical' analysis is much better equipped to deal with monopolistic and monopsonistic processes than classical and Marxian analysis.

In his later years Engels showed himself to be an alert observer of changing economic institutions. Like Marshall and J. B. Clark, he notes the rise of trusts and cartels, and also of joint-stock companies 'whose business is managed for them by paid employees' (Henderson, 1976, p. 679). He observes, too, Britain's declining relative position. He shows himself ready also to qualify basic Marxian doctrines such as the economic interpretation of history, and expresses acute distaste for the kind of followers whom his, and Marx's, teachings were increasingly attracting. He writes in letters of 1890:

Marx and I are ourselves to blame for the fact that the younger people sometimes lay more stress on the economic side than is due to it. We had to emphasize the main principle *vis-à-vis* our adversaries, who denied it, and we had not always the time, the place or the opportunity to give their due to the other elements involved in the interaction. . . I cannot exempt many of the more recent Marxists from this reproach, for the most amazing rubbish has been produced in this quarter, too. . . . There has been a students' revolt in the German Party. For the past 2–3 years, a crowd of students, literary men and other young declassed bourgeois has rushed into the Party, arriving just in time to occupy most of the editorial positions on the new Journals. . . All these gentlemn go in for Marxism, but of the kind you were familiar with in France ten years ago, and of which Marx said: 'All I know is that I'm no Marxist!' And of these gentlemen he would probably have said what Heine said of his imitators: 'I sowed dragons, and reaped fleas.' (pp. 611, 645)

Since 1890 the flea population has certainly multiplied with Malthusian profusion. But in one of his last and most discerning writings Engels went much further, with an admission never vouchsafed previously by him, or (of course) Marx, with regard to the prediction of revolutions, about which, in the face of repeated evidence, they had been wrong for decade after decade:

But we, too, have been shown to have been wrong by history, which has revealed our point of view of that time to have been an illusion. It has done even more: it has not merely destroyed our error of that time; it has also completely transformed the conditions under which the proletariat has to fight. The mode of struggle of 1848 is today obsolete from every point of view. (1895, p. 283)

Five months after writing this admission Engels was dead.

VII

A methodological postscript may be added. The Engelsian-Marxian dynamic theory of capitalist economic development and political revolution is one of the most grandiose examples of a general politicoeconomic theory. It was based on a vision which originated in Manchester in the early 1840s, and depends on assumptions seemingly appropriate at that time and place. These required that voteless and (largely) union-less workers were without economic and constitutional political power, while it was also essential to the model that the British economy at that time was the most, or among the most, advanced in the world. A huge general-theoretical model was constructed, and highly unqualified, and regularly falsified, predictions were derived, for decade after decade, by Engels and Marx, and subsequently, with increasing *ad hoc* adjustments and qualifications, by their followers.[5] In fact, the assumptions on which the model was based had, in England, ceased to be relevant long before Marx and Engels died, and far from representing a general case have seldom been fully realized elsewhere, and certainly not in those countries where 'Marxian' regimes have come to power. 'Marxian' thinkers have often attacked their 'bourgeois' opponents for claiming generality for theories based on assumptions for which only a transient or obsolete relevance could be validated. No theory is more wide open to this charge than their own.

Even more seriously, Marxians – like Keynesians – have not only claimed an unjustifiable generality for their theory or 'model'; their philosophical, or epistemological preconceptions, based on a kind of dogmatic, nineteenth-century scientism, have claimed an infallible correctness which has justified their intolerant, one-party totalitarianism. In conclusion, it must unfortunately be noted that Engels, in his writings on the philosophy of science, contributed significantly to this dogmatic, epistemological underpinning of the Marxian system, which culminated in the Marxian science policies of the Soviet Union. For Engels proclaimed dogmatically that dialectical materialism was a universal philosophical principle to which all science, natural and human, must submit. Thus scientists were told, in advance of their researches, what *kind* of answers they must discover:

Amid the welter of innumerable changes taking place in nature, the same dialectical laws of motion are in operation as those which in history govern the apparent fortuitousness of events. (1878, p. 15)

As Engels insisted, natural scientists will always be 'under the domination of philosophy' (1940, p. 243). For dialectical materialism laid down for all scientists overriding guidelines which 'possessed something that was superior to them even in their own special sphere' (Engels, 1940, p. 154).

As Professor Stanley Jaki has pointed out, it was the 'ramblings in science' of Engels which

were elevated into a canonical text whereby party philosophers tried to decipher what course science ought to follow. . . . The way Engels presented the respective roles of true philosophy (dialectical materialism) and science, anticipated with frightening concreteness the parlance of future party theoreticians in charge of laying down the line for scientists. (1966, pp. 481–3)

This culminating contribution of Engels, in his *Dialectics of Nature*, to the infallibilist methodology of Marxism, far outweighs, in the negative scale, any positive value in his contributions to Marxian political economy. The basis of Marxian dogmatism and intolerance is its claim to knowledge rooted in infallible scientific certainty. This is the basis of the totalitarian imperialism of Marxian states and of their final solutions of the world's political and economic problems. While a nihilistic scepticism is directed at all alternatives, an infallible scientistic 'correctness', certainty, and finality has been claimed for Marxian dogmas. Thus 'revisionism' which ought to be a constant duty, directed at reducing error, has often, for Marxians, represented an appalling sin against the absolute, infallible scientific truth of Marx and Engels, punishable often with death. Engels, unfortunately, contributed mightily to this scientistic epistemology, which is the source both of the pretentious intolerance of Marxism and of its fundamental intellectual weakness.[6]

Notes

1   Professor Henderson supplies a vivid glimpse of Engels's relief at being freed of his business duties:

> On the day of his retirement Engels wrote to Marx: 'Hurrah! I have finished with sweet commerce to-day and I am a free man'. . . . Eleanor Marx was visiting Engels at this time and she later recalled: 'I shall never forget the triumph with which he exclaimed: "For the last time." A few hours later we were standing at the gate waiting for him. We saw him coming over the little field opposite the house where he lived. He was swinging his stick and singing, his face beaming. Then we set the table for a celebration and drank champagne and were happy'. (Henderson, 1976, vol. 1, pp. 218–19)

2   'If Henry Frederick Demuth was Karl Marx's son, the new mankind's Preacher lived an almost lifelong lie, and scorned, humiliated, and disowned his only surviving son' (Raddatz, 1978, p. 134). Certainly, even the pettiest bourgeois could hardly have surpassed Marx in his obsequious regard for this kind of conventional respectability, nor have outdone the Marxian establishment in so strenuously suppressing the truth for as long as possible.

3   In the same year as Engels's *Condition of the Working Class in England*, Benjamin Disraeli published his *Sybil: or the Two Nations*. Regarding the class division in England, Disraeli wrote: 'Two nations; between whom there is no intercourse and no sympathy; who are as ignorant of each other's habits, thoughts, and feelings as if they were dwellers in different zones, or inhabitants of different planets; who are formed by a different breeding, are fed by a different food, are ordered by different manners, and are not governed by the same laws' (1845/1954, p. 73). See also Disraeli's description of 'Wodgate' and its proletariat in book 3, chapter 4.

4   Engels's warning regarding imbalances in the supply of trousers and trouser buttons has recently acquired embarrassing relevance for the system of planning priorities in Russia. Professor Alec Nove has cited a complaint in *Pravda* that, as regards priorities in supplies, 'in the clothing industry trousers are on the list of the "most important", but zip-fasteners are not.' See Nove, 1980.

5   On the other hand, regarding Marxist theories Imre Lakatos has asked:

> Has, for instance, Marxism ever predicted a stunning novel fact
> successfully? Never! It has some famous unsuccessful predictions. It
> predicted the absolute impoverishment of the working class. It
> predicted that the first socialist revolution would take place in the
> industrially most developed society. It predicted that socialist
> societies would be free of revolutions. It predicted that there will be
> no conflict of interests between socialist countries. Thus the early
> predictions of Marxism were bold and stunning but they failed.
> Marxists explained all their failures: they explained the rising living
> standards of the working class by devising a theory of imperialism;
> they even explained why the first socialist revolution occurred in
> industrially backward Russia. They 'explained' Berlin 1953,
> Budapest 1956, Prague 1968. They 'explained' the Russian-Chinese
> conflict. But their auxiliary hypotheses were all cooked up after the
> event to protect Marxian theory from the facts. (1978, vol. 1, p. 6)

There is not much sign here of Lakatosian 'patience' with a 'budding'
research programme. In fact, Lakatos here seems to be applying, very
rightly and relevantly, the 'positivist' and 'empiricist' criteria, in terms of
testing and predictions rejected by a priorists. As Mr J. Worrall has
pointed out, Lakatos's denunciation of Marxism was not, of course,
made simply on the ground that it offered no testable predictions (it
made many); nor because these predictions were unsuccessful (good
scientific theories *may* make unsuccessful predictions); but because the
Marxist programme was a degenerating one, shifting, on falsification,
'to a set of assumptions incapable of receiving support from more facts
than its predecessor' (see Worrall, 1978, pp. 55–6). However, it might be
pleaded by an extreme exponent of Lakatosian 'patience' that even as
obviously a degenerating programme as Marxism should be given a
chance to revive. But Lakatos's incisive judgement to the contrary is
surely the only justifiable decision and he should not be charged with
'impatience', or 'naïveté', for condemning so emphatically the Marxian
programme.
6   I am much indebted to the illuminating article by Gerard Radnitzky
(1976) to whom I owe the reference to Jaki's work which I have quoted
above.

References

Carlton, G. (1965), *Friedrich Engels, the Shadow Prophet*.
Cohn, N. (1972), *The Pursuit of the Millennium*.
Disraeli, B. (1845), *Sybil: or the Two Nations* (Penguin Books, 1954).
Engels, F. (1845), *The Condition of the Working Class in England*,

   translated by W. O. Henderson and W. H. Chaloner reprinted in
   Henderson (ed.), 1967.

   (1878), *Herrn Eugen Dührings Umwälzung der Wissenschaft*, reprinted
   1928.

   (1884), Preface to 1st German ed. of K. Marx, *The Poverty of
   Philosophy*; translation published by Foreign Languages Publishing
   House, Moscow, n.d.

   (1894), Preface to K. Marx, *Capital: A Critique of Political Economy*,
   vol. 3, Foreign Languages Publishing House, Moscow, 1959.

   (1895), Preface to new edition of K. Marx, *The Class Struggles in
   France*, in Henderson, (ed.) 1967.

   (1940), *Dialectics of Nature*, translated by C. Dutt, from *Dialektik der
   Natur* (1925).

Freedman, R., ed. (1962), *Marx on Economics*.

Henderson, William O. (1976), *The Life of Friedrich Engels*, 2 vols.

Henderson, William O. ed. (1967), *Engels, Selected Writings*.

Hess, M. (1842), 'Über eine in England bevorstehende Katastrophe',
   Rheinische Zeitung, vol. 177, 26 June.

Horwitz, M. J. (1976), 'The Legacy of 1776 in Legal and Economic
   Thought', *Journal of Law and Economics*, vol. 19, Oct., pp. 621–32.

Hutchison, T. W. (1957), Review of K. Marx, *The Poverty of Philosophy*,
   in *Economica*, Feb., p. 89.

Jaki, S. (1966), *The Relevance of Physics*.

Lakatos, I. (1978), *Philosophical Papers*, 2 vols, ed. J. Worrall and G.
   Currie.

McLellan, D. (1977), *Engels*.

Mayer, Gustav (1934), *Friedrich Engels. Eine Biographie*, 2 vols.

Nove, A. (1980), 'Planning Becomes a Nightmare for Moscow', *The
   Times*, 16 Apr., p. 19.

Payne, R. (1968), *Marx, a Biography*.

Raddatz, F. J. (1978), *Karl Marx, A Political Biography*, translated by R.
   Barry.

Radnitzky, G. (1976), 'Dogmatic und Skepsis: Folger den Aufgabe der
   Wahrheitsidee für Wissenschaft und Politik', in K. Hübner, N.
   Labkowicz, H. Lübbe and G. Radnitzky (ed.), *Die politische
   Herausforderung der Wissenschaft*.

Robinson, Joan (1966), *An Essay on Marxian Economics*, 2nd ed.

Schumpeter, J. A. (1954), *A History of Economic Analysis*.

   (1962), *Capitalism, Socialism and Democracy*, 3rd ed.

Worrall, J. ed. (1978), 'The Ways in which the Methododology of
   Scientific Research Programmes Improves on Popper's Methodolo-
   gy' in *Progress and Rationality in Science*, ed. G. Radnitzky and G.
   Andersson, pp. 45ff.

2

The Market Economy
and the Franchise,
or 1867 and All That

I

Both 'internal' and 'external' influences have shaped the questions or agenda for economists and the history of economic thought, in varying mixtures and combinations. Partly, or in some phases, it has been questions thrown up within the subject which economists have focused on, with regard to the development of a particular conceptual framework or idea, as happened with the application of the marginal concept to microeconomics in the initial decades of the neoclassical period. There are also, in between, sociological forces, intellectually 'external' but professionally 'internal', concerning the status or profession of economists, which influence criteria and intellectual objectives, as when economists became increasingly academic and began to go in for the more precise, and often more mathematical, formulation of economic theory – also in the neoclassical period. But what has often been more emphasized by economists have been the 'external' forces shaping the choice of questions and arising out of changing economic and political events and institutions.

Clearly the salient economic policy problems which have arisen in different periods have been of major importance in setting up the questions for economists. Though such problems arise partly out of economic events and developments, to an important extent they may arise from, or may be shaped by, changing political forces and changes in policy preferences and demands. In this account we are concerned with the main, broad shifts in political power in Britain in the nineteenth century and after, which led on to changing priorities and demands with regard to policies. First, this paper surveys the views of the English classical economists with regard to extending the franchise, and then proceeds to sketch in, very briefly, the more obvious consequences for economic policy of the great reforms of 1832, 1867, 1884 and subsequently. Second, comes an attempt to account for, and comment on, the assumptions of the broadly non-political, or would-be non-political or apolitical economics widely dominant in the first half of this century. In conclusion, there is a brief account of the modes and implications of the explicit reintroduction of politics into political economy since about the 1960s. We would simply add that in this broad survey 1867 is clearly a key year, and that, coincidentally, this date takes on a certain piquancy from the fact that Marx published his *Das Kapital* in that year, which is also exactly half a century before the Russian Revolution.

II

Let us take as a text with which to launch our historical observations, a remark from Professors Buchanan and Tullock's *The Calculus of Consent*: 'Constitutional democracy in its modern sense', they write, 'was born as a twin of the market economy' (1962, p. 306).

At least this makes the fundamental point of the close relationship between the two, and we would not for one moment venture to take issue with these authors on the aptness of their biological metaphor regarding the history of the United States. But if what they call 'constitutional democracy in its modern sense' implies, as one would surely expect, a widely extended suffrage, then this 'twin' metaphor, with regard to this country and probably most of Europe, is pretty inappropriate. A family relationship, even a brotherly relationship, or perhaps some sort of rather unharmonious husband-and-wife relationship, might be metaphorically justifiable. But, of course in this country, unlike the United States, the market economy was 'born' long before the suffrage was sufficiently extended to constitute anything describable as 'constitutional democracy in its modern sense'. It is, incidentally, worth pointing out what a crucial and perhaps traumatic effect early experiences may, as usual, have had in shaping the subsequent course of family relationships. How the eventual electoral majority, before it obtained political power, was treated by the market system, when this was unmodified and unshaped by a majority electorate, has obviously been crucial for the subsequent relationship between free-market institutions and electoral majorities in this country, as contrasted, to some extent, with the United States, where a metaphorical twin relationship, or a more nearly simultaneous birth, may be much nearer the mark.[1]

Anyhow, the first compact school of ardent free-marketeers, the Physiocrats under Quesnay, far from wanting free markets and constitutional democracy as twins, called for free markets under the aegis of an autocratic monarchy. But we shall confine these speculations to this country alone, and review now what our classical economists had to say about democratic political reform and the market economy.

One certainly might have thought that Adam Smith's eloquent pleas for the freedom of enlightened individual initiative in competitive markets would have suggested strong implications regarding political enfranchisement. In his 'simple system of natural liberty', 'every man, as long as he does not violate the laws of justice, is left perfectly free to pursue his own interest his own way, and to bring both his industry and capital into competition with those of any other man, or order of men' (1976, vol. 2, p. 687). If *every man*, or the general average of men, has the initiative and intelligence significantly to implement this 'simple system' on the economic side, in free markets, then it might seem broadly to follow that a widely based suffrage, or free political choice, might be indicated on the political side.

Adam Smith's treatment of politics in his lectures of 1763 is justifiably but tantalizingly cautious.[2] He gives, however, one rather contemporary-sounding example regarding the possibly misleading results of majority voting.[3] But to some extent he foreshadows – much more than his immediate classical successors – the non-political or apolitical attitude of the neoclassicals and modern economics. The political arena is apparently a chaotic irrational place, inhabited by 'that insidious and crafty animal, vulgarly called a statesman or politician, whose councils are directed by the momentary fluctuations of affairs'. The deliberations of the legislature are apt to be dominated 'by the clamorous importunity of partial interests', rather than by 'an extensive view of the general good'. Apparently, however, Smith relied merely on his eloquent philosophical advocacy and on an 18th-century trust in the power of reason, for getting the insidious and crafty animals to put through politically the fundamental reforms needed to establish and maintain his simple system of natural liberty, or the competitive market economy.

Anyhow, in 1776 electoral reform was simply not on the horizon. One could only try to clear an area for individual initiative in economic life, and keep it as free as possible from the 'clamorous importunities' of the political world.

It is with James Mill and Ricardo, in the heyday of Philosophic Radicalism after 1815, that political and electoral reform and economic reform to establish a free-market economy enter a kind of temporary twin relationship. Political reform was now clearly a possibility – so much so that it could be held that a substantial measure was essential for warding off violence or revolution, with the prospect of which James Mill tried to scare the Whigs (see Hamberger, 1963). Moreover, *some* measure of political reform was also essential, not simply for its own sake, but for getting through the main reforms necessary for reshaping the economy on competitive free-market principles, and particularly for securing the abolition of the Corn Laws. But although *some* electoral reform was necessary to establish the competitive market economy, the question arose: *how much* electoral reform, or how extensive a franchise, was compatible with the long-run maintenance of a competitive free-market framework, as the classicals conceived it, and above all with the essential principle described as the sanctity of private property?

James Mill was, on the whole, optimistic, but fairly cautious about how far the franchise should, in the short run, be extended down the wealth scale. In his remarkable *Essay on Government* he proposed, of course, a sex qualification, but also severe age and property qualifications. He actually mentioned forty as a suitable *minimum* age for the vote (1955, section VIII) – a proposal which it would be rather fun to have revived today, when contemporary Liberals would presumably rather take forty as a maximum, not as a minimum, age for voting. On the property qualification, Mill saw the problem as one of striking a balance between simply enfranchising a privileged minority and, on the other hand, so extending the franchise down the wealth scale as to give a majority, with little or no wealth, the power to exploit the wealthy minority. In the event he seems to have been satisfied with the reform of 1832, at least as a first instalment.

Ricardo was to a large extent the pupil of James Mill in political matters and was, with qualifications, even more optimistically and explicitly radical than Mill. He envisaged in the long run the eventual possibility of full adult suffrage. But in the short run Ricardo favoured considerable caution and emphasized strongly the possible dangers to property. The conclusion of his paper on Parliamentary Reform is so interesting, and so complex in its emphasis, as to deserve extensive quotation:

The last point for consideration is the supposed disposition of the people to interfere with the rights of property. So essential does it appear to me, to the cause of good government, that the rights of property should be held sacred, that I would agree to deprive those of the elective franchise against whom it would justly be alleged that they considered it their interest to invade them. But in fact it can be only amongst the most needy in the community that such an opinion can be entertained. The man of a small income must be aware how little his share would be if all the large fortunes in the kingdom were equally divided among the people. He must know that the little he would obtain by such a division could be no adequate compensation for the overturning of a principle which renders the produce of his industry secure. (1952, p. 501).[4]

One cannot be sure how precisely to interpret this passage, and to estimate how far it has or has not been borne out by subsequent history, without knowing just what Ricardo would have regarded as an 'invasion' of those sacred rights of property which were an indispensable condition of the market economy as he understood it. Certainly, if such an 'invasion' covers only a completely equal division or levelling, Ricardo's optimistic view of the compatibility of a wide franchise with the market economy has almost been borne out. But if considerable progression of income taxation, at 10 to 20 (or more) times 19th-century levels, would constitute 'invasion', then, of course, things have not gone quite as he hoped. Ricardo may not have had an accurate picture of the actual distribution and 'security' of property and income. Anyhow, there perhaps may have been some naïveté in trusting that the relatively poor majority, of those 'low in the scale of society', would be so convinced – by the teachings, presumably of Mrs Marcet and Miss Martineau – of their long-run gains in relative income and 'security' from a market economy that they would not, directed by rational self-interest, try to use their majority of votes to improve somehow their relative position.

It is difficult to say whether, in spite of his exaggerated rhetoric, Macaulay was not predicting more accurately, in his attack on James Mill, when he asked: 'How is it possible for any person who holds the doctrine of Mr Mill [favouring some extension of the franchise] to doubt that the rich, in a democracy, such as that which he recommends, would be pillaged as unmercifully as under the Turkish Pasha?' Anyhow, Lord Robbins suggests that it was this view of Macaulay's which 'was probably the majority view of mid-nineteenth century liberals' (1952, pp. 199–200).

The 1832 reform was, of course, vitally important as a first step. But, as Seymour very mildly states, it was 'in its first effects by no means a democratic measure' (1915, p. 486). It gave the vote to only about one seventh of the adult males in Great Britain, and there was no secret ballot. The increase in the total number of voters was not very large, and some labourers previously enfranchised lost the vote.

The upper-middle classes in the towns now had not exclusive but a considerable measure of political power. There is no doubt about the consequences for economic policy. It was on the political basis of the 1832 electorate, roughly the one seventh of adult males at or near the top of the wealth pyramid, or 'the scale of society', that the essential framework of the competitive market economy was established: with regard to the labour market in the 1834 reform of the Poor Law; with regard to the monetary framework in 1844; and, most important of all, with regard to agriculture and free trade in the abolition of the Corn Laws, which had of course a significance far transcending a mere reform of tariff policy.

As Professor Norman Gash, the authority on the Peel era, puts it: after 1832, 'it needed no special perspicacity to foresee the coming onslaught on the Corn Laws' (Gash, 1953, p. 6; see also Clark, 1951, p. 109). Or, as Trevelyan sums up: 'By the events of 1845/6 the £10 voter had at length asserted his power, to the extent of insisting that the economic and financial policy of the State should no longer flout his interests' (1955, p. 271).

After the 1832 reform many of the leading economists and surviving classicals would have liked to stop there, and were opposed to further extensions of the suffrage down the wealth scale. McCulloch was certainly not eager for further extension (1843, p. 57) and Senior expressed considerable alarm about granting electoral power to the poor (Senior, 1871, vol. 1, pp. 150–2, quoted in Robbins, 1952, p. 201). He considered that if a densely populated country was to be properly governed, in most cases the poor must either be excluded from political life or be kept under by military power. Not only Whigs like Senior but also adherents of Utilitarianism and Philosophical Radicalism were opposed to further extension of the franchise. Dicey calls attention to the 'curious historical phenomenon', as he describes it, of a number of 'rigid utilitarians' adopting, 'without any fundamental change of principle, a peculiar type of conservatism. They held that a Parliament constituted under the Reform Act of 1832 was more likely to legislate in accordance with utilitarian principles than would be any more democratic assembly' (1905, p. 164).

One of these conservative utilitarians was, for example, that interesting figure Robert Lowe, a rigid disciple of classical political economy, who might perhaps be described as an economist.[5] He is mentioned here because he upset his own Whig-Liberal government by leading the rebels in 'the cave of Adullam' in opposition to the extension of the franchise, and did so on what he insisted were the strictest utilitarian principles.

But if several of the later classical economists, Whigs or Utilitarians, were against extending the suffrage down the wealth scale, in some cases quite explicitly because they believed that the framework of the market economy as they conceived it would be endangered by enfranchising the poor, there was of course on the other side J. S. Mill, a host in himself. Mill, possibly, as Professor F. A. Hayek would suggest, under the sinister influence of Harriet, advocated votes for women, and also, with some apprehensiveness, the extension of the franchise to the labouring classes. But he was very fearful for the rights of minorities, just as in supporting the claims of trade unions he was apprehensive about how they might use their power. Hence his proposals regarding proportional representation (1861, chapters 7–10).

As Seymour says, the measure of 1867 was 'by no means a democratic revolution'. But '*in its immediate effects upon the electorate it was the most striking of all three* [of the nineteenth century reforms]. The increase in the number of electors far transcended that of 1832 and was proportionately greater than that of 1884' (1915, p. 487, italics added). The 1867 reform enfranchised roughly the lower-middle and artisan classes and the upper levels of the labouring classes. The extension was not granted in response to some great wave of popular agitation based on natural rights or adult suffrage. On the supply side it emerged from the rival manoeuvring of political entrepreneurs seeking to create and get a hold on a future political market, and at once seeking to satisfy the prospective new market's immediate demands as regards economic policy. On the demand side the new voters wanted their electoral power in order to get something quite definite, which they duly got. What they wanted was what Dicey described as 'a means for obtaining legislation (such, for example, as a modification of the combination laws), in accordance with the desires of trade unions';[6] and of course the Act of 1871 recognized and legally protected trade unions, the then craft unions of 'the aristocracy of labour', and the 1875 Act – with which Disraeli promptly outbid Gladstone – permitted picketing. Disraeli well understood the point made by Professor Gordon Tullock in his recent work on *Entrepreneurial Politics*: 'If a politician makes an offer to a group of voters which is not the maximum which can be given to them, then another politician can win their votes, or enough of them, to give him a majority by making a better offer' (1962, p. 3).[7]

One need hardly today stress the importance of the laws relating to trade unions for the whole framework and processes of a market economy. Of course primary education and a proto-meritocratic reform of the Civil Service and Army also followed at once. But the Trade Union Acts were perhaps even more significant as constituting, in the words of one authority, 'the first great legislative victory won by organised labour and a forecast of its power in the twentieth century' – in large measure due to, or linked with, the 1867 extension of the franchise (McCready, 1956, p. 141). In fact, according to Professor Hobsbawm: 'The Acts of 1871 and 1875 gave the unions a degree of legal freedom which conservative-minded lawyers have since, at intervals, attempted to whittle away'. Professor Hobsbawm continues regarding 1867: 'The Reform Act of 1867 (followed . . . by a whole crop of important legislative changes) accepted an electoral system dependent on working-class votes. It did not introduce parliamentary democracy, but it implied that the rulers of Britain reconciled themselves to its eventual introduction, which subsequent reforms (in 1884–5, 1918 and 1928), achieved with diminishing amounts of fuss.' (1969, p. 125)

The Second Reform Bill came in the same year as the appearance of vol. I of *Das Kapital*. The slight irony is, of course, that it was the former which was probably the preponderant agent in falsifying the revolutionary prophecies of the latter regarding the then leading capitalist country. (See the stimulating argument in Strachey, 1956, especially chapters IX and XIV.) The voteless and trade-unionless 'proletariat' of Marx's *Das Kapital* now had the ingredients of both political and economic power. As in the case of Keynes's *General Theory*, the institutional falsification of the Marxian politicoeconomic model began, as far as Britain was concerned, within a year of its publication.

Whether or not, or how long, the line could have been held without revolution at the 1832 franchise might be a matter for speculation. But speculation is hardly possible as to whether it could have been held at 1867. The 1884 reform was bound to follow soon after. Indeed, one might at this point insert one of those challenging apophthegms which are thrown at examinees with the exhortation to 'comment' or 'discuss', which might run as follows: 'The 1832 reform was essential for the establishment of the classical competitive market economy, of which the 1867 reform ensured the eventual complete transformation'.[8]

Anyhow, 1884 brought a further advance towards *man*hood suffrage, and again we at once have the spectacle of a great political entrepreneur, Joseph Chamberlain, like Disraeli before him, working for the extension of the franchise and then making a strong bid for the new political market he had helped to create. Political entrepreneurs, like or even more than economic entrepreneurs, have to anticipate, shape, and to some extent create their markets. 'This involves', to quote again from Professor Tullock's *Entrepreneurial Politics*, 'even more difficult problems than trying to anticipate consumer demands in the economic field, so sizeable errors are to be expected. Nevertheless, as in the economic field, the people who are most effective in making these difficult guesses will, over time, come to dominate the party system'. In 1885 Chamberlain produced his Radical Programme which came, as an alarmed *Times* explained, 'in a volume appropriately bound in the brightest of red covers'. Chamberlain proceeded to call for a 'direct progressive tax on income and property as the lever to which we shall look for social reform'. This was the first significant proposal for progressive taxation, overthrowing the classical principle of proportionality, made by a leading party politician in or approaching power (see Shehab, 1953, p. 190; Dicey, 1905, p. 225). Shortly after, in 1894, Harcourt, announcing that curious claim that they were all socialists then, duly introduced progression into the estate duty. As Professor Hobsbawm has summed up the development:

The foundations of laissez-faire crumbled in the 1860s and 1870s . . . As the working classes got the vote – in 1867, but especially in 1884–5 – it became only too obvious that they would demand – and receive –

substantial public intervention for greater welfare. . . The extension of the vote in 1884–5 gave the working class considerably increased political leverage on the other parties, especially the Liberals, normally anxious to retain their proletarian following. (1969, pp. 165, 237, italics added)

The subsequent electoral reforms of 1918 and 1928, doubling the electorate by extending the vote to women, have had, as far as one can guess, no obvious major implications for economic policies[9] comparable with those of the 19th-century extensions of the suffrage down the wealth scale, with their immense shifts in political or electoral power to the majority of wage-earners at the bottom, and bringing about, as Mr Anthony Downs has pointed out, the eventual supersession of the Liberal party by the Labour Party (1957, p. 129).[10] It certainly seems reasonable enough to emphasize the immediate and longer-run consequences for economic policy of the great reforms of 1867 and 1884. But though the thin, wispy, little saplings then planted – legal recognition of trade unions, and the introduction of a very slight degree of progression into the tax systems – have now grown to dominate our economic landscape and crucially to shape the framework and processes of the economy, when they were first planted they only *very* marginally affected the competitive market framework as it had been established earlier in the century. The contemporary outcry of bright-red socialism seems today quite grotesque, though not the anticipation that the thin end of what would eventually prove a pretty massive wedge was being inserted.

III

So much by way of a historical review. Next, moving from a historical tense to what might be called the historical-contemporary, comes a discussion of how 'neoclassical' economics, that is modern economics in one of its formative phases, largely severed political connections and came to be based on strictly non- or apolitical assumptions in contrast with the classical political economy it superseded.

There were two or three respects in which classical political economy was political, or was concerned with the interactions between politics and economics. There was also one respect in which it was *not* political, or only minimally so, in which our economy – though not yet our economics – is highly political, that is in respect of the share of total economic activity controlled or strongly influenced by the government. But classical political economy was political in that in its prime it had been concerned with the reshaping of the whole framework or constitution of the economy on competitive free-market principles. Hence it was inevitably involved with political values and objectives, as is seen particularly, in the concern of Adam Smith and J. S. Mill with the decentralization of power and with the values of individual initiative and self-reliance for their own sake, as distinct from, though as well as, with economic efficiency and growth. Furthermore, classical political economy, as we have seen, also inevitably got involved with the problems of political reform and the extension of the franchise, first as a condition for establishing, and then as regards preserving, the competitive free-market framework.

In the neoclassical period, however, from its formative phase in the 1860s and 1870s onwards, these major political concerns largely disappeared. There must, virtually always, be *some* significant interactions between economics and politics. But in the early years of Jevons and Marshall the interactions of politics and economics were, in spite of the extensions of the franchise and their initial effects, at something of an all-time low. There was comparatively little steam and mileage remaining in the crusade for the fundamental reshaping of the economy on the principle of free competitive markets. Except for marginal adjustments, the competitive market economy, with an assumed automatic monetary policy and balanced budgets at well under ten per cent of GNP, was taken for granted as 'normal', as Marshall called it, both in the assumptions of economists and by the leading competing political entrepreneurs. The final steps to adult suffrage were hardly controversial, and the vast consequences thereof were still well in the future, significant though the first results had been. The supersession of classical political economy by non-political economics sprang from this fleeting impermanent conjuncture, fundamentally one of politicoeconomic disequilibrium. Only the slow rate of adjustment of the new majority of relatively poor voters, in exercising their power over economic policy, provided the impression of mid-Victorian stability.

To appreciate the disappearance of the political element with the advent of neoclassicism one has only to contrast Professors Jevons, Marshall and Edgeworth, in terms of their political interests and involvement, with James Mill, David Ricardo MP and J. S. Mill MP. There are very few passages in the works of Jevons and Marshall expressing political interests, though there is the slightly surprising pronouncement of Jevons in 1867: 'It is very difficult to know what view to take of the reform agitation. I am not a democrat, as perhaps you know, and don't much care to adopt popular views to please the mob. However, I don't think any Reform Bill that is likely to pass will really upset our system here, while it may lead to many real improvements.' (1886, p. 232)

In the 1860s and 1870s, and for some time after that, non-political economics represented a slight abstraction but a reasonable one. It also represented a justifiable division of labour and, with economics developing particularly as an academic subject in the last quarter of the nineteenth century, it represented a judicious demarcation of professional, departmental responsibilities. But the justification of non-political economics sometimes got mixed up with the case for a politically neutral, value-free economics. A rather confusing, but common and still prevalent, use of the adjective 'political' began to emerge, equating it with 'normative' or 'ethical', with the implication that political behaviour and processes are not, or cannot be, or cannot usefully be, studied as positively or neutrally as economic 'scientists' study, or try or claim to study, economic behaviour and processes. In fact, this assumption might seem to have been lent some confirmation by the form which political studies and political philosophy then predominantly took.

At this time also, Robinson Crusoe emerged as the personification of neoclassical, non-political economics. For Crusoe's economic problems, decisions and activities represent purely economic problems, decisions and activities uninfluenced, unshaped, unrestricted, and uninterfered with, by any political power or political framework. One man on a desert island has economic problems but no political problems. There is a kind of economy, but no kind of polity, until Friday arrives on the scene, when non-economic problems of conduct and power arise, the answer to which may, and very probably will, crucially shape the economic activities of both parties (see Leoni, 1957, p. 239).

Needless to say, Jevons, Marshall, and even Edgeworth, were profoundly and keenly interested in economic policy, both in general principles and in particular current measures. In stressing the sense in which neoclassical economics went non-political, we were obviously not implying a lack of interest in *policy*. But economic policy was approached and treated *non*-politically, though not in the sense that the treatment was always politically neutral, or avoided value-judgements. Sometimes it was and sometimes it was not. But policy was treated non-politically: first, in the sense that the political effects and objectives of economic policies, so stressed by Smith and J. S. Mill, were increasingly neglected, often explicitly as with Pigou's concentration on 'economic welfare' as separable from 'total welfare'; and, secondly, in the sense that collective choices and government policies were not regarded as significantly determined, in some comprehensible regular way, by political processes. As Mr Downs has pointed out, according to economic theory, individuals motivated by self-interest would in different market situations, buy and sell various quantities of goods at various prices, competitive quantities and prices, or monopoly or monopsony quantities and prices, according to the market forces (Downs, 1957, p. 283). To *preach* that, regardless of the market situation, certain prices and quantities *ought* to be decided upon, that monopolists *ought* to charge at marginal cost, for example, would be considered, perhaps not entirely fairly, as the typically naive futility of non-economists (or of ministries of economic affairs).[11] But economists themselves did and do just that with regard to political processes, sometimes even apparently considering it to be somehow morally superior to disregard sordid political realities in their policy recommendations.

From this non-political attitude there arises, also the tremendous importance economists attach to one another's ideas, for better or for worse, in the determination of economic policy. Economists are apt to regard the abolition of the Corn Laws as some kind of rational fruit of Ricardian theorizing, as a triumph for 'good economics'. But as Leslie Stephen pertinently asked regarding the free-trade victory: 'Did it mark a triumph of logic, or was it due to the simple fact that the class which wanted cheap bread was politically stronger than the class which wanted dear bread?' (1900, vol. III, p. 164) Similarly, we find Professor Hayek complaining bitterly of the quite unjustifiable deduction by Edgeworth and others in the 1890s of a case for progressive taxation, from the assumption of diminishing marginal utility, which he sees as the fount and origin of contemporary progressive tax policies, without any reference to the electoral developments of the time (Hayek, 1960, p. 208).

It would be quite unjustifiable to rush to the other extreme of a wholesale dismissal of the role of ideas. But considerable scepticism is justifiable regarding Keynes's now rather hackneyed exaggeration to the effect that the ideas of economists, both when they are right and when they are wrong, are so powerful that the world is ruled by little else. Moreover, the more it is insisted that political choices are decisively and unambiguously determined, just like economic choices, by utility maximization, the narrower the scope for 'ideas'. Keynes's proposition should always be balanced by one from J. S. Mill : 'Ideas, unless outward circumstances conspire with them, have in general no very rapid or immediate efficacy in human affairs', – and the salient 'outward circumstances' here are, of course, prospective electoral advantage. (Keynes, 1936, p. 383; J. S. Mill, 1845, p. 503. See also below, chapter 5 and Hutchison, 1978, chapter 10.)

Certainly, Mill's proposition might have a much healthier realistic effect on the treatment of economic policy formation by economists, who seem often to have flown to extremes in their assumptions about political policy-makers. Either these are the 'insidious and crafty animals' of Adam Smith, or they are assumed to be, in Pigou's Platonic phrase, 'philosopher kings' who will at once find it in their interests to put through welfare-maximizing or welfare-optimizing changes when economists point them out.

IV

Let us conclude with a few brief observations on the contemporary situation, where, over several decades, an immense expansion in the role of government in the economy has generated a much wider range of interactions and interdependences between political and economic processes. Not only are economic processes substantially controlled or affected by political forces, but they react back on politics, through the ability of governments to improve their chances of holding on to political power by short-run economic manipulation. In fact, the last third of the twentieth century has been witnessing politicoeconomic interactions very different in nature from, and on a much greater scale and significance than, those which the classical political economists were concerned with, in this country, in the first two thirds of the nineteenth century. Whether with regard to shorter-term cyclical fluctuations, or the processes of inflation, or regarding the longer-term institutional framework for economic efficiency and growth, either in more developed or less developed economies, political forces have obviously become of massive and decisive importance for the workings of economies.

In view of the increasingly important and all-pervasive politicoeconomic interactions in recent decades, it is hardly surprising that economists have been concerning themselves increasingly, in a wide range of different ways, with political processes of one kind or another, whether those of voting arrangements, democratic elections, bureaucracies, or interest-group lobbies, as in the well-known works of Professors Arrow, Buchanan and Tullock, Downs, and Olson; while there has also been the notable example of Professor Hayek turning his attention from the economics of capitalism and socialism to the problems of political constitution-making, of limiting the powers of majorities, and of putting the monetary framework of the economy altogether outside the political process. From the other direction, writers such as, most notably, Professors Rawls and Barry have approached the analysis of economic policies, or the economic aspects of constitutions and institutions, from the standpoint of alternative political values.

One strand or impulse in this intellectual development could be said to have come originally from the side of economic welfare theory, that is Professor Arrow's analysis of how a social welfare function could or could not be constructed by a democratic voting procedure. But, on the whole, political analysis of collective choices and of economic policies should be regarded as a break with welfare economics and its assumptions, rather than a continuation. The essence of neoclassical welfare economics was the propounding of what were intended as *purely economic* criteria for policies on the basis of widely or universally acceptable value-judgements, without reference to political forces, while a quite Utopian degree of knowledge was assumed. To the extent that economic-welfare engineering was ever accepted or enforced, politics, which is about disagreement, would disappear. The investigation of how policies, and social choices, are, or may be, shaped by actual or hypothetical political and electoral forces, must strike out in a very different direction from that taken by economic welfare analysis.

However, much of the social choice analysis which underwent such a mushroom growth in the 1970s seems to share some of the fundamental limitations of abstract economic equilibrium theory and welfare analysis, from the point of view of practical, real-world applicability and predictive content, since it is dependent, in the same way, on the assumption of certainty and adequate knowledge.

In so far as recent attempts at an 'economic' theory of politics have been based on maximization analysis, it shares with much traditional economic theorizing the limitations or problems, of (1) the extent of knowledge, ignorance and uncertainty with which a maximand is pursued; and (2) the content of the maximand.

With regard to (1) the problems arise in seeking to get beyond the simplification of maximization under certainty and of selecting relevant case-studies of the appropriate types of uncertainty, ignorance and erroneous expectations. Indeed, it may not seem so extremely illuminating, in terms of practical, real-world predictions, to have shown that, even under conditions of certainty, with adequate knowledge and stable preferences, democratic voting procedures may not yield any ideally decisive and stable conclusion, but end in cyclical majorities, or deadlocks of one sort or another, when one is perfectly familiar, in the real world of uncertainty, ignorance and shifting expectations and preferences, with how often actual democratic voting procedures fall short of any clear-cut ideal decisiveness.

With regard to (2) maximands in economic theories, especially with regard to private firms, those that can be 'brought within the measuring-rod of money' – as Marshall put it – may have served as a proxy, or first approximation. But there is often no very obvious or easily definable second approximation, so that the maximand is liable to be reduced to the somewhat vacuous one of 'utility'. But trying to define a maximand for political theorizing involves one with even more qualitative or less precisely definable concepts. As Professor Herbert Simon has explained:

As economics expands beyond its central core of price theory, and its central concern with quantities of commodities and money, we observe in it the same shift from highly quantitative analysis, in which equilibration at the margin plays a central role, to a much more qualitative institutional analysis, in which discrete structural alternatives are compared. (1978, p. 6)

As Professor Simon goes on to observe, the more precise and 'rigorous' formulation of maximization analysis, on the lines of much traditional economic theory, may not have so very much that is highly significant to add, in terms of real-world applicability and predictive content, to the looser kind of institutional analysis of political theorists. Political theorizing which takes account of ignorance, uncertainty and complex political maximands cannot avoid, methodologically, a 'long march through the institutions'.

However, what this recent new political dimension to economic policy analysis has achieved has been to counter some of the sometimes highly naïve or even crude brands of politics which economists, explicitly or inexplicitly, have attached to their economics, or embodied in their political economy. Over the centuries the extent, explicitness and quality of the political element in political economy and economics has varied widely. With Adam Smith it attained a profundity and realism which it has hardly or seldom achieved since. Under the later classicals, under the influence, notably, of James Mill, a cruder, and more pretentious 'rationalist' utilitarianism was injected. With the neoclassicals the political element became much less obtrusive, while the analysis of policies, by such masters as Jevons, Sidgwick and Marshall, became more modest, empirical and realistic. In the interests of clarity a serious attempt was made to uphold the (not impossible) academic virtue of keeping the political element reasonably distinct (though not necessarily, of course, quite separate) from the economics. On the other hand, for some time the misleading notion was pursued of maintaining a kind of non-political analysis of economic policies on the basis of the 'economic welfare' concept.

However, when, with the extensive growth of the role of government, political forces inevitably had to be taken account of, and a return to political economy – though of a very different type from that of the classical economists – was proclaimed, then sometimes the politics injected was of a highly questionable nature. Sometimes the Utopian assumption seems to have been resorted to (as we have seen Pigou, in his later years complaining) that economists only had to expound their socially maximizing or optimizing formulae for democratic politicians to seek immediately to implement them in their economic policies. Sometimes Utopian models of social maxima and optima, depending on assumptions of omniscience, were used as a basis for criticizing tendentiously and irrelevantly particular kinds of actual, human, real-world institutions. Sometimes reinserting the adjective 'political' in political economy was taken as a licence for the introduction of the crudest kinds of ideology, sometimes of a totalitarian nature. But there has also been emerging the development and prospect of a more realistic, empirically based treatment, by economists, of political processes, institutions, and politicoeconomic interactions, and hence the creation of a genuine discipline of 'political economy' in respect of both the component parts of that term.

Notes

1　See the quotation from Horwitz about the US in the previous chapter (p. 9): 'at the beginning of the nineteenth century . . . the market was thought to be the most powerful institutional expression of the ideal of equality of opportunity'. Contrast, on the other hand, what J. S. Mill had to say in 1852 about 'the present state of society with all its sufferings and injustices' – that is the *English* 'capitalist' market economy, based on 'the principle of private property'. This principle, according to Mill:

> has never yet had a fair trial in any country; *and less so perhaps in this country than in some others.* The social arrangements of modern Europe commenced from a distribution of property which was the result, not of just partition, or acquisition by industry, but of conquest and violence: and notwithstanding what industry has been doing for many centuries to modify the work of force, the system still retains many and large traces of its origin. The laws of property have never yet conformed to the principles on which the justification of private property rests. They have made property of things which never ought to be property, and absolute property where only a qualified property ought to exist. They have not held the balance fairly between human beings, but have heaped impediments on some, to give advantages to others; they have purposely fostered inequalities, and prevented all from starting fair in the race. That all should indeed start on perfectly equal terms is inconsistent with any law of private property: but if as much pains as has been taken to aggravate the inequality of chances arising from the natural working of the principle, had been taken to temper that inequality by every means not subversive of the principle itself . . . the principle of individual property would have been found to have no necessary connexion with the physical and social evils which almost all Socialist writers assume to be inseparable from it. (1909, pp. 208–9)

> See also my chapter in *The Emerging Consensus?* ed. A. Seldon, 1981.

2　According to J. Viner (1965, p. 85): 'Smith did believe in "representation" in the law-making authority, including representation on a territorial basis, but his criteria of "representation" were not democratic ones and he never expressed dissatisfaction with the Scottish situation, where only a tiny minority had a vote, and on as fortuitous and irrational a basis as can be imagined.'

3 See Smith, 1896, p. 54: 'When there are 100 votes and three candidates, it is possible that the person who is most odious may be elected. If A, B and C be candidates, there may be 34 votes for A, and 33 for B, and as many for C. Thus, though there are 66 votes against A, he carries it. This must be still more the case when a criminal is brought before this assembly, for 34 may think him guilty of murder, 33 of manslaughter, and 33 of chance medley, yet he must suffer for murder.'
4 Ricardo goes on:

> Whatever might be his gains after such a principle had been admitted would be held by a very insecure tenure, and the chance of his making any future gains would be greatly diminished; for the quantity of employment in the country must depend, not only on the quantity of capital, but upon its advantageous distribution, and, above all, on the conviction of each capitalist that he will be allowed to enjoy unmolested the fruits of his capital, his skill, and his enterprise. To take from him this conviction is at once to annihilate half the productive industry of the country, and would be more fatal to the poor labourer than to the rich capitalist himself. This is so self-evident, that men very little advanced beyond the very lowest stations in the country cannot be ignorant of it, and it may be doubted whether any large number even of the lowest would, if they could, promote a division of property. It is the bugbear by which the corrupt always endeavour to rally those who have property to lose around them and it is from this fear, or pretended fear, that so much jealousy is expressed of entrusting the least share of power to the people. But the objection, when urged against reform, is not an honest one, for, if it be allowed that those who have a sacred regard to the rights of property should have a voice in the choice of representatives, the principle is granted for which reformers contend. They profess to want only good government, and, as a means to such an end, they insist that the power of choosing members of Parliament should be given to those who cannot have an interest contrary to good government. If the objection made against reform were an honest one, the objectors would say how low in the scale of society they thought the rights of property were held sacred, and there they would make their stand. That class, and all above it, they would say, may fairly and advantageously be entrusted with the power which is wished to be given them, but the presumption of mistaken views of interest in all below that class would render it hazardous to entrust a similar power with them – it could not at least be safely done until we had more reason to be satisfied that, in their opinion, the interest of the community and that of themselves were identified on this important subject.

This concession would satisfy the reasonable part of the public. It is not Universal Suffrage as an end, but as a means, of good government that the partisans of that measure ask it for. Give them the good government, or let them be convinced that you are really in earnest in procuring it for them, and they will be satisfied, although you should not advance with the rapid steps that they think would be most advantageously taken. My own opinion is in favour of caution, and therefore I lament that so much is said on the subject of Universal Suffrage. I am convinced that an extension of the suffrage, far short of making it universal, will substantially secure to the people the good government they wish for, and therefore I deprecate the demand for the universality of the elective franchise – at the same time, I feel confident that the effects of the measure which would satisfy me would have so beneficial an effect on the public mind, would be the means of so rapidly increasing the knowledge and intelligence of the public, that, in a limited space of time after this first measure of reform were granted, we might, with the utmost safety, extend the right of voting for members of Parliament to every class of the people.

In an article on Ricardo, Professor George Stigler with perhaps more relevance to the period after 1832, writes (1965, p. 324): 'The truths of economics then led directly to good social policy, which only an unrepresentative, soon to be reformed, Parliament sometimes prevented from being translated into immediate action. The possibility that good economics will not inevitably carry the day in a democracy, of which we are acutely aware, also dwelled in the unpredicted future.'

5   Lowe presided over the Political Economy Club, as Chancellor reduced income-tax to an all-time minimum of 2d. in the pound, and coined the phrase (after 1867): 'We must induce our future masters to learn their letters.' Another Philosophic Radical later to oppose extension of the franchise was John Austin, Professor of Law at University College, at one time accepted, as Leslie Stephen puts it, 'as the heir-apparent to Bentham in the special department of jurisprudence' (1900, vol. 3, p. 317).

6   See Dicey, 1905, p. 253; and on the 1867 Reform Act, McCready, 1956, and Hanham, 1959.

7   As Mr M. Cowling has written of 1867 and after: 'Disraeli did not revert to being a Radical. Derby did not suddenly discover Marx. Since there was to be a predominantly working-class electorate in the boroughs, they had to put themselves right with it. . . . The result was a Tory social policy in the seventies.' (1967, p. 310)

8   Reviewing the first volume of *Das Kapital* in 1868, Engels remarked: '*Universal suffrage compels the ruling class to court the favour of the workers.* Under these circumstances, four or five representatives are a *power*, if they know how to use their position' (Engels's italics). This is very

different from any Marxian state in the twentieth century. See Marx, 1942, quoted by Prager, 1967, p. 208.

9   See, however, J. Pickett and R. L. Alpine, 1965, p. 51, who examine the electoral implications of the considerable differences in economic 'knowledgeability' which they claim exists between men and women.

10   Lloyd George showed his awareness of the danger to the Liberal Party in 1904: 'We have a great Labour Party springing up. Unless we can prove . . . that there is no necessity for a separate party to press forward the legitimate claims of labour, you will find that . . . the Liberal Party will be practically wiped out and that, in its place, you will get a more extreme and revolutionary party.' (Grigg, 1978, p. 77)

11   Such an accusation is not entirely fair or realistic. Simplifiers, or oversimplifiers, are apt to regard either free-market prices or governmentally and legally fixed prices as the only logical alternatives, excluding any ambiguous middle ground. This oversimplification is based on the oversimplification of textbook price theory, which usually assumes that firms and consumers *know*, at every moment, with completeness, certainty and precision, exactly what their maximizing or optimizing prices and quantities are, and exactly when they change. It follows that only governmental or legal restraints will prevent self-interested individuals or units from charging the prices which they *know*, *with certainty and precision*, to be in their own best interests as they clearly see them. But, of course, actual firms do *not* know with certainty and precision what their profit (or other) maximizing price is, or exactly where their own best interest lies. Consequently they are open to persuasion, or what Sir Dennis Robertson called 'ear-stroking'. Much of economic policy, or 'planning', has been based on this technique, in this country, sporadically in the US, and even in Germany. The limits for its successful operation may be narrow or precarious, but at least its possibility exists, as would immediately be conceded for political behaviour.

References

Buchanan, J. M. and Tullock, G. (1962), *The Calculus of Consent*.

Clark, Kitson (1951), 'The Electorate and the Repeal of the Corn Laws', *Transactions of the Royal Historical Society*.

Cowling, M. (1967), *Disraeli, Gladstone and Revolution*.

Dicey, A. V. (1905), *Lectures on the Relation between Law and Opinion*.

Downs, A. (1957), *An Economic Theory of Democracy*.

Engels, F. (1868), Review of K. Marx, *Capital*, vol. 1, reprinted in K. Marx, *Selected Works*, vol. 1, 1942.

Gash, N. (1953), *Politics in the Age of Peel*.

Grigg, J. (1978), *Lloyd George, The People's Champion*.

Hamberger, J. (1963), *James Mill and the Art of Revolution*.

Hanham, H. J. (1959), *Elections and Party Management: Politics in the Time of Disraeli and Gladstone*.

Hayek, F. A. (1960), *The Constitution of Liberty*.

Hobsbawm, E. (1969), *Industry and Empire*.

Horwitz, M. J. (1976), 'The Legacy of 1776 in Legal and Economic Thought', *Journal of Law and Economics*, vol. 19, Oct., pp. 621ff.

Hutchison, T. W. (1978), *Revolutions and Progress in Economic Knowledge*.
    (1981), 'The Changing Intellectual Climate in Economics', in *The Emerging Consensus*, ed. A. Seldon.

Jevons, W. S. (1886), *Letters and Journal*, ed. H. A. Jevons.

Keynes, J. M. (1936), *The General Theory of Employment, Interest and Money*.

Leoni, B. (1957), 'The Meaning of "Political" in Political Decisions', *Political Studies*, pp. 239ff.

McCready, H. W. (1956), 'Britain's Labour Lobby 1867–1875', *Canadian Journal of Economics and Political Science*, May, pp. 141ff.

McCulloch, J. R. (1843), *Principles of Political Economy*.

Marx, K. (1942), *Selected Works* (vol. 1).

Mill, J. (1955), *Essay on Government*, ed. C. V. Shields.

Mill, J. S. (1845), 'The Claims of Labour', *Edinburgh Review*, Apr., pp. 503ff.
    (1861), *Representative Government*.
    (1909), *The Principles of Political Economy*, ed. W. J. Ashley.

Pickett J., and Alpine, R. L. (1965), 'Economic Knowledge and Political Behaviour', *Journal of Economic Studies*, vol. 1, no. 1, p. 51.

Pigou, A. C. (1902), 'A Parallel between Economic and Political Theory' *Economic Journal*, vol. 12, pp. 274ff.
    (1939), Presidential Address to Royal Economic Society, *Economic Journal*, vol. 49, pp. 215ff.

Prager, T. (1967), 'On the Political Compulsions of Economic Growth', in C. H. Feinstein (ed.), *Socialism, Capitalism and Economic Growth, Essays Presented to Maurice Dobb*.

Ricardo, D. (1952), *Works and Correspondence*, ed. P. Sraffa, vol. 5.

Robbins, L. C. (1952), *The Theory of Economic Policy*.

Senior, N. W. (1871), *Journals Kept in France and Italy from 1848 to 1852*, 2 vols.

Seymour, C. (1915), *Electoral Reform in England and Wales*.

Shehab, F. (1953), *Progressive Taxation*.

Simon, H. (1978), 'Rationality as Process and as Product of Thought', *American Economic Review*, vol. 68, May, pp. 1ff.

Smith, A. (1896), *Lectures on Justice, Police, Revenue and Arms*, ed. E. Cannan.
    (1976), *The Wealth of Nations*, ed. R. H. Campbell and A. S. Skinner and W. B. Todd, 2 vols.

Stephen, L. (1900), *The English Utilitarians*, 3 vols.

Stigler, G. J. (1965), *Essays in the History of Economics.*
Strachey, J. (1956), *Contemporary Capitalism.*
Trevelyan, G. M. (1965), *British History in the Nineteenth Century and After.*
Tullock, G. (1962), *Entrepreneurial Politics*, Research Monograph, Thomas Jefferson Centre for Studies in Political Economy.
Viner, J. (1965), *Guide to John Rae's Life of Adam Smith.*

3

The Philosophy and Politics
of the Cambridge School

I *Introduction*

The Cambridge school, which may be said to have come into existence with the accession of Marshall to the chair in 1885, occupied, for much of the first half of the twentieth century, a leading and, for a time, almost a monopolistic position in British economics. The school included two of the most important English economists of their own, or any other, time, and in its heyday achieved a degree of exclusive prestige only surpassed by the classicals. In the main controversies over British economic policy in the earlier part of the century its members played a dominant part, as, for example, in the resistance to the tariff reform campaign in the first decade of this century, and on behalf of 'welfare' and employment policies in the interwar years. In so far as economic policy in Britain, in the first half of the twentieth century, was influenced – if at all – by contemporary economic theorizing or economists, then it must have been largely by Cambridge economic theorizing and economists. Also, in the emergence of various interpretations of Marxian economics in the second quarter of this century, it was one or two Cambridge economists who played a leading and vitally influential role.

It might be argued that the term 'school' is hardly applicable to the Cambridge economists because of the profound divergences and fierce disagreements in interests and doctrines, both between generations and between members of the same generation. Controversies, and even feuds, of a quite fundamental and persistent nature have seldom been absent from Cambridge economics since the quarrels of Marshall and his second-in-command Foxwell. Certainly, if there has been a Cambridge school, then Marshall was its founder. But it will be a recurrent theme of this chapter that several of Marshall's most important interests and methodological prescriptions almost completely disappeared, or were significantly eroded, even before his death in 1924. In fact, a considerable part (but not, of course, all) of the fulsome tributes to Marshall paid by his immediate successors had an element of lip-service about them, while some of his most fundamental ideas and interests were being quietly abandoned.

On the other hand, a remarkable feature of Cambridge economists in, roughly, the first half of the century, which could be said to justify the use of the term 'school', was that they tended to spend their whole, or almost their whole, careers as economists, from Freshman to Emeritus, in Cambridge, except for wartime breaks, or the odd session in foreign parts. These locational limits were reinforced by rather concentrated reading habits, and they tended to impart, in some cases, a considerable degree of what Dr Gunnar Myrdal once called that 'attractive Anglo-Saxon kind of unnecessary originality' (1939, p. 8), which comes from confining reading largely – though not entirely – to the works of one's immediate colleagues. Thus, outside influences, in so far as they penetrated at all significantly – even the later influence of Marx – had to pass through a filter of Cambridge preconceptions. (Not that any such restraints had originally applied to Marshall, who spent some years as far afield as Bristol and Oxford, and, who, moreover, in his early years had read very widely and enterprisingly among then very little-known French and German authors, notably Cournot and von Thünen.)

This chapter is confined to some of the main philosophical, methodological, political and policy ideas of Cambridge economists roughly down to the mid-fifties of this century, after which time some dilution set in. It is confined to economists who spent the whole, or almost the whole, of their careers, from first-year undergraduates onwards, in Cambridge, and who contributed importantly to the philosophy, methodology and politics of economics. Obviously Sidgwick and Marshall were the founding fathers, together with J. N. Keynes, with his important book on scope and method. They were succeeded by Pigou and J. M. Keynes. Then came the introduction of the Marxian element by Dobb and Professor Joan Robinson. Lesser roles in this story were played by Foxwell, Robertson, Shove, and Dr Sraffa. The last-named was to some extent the joker in the pack in coming so influentially into Cambridge economics from right outside as early as he did. But Dr Sraffa did not come fully into his own until the 1960s, with the publication of his text *Production of Commodities by Means of Commodities* (1960), some time after our period is coming to an end.

II *Sidgwick*

Henry Sidgwick (1838–1900) is of fundamental importance in the history of Cambridge economics, both in his own right and as Marshall's 'spiritual father and mother' – as the latter himself described their relationship. It was Sidgwick, son of an Anglican clergyman, who, on losing his Christian faith, in the late 1850s or early 1860s, was the first in Cambridge, in his search for a kind of religious replacement, to take the spiritual and intellectual route to the social (or 'moral') sciences and economics – a route subsequently followed by Marshall. Writing of 'the new influx of ideas' led and provoked by Comte, Spencer, Darwin and others in the 1860s, Sidgwick stated:

What we aimed at from a social point of view was a complete revision of human relations, political, moral and economic, in the light of science directed by comprehensive and impartial sympathy and an unsparing reform of whatever, in the judgement of science, was pronounced to be not conducive to the general happiness. (A. and E. Sidgwick, 1906, p. 39)

Similarly, describing what she called 'the mid-Victorian trend of thought and feeling', Beatrice Webb (whom we shall meet later discovering 'A New Civilization' in Stalin's Russia) wrote:

There was the current belief in the scientific method, in that intellectual synthesis of observation and experiment, hypothesis and verification, by means of which alone all mundane problems were to be solved. And added to this belief in science was the consciousness of a new motive; the transference of the emotion of self-sacrificing service from God to man. (1938, p. 153; see also Hutchison, 1953, p. 9)

This attitude had come down from the Enlightenment. What was characteristic in this phase of the 1860s and 1870s was the combination of missionary fervour for social and economic reform, with the belief in science and scientific method. Of course, there were varying interpretations of what 'science and scientific method' required. But this combination of belief in 'the light of science' together with the driving force of 'social enthusiasm' – as Pigou was later to call it – characterized a general, and not simply a Cambridge movement. Cambridge, however, provided what was in some ways a specially favourable site, or soil, for its growth, because science had begun to win there a prestige and devotion not yet achieved to the same extent elsewhere in Britain.

The danger was, of course, that the empirical discipline of science might be eroded or discarded when fused with the missionary fervour and social enthusiasm of some of the new practitioners of social and economic science. In some cases a naïve, pretentious, dogmatic and undisciplined 'scientism' emerged, fulfilling the role of a kind of surrogate for religious faith. But, for Sidgwick, 'the light of science' implied a firm control over the driving force of his 'comprehensive sympathy', by a seriously understood, and conscientiously upheld, scientific method. The balance, however, between discipline and enthusiasm was bound to be precarious and subsequently was not always maintained with the same austere caution as it had been by Sidgwick. For Sidgwick could be regarded, as J. M. Keynes later claimed, as having carried on in Cambridge, 'in direct succession', the English tradition of Locke, Berkeley, Hume and Mill, 'who in spite of their divergences of doctrine, are united in a preference for what is matter of fact, and have conceived their subject as a branch of science rather than the creative imagination, prose writers, hoping to be understood' (1921, p. v).

As Keynes implied, Sidgwick's position, as an upholder of this tradition, imposed a commitment to clarity and to empirical, factual testing. It implied also, for Sidgwick, a degree of caution, and even scepticism, regarding policy pronouncements, together, in particular, with the more precise methodological prescription of the normative-positive distinction. This distinction had been introduced into political economy in the later classical period by Whately and Senior, and upheld by J. S. Mill and Cairnes. Sidgwick insisted that 'the economist's ultimate aim is to explain and predict facts. . . . We shall gain in clearness by distinguishing the problems of economic science from the political or ethical problems that are commonly combined with them.' (1883, p. 24)

Sidgwick went on to warn against the exaggerations of some of the classicals: 'I certainly think that the language sometimes used by economic writers, suggesting as it does that the doctrines they expound are entitled in respect of scientific perfection to rank with those of Physics, is liable to be seriously misleading' (p. 45). He, surely very wisely, rejected the then Oxford conclusion, that Political Economy ought to be treated 'unscientifically,' (as Professor Bonamy Price had advocated) and concluded with admirable balance:

My inference would rather be, not that we ought not to aim at being as scientific as we can, but that we ought to take care not to deceive ourselves as to the extent to which we have actually attained our aim: that, for instance, so far as we are treating Political Economy positively, we should avoid mistaking a generalisation from limited experience for a universal law. (*ibid*., italics added)

Sidgwick's approach to politics and policies was cautious and empirical. Though he was penetrating and discerning regarding the problems of a market economy, he was, as a political realist, well aware that the intervention of governments might only make such problems worse: 'It does not follow, of course, that wherever *laissez-faire* falls short governmental interference is expedient; since the inevitable drawbacks and disadvantages of the latter may, in any particular case, be worse than the shortcomings of private industry' (1883, p. 419). He went on to warn against the dangers of political power and influence being used for corrupt purposes, of misusing the economic functions of government to gratify politically influential sections of the community, and of 'wasteful expenditure under the influence of popular sentiment'.

Sidgwick's addition to the functions of government, that of 'rightly distributing produce among members of the community', was a significant and consequential step beyond the classical position. But he insisted on a point on which there was later to be much strenuous confusion in Cambridge and elsewhere:

There is no obvious and simple connexion between an investigation of the actual facts of the division of wealth among labourers, employees and owners of capital or land, and a discussion of the principles on which it ought to be shared among the classes; and there is no generally accepted axiom of ethics or politics which can be taken as a principle for judging of the rightness or goodness of different modes of division. (1883, p. 26)

He warned regarding a socialistic method of redistribution that 'it would have so much less to divide' (1887, p. 516), and he was apprehensive of socialism being accompanied by what he called 'Caesarism'.

On the subject of free trade *versus* protection, which was to become a major issue of controversy, in which Marshall and Pigou later also put forward very strong and decisive views, Sidgwick rejected vigorously the a priorist free-trade case. He insisted that arguments for protection:

require to be met by a line of argument different from that which English economists have usually adopted. I think it erroneous to maintain, on the ordinary economic grounds, that temporary Protection must always be detrimental to the protecting country, even if it were carried out by a perfectly wise and strong Government, able to resist all influences ·of sinister and sectarian interests, and to act solely for the good of the nation. *The decisive argument against it is rather the political consideration that no actual Government is competent for this difficult and delicate task; that Protection, as actually applied under the play of political forces, is sure to foster many weak industries that have no chance of living without artificial support, and to hamper industries that might thrive independently* . . . so that it turns out a dangerous and clumsy, as well as costly, instrument. (1962, p. 81, italics added)

In fact, the politics in Sidgwick's political economy were informed by a political-philosophical culture, and a conscientious realism and empiricism, which was not to survive unscathed amid the enthusiastic policy and political ambitions of twentieth-century Cambridge.

III *Marshall, J. N. Keynes and the Scope and Method of Positive Economics*

The same wave of ideas, from the sixties of the nineteenth century, with its somewhat precariously balanced fusion of optimistic confidence in 'the light of science', together with social reformist moral fervour, which brought Henry Sidgwick to the study of political economy and 'the social sciences', also brought Alfred Marshall, four years his junior, to dedicate himself to political economy and economics. The motivating force, therefore, of this powerful tide of ideas was significant for the general approach of the Cambridge school.

It is well known how Marshall's moral fervour as an economist supervened on an earlier ambition, as an undergraduate, to become a Christian missionary. Indeed Marshall's peculiar greatness as an economist stemmed from the strength and balance with which he upheld and combined the two principles, not easily kept in harmony, first that economics could and should be 'a handmaid of ethics and a servant of practice', in Pigou's phrase (Pigou, ed., 1925, p. 84), concentrated on urgent, real-world social and economic problems; and second, at the same time, that the economist's efforts must be based on a strict and conscientious code of scientific discipline. The time was ripe, Marshall urged, in his Inaugural Lecture (1885), with the lifting of what Cairnes had called 'the great Malthusian difficulty', for proclaiming and implementing 'the faith', denied to their classicial predecessors, which 'modern economists have, in the possibility of a vast improvement in the condition of the working classes' (Pigou, ed., 1925, p. 155). In a rousing peroration to this lecture Marshall proclaimed his hopes for Cambridge economics:

It will be my most cherished ambition, my highest endeavour, to do what with my poor ability and my limited strength I may, to increase the numbers of those, whom Cambridge, the great mother of strong men, sends out into the world with cool heads but warm hearts, willing to give some at least of their best powers to grappling with the social suffering around them. (p. 174)

Marshall might have been somewhat surprised at some of the more extreme directions in which 'warm hearts' and perhaps not so 'cool heads' led some subsequent alumni. He would certainly have been quite appalled to learn, a century later, that according to the *doyen* of English theoretical economists, 'much of economic theory' (including, presumably, much or some in Cambridge) was being 'pursued for no better reason than its intellectual attraction; it is a good game' (Hicks, 1979, p. viii).

It was his overriding concern with real-world problems which drew Marshall to history and away from mathematical methods. As Pigou said:

Though a skilled mathematician, he used mathematics sparingly. He saw that excessive reliance on this instrument might lead us astray in pursuit of intellectual toys, imaginary problems not conforming to the conditions of real life: and further, might distort our sense of proportion by causing us to neglect factors that could not easily be worked up in the mathematical machine. (Pigou, ed., 1925, p. 84)[1]

Indeed what was unique to Marshall among leading Cambridge economists, and others, was his concern with the historical method and with institutional relativism. He did not go all the way with the German historical school, but went significantly further than J. N. Keynes. Marshall wrote to Foxwell: 'Most of the suggestions which I made on the proofs of Keynes' *Scope and Method* were aimed at bringing it more into harmony with the views of Schmoller. . . . As regards method I regard myself as midway between Keynes *plus* Sidgwick *plus* Cairnes and Schmoller *plus* Ashley.' (Coase, 1975, pp. 27–8) Professor Coase adds:

Although Marshall claims to occupy this middle ground, and in a sense he does, if we study what Marshall says, it seems to me that he always emphasises induction, the collection and assembly of facts, and plays down what we would term 'theory', a word which, as we have seen, he did not much like when applied to economics. Indeed in one letter to Foxwell he says that in economics there is 'no theory to speak of'. (1975, p. 28)

Marshall's historical-institutional method was deployed most effectively in *Industry and Trade*, which, in so far as it deals with monopolistic tendencies rather than the competitive model, could be considered, in terms of method and real-world relevance, as more significant than his *Principles*. But *Industry and Trade*, and its method, were almost completely disregarded by Marshall's successors in Cambridge. In particular, what came to be called 'the theory of the firm' was later developed on methodological lines, rejected by Marshall, which shunted the subject into what has been called 'one of the most notorious blind alleys in twentieth century economics' (Loasby, 1976, p. 174; see also Williams, 1978).

Anyhow, like his mentor Sidgwick, Marshall conscientiously subjected his moral, activist fervour as an economist to the discipline, demarcations, and distinctions of a scientist. Marshall later (1906) wrote to Foxwell: 'I am never roused to great enthusiasm about anything which does not seem to me thoroughly scientific' (Keynes, 1972, vol. 10, p. 292). For Marshall, 'scientific' was no hollow, tendentious prestige term. It meant observing and respecting, as scrupulously as is humanly possible, and not blurring and fudging, crucial distinctions and demarcations. It especially implied a conscientious caution in policy pronouncements. In his inaugural lecture Marshall warned:

It is true that an economist, like any other citizen, may give his own judgment as to the best solution of various practical problems. . . . But in such cases the counsel bears only the authority of the individual who gives it: he does not speak with the voice of his science. And *the economist has to be specially careful to make this clear*; because there is much misunderstanding as to the scope of his science, and undue claims to authority on practical matters have often been put forward on its behalf. (Pigou, ed., 1925, p. 165, italics added)

Perhaps Marshall was over-optimistic in believing that preaching by economists was ineffective (and evidently some of his successors have not agreed):

I think that, when the academic student takes on himself the role of a preacher, he is generally less effective than when he treats the problems of life objectively; that is when he assumes no major premises based on his own views of duty, his own ideals of social life. (*ibid.*, p. 397)[2]

In fact, in the late eighties and early nineties, in his first decade in the Cambridge chair, Marshall successfully conducted a minor and restrained *Methodenstreit* against a young Oxford group who were enthusiastic for a much broader social, historical and unrestrictedly ethical conception of political economy, more on the lines of the *Verein für Sozialpolitik*, and rejected Marshall's Cambridge conception of economic science marked off by a regard for narrower scientific distinctions and demarcations from ethical, political and social factors. (I am indebted on this point to the as yet unpublished work of Dr A. Kadish, on Oxford's Young Economists during the 1880s and early 1890s.)

Certainly it can be argued that Marshall (and Sidgwick too) did not always, in all their concepts, interpret their commitment to 'science' as strictly and precisely as they should have done. But what is undeniable is the effort and stand they made, which was for a time successful and influential for the development of economics in Britain. Indeed it was Marshall, with his *Principles*, and later his Tripos, who was more responsible than anyone else for the introduction of the term 'Economics', which was certainly not intended merely as a terminological abbreviation. To some extent this change of name was related to a new kind of 'professional' aspiration, keenly cherished by Marshall. The introduction of the new term was also related to the renewed emphasis on the positive-normative distinction, which had come down from Senior. (In fact this distinction was an important part of the sense in which, as far as Marshall was concerned, 'neoclassical' meant 'renewing the (later) classical method'.)

But the new term 'Economics' made a further point with regard to the interactions between politics and economics. The earlier classical economists had been concerned with changing the framework of the economic order to that of a thoroughgoing market economy, obviously a highly political process. But that change had been completed by the middle of the century. The framework of the market economy was then taken as broadly given, with the political involvement of government at first at a very low level. Certainly a significant expansion of the role of government, in various directions, especially with regard to the mitigation of poverty, was envisaged by Marshall. Indeed, it is highly misleading to maintain that Sidgwick, Marshall, and the 'neoclassical' economists generally, 'were able ‚to retain unimpaired the classical bias, towards economic individualism and *laissez-faire* up to 1914' (Deane, 1978, p. 101); or that: 'For the neoclassicals, *laissez-faire* became a dogma' (Robinson and Eatwell, 1973, p. 47). A much less inaccurate assessment was given by Maurice Dobb (not likely to be unduly flattering to 'neoclassicals'): 'Marshall was the first economist in the Ricardian tradition to pass from specific exceptions to the harmony of *laissez-faire* to a general stress on its limitations; in the work of Pigou, who succeeded him, these exceptions have formed the special theme' (1931, p. 368).[3]

But the most accurate account of 'the age of Marshall' is given in Professor Jha's scholarly work of that title, where he emphasizes that *The Economic Journal* for 1891–1915 shows English economists interested in all types of projects for economic and social reform. According to Professor Jha:

The neo-classical economists were deeply concerned with the various aspects of poverty. . . .
[They] saw clearly the relation between poverty, unemployment and the trade cycle. . . . It was increasingly realised that markets did not necessarily lead to the maximum satisfaction of the consumer under the conditions of *laissez-faire*. . . . The support given to the extension of state activity . . . continued to increase. (1973, pp. 201–3)

The expansion of the role of government, supported by the English neoclassicals, from the minimal base of the 1860s was highly significant (including sooner or later a much stronger role for trade unions, a new attitude to the poverty problem, support for progressive taxation and for counter-cyclical public works).

But for Marshall, when writing his *Principles*, the interactions between politics and economics, within the framework of a market economy, and of what Pigou was later to call 'a stable general culture', were still at a very low level. So the assumptions of a more or less non-political economics continued to be less unrealistic than at almost any other period in Britain (still worlds away from the developments of the second half of the twentieth century after two world wars and the intensification of democratic politics). But by the latter part of the twentieth century in Britain, non-political economics, as Marshall envisaged it, that is, as concerned overridingly with policy relevance (rather than with 'a good game'), was left with a very tenuous and dubious area of relevance. Politics had inevitably come back into political economy.

The most forthright insistence in Cambridge on the normative-positive distinction, and the demarcation it implies, came from J. N. Keynes (whose ideas have largely been rediscovered by Professor Milton Friedman, the leading Neo-(J.N.)Keynesian, who goes much further than Keynes did in insisting on the closest parallels between economics and the natural sciences). Marshall seems to have differed from Keynes's emphasis with regard to history and induction, but not significantly with regard to the normative-positive distinction.

Keynes begins by summarizing the later classical views of Senior, J. S. Mill, Cairnes and Bagehot as implying that: 'A sharp line of distinction is drawn between political economy itself and its applications to practice. . . . Political economy is, in other words, a science, not an art or a department of ethical enquiry' (1890, p. 12). Keynes insists on 'recognising a distinct positive science of political economy', and that it shall be 'pursued in the first instance independently' (pp. 46–7). His reasons are:

> Our work will be done more thoroughly, and both our theoretical and our political conclusions will be the more trustworthy, if we are content to do one thing at a time. . . .
> The attempt to fuse together enquiries as to what is, and enquiries as to what ought to be, is likely to stand in the way of giving clear and unbiased answers to either set of questions. Our investigation, for instance, of the laws that determine competitive wages cannot but be very seriously hampered, if the very same discussion is to serve for a solution of the problem whether wages so determined are fair wages. (p. 48)

Keynes insisted on a commitment to *clarity* and the normative-positive distinction, not only with regard to policy, but with regard to methodological issues:

The endeavour to merge questions of what ought to be with questions of what is tends to confuse, not only economic discussions about economic method. The relative value to be attached to different methods of investigation is very different, according as we take the ethical and practical standpoint, or the purely scientific standpoint. (p. 63)

J. N. Keynes's was a notable Cambridge statement, broadly supported by, and at times explicitly argued by Marshall. It is an indication of how dominant completely contrasting views later became in Cambridge, and how completely forgotten the views of J. N. Keynes and Marshall became, that some seventy years later a very influential Cambridge economist could write: 'In Cambridge we had never been taught that economics should be *wertfrei* or *that the positive and normative can be sharply divided* (Robinson, 1962, p. 74, italics added).

IV *Marshall on Policy, Politics and the British Economy*

The philosophical preconceptions and methodological doctrines of economists often reflect, or are closely linked with, their policy ideas and proposals. Economists are apt to argue for those 'methods' which seem to lead to the kind of results they want. But the relationship may also be partly or mainly one of 'mood', in that the unqualified forthrightness and confidence with which an economist recommends particular types of policies, or intervention or non-intervention by government in the economy, will tend to reflect his methodological or epistemological tenets.

An economist who is cautious, fallibilist and empiricist, distrustful of *a priori* axioms and introspection, will tend to be cautious and tentative regarding politics and policies; while a confidence in securely established 'laws' of economics will tend to make for more sweeping and ambitious policy recommendations. In spite of his youthful and recurring anxiety 'to do good' – as Keynes (J.M.) put it – Marshall's conscientious concern for scientific discipline rendered him highly cautious and restrained in his public pronouncements on policy. He was *extremely* chary about using his almost unique intellectual or scientific prestige on behalf of the policies he favoured. Tom Stoppard has observed of more recent fashions that 'it's better to have halitosis than no opinion'. But Marshall was quite ready to ask regarding such a pressing and poignant economic problem as that of low wages: 'Why should I be ashamed to say that I know of no simple remedy?' (Pigou, ed., 1925, p. 387). In fact, Marshall's policy views can sometimes only be discerned in minor writings or letters and are only hinted at in his best-known books. His very thorough investigation of the most celebrated policy issue of the day – tariff reform – remained for years unpublished.

No attempt is made here to review in any detail Marshall's contributions on economic policy. On some of the main branches of economic policy Marshall's ideas both followed those of Sidgwick and were followed, in turn, by his successors. For example, regarding the possibilities of redistribution, Marshall decisively marked off his position from that of the classicals. He referred to 'doctrines that were universal among the economists of the beginning of the century', to the effect that: 'if you tax the rich, and give money to the working classes, the result will be that the working classes will increase in number, and the result will be you will have lowered wages in the next generation; and the grant will not have improved the position of the working classes on the whole.' But Marshall firmly insisted: '*As regards this a change has come, which separates the economics of this generation from the economics of the past*' (1926, p. 225, italics added).

Indeed, Marshall claimed with pride regarding the change in policies since the classical era: 'The great glory of the fiscal policy of the latter two-thirds of the nineteenth century is, that it found the working classes paying a very much greater percentage of their income in taxes than the rich did, and that it left them paying a less percentage' (p. 410). However, he warned very realistically against the adverse effects on production of 'reckless' schemes of redistribution: 'Many of the social reformers of today, in their desire to improve the distribution, are reckless as to the effects of their schemes on the production of wealth' (Pigou, ed., 1925, p. 162).

Though he did not foresee the very serious unemployment problems which developed after his death, he was ready, in thoroughly anti-Ricardian terms, to support relief works during a slump. Certainly, also, Marshall took very seriously problems of monopoly and restrictive practices, devoting his largest work mainly to such problems, and he was acutely concerned about the increasing powers of unions.

But there was one main problem, in particular, which his realistic grasp of the forces making for and against economic growth enabled Marshall to discern. This was the emerging problem, towards the end of the nineteenth century, of Britain's relatively slow rate of growth, compared with her main competitors. Marshall showed his anxiety about this trend in some powerful letters around the turn of the century, and it is a recurring theme in his *Industry and Trade* (1919). In a letter of 1901 Marshall warned:

Our real danger is that we shall be undersold in the product of high class industries, and have to turn more and more to low class industries. There is no fear of our going back absolutely, but only relatively. The danger is that our industries will become of a lower grade relatively to other countries: that those which are in front of us will run farther away from us, and those which are behind us will catch up. This might be tolerable if peace were assured; but I fear it is not. Here I am very sad and anxious. . . . (Pigou, ed., 1925, p. 393)

In his *Memorandum on the Fiscal Policy of International Trade* (completed in 1903 but not published until 1908) Marshall viewed 'the future of England with grave anxiety'. It should be noted how completely Marshall rejected the remedy of tariff reform. If economists can be said to have exercised any influence on major policy decisions in the opening decades of this century, then Cambridge economists may have done so with regard to the rejection of protective tariffs. Just as Pigou followed Marshall on this important policy issue, so Marshall followed Sidgwick. In particular, with a clear perception of the increasing power of trade unions, Marshall saw the great dangers of the abuse of that power in respect of economic and fiscal policy. England, Marshall estimated:

excels all other countries in the solid strength of her Trade Unions; and perhaps *her greatest danger* is that they be tempted to use that strength for the promotion of the interests of particular groups of workers at the expense of wider interests, as the landowning classes did when they had the power. (1926, p. 396, italics added)

It is clear that, although Marshall had marked off 'economics' from politics, when he had to bring back politics into the appraisal of economic policies (as he recognized was inevitable) the politics which he brought back were, like his mentor Sidgwick's, of a thoroughly realistic and empirical nature. He was keenly aware of the possibilities, indeed probabilities, of 'government failure', and would never have committed the unrealistic tendentiousness of describing as 'market failure' a 'failure' to achieve what only a government of perfectly omniscient, omnipotent, and altruistic angels might conceivably achieve, but which no actual human being, or human group, *could* practicably achieve, or was usually likely even to approach. Marshall observed to the Industrial Remuneration Conference (1885):

Even as human nature is, an infinitely wise, virtuous, and powerful Government could, I will admit, rid us of many of our worst economic evils. But human nature is unfortunately, to be found in Government as elsewhere; and in consequence Government management, even if perfectly virtuous, is very far from being infinitely wise. . . . Wastefulness is the least evil of Government management. A greater evil is that it deadens the self-reliant and inventive faculties, and makes progress slow. But the greatest evil of all is that it tends to undermine political, and through political, social morality. (IRC Report, 1885, p. 174)

Marshall concluded:

Whatever tends to bring money into politics leads to great loss to all, *particularly to the working classes.* (p. 175, italics added)

With regard to the problem, around the turn of the century, of the relative decline of Britain's rate of growth and economic power, Marshall put forward no oversimplified, monocausal explanation. He emphasized failures in technical education and mentioned 'the apathy of many employers' (Pigou, ed., 1925, p. 399). He also expressed much sympathy with some of the earlier activities of unions. But he repeatedly assigned primary emphasis to what he called 'the dominance in some unions of the desire to make work and an increase in their power to do so' (p. 399). He maintained:

The anti-social side of English Trade-Union regulations for the maintenance of a standard wage seems to be mainly responsible for the result that some tens of thousands of Englishmen are doing unskilled work at low wages in order that a small group of people, by cruel apprenticeship regulations, etc., may sustain their standard rate a few shillings higher than it otherwise would have been. (p. 385)

Marshall condemned 'the most malignant of all social evils – the expulsion of the masses of the people from the best work which they are capable of performing' (p. 384). He singled out the engineers and the bricklayers. As a result of the demands of the Amalgamated Society of Engineers: 'The progress upwards of the English working classes, from the position of hewers of wood and drawers of water, to masters of nature's forces will, I believe receive a lasting check' (p. 398). Similarly: 'If bricklayers' unions could have been completely destroyed twenty years ago, I believe bricklayers would now be as well off and more self-respecting than they are: and cottages would be 10 or 20% larger all round' (p. 400; see also Marshall, 1919, p.409).

At one point Marshall offers a rough quantitative estimate of the respective responsibilities for the American lead in productivity:

The balance against us, allowing for the superior weight of American locomotives, comes out at about 3:1, i.e. 3 Glasgow men needed to do the work of 1 American. I should put (say) a quarter of this to account of our employers, a half to account of new-unionism, and the remaining quarter to no account at all. I mean that, when a man works in a leisurely way and for relatively short hours, he does get some gain which may be set off against the loss in his efficiency. (Pigou, ed., 1925, p. 401, in a letter of 1897)

In *Industry and Trade* Marshall emphasized the danger in some industries 'that a modern American machine is less likely to be worked grudgingly and to less than its full capacity in Germany than in England' (1919, p. 137). He suggested that the emergence of those practices which were playing such an important part in Britain's relative decline was to be explained as follows:

This evil side of trade-union policy was developed at a time when Britain's machine industries were so far ahead of those of any other country, that they had little to fear from external competition, while in other countries the necessity of making the most of relatively imperfect appliances, in order to make way against British competition, was so urgent and so prominent that vested interests in the sectional control of machinery had little chance of being developed. (1919, p. 641)

For Marshall the study of economic growth had to be pursued historically and institutionally and was intended to promote not 'a good game', but a grasp of real-world processes and problems. He would, presumably, have been very little interested in the construction and manipulation of countless highly abstract and oversimplified 'models' of growth, or of the accumulation of capital. Certainly, in the first half of the twentieth century, the problem of Britain's declining relative economic power was, to some extent, an intermittent, background development. But it was to be a very long time, well into the second half of the century, before Marshall's successors seemed to discern or interest themselves in this overriding British problem. (One can only wonder what Marshall would have made of Cambridge economists, some three quarters of a century later, allying themselves with union officials in developing the senile industries argument for an extensive system of protective tariffs.)[4]

V *Foxwell and Pigou*

Foxwell, Marshall's first pupil and long-serving second-in-command, diverged fundamentally in philosophy and approach from the Cambridge pattern set by Sidgwick and Marshall, in that he shared little or nothing either of their social enthusiasm or of their scientific standards or ambitions. He was a historian and scholar, and as Keynes (J.M.) put it, 'in the literal sense of the word a conservative. . . . He was wholly free from the *Verbesserungs* malady' (1972, vol. 10, p. 292) – which, of course, Keynes himself was liberally blessed with, or suffered from. But, though a 'conservative', Foxwell, as an economist, and certainly as a Cambridge economist, was not orthodox. For example, he condemned Ricardo. However, according to Keynes, (p. 271), in spite of the political repugnance he felt for Marx, Foxwell was 'the first English economist to appreciate his importance'. Incidentally, Foxwell was also perhaps the first academic economist after Malthus, half a century before, to emphasize the importance of the unemployment problem, and, as a forthright anti-Ricardian, he agreed with the charge that 'economists as a body' had 'in some respects helped to increase' unemployment (1886, p. 262). But Foxwell did not get the chair and had virtually no influence on economics in Cambridge in the twentieth century.[5]

A. C. Pigou, who succeeded Marshall in the Cambridge chair in 1908 at the age of 31, apparently with the strong support of his predecessor, seemed to fit admirably into the mould set by Sidgwick and Marshall himself, combining and balancing, as they did, an ardent missionary, or reformist, enthusiasm with adequately positive 'scientific' professions.

In his Inaugural Lecture, entitled 'Economic Science in Relation to Practice', Pigou maintained: 'Our science is not a normative but a positive science. It is concerned not with what ought to happen, but with what tends to happen.' (1908, p. 13) On the other hand, for Pigou, the most valuable kind of motivation for the economist was not so much that he might be 'interested by Professor Edgeworth's *Mathematical Psychics* or Dr Fisher's *Appreciation and Interest*', but rather that he should be possessed by 'social enthusiasm' – 'because he has walked through the slums of London and is stirred to make some effort to help his fellow men. . . . *Social enthusiasm, one might add, is the beginning of economic science.*' (pp. 12–13, italics added)

In this 'glad confident morning' of Cambridge economics such a programme appeared quite unproblematic. What would happen, or 'give', if the 'positive science' seemed or tended to exclude or dilute what the 'social enthusiasm' was enthusing after? Or what if the 'social enthusiasm' ran away with the scientific discipline? These were questions which naturally aroused little interest. Nor was confidence in the real-world relevance and applicability of the austere, abstract model-building in which Pigou and his colleagues were often engaged, clouded over by suspicions that 'much' of it might simply become 'a good game'. As he later claimed: 'The complicated analyses which economists endeavour to carry through are not mere gymnastic. They are instruments for the bettering of human life' (1920, p. vii).

The early Pigovian period, or the first 20 years of his tenure of the chair, down roughly to the great slump, was a time, in Cambridge, of considerable confidence regarding the philosophy and method of the subject, and of impatience with methodological questioning. Seldom has there seemed in Cambridge to have been more of a fundamental consensus or fewer dissensions and disagreements. The intellectual atmosphere of this period was admirably summed up by Sir Dennis Robertson. Regarding the 'topic of what sort of study economics is and what it was all about', Sir Dennis explained:

This is a topic which, when I started to read economics at Cambridge in 1910, it was not, I think, fashionable among us to think much about – less fashionable, I dare say than it may have been a few years previously, when the separate course in economics had not yet been extracted like

Eve from the ribs of the Moral Science Tripos. To us, I think, it seemed a topic more suitable for discussion by Germans than by Englishmen. There was on our reading-list what I have since come to regard as a good, if dry book about it, J. N. Keynes's *Scope and Method of Political Economy*, but to be quite honest I doubt if many of us read it. We thought we knew pretty well what sort of things we wanted to know about. (1951, p. 14)

Anyhow, if this might seem to describe a somewhat overconfident or uncritical intellectual condition, Sir Dennis went on:

A little later something happened which enabled and compelled us to formulate our ideas a little more sharply – namely the birth in 1912 of the great work by Pigou which in its christening-clothes bore the name of *Wealth and Welfare*. Thenceforth we went armed with a picture of what we were supposed to be doing. (p. 14)

The picture which Cambridge economists went 'armed with' was one of 'economic welfare' as the 'ultimate subject-matter' of economics.

Certainly there are one or two of Marshall's concepts – like consumers' surplus – which may be criticized as ambiguous or dubious in one way or another. But Marshall's scientific caution warned him against putting excessive weight on such ideas. As Keynes (J.M.) put it, Marshall knew where the ice was thin. Neither Sidgwick nor Marshall, in their admirable treatments of economic policy, had found it necessary or desirable to indulge in the concept of 'economic welfare', with its fundamental normative-positive ambiguity, its dubious testable content, and its overtones of ethical uplift. Much less had Sidgwick and Marshall sought to put such a concept right at the centre of the subject. Nor was this concept necessary for the significance and validity of the extensive policy analysis which Pigou was presenting. But with the somewhat fuzzy notion of 'economic welfare', the discipline of positive economics on which Sidgwick, Marshall and J. N. Keynes had so clearly and emphatically insisted, was to some extent undermined. For the welfare concept fosters a pretentiousness about the kind of judgements economists are qualified to make. Perhaps the change was one of shades of emphasis, but such shades can be crucial, just as a pebble can set off an avalanche. Gunnar Myrdal has insisted on the scientist's duty 'to keep concepts and terms clean, disinfected, logical and adequate to reality', and that 'we should never compromise with our duty to the language of strict science' (1973, pp. 157, 165–6). It was compromising with this scientific duty, which Sidgwick, Marshall and J. N. Keynes had laid down, to put such an ambiguous concept right at the centre of economics. Though few economists outside Cambridge had very much use for it, in Cambridge itself this concept of 'economic welfare' was widely supported and employed, right across the political spectrum from Sir Dennis Robertson to M. H. Dobb. In fact, perhaps not deliberately, more by unintended ambiguity than by a conscious change of programme, Pigou brought about a slight but significant shift in the balance of the Sidgwick-Marshall approach as between 'social enthusiasm' and scientific discipline. Following this shift, introduced by Pigou, the conception of a disciplined positive economics, as propounded by Sidgwick, Marshall and J. N. Keynes, was to be further eroded, and then abandoned, in pursuit of much more fundamental and 'revolutionary' aims and claims.

There were other important respects in which Pigou shifted the balance of the Sidgwick-Marshall approach to method and policy, or even departed, significantly, from Marshall's methods and interests. First, while both Sidgwick and Marshall had emphasized the redistribution of income as a dimension of economic policy, they had insisted strongly on the qualification regarding the possible damaging effects of redistribution on production. Certainly this vital qualification appears in Pigou's *Economics of Welfare*, but less emphatically and constantly than when Marshall had complained (as we have seen above) about how '*reckless*' many social reformers were as to 'the effects of their schemes on the production of wealth', or when Sidgwick had predicted that socialism would 'have so much less to distribute'.

In fact, Pigou did not share to the same extent Marshall's keen interest in the longer-run growth of production and productivity and in the forces promoting or discouraging this. The size, or the 'production' dimension of 'the national dividend', and hence of 'economic welfare', was envisaged by Pigou mainly in pretty short-run terms and was studied by him with regard, for example, to how monopoly, or state intervention, might affect the dividend via the allocation of resources. The longer-run growth-rate does not have an important place in Pigou's *Economics of Welfare*. In fact, Pigou, though he came to economics from history, did not share Marshall's intense concern with the historical dimension of economic processes, which, in fact, largely faded from the Cambridge scene with Marshall's departure. At the same time,

Pigou never showed much interest, in his main writings, in the particular, real-world, national growth process and problem which his predecessor had discerned with such anxiety at the turn of the century: that is, the emerging problem of the relative decline of Britain's economic position and growth-rate. Nor did Pigou show much interest or anxiety regarding what Marshall had seen as Britain's 'greatest danger': that is the way in which trade unions were exercising their increasing power.

Thus, it may be maintained that, in various respects, Pigou's *Economics of Welfare*, if it did not actively encourage, at least may have facilitated or permitted the development of the wishful notion, later to become influential in Britain, that it was primarily by redistribution, rather than by increasing productive efficiency and growth, that poverty could and should be attacked.

There were further ambiguities in Pigou's presentation of one of his most celebrated contributions, that is, the analysis of the distinction between private and social costs and products. Here again the idea is present in the writings of Sidgwick and Marshall. But Pigou developed the distinction much further, claiming that he is seeking 'to bring into clearer light some of the ways in which it now is, or eventually may become, feasible for government to control the play of economic forces in such wise as to promote the economic welfare, and through that, the total welfare, of their citizens as a whole' (1929, p. 131–2). It might appear that Pigou is building up a case for state intervention in market processes. But it is difficult not to sympathize with the criticisms of Professor R. H. Coase regarding the 'almost insuperable difficulties of interpretation' which Pigou's arguments raise, and their 'extremely elusive' character. As Professor Coase observes:

> The Pigovian analysis shows us that it is possible to conceive of better worlds than the one in which we live. But the problem is to devise practical arrangements which will correct defects in one part of the system without causing more serious harm in others. . . .
> Nothing could be more 'anti-social' than to oppose any action which causes any harm to anyone. (1960, pp. 34–5)

It may be unfair to blame Pigou for the misuse of his arguments by successors. But his vagueness may have facilitated exaggeration and distortion. For example, two of Pigou's successors in Cambridge later proceeded to assert, in an introductory textbook, regarding pollution as one of the problems of 'capitalist nations' (but not of 'socialist states'):

Pigou pointed out that it is a serious defect in the system of *laissez-faire* that producers bear only the costs that they pay for. The production of commodities throws costs upon society that are not paid for and do not enter into prices. He took the mild example of the smoke nuisance. In recent times, the poisoning of air and water, destruction of amenities, and consumption of irreplaceable natural resources have reached such a stage that even the most complacent apostles of *laissez-faire* have had to take notice of them. (Robinson and Eatwell, 1973, pp. 309–10)

One might hope, of course, that 'complacent apostles' of socialist planning have also taken note of this problem in view of the appalling pollution that goes on in Russia.

However, Pigou, some 25 years after he had originally propounded his celebrated doctrine regarding divergences between private and social costs, himself insisted:

While, therefore, it is true that, under capitalism the allocation of resources among occupations is faulty on account of divergences between private and social cost, there is serious doubt whether socialism could remedy these faults. Their existence, therefore, under the present system has little bearing on our choice between that system and its rival. (1937, p. 44)

Pigou explains that for the necessary improvement in the allocation of resources:

The relevant knowledge is of a sort that we do not at present possess, and *the eventual winning of which is no more likely under the one system than under the other.* (p. 44, italics added)

But it is difficult not to suspect that the original and persisting ambiguities in Pigou's treatment of divergences between social and private costs, and even, in fact, his subsequent use of the term 'faults' in 'the present system', *may* have helped, or unfortunately permitted, the emergence of persuasive doctrines that 'market failure' occurs when real-world markets do not achieve as perfect and ideal a solution as might be achieved by omniscient and omnipotent angels. Such a fallacy should have been the more easily avoidable in Cambridge because Marshall and Sidgwick had, as we have seen, explicitly warned against the assumption of perfectly virtuous and infinitely wise governments.

Certainly in his later years, Pigou's views regarding the actual tendencies of statesmen and governments became rather more realistic, and he explicitly disclaimed his earlier optimistic visions:

> The ambition, I have claimed elsewhere, of most economists is to help in some degree, directly or indirectly, towards social betterment. Our study, we should like to think, of the principles of interaction among economic events provides for statesmen data, upon which, along with data of other kinds, they, philosopher kings, build up policies directed to the common good. How different from the dream is the actuality! How very unlike philosopher Kings actual politicians are! . . . In view of these things, the hope that an advance in economic knowledge will appreciably affect actual happenings is, I fear, a slender one. (1939, pp. 220–1)

Unfortunately, as is apt to happen, this realization of Pigou's came long after his main and most influential work had appeared. He might not have ended up so disillusioned if, instead of investing so heavily in the concept of 'economic welfare', he had followed up the kind of realistic political analysis outlined in his paper of 1902, entitled 'A Parallel between Economic and Political Theory'.

Though one may venture to criticize Pigou's elusiveness as to the significance of his analysis of private and social costs, his caution in proclaiming his conclusions, or preferences, regarding capitalism and socialism, not only in respect of values, but in positive terms as to 'what will work', has something admirably Marshallian about it:

> In this field an economist has no special qualification. Indeed, as a more or less cloistered person, he is worse qualified than many others, who, may be, have less knowledge of the relevant facts. A wide experience of men and affairs and a strong 'feel' for what, with the human instruments available, will or will not work, are needed here. These the present writer, like most academic persons, does not possess; and, unlike some academic persons, he is aware that he does not possess them. (1937, p. 137)

Nevertheless, in the conclusion to his *Socialism versus Capitalism* (1937) Pigou committed himself to a programme somewhat resembling that put through in Britain ten years later by the Attlee government of 1945–50, including the reduction of 'glaring inequalities of fortune and opportunity', and public control, or nationalization, of the Bank of England, of the manufacture of armaments, probably of the coal industry, and possibiy of the railways (p. 138). Pigou also favoured some 'planning' of investment, and emphasized, as Marshall would have done, that 'the most important investment of all is investment in the health, intelligence and character of the people' (*ibid.*). Unfortunately, Pigou is quite unspecific as to how this kind of 'investment' is to be channelled, and his claim that, on this point, he would 'take a leaf from the book of Soviet Russia' could hardly be more ominous.

Here may be noted a curious, even paradoxical omission from Pigou's extensive treatment of the economics of welfare, which has very little or nothing to say about health, education and housing. Presumably it is not '*economic*' welfare to which health, education and housing are relevant, and their vital economic aspects are omitted. Though Marshall had expressed stern opposition to municipal housing (Pigou, ed., 1925, p. 445), Pigou had no criticism, in his *Economics of Welfare*, of current developments in housing policy, nor about the creation of huge bureaucracies to control health and education services.

For an impression of Pigou's later philosophical and political inclinations two of his reviews of celebrated and widely contrasting politicoeconomic works of that period may be noticed: the Webbs' *Soviet Communism: A New Civilisation?* and Hayek's *Road to Serfdom*. Though elaborately polite to the authors of both works, Pigou may be seen to distance himself distinctly further, in general philosophy, from Hayek than from the Webbs. Pigou, of course, accepts Hayek's condemnation of central planning in the case of the regimes of Hitler and Mussolini, but claims that central planning is simply a means, and rejects Hayek's 'historical thesis' that its tendency is to destroy liberty and personal responsibility (1944, pp. 218–19).

The Webbs' *Soviet Communism: A New Civilisation?* (the question mark in the title of the original edition soon disappeared) has been not very unfairly described as perhaps the most ridiculous book ever published by authors with a previously well deserved reputation for the highest seriousness. For Beatrice, this work represented the ultimate expression of that 'mid-Victorian trend of thought' in which she had participated, with its union of faith in the scientific method with the 'transference of the emotion of self-sacrificing service from God to man'. In his ten-page review-article Pigou accepts, mainly uncritically, the Webbs' account of the 'New Civilisation' then blossoming under the leadership of Stalin. Following the Webbs, Pigou concludes:

Of course, in all these things what is attempted is often very imperfectly attained. . . . From an educationalist's point of view, the strenuous inculcation into every child, however young, of the communist creed is anything but attractive. All this must be granted. But, none the less, *to have enshrined in the actual policy of a great country the doctrine that it is life, not machinery, which matters in the end, that the supreme commodity is man himself, and that the approaches to civilisation should be free to all not a privilege of a few, is to have made a unique contribution to history.* (1936, p. 94, italics added)

Pigou condemned, like the Webbs, 'the disease of orthodoxy', but he expressed the hope that the right diagnosis 'is growing pains, not premature hardening of the arteries' (p. 95). The only point on which Pigou dissents at all sharply from the Webbs is with regard to their attack on 'the deductive economists of the western world', for having allegedly asserted that 'the operation of the price mechanism in an absolutely free market necessarily secures the maximum satisfaction then and there possible of the whole aggregate of consumers'. Pigou proceeds to ridicule this 'absurdity' of the Webbs – though it was an absurdity which was to be propagated in a Cambridge textbook three or four decades later.

In conclusion, let it be remarked that it is neither necessary nor desirable to lay *too* much emphasis on Pigou's various departures from the methods and interests of Marshall, as contrasted with the extent of his adherence to them. But his placing of the concept of 'economic welfare' at the centre of the subject, his discarding of the historical method, his lack of interest in growth processes, and, in particular, in the emerging relative growth-rate problem of the British economy, together with his ambiguities regarding the possibilities, or probabilities, of government intervention improving on the performance of markets – these, with his comparatively sympathetic attitude to the Russian economy, add up to a significant and consequential list, to be followed by other much more extreme departures in subsequent decades.[6]

VI *J. M. Keynes*

Like Pigou, Keynes did not write very much on scope and method, and from what he did have to say rather contrasting views emerge. Regarding the formulation of economic advice on policy, he was, on occasion, prepared to recognize 'the enormous part to be played in this by the scientific spirit as distinct from the purely party attitude' (*Memorandum*, quoted by Howson and Winch, 1977, p. 21). Also, in letters, and in his criticism of econometrics, Keynes insisted illuminatingly on the historical dimension of economics – though this hardly amounted to Marshall's concern with the historical method and historical processes. He also warned against the danger of economists treating their material as constant and homogeneous (1973, p. 300).

However, Keynes also maintained that 'economics is essentially a moral science and not a natural science. That is to say, it employs introspection and judgements of value' (*ibid* p. 297). And he added: 'It deals with motives, expectations, psychological uncertainties' (p. 300). These are somewhat ambiguous propositions. Certainly *all* sciences – including natural sciences – can be said inevitably to 'employ judgements of value'. But, as Schumpeter once put it: 'What is meant by "*Wertfreiheit*" is merely freedom from value judgements of a *particular kind*, viz. from judgements about how it would be desirable for the phenomena under study to behave' (n.d.).

Keynes's statements might be (and have been) interpreted as supporting a rejection of the distinctions, demarcations and discipline of scientific method, as insisted on by Sidgwick, Marshall, and his father. But it is none too clear from Keynes (J.M.)'s statements just how far they conflict with those of Keynes (J.N.), of nearly half a century previously. Regarding the description of political economy as a 'moral science', Keynes (J.N.) had maintained:

In order to mark off political economy from the physical sciences, it is spoken of sometimes as a moral science, sometimes as a social science. Of these descriptions, the latter is to be preferred. The term moral science is, to begin with, not free from ambiguity. This term is no doubt sometimes used in a broad sense as including all the separate sciences that treat of man in his subjective capacity, that is, as a being who feels, thinks, and wills. But more frequently it is used as a synonym for ethics; and hence to speak of economic science as a moral science is likely to obscure its positive character. (1890, p. 87)

It is not at all clear just how far Keynes (J.M.), 48 years later, was concerned to 'obscure' the 'positive character' of economics, nor how far he (J.M.) would have regarded it as important to contradict J.N. when the latter had asserted:

> Economic phenomena depend upon the activity of free agents, whose customary behaviour may be modified not merely by legislative interference, but also by changes in their own moral standard, or in the social pressure brought to bear upon them by public opinion. . . .
>
> It involves confusion of thought, however, to suppose that economic phenomena are for the above reason incapable of being studied positively or that in our investigation of them we are bound to pass a judgement upon their moral worth. (*ibid.*, pp. 43–4)

Anyhow, we have seen that Pigou in his philosophy of economics, though seemingly at first fitting closely into the mould set by Sidgwick and Marshall, began to depart, unobtrusively and perhaps unintentionally, but highly consequentially, from the always precarious balance of scientific discipline and 'social enthusiasm' maintained by his predecessors. Keynes, though sharing some of the Sidgwick-Marshall presuppositions, in some ways departed, from the start, much more explicitly from the approach of the founding fathers in Cambridge. This explicit departure was partly in respect of philosophical preconceptions, and partly because Keynes was launched at the start of his career on an activist, not strictly academic approach to the subject – unlike Sidgwick, Marshall and Pigou, who had all fundamentally been concerned with academic standards.

Keynes was considerably fortified, in his confidence as an economist, by his belief in a version of the philosophical doctrines of G. E. Moore.[7] In his essay 'My Early Beliefs' (1938) Keynes explained that the version of Moore's philosophy which he and his apostolic friends espoused was a highly selective one:

> What we got from Moore was by no means entirely what he offered us. He had one foot on the threshold of the new heaven, but the other foot in the Sidgwick and the Benthamite calculus and the general rules of correct behaviour. There was one chapter in the *Principia* of which we took not the slightest notice. We accepted Moore's religion, so to speak, and discarded his morals. (1949, p. 82)

Keynes went on to claim that these beliefs (or 'Moore's religion') protected him and his apostolic friends against Marxism, which he, rather strangely, described as 'the final *reductio ad absurdum*' of Benthamism. On the other hand, according to

Keynes, the influence of Sidgwick would have been in the direction of Marxism – an extraordinary suggestion at which Dr Leavis was well justified in expressing much amazement (1967, p. 259).

The 'religion', or religious surrogate, which Keynes and his apostolic associates adopted from Moore certainly contained a confident and intense conviction of the certainty and infallibility of their knowledge of what was 'good':

> How did we know what states of mind were good? This was a matter of direct inspection, of direct unanalysable intuition about which it was useless and impossible to argue. In that case who was right when there was a difference of opinion? . . . It might be that some people had an acuter sense of judgement, just as some people can judge a vintage port and others cannot. On the whole, so far as I remember, this explanation prevailed. *In practice victory was with those who could speak with the greatest appearance of clear, undoubting conviction and could best use the accents of infallibility. . . .*
>
> Broadly speaking we all knew for certain what were good states of mind. (*ibid.*, pp. 84–6, italics added)

This certainty and infallibility, Keynes maintained, was based on '*science*':

> We regarded all this as entirely rational and *scientific* in character. Like any other branch of science, it was nothing more than the application of logic and rational analysis to the material presented as sense data. . . .
>
> Indeed we combined a dogmatic treatment as to the nature of experience with a method of handling it which was extravagantly scholastic. (p. 86)

In other words Keynes possessed 'scientific' pretensions, or ambitions (like Sidgwick, it might be thought). But Keynes was conceiving of 'science' rather in the dogmatic, infallibilist terms of nineteenth-century rationalists, which incidentally was one of the fundamental features of the Marxian philosophy (as later also maintained by a small elite of apostolic party members). Thus equipped, philosophically, as Keynes went on to explain: 'We recognised no moral obligation on us, no inner sanction to conform and obey. Before heaven we claimed to be our own judge in our own case. . . . We had no respect for traditional wisdom or the restraints of custom. We lacked reverence.' (pp. 98–9)

There was a further vital dimension of Keynes's philosophy. He was possessed by what he called, 'the *Verbesserungs* malady', and an 'impatience to short-cut normal long-run tendencies and influence events in the direction he desired' (Moggridge, 1976, p. 38). Keynes described himself as belonging with 'the Utopians, the meliorists as they are sometimes called, who believe in a continuing moral progress by virtue of which the human race already consists of reliable, rational, decent people, influenced by truth and objective standards, who can be safely released from the outward restraints of convention and traditional standards.' (p. 99)

Thus, for Keynes, the belief in progress was buttressed by an ardent belief in 'rationality'. Though by 1938 he still held that his early beliefs, or 'this religion of ours', remained 'nearer the truth than any other that I know' (p. 92), Keynes had come to regard this 'rationalist' tenet as superficial and misconceived – though he admitted that he was still dominated by it:

As cause and consequence of our general state of mind *we completely misunderstood human nature, including our own.* The rationality which we attributed to it led to a superficiality, not only of judgement, but also of feeling. . . .
I still suffer incurably from attributing an unreal rationality to other people's feelings and behaviour (and doubtless my own, too). (p. 100, italics added)[8]

Certainly, it may be somewhat dangerous for those urging extensive economic, social and political reforms and policies, completely to misunderstand human nature (including their own). However, it might well be maintained that Keynes (like Beatrice Webb) started from a variant of the Sidgwick-Marshall, mid- and late-Victorian spirit of the age, combining an enthusiasm for human or social progress with a confident belief in 'the light of science'. But the scientific ambitions of Sidgwick and Marshall were upheld in a much more cautious, empirical and even slightly sceptical mood, with a careful regard for academic discipline. Confidently armed with his apostolic version of Moore's philosophy, Keynes largely rejected the caution and academic restraints maintained by Marshall, whose reticence and reluctance in public policy debate may have seemed to him faintly pathological – something like sexual repression. Though Keynes claimed – to some extent justifiably – to follow in the English empirical traditions of Locke, Hume, Mill and Sidgwick, in some directions he veered rather dangerously away from them. As contrasted with Sidgwick and Marshall, Keynes felt he belonged to an apostolic elite of *connoisseurs*, whose beliefs were imbued with an infallible, scientific, certainty, and which included a confidence in human progress and in their own ability to bring it about.

This infallibilist confidence in the scientific (or rather scientistic) certainty of one's beliefs, fused with an intense trust in beneficent progress, and with a complete rejection of all restraints, conventions, or traditional standards – both those of academics and those of civil servants – obviously make up a dangerous combination, though not violently dangerous in the genteel, humane, largely aesthetic form entertained by Keynes and his apostolic associates. But this is, of course, exactly the ideological blend, of a belief in scientific certainty and progress, with a rejection of all conventions and restraints, which has made many Marxians so inhumanly intolerant. Keynes could hardly have distanced himself further from such intolerance. But epistemologically he and his apostolic friends had camped on a slippery slope.

The nearly two years which Keynes spent in the Civil Service (1906–8), before becoming a Cambridge economist, might well have bolstered and encouraged in other directions those elitist tendencies which Keynes had developed as a Cambridge apostle – this admittedly appallingly misused term 'elitist' *does* seem appropriate in this case. At the India Office Keynes became one of a very small group of officials overseeing the political and economic problems of India, and in a very few years had become the outstanding expert concerned with reshaping the monetary framework for the millions of Indians. No more than a handful of officials, of whom Keynes, with brilliant rapidity, became the outstanding authority, possessed the knowledge or opportunity to argue influentially, and there was little in the way of clamorous, democratic political pressure to contest, or protest, his beneficent, apostolic recommendations – and let it be recognized how superbly conceived and scintillatingly expressed his beneficent, apostolic recommendtions were.

This early experience, reinforcing his confident 'rationalist' belief in human progress, shaped Keynes's activities as an economist, which took in ten further years as a civil servant. But, in the roughly forty years of Keynes's career, political realities and the political environment in Britain, with regard to the shaping and implementation of economic policies, were to be transformed completely from how they may have seemed to a young apostolic mandarin in the India Office in 1906–8.

As to the role of the academic economist, Pigou once wrote on this point, faithfully following Marshall, in this case:

> While it is natural and right in the present deplorable state of the world's affairs that many economists should seek to play a part in guiding conduct, that is not their primary business. They are physiologists not clinical practitioners; engineers not engine drivers. The main point of such contributions as they may hope to make must be indirect; in the study, not in the pages of newspapers or even in the council chamber. (1933, p. v)

Keynes completely rejected such Marshallian-Pigovian restrictions. First by his apostolic confidence in rationalist, 'scientific' certainties, and by his enthusiasm for '*Verbesserung*', he was prepared for the sweeping away of obsolete restraints and traditional conventions. Keynes saw himself not simply as an engineer but as an engine driver, or at least on the footplate guiding the driver's hand; while, at the same time, he was the most effective spokesman for the passengers regarding the speed and destination of the train. Moreover, being neither a regular civil servant, nor a full-time academic, Keynes had no very meticulous regard for the restraints and disciplines of either profession.

Thus the example of Keynes, like that, less explicitly and in a very different way, of Pigou, promoted the erosion of the austere, restrained disciplines and distinctions of Sidgwick, Marshall and J. N. Keynes.

Certainly there are some parallels between Keynes's political attitudes and those of Marshall. For example, Keynes, like Marshall, had no illusions about trade unions. Three months before the general strike of 1926 Keynes referred to 'the Trade Unionists, once the oppressed, now the tyrants, whose selfish and sectional pretensions need to be bravely opposed' (1972, vol. 9, p. 309).[9] Here indeed Keynes's language is quite Marshallian. But, unlike Beveridge, in his *Full Employment in a Free Society* (1944), Keynes does not seem to have envisaged that the implementation of 'full', or high, employment policies should be accompanied by any modification of the laws relating to strikes and union power (see Beveridge, 1944, p. 200). It should be emphasized, however, that Keynes recommended fairly moderate employment targets compared with the very high levels advocated by 'Keynesians' after his death (see below, chapter 4). However, the problems of growth and of Britain's relative position and rate of growth hardly finds a place in the world as Keynes saw it, which was so overwhelmingly dominated by the unemployment problem and, in the long run, by stagnation and by interest rates falling to near zero.

On the broader principles of economic policy Keynes's best-known essay has probably been 'The End of Laissez-Faire' (1926). The title may be rather unfortunately misleading. For one thing, the end of '*laissez-faire*' could be said to have come about half a century or more previously, around 1870 – as Professor Hobsbawm, for example has suggested. Anyhow, '*laissez-faire*' is a highly ambiguous concept. Certainly, since around 1870, a strong case had developed for major government action to revise and adapt the framework of the market economy in face of new political demands for less economic inequality, instability, and insecurity, as well as to curb the growth of monopoly and monopolistic practices, which Marshall (and J. B. Clark) had seen as one of the most serious problems of the age. But this did not mean, and should not have meant, a widespread overriding and frustration of market processes and principles by government, but rather adapting and extending the framework of the market economy to changed political and technological conditions and to the growth of public goods and services – such as the 'social services', as they were coming to be called. After all, as Keynes emphasized in the conclusion to his *General Theory*, what he called 'the existing system', or, in other words, market processes, allocated reasonably satisfactorily the 90 per cent of factors of production that were assumed to be employed. Therefore Keynes could not have meant by 'the end of *laissez-faire*' the end of market processes, and he could and should have made this much plainer than he did, considering the broad reliance which he wished still to be placed on markets. Indeed, at the end of his life, there were a number of signs that in the postwar world he was prepared to place an increased emphasis in British economic policy on free markets and free trade.

Finally, a mention should be made of Keynes's version of, or his method of writing, the history of economic thought. His 'revolutionary' version followed, in some respects, the method of previous would-be revolutionaries – Smith, Marx, and Jevons – by identifying an all-pervasive error vitiating the previous orthodoxy. In fact, Keynes was not concerned to produce a

thorough and well-balanced account, but a 'revolutionary' historical setting for his own ideas. But it must be recognized that his
treatment of the mercantilists has been found illuminating and
valid by a number of distinguished economic historians. Certainly
also the 'classical' theory and model, in Keynes's sense, had
wielded a powerful influence on policy and teaching, through
Smith, Ricardo, and, on the whole, J. S. Mill, for about a century.
It was in his treatment of his contemporaries and of the previous
half-century of business cycle theory, that Keynes's concept of
'classical' economists, and 'classical' theory, was confusing and
unjustifiable. Among other peculiarities, it led to the condemnation as 'classical' of Pigou and Henderson, who had advocated
'Keynesian' policies, while proclaiming as 'never' classical, Haw-
trey, who had been a main opponent of 'Keynesian' policies (see
Hutchison, 1978, chapters 5 and 8).

Indeed the whole enterprise of drawing up a 'revolutionary'
version of the history of the subject, as a kind of persuasive
historical setting for one's theories, set a rather dangerous
example, which was very soon imitated in Cambridge, in much
more extreme terms, only six years after the publication of *The
General Theory*.

VII *M. H. Dobb*

In 1919, with his *Economic Consequences of the Peace*, Keynes had
established himself as a major public figure, and as a highly
political economist very different in style from the academic
'founding fathers', Sidgwick and Marshall. In fact, Cambridge
economics emerged in the early twenties in a state of considerable
confidence and prestige, with, for some years, an unusually broad
measure of consensus among its leading figures. This mood was
expressed in Keynes's introduction to the Cambridge Economic
Handbooks, which he edited, and to which such distinguished
authorities as H. D. Henderson, D. H. Robertson and M. H.
Dobb were early contributors. According to Keynes:

Even on matters of principle there is not yet a complete unanimity of
opinion amongst professors. Generally speaking, the writers of these
volumes believe themselves to be orthodox members of the Cambridge
School of Economics. At any rate, most of their ideas about the subject,
and even their prejudices, are traceable to the contact they have enjoyed

with the writings and lectures of the two economists who have chiefly
influenced Cambridge thought for the past fifty years, Dr Marshall and
Professor Pigou. (1922, p. vi)

However, by now 'the Cambridge School of Economics', in so
far as a generalization is possible, and in so far as Keynes was
representative of the school, was considerably more inclined to be
critical of established institutions and established positions in
politics and economic policy, especially conservative policies, than
it had been a quarter of a century previously, under Marshall.
Moreover, Cambridge economists, like Keynes and Henderson,
were prepared to express their criticisms much more eloquently
and outspokenly in the press and in party-political debate. But, at
this juncture, the Cambridge school would still have been
virtually united against proposals for protective tariffs.

At this time, in the early twenties, the tide of mid-Victorian
ideology, which had come down from the Enlightenment, and
had carried away the young Sidgwick and Marshall (not to
mention Beatrice Webb), was by no means spent, with its
powerful combination of a faith in 'the light of science' together
with 'the transference of the emotion of self-sacrificing service
from God to man'. This combination continued to provide a
framework – though a rather precariously balanced one – within
which the search for a substitute religion could be pursued.
Certainly the appalling slaughter of World War I, swiftly followed
by the very severe slump of 1921, may have stimulated an even
more urgent search for some kind of 'complete revision of human
relations, political and economic' (as Sidgwick had described his
quaesitum).

Though still with a very minute following in England,
Marxism, with its scientific (or scientistic) claims, and its burning
'social enthusiasm' fitted quite aptly, as an extreme species, into
this broader ideological pattern or genus.[10] Certainly, the ponderous Teutonic terminology of Marxism may have been found
unpalatable by some. But its 'difficulty', and its aura of intellectual
profundity, was for some a highly attractive characteristic. (For
many intellectuals an admixture of the unintelligible is almost
essential for success.) Joining up as a Marxian then also had
something of the appeal of belonging to a select, almost apostolic,
and, in some ways conspiratorial group of inspired social
enthusiasts. But the great new attraction, as it seemed at this
juncture, of the Marxian creed, was that, with the revolution in

Russia, believers could now focus not on some disembodied ideal but on an actual realization of Utopia on earth. The future *was* working (it seemed possible to believe). Certainly sceptics like H. G. Wells and Bertrand Russell returned unconverted, and Keynes's verdict was mainly condemnatory. But there were many others prepared to pin their glowing hopes to the new Utopia. (See the illuminating treatment in David Caute, *The Fellow-Travellers*, 1973, especially the opening chapters: 'The Future is There', and 'Thinking of Russia'.)

M. H. Dobb (1900–76) was the first important Marxian recruit to the Cambridge Faculty of Economics. Except for a brief sojourn as a graduate student at the London School of Economics – and, of course, for his pilgrimages to the Soviet Union – Dobb spent his entire career from Freshman to Emeritus Reader at Cambridge. For Dobb, as a dedicated Marxian and almost lifelong party member, the ideas of Sidgwick and Marshall on the scope and method of economics, and on the role of the economist, must have seemed quite misconceived, at best containing and fostering major illusions, at worst a bogus (or bourgeois) deception. Of course, some of the purely technical aspects of Marshallian economics may have been of use even to a Marxian economist. But, the positive-normative distinction, for example, as upheld by Sidgwick and Marshall, and especially by J. N. Keynes, was hardly compatible with Marxian tenets. For, according to the often-quoted pronouncement of Marx, all bourgeois economists, with very minor exceptions, after the year 1830, had been unmasked as 'hired prizefighters':

> Thenceforth, the class-struggle, practically as well as theoretically, took on more and more outspoken and threatening forms. It sounded the knell of scientific bourgeois economy. It was thenceforth no longer a question, whether this theorem or that was true, but whether it was useful to capital or harmful, expedient or inexpedient, politically dangerous or not. In place of disinterested inquirers, there were hired prize-fighters; in place of genuine scientific research, the bad conscience and the evil intent of apologetic. (1961, p. 15)

Dobb, like other Marxian economists, when writing at the appropriate level, repeatedly quoted this famous passage with enthusiastic approval, in order to denounce bourgeois economists (see, for example 1937, p. 138 and 1973, pp. 28–9, 96n, 110). Thus he described applied economics as 'an unscientific system of apologetics' (1924, p. 397), and 'the traditional basis upon which economic theory in the nineteenth century was built as an elaborate apologetic of capitalism' (1955, p. 105). But, as a sophisticated Marxian, Dobb was ready also to don his academic cap and gown and argue on a very different level. To persist in maintaining, among serious mature students, that, for example, Alfred Marshall was 'a hired prizefighter' might seem to be going *just a little* too far. So Dobb sought to maintain that Marx had not *really* meant what he had plainly stated in the carefully considered *Nachwort* which he had appended to his single master volume on political economy published in his lifetime. Dobb explained that Marx 'was careful to discriminate and by no means treated all economists as "hired prizefighters" ' (1973, p. 29). Apparently all Marx had *really* meant to say was something rather like what Schumpeter later maintained, that is, that all economists start from a 'vision' of economic phenomena which may well be inbued with normative, value-laden elements. But, of course, in actual fact, Marx regularly, and with only minor exceptions, treated bourgeois economists in the terms of his *Nachwort*, and Marxian economists, including notably Dobb, have repeatedly and enthusiastically quoted Marx's words, and further elaborated and extended his general condemnation to include, in particular, the neoclassicals.

In some of his last contributions Dobb took the more sophisticated line, explaining that it involved a '*mis*interpretation' of bourgeois economics to represent it as concerned with making 'a propaganda case': 'One might even call it the *vulgar* interpretation of ideological influence on theory' (1975, p. 357, italics in original). Now, of course, for any self-respecting Marxian intellectual, '*vulgarity*' constitutes the most appalling *faux pas* one can commit – (like wearing brown shoes with a blue suit). Any Cambridge Marxian worth his, or her, salt would shudder with horror at the thought of perpetrating anything '*vulgar*' (though, of course, it remains quite in order to put the '*vulgar*' boot in, now and then, in a context in which one can expect to get away with it – as Dobb himself, in his younger days, and so many Marxian economists, have constantly done).[11]

Of Dobb's earlier work, much, naturally enough for a Marxian, was devoted to the economy of the Soviet Union, which many students must first have learnt about from him. From any point of view, what was happening in Russia in the twenties and thirties, and the claims that were being made for Russian planning, were bound to be of much interest to economists, especially with the onset of the great slump. Dobb's enthusiasm for this new chapter in human progress was unbounded:

It is this novelty . . . which is causing Soviet Russia to hold the attention of the world today as no country has ever held it before. . . . Today the almost universal lure, whether joined with hatred or with affection, is the Planned Economy of the Soviet Union. But this interest does not lie merely in details of organisation – in the way in which the apparatus of this novelty of a Planned Economy is designed. . . . Nor does it lie merely in the size of the novelty – in the fact that a Planned Economy . . . covers in all about a sixth of the land-surface of the globe. Nor does interest lie alone in the dimensions of what it aims to achieve. What is unique about the Soviet Union is the combination of all these elements in a social system which represents, in a revolutionary sense, a new historical type: a type which is entirely new . . . a new chemical composition. (1932, pp. 6–7)

(It may be noteworthy that, about a quarter of a century later, another Cambridge economist, moved by 'social enthusiasm', was making similar sweeping claims of 'novelty' on behalf of the 'Great Leap Forward' and the Cultural Revolution in China.)

Anyhow, it was to this striking new phenomenon that Dobb devoted much of his voluminous writings. To judge of the nature and mood of Dobb's work in this field one might very suitably consider his treatment of the striking episode of Stalin's collectivization of agriculture (*c*. 1930–33). The campaign for collectivization was (according to Dobb) the conception of Stalin, 'with his unerring instinct' (1960, p. 216). Moreover: 'The actual success of the campaign for collectivization must constitute the most spectacular transformation in economic history' (1932, p. 29). Indeed, with regard to the whole Soviet policy of planned industralization it was 'the policy with regard to agriculture' which was '*the cornerstone of this imposing arch*' (1941, p. 14, italics added).

Dobb continued:

This policy was clearly an act of political genius, comparable to Lenin's decision eight years before with regard to NEP and his decision in 1917 that, despite Russia's backwardness, the situation was ripe for a seizure of power by the Soviets. It consisted in nothing less than the transformation of peasant agriculture on the basis of cooperative or collective farming in large units, on which up-to-date and mechanised methods of cultivation could be employed; a revolution in the social and economic basis of the village, within the space of half a decade, on a scale that history can rarely, if ever, have witnessed before. Few would dispute that it was an act of great political courage as well as of genius. (1941, p. 14; italics added)

Certainly Dobb recognized 'some bad mistakes in the first two years of the policy'; and that 'this collectivization of what was almost a continent was not achieved except at a considerable cost'. Indeed:

A number of *Kolhoze*, moreover, at the onset were farmed very badly. All this coinciding with unfavourable weather conditions and crop failures in some districts both in 1931 and 1932, resulted in *something approaching* famine conditions in certain areas. But it is less remarkable that such things should have occurred than that *so immense an undertaking should have succeeded*. (1941, p. 16, italics added)

Now it has long been widely recognized, and accepted by competent authorities outside the Soviet Union, that what happened in these years was a purely man-made, peacetime famine in one of the most richly fertile agricultural areas in the world, in which millions of people died of starvation. However, as transmuted by Dobb's Marxian scholarship, this became one of the most triumphant successes, and one of the most extraordinarily courageous strokes of genius, in the whole economic history of the world. *Moreover, what is most interesting is that, according to Dobb, Stalin's agricultural policy of the early thirties was typical of, and comparable with, the entire Russian revolution and its economic planning as a whole.* It might, incidentally, be added that, as Professor Nove has pointed out, between the years 1929 to 1939, according to official Soviet population statistics, 'well over 10 million people had "demographically" disappeared' (1972, p. 180) – through, of course, besides famine, other factors, such as the purges and the 'Gulags' (also emanations of Stalin's 'unerring instinct') were at work.[12]

One significant feature which Marxian economics, as cultivated by Dobb, shared with Marshallian economics, was the concern with the fundamental *historical* dimension of economic processes and problems. To some extent, the Marxian and the Marshallian concern with the historical dimension shared a common German ancestry, and before that, in the eighteenth century, common Scottish and French forerunners. In other respects there was not much shared ground. Certainly, however, the Marxian concern with historical methods and processes should have rendered Dobb both more interested in, and perhaps better equipped to deal with, longer-run growth processes. Moreover, to this historical concern Dobb added the expertise of growth modelling, when this fashion spread to Cambridge in the fifties.

Presumably the outcome, or 'fruit', of the study of economic growth, whether on Marxian or Marshallian lines, should have been demonstrated in a grasp of real-world growth tendencies, and growth potentials, in the various actual types of economy in the world. If growth modelling, and the broader study of growth, were not pursued simply as a 'good game', then presumably they should have promoted a sharper discernment of the kinds of institutions, economic and social, which were actually making for higher or lower growth-rates in the different economies in the real world. Dobb, equipped with both Marxian historical perspective and an expertise with the new growth models, should presumably have produced the most prescient and reliable predictions and judgements about the growth prospects of the leading economies in the world.

In his lectures in Delhi (1951), *Some Aspects of Economic Development*, Dobb produced some significant judgements regarding the prospects of the US economy at that time, which was, of course, just entering on a long period of remarkable growth and stability. Though for the most part he fundamentally rejected Keynesian theories and policies as being concerned with making capitalism work, Dobb enthusiastically embraced the Keynesian stagnation thesis at this time. With remarkable timing, Dobb chose this juncture to proclaim:

Gone is the old optimism, even in America. . . . A diminishing number of American economists, and few, if any, outside America, would be found today to argue with any assurance that capitalism in its moribund state of today was capable of being an agency *par excellence* of economic development and progress. (1967, pp 67–8)

But then what *could* a Marxian economist be expected to proclaim to the eager students of Delhi (whose country was receiving, or about to receive, such unprecedented quantities of aid from the 'moribund' capitalist economy of the USA) other than the same predictions about the decline and breakdown of capitalism, which Marx and Engels had first proclaimed in the

1840s, and had repeated, decade after decade, through the heyday of Victorian 'capitalism'? Naturally Dobb had little or nothing to say about the German or Japanese economies.

Obviously, with regard to comparisons between the Russian economy and those of the capitalist West, it seemed extremely probable, Dobb suggested, that the former would soon be overtaking the latter, in terms of key economic and industrial indices. In a paper 'Rates of Growth under the Five-Year Plans' (1953), Dobb cited (as usual, with full approval) some official Russian statistics of 'Mr Beria'. By projecting Mr Beria's figures, Dobb estimated that, with regard to the fundamental 'metal-fuel-power group' of industries:

We reach the conclusion that Soviet output of this metal-fuel-power group will surpass that of Western Europe thus projected during the second half of the 'fifties, and that of USA thus projected during the first half of the 'sixties. This is to speak in terms of *absolute* output: if we speak of output *per capita* of population, then equality would be reached a year or two earlier with Western Europe . . . and a few years later with USA (1955, pp. 128–9)

Of course, Mr Beria's figures, relied upon, as usual, for his projections by Dobb, were not concerned with consumption and living standards.[13] Certainly, moreover, Dobb would have insisted on making allowance for the far-flung 'peace-keeping' activities of Soviet Russia, in Czechoslovakia, Hungary and elsewhere. But Stalin himself, as quoted by Dobb (p. 130), had emphasized that 'the basic law of socialism' is 'the maximum satisfaction of the constantly rising material and cultural requirements of the whole of society'. So Dobb suggested that the same tendencies and projections revealed by Mr Beria's figures for the heavy industries, would, in due course, become apparent in the consumer goods sector – though he also cited the warnings of Mr Molotov regarding 'the international situation'.

Let it be emphasized that we are not concerned here to press, or even to raise, any normative or moral questions regarding Stalin's methods of economic planning: we are simply looking at Dobb's positive judgements and predictions about comparative growth-rates in the Soviet Union, the United States and elsewhere.

Anyhow, throughout his work on the Soviet economy, not only did Dobb display an enthusiastic reliance on the pronouncements of Stalin, Mr Beria, Mr Molotov, and other such Soviet dignitaries, but throughout the whole quarter-century of the Stalin regime, and long after, Dobb's attitude was thoroughly uncritical and unquestioning of official Russian statistics and claims. As Ernest Mandel pointed out, Dobb 'has always faithfully interpreted the official theses of the leading circles in the USSR' (1968, p. 552, italics added).

Nor did Dobb, throughout the quarter-century of the Stalin regime, and long after, ever permit himself to publish a syllable of criticism of the appalling intellectual degradation of the study of political economy which took place in the Russian Empire in these decades and subsequently. As Mandel has emphasized, the Stalinist economists were concerned in their theorizing to hide the facts about the Soviet economy and thereby 'justified the continued existence of social inequality and alienation of labour in this strange "socialist society" ' (p. 724). Mandel stresses how, with the coming of the Stalin regime:

The next two decades saw the stifling of all independent development of critical thought. The degeneration of Marxism into a form of apologetics transformed it at the same time into a form of scholasticism incapable of responding to genuine and fresh problems otherwise than with a sterile juggling with quotations. (p. 726)

All this economic Lysenkoism never, while it flourished, evoked from Dobb any significant expression of disapproval.

However, at last, recalling events of 1956, Dobb recounts in his 'Biographical Notes' how 'he was a member of the party of English economists invited to Poland by Polish economists. Here he was a witness of the "Poznan events" – from which painful event came the first full realisation that contradictions were possible in a socialist society' (1978, p. 120). It might seem grotesque that apparently, after 37 years' study of economics, and after about 30 years' intense research on the leading socialist economy, Dobb could only then, by being brought face to face with reality on the spot, achieve a 'first full realisation' of what ought to be obvious. It was not a question so much of norms, ethics or politics, as of fundamental positive economic analysis. However, even after 1956, it was many years before any significant criticism was forthcoming, in print at any rate, from Dobb. Only long after Stalin's death, when he himself was approaching 70, did Dobb permit himself the faintest, mildest, critical comments. Certainly full credit should be granted for septuagenarian repentances. But for Dobb, throughout his main writings, as long as it lasted, the regime of Stalin was one with which it should be the overriding aim of policy in all other countries, including Britain, to be aligned. (See the comments by Dobb quoted by Eatwell, 1979, p.143, and Dobb, 1970, pp. 62, 68-9.)

No significant corrections of his earlier enthusiastic claims about the Stalinist economy were ever published by Dobb. As Professor Hobsbawm has pointed out, Dobb persisted in his member-ship of the Communist Party for longer than any of those who joined up in Cambridge, when he did, in 1921: 'He proved to be the most persistent of his contemporaries' (Hobsbawm, 1967, p. 3). This 'persistence' lasted through most of a period when being a committed Marxian usually meant being a loyal supporter of Stalin. Perhaps Dobb's 'persistence' should be described as a kind of loyalty – Professor Hobsbawm mentions Dobb's some-what surprising 'loyalty' to his former, highly superior, public school, Charterhouse, which, in his 'Biographical Notes' Dobb not very loyally referred to as 'of the second rank'. But another factor, perhaps difficult to distinguish from loyalty, though very different in nature, may be a kind of hubris, persistently refusing to recognize mounting evidence or admit even the possibility of monstrous error, – fortified by Marxian infallibilist scientism.

VIII *Joan Robinson and G. F. Shove*

The efflorescence of Marxian doctrines in Cambridge in the thirties has become a much scrutinized phenomenon. But Cam-bridge economics was not very much affected at the time. Dobb remained the sole important Marxian teacher (with Dr Sraffa, who had arrived in the mid-twenties, somewhere in the back-ground). Of course Marxism attracted some support among undergraduates studying economics. But among the subsequently more notorious enthusiasts for Stalin (whom Cambridge, as Marshall had put it, 'the great mother of strong men sends out into the world with cool heads but warm hearts') in the thirties only one was an alumnus of the Economics Tripos. For, in Cambridge economics, the thirties was a period of strenuous and optimistic new developments directed at the solving of the crucial economic problem of the day on quite un-Marxian, indeed anti-Marxian, lines. Though policies for counter-cyclical relief works against unemployment had, for decades, been supported probably by a majority of English economists, 'the Keynesian Revolution', with its 'General Theory', was the centre of much confident and optimistic intellectual excitement.

Let it be emphasized that in spite of its coming too late to mitigate the great slump, and to prevent the accession of Hitler; in spite of excessive claims to generality; and in spite of the degeneration of subsequent decades into 'modernist stuff gone wrong and turned sour and silly', the impetus of Keynes's ideas in the crisis of the thirties did provide some valid grounds for hope, and some of that hope was, arguably, fulfilled. The main alternative ideas at that time, of Hayek and the Austrians, would only have served to aggravate 'the great contraction', and at the time of the breakdown of the gold standard there was no properly articulated alternative on 'monetarist' lines. On the other hand, the catastrophic Marxian prophecies of the thirties were, as usual, falsified: capitalism did not 'break down', and British 'capitalism' did not rescue itself by an alliance with Hitler. (It was Stalin's divisive policies which helped Hitler to power in Germany at the beginning of the thirties, and Stalin who made a pact with Hitler at the end of the decade.)[14] One may argue over how far Keynes's work was important in falsifying Marxian predictions. But in the Cambridge of the thirties, among the economists especially, it provided an effective alternative.

Anyhow, to a much lesser, but significant extent, in the early thirties, just before the outbreak of the Keynesian Revolution, the new analysis of imperfect competition, to which Joan Robinson was a leading contributor, was hailed as marking a striking new advance in price theory.

Mrs Robinson, the great-grand-daughter, via two distinguished generals, of the Christian socialist theologian F. D. Maurice,[15] has provided some rather puzzling vignettes of her education in economics as a Girton undergraduate in the early twenties. She has recalled that 'the doctrine of the universal benefits of free trade . . . was imposed upon our young minds, as a dogma' (1973b, vol. 4, p. 1). Moreover: 'I was a student when vulgar economics was in a particularly vulgar state. There was Great Britain with never less than a million workers unemployed and there was I with my supervisor teaching me that it is logically impossible to have unemployment because of Say's Law.' (*ibid.* p. 264)

We have seen above how, in previous decades, both Sidgwick and Marshall, though supporting a free trade policy for Britain, had explicitly denounced any *dogma* 'of the universal benefits of free trade'. Moreover, Pigou, in his inaugural lecture (1908), had fundamentally attacked Ricardian policies on unemployment based on Say's Law. What the explanation may be, it is impossible to say, of the glaring discrepancy between the actual teachings of Sidgwick, Marshall, Pigou and Robertson and the 'dogmas' imposed upon the undergraduate Joan Robinson.[16] (The answer, perhaps, is wrapped up in that 'psychological riddle' which Schumpeter later discovered in her *Essay on Marxian Economics* – as we shall discuss below.)

However, Professor Robinson did remain grateful for what she regarded as an overriding advantage which she derived from her education in what Keynes was then calling 'the Cambridge School of Economics': 'I was brought up at Cambridge . . . in a period when vulgar economics had reached the depth of vulgarity. But all the same, inside the twaddle had been preserved a precious heritage – Ricardo's habit of thought.' (1973b, p. 266) (Some would describe this 'habit of thought' as 'the Ricardian vice of implicit theorizing', which excludes all relevance to what Professor Robinson was later to call 'historic time'.)

Although decades later she asserted that 'the analysis of imperfect competition was conceived as an attack upon orthodoxy' (1979b, p. 155), in her first book, *The Economics of Imperfect Competition* (1933), Mrs Robinson claimed to have 'endeavoured to build on the foundations laid down by Marshall and Pigou' (p.v). In fact, she was turning away from the methods of Marshall, as developed in *Industry and Trade* to follow a path more akin to that of Cournot and Pareto (as had been suggested by Dr Sraffa). Her method then, as ever since, was essentially abstract and geometrical (or Ricardian). Although she has complained that 'Pigou emptied history out of Marshall' (1979, p. 54) she proceeded to accept such emptiness and to depart far from the historical and institutional methods of Marshall, as then did other leading figures at Cambridge. On the other hand, she admirably defended the Marshallian academic duties of caution, patience, and detachment. Following Pigou, she described her work as that of a 'tool-maker'. However, she warned:

It is natural enough for the practical man to complain that he asks for bread and the economist gives him a stone. . . . *The practical man must be asked to have patience*, and meanwhile the economist must perfect his tools

in the hope of being able sooner or later to meet the practical man's requirements.
Such an ideal is still far distant. (1933, pp. 1–2, italics added)

What, however, Mrs Robinson then saw as the criterion, or epistemological *quaesitum*, of the theoretical economist was *logical consistency*, with empirical criteria such as testability, evidence and realism having, apparently, little explicit role (in accordance with 'Ricardo's habit of thought'). Anyhow, at this stage she argued that the economist must turn his (or her) back on real-world 'fruit', or 'gold':

> Unless economics is content to remain for ever in the age of Alchemy it must resolutely turn its back on the pursuit of gold, however precious it may be to human welfare, and embark upon the path of an austere and disinterested search, not 'for the Truth' but for a single self-consistent system of ideas. (1932, p. 4)

Marshall himself would have applauded Mrs Robinson's admirable call for caution, which was, in the best sense, academic, though her judgement of the past record was somewhat severe (but then so had been Sidgwick's regarding the English classicals, especially the Ricardians):

> Just as inadequate knowledge of physiology has led in the past to a medicine which killed more patients than it cured, so, in the history of the last hundred years, an economics, at once primitive and over-confident, has done more harm than good in the sphere of political life. (Robinson, 1932, p. 13)

However, Mrs Robinson was not advocating nihilism:

> It does not at all follow that economists should refrain from giving governments the benefit of their advice. . . . What the economist, in his capacity of amateur doctor, should do, is to explain frankly the limitations of his knowledge. It is the unjustified self-assurance of the economists which has alienated the governments. (p. 14)[17]

Within a very few years, it would seem, the dangers of a 'primitive and over-confident' attitude by economists, or of 'unjustified self-assurance', had faded in the rosy dawn of 'the Keynesian Revolution'. However, it must be recognized that in her earlier 'Keynesian' writings on 'the theory of employment',

Mrs Robinson was reasonably modest and cautious with regard to unemployment targets, which she envisaged in terms very different from the highly ambitious levels which she was to insist on a quarter of a century later, when she denounced a two per cent unemployment target as 'cold-blooded' and 'out of the question' (1966, p. 20). Earlier, in the thirties and forties, Mrs Robinson had argued (as had Keynes himself) that 'something appreciably short of full employment must be regarded as the optimum' (1937, p. 26). In fact, in 1946, she was maintaining that to reduce unemployment below five per cent 'would involve great sacrifice of liberty', while to reduce it below two per cent 'would involve complete conscription of labour' (1951, p. 106).

Nevertheless, it seems doubtful whether Mrs Robinson ever really accepted the positive, constructive side of Keynes's 'revolution' in so far as it was – as Dobb had quite validly maintained – concerned with making 'capitalism' work more effectively. Mrs Robinson simply embraced enthusiastically, and later emulated, Keynes's negative, denunciation, or 'overthrow', of 'orthodox economics'.

The publication in 1942 of Joan Robinson's *Essay on Marxian Economics* (together with the review article on it by G. F. Shove, 1944) surely marks, in retrospect at least, a significant happening in the history of the Cambridge school (and perhaps signifies a turning point in her intellectual biography). One main purpose of the essay was to give a sympathetic account of Marxian economics, some aspects of which had certainly deserved much more attention than they had been receiving. However, Mrs Robinson was highly critical of Marx on several points, though some of these criticisms were to be revised or withdrawn in subsequent decades. But no influence from the direction of Dobb is apparent, who would never have countenanced such a treatment of the prophet.

But the *Essay* opens on page 1, like Keynes's *General Theory*, with what amounts to a sweeping extension of the Keynesian approach to the history of economic thought. For Mrs Robinson begins with a root-and-branch denunciation of what she calls 'traditional orthodox economics', and 'orthodox economists', who are alleged to 'accept the capitalist system as part of the eternal order of nature', and to 'argue in terms of a harmony of interests between the various sections of the community' (1942, p. 1).

This unmasking of 'orthodox economics' was not developed as

comprehensively as in some subsequent portrayals (such as that in the introductory textbook of 1973). But a salient characteristic of this denunciation, subsequently almost invariably retained, was that few, if any, *actual quotations* from the works of 'orthodox' economists were supplied.[18] (Keynes had at least provided a small but very interesting selection.)

In G. F. Shove, the pacifist, socialist, Fellow of Kings, Lord Keynes, as editor, certainly enlisted a conscientious reviewer, of the highest scholarly and critical standards (whose own publications on economics, unfortunately, would perhaps, in their collected entirety, hardly have filled the pages of Mrs Robinson's *Essay*). He devoted fifteen pages to his review article, three and a half of which were occupied with approving comments on Mrs Robinson's treatment of Marx. The rest are concerned with her 'onslaught' on the 'orthodox economists', which Shove maintains 'is not nearly so well documented. We are not even told who the "orthodox economists" are, and an attempt to identify them by the doctrines attributed to them encounters difficulties' (1944, p. 50).

Shove then patiently proceeded, by means of precise and detailed quotations and references, to demonstrate that Smith, Ricardo, J. S. Mill, Marshall, Malthus, Cairnes, Sidgwick, Jevons, Edgeworth and Pigou had, in fact, expressed very contrasting doctrines to those comprehensively attributed to 'orthodox economists' by Mrs Robinson. Shove's conclusion may be cited at some length, since, although Mrs Robinson's views on 'orthodox economics' have frequently been repeated and elaborated in subsequent writings, no one in Cambridge has followed Shove (who died a few years later) in devoting painstaking scholarship to the task of critical refutation. Shove, incidentally, supported Keynes against Pigou in the thirties, but regarding 'Mrs Robinson's onslaught on "orthodox economics" ', he concluded:

The impression which it makes on one reader at any rate is that *she has allowed her moral sentiments to run away with her*. So shocked is she by the injustice of our 'absurd' (p. 80) social system, that *she will seize on any stick with which to beat any doctrine that has been, or might conceivably be, twisted into an apology for it.* This makes her attack much less effective than it might have been. The prominent economists whom she assails may have been as biased as she supposes. They were certainly not so lacking in sense and subtlety, and their theories, though far from a complete and satisfactory solution of the problems they set out to solve and throwing less light than Marx does on some of the fundamental characteristics of capitalism, cannot be 'disintegrated' or 'overthrown' so easily. What is wanted, indeed (here as in the case of Marx), is not an attempt to overthrow or disintegrate but rather an effort, *as detached as possible*, to understand, to sift truth from error and to formulate precisely the problems which have been left unsolved. *That task can be accomplished only by the methods of exact scholarship. It would perhaps be made easier if both socialists and non-socialists would realise that acceptance of, say, Marshall's theory of value and distribution does not by any means imply acceptance of the present social order.* (1944, p. 60, italics added).

Apart from the issue of the requirements of a scholarly version of the history of economic thought, what Shove repeatedly had to emphasize here is the significance of the normative-positive distinction, so powerfully and explicitly insisted upon by Sidgwick, Marshall and J. N. Keynes. Notable also is Shove's formulation of 'what is wanted', intellectually and epistemologically, as, 'an effort, *as detached as possible*, to . . . sift truth from error'. Obviously such an effort required carefully considered epistemological criteria, more adequate simply than logical self-consistency in accordance with 'Ricardo's habit of thought'.

Schumpeter, in a reference to Mrs Robinson's *Essay*, discerningly described it as 'something of a psychological riddle' (1954, p. 885). One can see what Schumpeter meant. Certainly the 'riddle' was to be prolonged, with continuing convolutions and considerable repetitions, over the ensuing decades. It would seem that an approach to an answer to the 'riddle' – not itself an answer – might start from Shove's suggestion that Mrs Robinson had 'allowed her moral sentiments to run away with her'. In other words, the precarious balance between scientific discipline and 'social enthusiasm', which had been established by Sidgwick and Marshall, and which had been endangered, though not irreparably upset, by some of the concepts, presuppositions and methods of Pigou and Keynes (J.M.), had now, in Mrs Robinson's *Essay* of 1942, been 'overthrown' or 'disintegrated'.

Perhaps a specially significant clue in Mrs Robinson's *Essay* was the comparison she drew, in Marx's favour, as between his economics and 'the gentle complacency of the orthodox academics'. Marx 'is more encouraging than they, for he releases hope as well as terror from Pandora's box while they preach only the gloomy doctrine that all is for the best in the best of all *possible* worlds' (Robinson, 1942, p. 5).

Thus Mrs Robinson was searching for '*hope*', and was presumably ready to pay some price for it – even perhaps in terms of realism and the relaxation of scientific discipline. Moreover, apparently Marx promised 'hope', either at no price, or at a price in 'terror' – for Marx released 'terror' too – which Mrs Robinson seemed to be quite willing to pay. However, just where the 'hope' in Marx's writings was to be discerned, three quarters of a century after the publication of his magnum opus, was not precisely elucidated. Notoriously, Marx had made no attempt to reveal how the future socialist economy would work and had simply prophesied the 'overthrow' or 'disintegration' of capitalist economies. But what is clear is that the Keynesian Revolution, in which she had played such an active part, by 1942 was obviously not providing Mrs Robinson with enough 'hope'. Fortunately she was soon able to discern a real–world fulfilment of Marxian economic 'hope' in Stalin's Russia.

What was extraordinary about Mrs Robinson's pilgrimage to Moscow in quest of Marxian hope (and in her proclamation of having discovered it) was the extreme lateness of the date: 1952. Dobb's first hopeful mission had taken place about a quarter of a century previously, near the beginning of the Stalin era. Mrs Robinson left it to the last year of Stalin's reign, when he was engaged in a final frenzied fling on the occasion of 'the Doctors' Plot'. Judging from the impressions recorded in her remarkable pamphlet *Conference Sketchbook: Moscow 1952* (an exquisite example of its genre) Mrs Robinson was able to find the 'hope', originally 'released' by Marx, amply implemented and fulfilled in Stalin's Moscow, as exemplified in the fine taste of the hotel architecture, in the absurdity of the suspicions that foreigners might be followed and watched, and, in particular, in Stalin's prompt and humanitarian personal interventions in the direction of labour.

Unfortunately, however, the Marxian hope discovered in Stalin's Moscow proved as fleetingly evanescent as Mrs Robinson's discernment of it had been belated. Within a few years Mrs Robinson was comparing 'Stalinist' with 'McCarthyist persecution' (1965, p. 157), in a paper of 1962, a comparison which surely displays a remarkable political sense of proportion). But by the early sixties, with the Great Leap Forward in China, and the Cultural Revolution on the way, a new and rosier hope was dawning further east. By 1960 it appeared that in China: 'Even upon cautious estimates, the rate of growth of industrial capacity is probably the most rapid the world has ever known, but this is only a matter of degree' (1960, p. 410).[19]

One is reminded by Mrs Robinson's verdict on China of Dobb's enthusiastic judgements about Stalin's collectivization of agriculture thirty years previously. For the 'Great Leap Forward', and its dislocations, were followed by famine. As David Caute comments:

> In 1969 Joan Robinson wrote: 'It is true that there was a tight period following the Great Leap Forward. The historical analogue of this is the Russian famine of 1921. . . . No doubt many elderly people died sooner than they would have done, but no one is able to find evidence of famine.' Except, perhaps, the 'elderly people' who died. (1973, p. 376, quoting Robinson, 1969)

Another parallel with Dobb, thirty to forty years previously, was Mrs Robinson's enthusiasm for the 'novelty' of the Cultural Revolution. Under the striking title 'Something to Live For', Mrs Robinson proclaimed:

> The Cultural Revolution is something new in history. For the first time, a second wave of popular uprising, mounted against the New Class that inherited power from a successful revolution, has carried socialism back (for one more generation) onto the line of its original ideals. . . .
> The people are conscious of taking part in a great political experiment. They are being given not only something to eat but something to live for. . . .
> The village is gay now. 'They are always striking up some song.' (1971, p. 631)

Professor Robinson in particular expressed enthusiastic hope regarding the rounding up of students and 'intellectuals' for compulsory agricultural labour.[20]

But alas, here again Marxian 'hope' has proved all too fleeting. Within a few years, Maoism was virtually abolished, the Cultural Revolution denounced, and the much excoriated 'rightist' followers of 'the capitalist road' back in power, striving to get their country to make up some of the immense economic leeway *vis-à-vis* such neighbours as Japan, South Korea, Taiwan and Hong Kong. Indeed the world seems to be running rather short of Utopias to which to pilgrimate in the quest for Marxian 'hope'. So what the next turn may be, in the 'psychological riddle' discerned by Schumpeter, is not easy to predict. What would be *really* interesting would be a repudiation by Professor Robinson, as frank and complete as her repudiation of her neoclassical work in her earlier years, of all her subsequent Stalinist, Maoist and Marxian enthusiasms. But perhaps this is too much to hope for. It might be argued that the validity and quality of Professor Robinson's more abstract theoretical, or analytical work on capital, growth etc., are quite independent of her judgements regarding real-world policies and growth-rates in Mao's China, Stalin's Russia, and North Korea, and regarding the political processes in these countries. Logically, this distinction is quite clear and it is one which should often be insisted upon. But if one takes the view, traditionally prevalent in Cambridge, that economics should be regarded, and judged, above all as a fruit-bearing subject, of which its contribution to realistic policy-making is the vital criterion, then the real-world outcome, upshot, or cash value for policy guidance of Professor Robinson's work may be regarded as embodied in the judgements about communist politico-economic performance which we have been concerned to emphasize.

IX *Conclusion*

By concluding this chapter at this point, with the contributions of Maurice Dobb and Professor Robinson, it is not, of course, being suggested that Marxian, or pro-Marxian, doctrines on the philosophy and politics of economics subsequently dominated in Cambridge, to the exclusion of the teachings of the founding fathers. Certainly Marxian doctrines obtained a powerful hold. But the philosophical and political views of Sidgwick and Marshall have survived in the work of other Cambridge economists, though mainly inexplicitly and unarticulated. Anyhow, Dobb and Professor Robinson were the last of the 'pure' Cambridge economists who have contributed importantly to the philosophy and politics of the subject, and who spent virtually their whole careers, from Fresher to Emeritus, in Cambridge. Some of the subsequent 'neo-' and 'post-Keynesian' contributions to policy-making are discussed in the next chapter.

We have seen how the original difficult and delicate balance between moral and social enthusiasm and scientific method, which motivated and was, on the whole, scrupulously preserved by Sidgwick and Marshall, was distorted, though not irreparably, by some of the concepts and assumptions of Pigou and Keynes

(J.M.), and then was denounced by Marxian and pro-Marxian doctrines. We have seen, also, how, after his death, with the fading of Marshall's fundamental interest in historical and institutional processes, much of the theorising on firms and industries became more geometrical, unempirical and unhistorical, empty of the rich content on monopolistic conditions and processes which is to be found in *Industry and Trade*. Marshall's anxious concern with the historical problem of the relatively slow rate of growth of the British economy also disappeared for a long time.

Moreover, limitations increasingly emerged, in the second half of the twentieth century, in Marshall's attempt to replace political economy by a more or less non-political 'economics'. So long as the role of government in the economy was comparatively small, as, in Britain, at the beginning of this century, and so long as economic theorizing could proceed on the basis of a consensus regarding 'a stable general culture' (as Pigou called it), or a stable socioeconomic framework, then the assumptions of a non-political economics remained largely valid. But with a much greater role for government, and with much more comprehensive issues of policy on the agenda, including questions of the kind of economic order or framework (such as capitalism versus socialism), then a non-political economics soon began to lose relevance. Politics inevitably came back into the subject, not simply in normative terms in providing value-judgements and policy objectives, *but also in positive terms* with regard to how institutions work and how political man behaves.

Sidgwick, as an inheritor and upholder of the English philosophical tradition of Locke, Hume and J. S. Mill, and his philosophical-political disciple Marshall, possessed an admirable measure of political culture and methodological discipline. Certainly also, for example, Pigou's mature essay, *Socialism versus Capitalism*, was for the most part, informed, as far as it went, by a Marshallian realism in its assumptions about political processes and values. But the younger Pigou, in his treatment of 'welfare' policies, had disregarded – as the mature Pigou admitted – some of the vital, realistic political warnings of Sidgwick and Marshall in implying that policies could be assessed in terms of the failure of markets to achieve ideal maxima and optima, apparently on the assumption that, if these cases of failure were pointed out by economists, then politicians would, like omniscient, omnipotent, altruistic angels, rush in to implement such ideal welfare optima and maxima. The young Keynes, moreover, equipped himself with an apostolic philosophy, imbued with what may validly be described as highly 'elitist' assumptions which, as the older Keynes admitted, rested on a kind of 'pseudo-rationalism' which 'completely misunderstood human nature' – hardly a very reliable basis for realistic politics and policies.

Economic theorizing can proceed reasonably satisfactorily within the limits of non-political economics if pursued as no more than 'a good game'; and may even go beyond that, if its real-world policy relevance is restricted to an agreed or given social and political framework. But if larger-scale policies are at issue, or especially if comparisons of alternative politicoeconomic systems are involved – as in much of Marxian theorizing – then non-political economics develops inadequacies. There has to be a return to political economy. *But the quality of the political economy will depend crucially on the quality of the political input, positive and normative, which is brought back in.* The quality of economic theorizing *can* be virtually independent of the economist's politics: the quality of his political economy cannot. One might find acceptable, or unacceptable, the positive and normative politics of a Sidgwick or a J. S. Mill, or of an Adam Smith or Hume, but their seriousness can hardly be in dispute. If, however, the political element derives largely from the doctrines of Stalinism, or of Mao's 'Cultural Revolution', then the political economy which emerges will be imbued with a corresponding quality. It is not only a question of norms or morals, but of the positive processes of political institutions and behaviour – as well as of the positive processes of economic institutions as reflected for example in growth rates. As noted previously, E. M. Forster, at the end of the thirties, rightly rejected the Marxian politics, influential in Cambridge and elsewhere in that decade, by insisting that: 'I don't believe the communists know what leads to what'. It must also be remembered, however much Marxians may wish to forget, that, for decades, to be a Marxian was virtually to be an ardent supporter of Stalin.

The transition, in Cambridge, from the political and philosophical attitudes of Sidgwick, Marshall, and J. N. Keynes, to those of Dobb and Professor Joan Robinson, may seem like something of a cautionary tale, revealing what happens when discipline, distinctions, and empirical constraints disintegrate, and 'anything goes', while an extreme political urge, or anxiety 'to do good' persists.

Professor Moggridge has, surely correctly, emphasized regarding Keynes:

Unlike some of his predecessors such as W. S. Jevons or Marshall who
made some attempt to study and understand the lives of ordinary people
and had decided to pursue political economy as a result of what they had
learned, Keynes's conception of the desirable society was based much
less on widespread observation and experience. (1976, p. 41)

This contrast, in respect of the empirical study of the lives of
ordinary people, persists even more strongly with regard to the
successors of Keynes than it holds as between Keynes and
Marshall. It, therefore, makes it all the more strangely paradoxical
that Keynes should have charged Marshall with being 'too anxious
to do good' (1972, vol. 10, p. 200).

*On the contrary, it is not Marshall, but his successors, increasingly
from Pigou onwards, who should be charged with being 'too anxious'
(much too anxious, in some cases) 'to do good'.* For anxiety to do good
may sometimes be highly pretentious or presumptuous, expressing a will to manage and manipulate, and even rather to do harm
to others as much as 'good' to some. But, for the academic
economist, the anxiety to do good *can* be legitimized and validated
to the extent – but only to the extent – that it is balanced, *first*, by a
corresponding anxiety to study and understand ('with painful
care', as Jevons put it) the lives of the ordinary people which there
is such an anxiety to improve; and *secondly*, by a corresponding
anxiety to maintain standards of scientific caution and epistemological discipline in the economic theorizing out of which,
somehow, the 'good' is to emerge.

Marshall's 'anxiety to do good' was justified insofar as it was
firmly balanced and controlled by these two complementary
anxieties. But, after Marshall, the balance was not preserved.
Pigou's central concept of 'economic welfare' might be regarded,
in itself, as expressing a slightly excessive, intellectually, pretentious, anxiety 'to do good'; as might also what Professor
Moggridge describes as Keynes's 'impatience to . . . influence
events in the direction he desired' (1972, vol. 10, p. 38). However,
with regard to these two great men, Pigou and Keynes, it might
well be concluded that although their epistemological standards
and empirical caution came under excessive pressure from their
anxiety to do good, or their '*Verbesserungs* malady', as Keynes
called it, preponderantly, in their great works, a reasonable

balance was preserved. But subsequently the anxiety to do good so completely preponderated as to destroy the balance exemplified by Marshall, Sidgwick, and J. N. Keynes; or, as Shove stated of Mrs Robinson, 'moral sentiments' were allowed 'to run away with' the economics. As illustrations of how completely the principle of 'anything goes' took over, and empirical constraints were jettisoned, it is only necessary to contemplate Dobb's and Professor Robinson's practical, real-world judgements about comparative growth-rates, and, in particular, about the unique record-breading growth-rates, or other economic achievements, of Stalin's Russia, Mao's China and Cultural Revolution, or of North Korea, that is, in an area of economics where their strenuous and massive theoretical and analytical labours *might* have been expected to provide some kind of guidance. But *either* such theorizing does not, in fact, help to improve the accuracy of real-world predictions as to the growth rates and growth potentials of different economies; *or* an excessive anxiety to do good has cancelled out any illumination, or paralysed any guidance, which such rigorous abstract theorizing or model-building might have yielded.[21]

Notes

1   Marshall would have sympathized with Edward Gibbon: 'As soon as I understood the principles I relinquished for ever the pursuit of mathematics; nor can I lament that I desisted before my mind was hardened by the habit of rigid demonstration, so destructive of the finer feelings of moral evidence, which must, however, determine the actions and opinions of our lives' (1796–1911, p. 71).

2   See also Marshall, 1919, pp. 675–6:

> All opinion is liable to be tainted by unconscious bias; but *that taint can be kept low* in matters in which every serious student can equip himself with the knowledge and the implements for investigation and reasoning, that have been accumulated by the progressive labours of many generations of strong workers in the same field. . . .
>
> Economic studies are not to be limited to matters, which are amenable to strictly scientific treatment. But those conclusions, whether in detail or in general, which are based on individual judgements as to the relative desirability of different social aims, or as to matters of fact which lie beyond the scope of any individual's

special studies, *should be clearly distinguished* from those which claim to have been reached by scientific method. (Italics added)

3   It is interesting to find Dobb, in this article (p. 369), using the term 'neoclassical' explicitly for the Marshallian school (or theory) as contrasted with the Walrasian: 'The neoclassical theory of value is a theory of particular equilibrium as contrasted with the theory of general equilibrium characteristic of some other schools, especially the Lausanne, or mathematical school'. There is some logic behind this usage, but it is uncommon.

4   I am much indebted to an article of Mr A. Petridis who concludes: 'The gradual change in Marshall's attitude toward trade unions from a favourable and hopeful one in the 1870s to one of doubt and uncertainty in the 1880s and to a final position bordering on hostility is consistent with his interpretation of British economic history of the period' (1973 p. 183). It is very strange that economic historians concerned with the problem of Britain's relative industrial decline have hardly ever referred to the very emphatic views of Alfred Marshall. Possibly they have been inhibited by fears of being accused of 'union-bashing' – almost as terrible an accusation as 'McCarthyism'. Mr A. L. Levine's treatment in his work on industrial retardation in Britain is typical. After quoting Marshall on the subject of failures of management, he never so much as mentions Marshall in the chapter on unionism, which comes to very lenient conclusions regarding the unions. See Levine, 1967.

5   Foxwell's denunciation of Ricardo and Marx was cited by Dobb as 'significant of the temper' of neoclassicals (1937, p. 139). But Foxwell also denounced 'the fatalistic, crude, anti-social doctrine of *laissez-faire*', alleged to be a hall-mark of neo-classicism by Profs Robinson and Deane and Mr Eatwell.

6   It has been asserted by R. Deacon (*The Guardian*, 30 May 1977), that Pigou was 'the most secret and in many respects one of the most effective Russian agents in Britain over a period of 50 years'. This is quite incredible. However, perhaps some black amusement may be derived from the thought that the famous 'Pigou effect', which purported to demonstrate the stability of a capitalist economy, was really an elaborate 'cover' device. It would also be tempting to speculate as to the significance of left-wing denunciations, as a spokesman for *laissez-faire* capitalism, of this most subtle and effective of Russian agents, and of the allegations that his one remedy for depressions was cutting the workers' wages.

7   I am indebted to an, at present, unpublished paper by Mr R. Miller of the Institute of Economic Affairs on the subject of Keynes's philosophical beliefs.

8   Examples of Keynes's 'attributing an unreal rationality' to other people's behaviour which promoted erratic misjudgements on his part could certainly be found in the field of foreign policy. For example:

(1) As a high civil servant in World War I, under the pseudonym 'Politicus', Keynes wrote articles in the press criticizing the government's failure to pursue a peace policy in April 1916. Regarding signs of 'how intense and widespread is the discontent and disillusionment' in Germany, and how such signs might sustain a belief in 'victory', Keynes concluded: 'It is a far safer inference that the German people will be cured for a generation at least of warlike notions and pan-Germanic dreams. . . . The military issue of the war will be a deadlock and, for the future, there is already a deep-rooted hatred of war before which even Kaisers and Junkers will have to bow.' (1971, vol. 16, pp. 182–3) Subsequently Keynes maintained regarding France: 'That she has anything to fear from Germany in the future which we can foresee, except what she may herself provoke, is a delusion. When Germany has recovered her strength and pride, as in due time she will, many years must pass before she again casts her eyes westward.' (1971, vol. 3, p. 128)

(2) Again, in 1945, Keynes seriously misjudged the intentions of the US government as regards their providing Britain with a grant-in-aid or an interest-free loan. (See Lord Robbins, 1971, p. 205, who described Keynes's judgements on this issue as 'a case of a sort of brainstorm in which he was carried away by over-confidence in his own ability and a vision of what it might accomplish').

9   Also, regarding the Labour Party, Keynes would presumably not have wanted to revise his view of 1925 half a century or more later:

> I do not believe that the intellectual elements in the Labour Party will ever exercise adequate control; too much will always be decided by those who do not know *at all* what they are talking about; and if – which is not unlikely – the control of the party is seized by an autocratic inner ring, this control will be exercised in the interests of the extreme left wing – the section of the Labour Party which I shall designate the party of catastrophe. (p. 297)

10   As Dr Ronald Meek, one of Maurice Dobb's most enthusiastic disciples, later put it: 'In our own times, new doctrines concerning "the perfectibility of man and of society", *scientific rather than utopian in character*, have come to guide the practical day-to-day activities of large sections of mankind. Inspired by Marxism, tremendous social revolutions have occurred in the Soviet Union, China and the People's Democracies.' (1953, p. 40, italics added)

11   For example in the Introduction to a volume of papers in which the essays of such leading Cambridge *illuminati* as Dobb, Sraffa and Joan Robinson figure prominently, the editors proclaim: ' "Severely rational modern economics", the austere science, is being seen to function essentially as a pseudo-sophistication proclaiming the greatest beneficence while the wretched of the earth are starved, clubbed, gassed and bombed into submission' (Hunt and Schwartz, 1972, p. 32). In his later

years Dobb might have found this sort of thing, perhaps, *slightly* 'vulgar'.

12   *We are not aware that Dobb ever published any revision of his assessments of Stalin's agricultural policies in the early thirties.* Indeed, it is interesting to find Ronald Meek, as late as 1953, focusing one of his more far-reaching claims on behalf of the policies of 'the great scientist' Stalin (as he described him) on the achievements of Russian agriculture, inviting his readers to 'look around you at what is going on in the Soviet Union, where the great plans for the increase of food production are making a mockery of the Malthusian theory of population and the "law of diminishing returns" ' (1953, p. 49). Regarding Dobb's capacity for reacting to empirical evidence, it may be noted that, after many years of the activities of Yagoda, Yezhov, *et al.*, he was able to assert that the evidence for police torture to extract confessions in the Soviet Union was of 'very low' credibility, and that 'I had occasion to go as carefully as I could into this question' (Dobb, 1940, pp. 366 and 433).

13   Regarding Dobb's credulity, as Professor A. Erlich has noted: 'It is . . . *somewhat astonishing* that Professor Dobb seemed to take the targets of the First Five Year Plan *quite seriously*' (1960, p. 166n, italics added).

14   See Skidelsky, 1980. On the Marxian myths of the thirties, Professor Skidelsky writes (p. 27): 'The Marxist generation was wrong about the condition of the economy, wrong about the intellectual resourcefulness of capitalist democracy, wrong about the Spanish civil war, wrong about the nature of the menace facing the West, wrong about the motives of the British Government, wrong about the Soviet Union'. As E. M. Forster wrote at the end of the decade: 'I don't believe the Communists know what leads to what. They say they are becoming conscious of the causality of society. I say they don't know.' (1938, p. 972)

15   F. D. Maurice (1805–72) was apparently one of the founders of the Apostles, the Cambridge secret society. He was deprived of his professorship at Kings College London for unsound theology. He worked strenuously for the education of women and for the Working Men's College, founded in London in 1854. Later he was a professor of Moral Philosophy at Cambridge. Maurice seems to have inspired the most extremely contradictory judgements among his contemporaries. J. S. Mill's opinion was interesting:

> I have so deep a respect for Maurice's character and purposes, as well as for his great mental gifts, that it is with some unwillingness I say anything which may seem to place him on a less high eminence than I would gladly be able to accord him. But I have always thought that there was more intellectual power wasted in Maurice than in any other of my contemporaries. Few of them certainly have had so much to waste. Great powers of generalization, rare ingenuity and subtlety, and a wide perception of important and unobvious truths,

served him not for putting something better into the place of the worthless heap of received opinions on the great subjects of thought, but for proving to his own mind that the Church of England had known everything from the first. (1873/1924, pp. 129–30)

16 At this time, in the early twenties, the Cambridge Economic Handbooks, edited by Keynes, were very widely used standard texts. They certainly did not propagate the kind of 'dogmas' apparently 'imposed' on Joan Robinson. Indeed, the preface, signed by Joan Robinson, to a new 'Modern' Cambridge Economics Series, claims that these new handbooks are 'designed in the same spirit as and with similar objectives to the series of Cambridge Economics Handbooks launched by Maynard Keynes' (Robinson 1979b p. v).

17 See the pamphlet *Economics is a Serious Subject* (1932). One may find entirely inadequate, the Ricardian criterion of logical self-consistency. But there can be no more valuable message for the beginner student than that inculcated then by Mrs Robinson: an austere warning as to the very limited, immediate, 'fruit-bearing' policy-potential of economics, combined with a rejection of nihilism. I remain intensely grateful for having been given this pamphlet by Mrs Robinson herself, as my first reading on the 'serious subject' of the philosophy and method of economics. However, it might seem somewhat bewildering that most of what she taught me (1932–34) has long since been repudiated in disgust by Mrs Robinson; nor have I found at all palatable 'the Ricardian habit of thought'.

18 It may be noted that only a year or two previously Mrs Robinson had intervened to defend 'professional economists', in general, against the charge of hostility to generous, public old age pensions, holding that 'the type of *laissez-faire* economist opposed to such ideas, far from being orthodox', was 'nowadays a rare and silent bird' (1940, p. 682).

19 Almost as remarkable was the 'Economic Miracle' discovered in North Korea in 1964: 'All the economic miracles of the post-war world are put in the shade by these achievements. . . . As the North continues to develop and the South to degenerate, sooner or later the curtain of lies must surely begin to tear.' (1965, pp. 208–15) It might have been interesting to examine the actual statistics on which Professor Robinson's claims for the North Korean miracle, as for the record growth-rates in China, but she did not provide any.

20 David Caute's comments (1973, pp. 376–7) are worth noting. Regarding, for example, the Cultural Revolution, he remarks:

'The most ardent justification came from the pen of Joan Robinson in a short book which combined gullibility with latent authoritarianism in doses which were virtually standard among fellow-travellers of a certain stamp.' See Robinson, 1969 pp. 16–19, 29, 106; and 1973(a).

21 It may be noted that in complete contradiction of this chapter, Lord Vaizey (1972), a once devoted pupil of Professor Robinson, has stressed the continuity from Marshall to the 'Radical Economics', as he called it, of Prof. Robinson, Dr Sraffa, and Lords Kahn and Kaldor, whom he held to be continuers of 'the high intellectual tradition of Marshall and Keynes', and 'the most powerful intellects of the twentieth century'. 'Yes, I'm glad I'm a Radical Economist' concluded Lord Vaizey. However, seven years later, some flexibility in the principles of 'Radical Economics' emerged when, following a change of government, Lord Vaizey announced his ardent allegiance to the strenuous free-market policies of Mrs Thatcher.

References

Beveridge, W. (1944); *Full Employment in a Free Society*.

Caute, D. (1973), *The Fellow-Travellers*.

Coase, R. H. (1960), 'The Problem of Social Cost', *Journal of Law and Economics*, vol. 3, Oct., pp. 1ff.

(1975), 'Marshall on Method', *Journal of Law and Economics*, vol. 18, no. 1, pp. 25ff.

Deacon, R. (1977), 'Climbing to Power', *The Guardian*, 30 May.

Deane, P. (1978), *The Evolution of Economic Ideas*.

Dobb, M. H. (1924) *Capitalist Enterprise and Social Progress*.

(1931), 'Economics: The Cambridge School', in E. R. A. Seligman (ed.), *Encyclopaedia of the Social Sciences*, pp. 368ff.

(1932), *Soviet Russia and the World*.

(1937), *Political Economy and Capitalism*.

(1940), Letters in *New Statesman and Nation*, March 16 and 30, 1940, pp. 366 and 433.

(1941), *Soviet Economy and the War*.

(1942), *Soviet Planning and Labour in Peace and War*.

(1955), *On Economic Theory and Socialism*.

(1960), *Soviet Economic Development since 1917*, 5th ed.

(1967), *Papers on Capitalism, Development and Planning*.

(1970), *Socialist Planning: Some Problems*.

(1973), *Theories of Value and Distribution*.

(1975), 'Revival of Political Economy: An Explanatory Note', *Economic Record*, Sept., pp. 357ff.

(1978), 'Random Biographical Notes', *Cambridge Journal of Economics*, vol. 2, no. 2, pp. 115ff.

Eatwell, J. (1979), 'Dobb, Maurice H.', in *International Encyclopaedia of the Social Sciences, Biographical Supplement*, pp. 142ff.

Erlich, A. (1960), *The Soviet Industrialization Debate*.

Feinstein, C. H. ed. (1967), *Socialism, Capitalism and Economic Growth, Essays Presented to Maurice Dobb*.

Forster, E. M. (1938), in *New Statesman and Nation*, 10 Dec., p. 972.

Foxwell, H. S. (1886), 'Irregularity of Employment and Fluctuations of Prices' in *The Claims of Labour*, by J. Burnett *et al*.

Gibbon, E. (1796), *Autobiography* (Everyman ed., 1911).

Hicks, Sir John (1979), *Causality in Economics*.

Hobsbawm, E. (1967), 'Maurice Dobb', in Feinstein (ed.), 1967.

Howson, S. and Winch, D. (1977), *The Economic Advisory Council 1930–1939*.

Hunt, E. K. and Schwartz, J., ed. (1972), *A Critique of Economic Theory*.

Hutchison, T. W. (1953), *A Review of Economic Doctrine 1870–1929*.

(1978), *Revolutions and Progress in Economic Knowledge*.

Jha, N. (1973), *The Age of Marshall*, 2nd ed.

Keynes, J. M. (1921), *A Treatise on Probability*.

(1922), Introduction to Robertson, 1922.

(1949) *Two Memoirs*.

(1971), *Collected Writings*, ed. D. E. Moggridge, vols 3 and 16.

(1972), *Collected Writings*, ed. D. E. Moggridge, vols 9 and 10.

(1973), *Collected Writings*, ed. D. E. Moggridge vol. 14.

Keynes, J. N. (1890), *The Scope and Method of Political Economy*.

Leavis, F. R. (1967), *The Common Pursuit*.

Levine, A. L. (1967), *Industrial Retardation in Britain 1880–1914*.

Loasby, B. J. (1976), *Choice, Complexity and Ignorance*.

Mandel, E. (1968), *Marxist Economic Theory*, translated by B. Pearce.

Marshall, A. (1885), 'How far do Remediable Causes Influence Prejudicially (a) the continuity of employment, (b) the Rate of Wages?', *Industrial Remuneration Conference, Report of Proceedings and Papers*, pp. 173ff.

(1919), *Industry and Trade*.

(1926), *Official Papers*.

Marx, K. (1961), *Capital*, vol. 1, Moscow.

Meek, R. L., ed. (1953), *Marx and Engels on Malthus*.

Mill, J. S. (1873), *Autobiography*, World's Classics, 1924.

Moggridge, D. E. (1976), *Keynes*.

Myrdal, G. (1939), *Monetary Equilibrium*.

(1973), *Against the Stream*.

Nove, A. (1972), *An Economic History of the USSR*.

Petridis, A. (1973), 'Alfred Marshall's Attitudes to and Economic Analysis of Trade Unions', *History of Political Economy*, vol. 5, no. 1, pp. 165ff.

Pigou, A. C. (1902), 'A Parallel between Economic and Political Theory', *Economic Journal*, vol. 12, June, pp. 274ff.

(1908), *Economic Science in Relation to Practice*.

(1920), *The Economics of Welfare*, 1st ed.

(1929), *The Economics of Welfare*, 3rd ed.

(1933), *The Theory of Unemployment*.

(1936), Review of B. and S. Webb, *Soviet Communism: a New Civilisation?*, in *Economic Journal*, vol. 46, Mar. pp. 88ff.

(1937), *Socialism versus Capitalism.*

(1939), Presidential Address to Royal Economic Society, *Economic Journal*, vol. 49, pp. 215ff.

(1944), Review of F. A. Hayek, *The Road to Serfdom*, in *Economic Journal*, vol. 54, June, pp. 217ff.

Pigou, A. C., ed. (1925), *Memorials of Alfred Marshall.*

Robbins, Lord (1971), *Autobiography of an Economist.*

Robertson, D. H. (1922), *Money*, Cambridge Economic Handbooks.

(1951), *Utility and All That.*

Robinson, J. (1932), *Economics is a Serious Subject.*

(1933), *Economics of Imperfect Competition.*

(1937), *Essays in the Theory of Employment.*

(1940), Letter in *New Statesman*, Dec. 28, p. 682.

(1942), *An Essay on Marxian Economics.*

(1951), *Collected Economic Papers*, vol. 1.

(1952), *Conference Sketchbook, Moscow 1952.*

(1960), Review of *The Economic Development of Communist China 1949–1958* by T. J. Hughes and D. E. T. Luard, *Economic Journal*, vol. 70 pp. 409–10

(1962), *Economic Philosophy.*

(1965), *Collected Economic Papers*, vol. 3.

(1966), *Economics: an Awkward Corner.*

(1969a), *The Cultural Revolution in China.*

(1969b), Letter to *Tribune*, London, 24 Jan.

(1971), 'Something to Live For', *New Statesman*, 7 May, p. 631.

(1973a), *Economic Management in China 1972.*

(1973b), *Collected Economic Papers*, vol. 4.

(1979), *Aspects of Development and Underdevelopment.*

Robinson, J. and Eatwell, J. (1973), *An Introduction to Modern Economics.*

Schumpeter, J. A. (n.d.), 'The Meaning of Rationality in the Social Sciences', unpublished typescript.

Schumpeter, J. A. (1954), *History of Economic Analysis.*

Shove, G. F. (1944), 'Mrs Robinson on Marxian Economics', *Economic Journal*, vol. 54, pp. 47ff.

Sidgwick, A. and E. (1906), *Henry Sidgwick, a Memoir.*

Sidgwick, H. (1883), *Principles of Political Economy*, 1st ed.

(1887), *Principles of Political Economy*, 2nd ed.

(1962), 'The Scope and Method of Economic Science', in R. L. Smyth (ed.), *Essays in Economic Method.*

Skidelsky, R. (1980), 'Exploding Certain Convenient Myths of the 1930s', *Encounter*, vol. 54, no. 6, pp. 23ff.

Vaizey, Lord, (1972), 'Radical Economist', *New Statesman*, May 12, p. 645.

Webb, B. (1938), *My Apprenticeship*, 2 vols.

Williams, P. L. (1978), *The Emergence of the Theory of the Firm.*

4

Keynes *versus* the Keynesians

Three different sources of weakness and inadequacy may be distinguished in the process of decline and crisis of a once successful, or 'orthodox', system of theory, 'paradigm', or 'research programme' in economics, such as that of English Classical Political Economy or 'the Ricardo–Mill economics', as Jevons called it, or, a hundred years later, Keynesian economics.

First, there may be discovered original 'internal', logical or empirical weaknesses, of the kind which arise in the natural sciences, which may accumulate to create a 'crisis'. Keynesian economics, over the last four decades, has undergone interminable examinations and re-examinations in these terms which we do not resume here.

Secondly, in economics and the social sciences, a very important source, often cumulative, of weakness and inadequacy (unlike, usually, in the natural sciences) consists of changes in historical conditions and institutions. Such changes both give rise to new weaknesses and inadequacies and magnify old ones, by creating empirical anomalies or irrelevances in once more acceptable 'orthodox' doctrines.

In the roughly half-century before the 1860s, for example, institutional and historical changes had rendered the basic theoretical and policy concept of the 'natural wage' much more obviously invalid or inadequate – that is, either empirically false, or empty. The natural-wage proposition had always been at least questionable, but it remained absolutely central to the theoretical and policy doctrines of 'the Ricardo–Mill economics'. Furthermore, institutional changes had rendered more serious the inadequacies of the orthodox treatment, or non-treatment, of such increasingly important questions as relative wages and the pricing of public utilities and monopolies. Keynesian economics has also been subject to this source, or type, of historical-institutional obsolescence.

But the degeneration of systems, 'paradigms', or 'research programmes' in economic theory and political economy (and the rise of 'counter-revolutionary' ideas, or 'antitheses') may have a third kind of source: the way in which they come to be adapted or altered by disciples, successors, or popularizers. As Professor Martin Bronfenbrenner has explained:

With the passing of the generations, a thesis hardens from doctrine to dogma. Its choirs of angels become choirs of parrots, chanting 'supply and demand', 'full employment', or 'planned society', as the case may be. . . . At the same time . . . there is leached out of the original thesis whatever implications seem threatening to the ruling class. . . . Because the thesis turns apologetic, repetitive, and lifeless, and also because problems arise for which the answers stemming from orthodox paradigms are either lacking or unacceptable, there develop antitheses to every thesis. (1971, p. 139)

As regards the 'hardening into dogma', the overconfidence and pretentiousness generated by the initial 'revolution' may be reinforced by short-run, and/or apparent, or superficial, success in policy. That nothing fails like success is liable to be true also in the history of economic thought. For when, and in so far, as the original doctrines are hardened overconfidently into dogmas and protected against testing and re-testing, the flexibility and sensitivity to changing real-world conditions which contributed to the success of the work of the original 'revolutionary' leader may be lost by the epigoni.

Furthermore, the attitude of regarding economic theories – including especially a new 'revolutionary' theory – as on a par, epistemologically, with the theories of the natural sciences (and Keynes was compared with Einstein) may encourage a more exaggerated belief than is justified in the relative durability, and resistance to obsolescence, of the new economic theory or discovery. A more serious development may be that the hardening into dogma and mystique of the original doctrines may bring significant alterations, in emphasis or content, as qualifications and exceptions are forgotten or modified.

This third type, or source, of degeneration may, of course, be combined with the second historical–institutional source. To some extent, for example, both these kinds of process were present during the decline and fall of classical political economy, in which the exaggerations and dogmatisms of oversimplifiers and popular-izers played a significant part in rendering the orthodox doctrines more open to attack. During the critical period of the 1860s, for example, such figures as Fawcett and Lowe might be mentioned.[1] It may be still more serious if the epigoni bend the doctrines of the original 'revolutionary' leader in favour of their own policy predilections, or in favour of political forces or trends on whose wave, or 'bandwagon', they may wish to advance – such as, for example, in the sixties and seventies in Britain, the trade union bosses and the bureaucratic planners. The central theme of this essay relates mainly to this third source of weakness, or process of decline.

II

Our main concern is with the wide divergences between the policy objectives which Keynes formulated in the last decade of his life, and those propagated in his name in the decades after his death.

Before passing to this main theme we touch, all too briefly, upon the peripherally related question, recently raised, that because 'Keynesian' policies had, in their country of origin, run into obviously very serious difficulties by the 1970s, *therefore* Keynes's own doctrines were fundamentally and fatally flawed from the start. Certainly by the 1970s it could hardly have failed to escape the attention of open-minded observers that, as Mr Walter Eltis has remarked:

Inflation has accelerated throughout the world, and it must be particularly disturbing to Keynesian policy-makers that the countries where their influence was greatest are those which have suffered most. . . . So how is it, a sensible Keynesian might ask, that the countries where those in power and influence have the most correct understanding of how economies work managed to achieve the worst results and to be among the world's perpetual candidates for inter-national financial support? Ironically, most of this [support] has to come from countries which are managed in non–Keynesian ways. (1976, p. 1)

There is obviously a justifiable and searching question here. However, more fundamental criticisms have been expressed to the effect that Keynes's main doctrines were, in their origins, fundamentally invalid or unnecessary, and that their influence, and the whole phenomenon of 'the Keynesian revolution', was irrelevant or even disastrous. Professor F. A. Hayek, for example, has (1975) referred to '*the fatal idea* that unemployment is predominantly due to an insufficiency of aggregate demand' (1975, p. 19, italics added). Professor H. G. Johnson, on rather different lines, has argued that Keynes's main doctrines were quite misconceived for dealing with a problem which amounted simply or largely to the overvaluation of sterling between 1925 and 1931: 'Had the exchange value of the pound been fixed realistically in the 1920s – a prescription fully in accord with orthodox economic theory – there would have been no need for mass unemployment, hence no need for a revolutionary new theory to explain it' (1975, p. 110 and 1974, p. 273).[2]

While fully conceding the force of Mr Eltis's question regarding the difficulties which 'Keynesian' policies had run into by the 1970s, we do not agree with the views of Professors Hayek and Johnson that Keynes's doctrines were fatally erroneous or irrelevant *from the start*. Obviously the passages quoted raise much larger and more complex questions than can be dealt with here. But, very briefly and summarily, there are five main grounds for disagreeing with their fundamental and comprehensive dismissal of Keynes's original doctrines:

(1) It seems to amount to a considerable misconception of the order of magnitude of the crisis of depression and unemployment during the interwar years to suggest that it could all have been avoided by fixing the gold parity of the pound rather differently between 1925 and 1931. The outcome from a lower parity would in any event have depended on the conduct of the money supply. Also, incidentally, the abandonment of the prewar gold parity would have represented, as Pigou warned at the time, a crucial step – inevitable perhaps in the long run – towards the political control of money, which has indeed followed the later abandonment of gold. Anyhow, the most powerful monetary orthodoxy at the time was in terms of the unchanging *gold* parity of the pound. While leading the attack on it, Keynes showed a reluctant respect for the psychological power, in terms of 'confidence', of this long-entrenched orthodoxy, by his refusal to support an abandonment of the gold parity before the final crisis of 1931. It

would seem, also, that modern 'monetarist'·prescriptions might have run into serious conflicts with the gold-standard orthodoxy.

(2) Professor Hayek, in the early 1930s, thought that deflation could restore 'the functioning of the system'. Forty years later (1975) he thought differently: 'I then believed that a short process of deflation might break the rigidity of money wages. . . . I no longer believe it is in practice possible to achieve it in this manner.' (1975, p. 26) By 1939 Professor Hayek agreed also that: 'There may be desperate situations in which it may indeed be necessary to increase employment at all costs, even if it be only for a short period' (1939, p. 63n, quoted in 1976, p. 11). He admitted that Germany under Brüning in 1932 may have been such a case. But in Britain in 1932, with unemployment at over 22 per cent, Professor Hayek opposed a proposal for increased public spending put forward by Keynes, Pigou and others. We would maintain that, in the circumstances of 1932, Keynes and Pigou were right and that Professor Hayek and his colleagues from the London School of Economics were wrong.[3] Professor Hayek's main policy maxim at that time was to keep the quantity of money constant, with the price level falling if the economy was growing. His main and repeated warning was of the dangers of an increase in the quantity of money. He never seemed to refer to the dangers of a contraction or to have envisaged such dangers as currently serious (1935, lecture 4).

(3) Unemployment in Britain, between 1921 and 1939, seems almost continuously to have been above anything describable as a 'natural' level, as it may well also have been periodically during the depressions of the pre-1914 business cycle. Unemployment was widely regarded as an increasingly serious problem in Britain well before World War I. In the interwar years economic instability and unemployment were leading, outside Britain, to profound social upheavals. It was unemployment between 1930 and 1933 that was to a large extent responsible for bringing Hitler to power, and hence for World War II.

(4) There was in Britain no effective alternative to the Keynesian policy proposals in the interwar years. Indeed, Keynes's proposals were supported by a considerable majority of leading economists, *including Pigou and Robertson*. It would be misleading, and a very unjust reflection on the creative originality of Professor Milton Friedman, to suggest that there was some effective, operational 'monetarist' doctrine, or 'orthodoxy', equipped with adequate statistical material, to combat the overriding problem of unem-

ployment in the interwar years. (One is reminded of the great Groucho's indignant exclamation in *Go West* when someone suggested he telephone an urgent message: 'Telephone? This is 1870. Don Ameche hasn't invented the telephone yet.')

Moreover, the predictions in 1929 of the leading quantity theorist and forerunner of 'monetarism', Irving Fisher, do not suggest that any effective, operational alternative then existed in that direction.[4] Keynes's policy doctrines were not without weaknesses and dangers, but in a profoundly and acutely critical world economic situation they were the best, and almost the only coherent proposals in Britain at the time.

(5) Anyhow, the Keynesian 'revolution' was followed after 1945 by what Professor Hayek describes as 'a unique 25-year period of great prosperity . . . [which lasted] for a much longer time than I should have thought possible' (1975, p. 15). This is quite a long success, and one cannot help wondering why, since this great prosperity – whether or not it owed anything or much to Keynes's teachings – survived for so long, more caution and moderation could not have kept it going still longer. For, as we shall see, a most influential group of self-styled 'Keynesian' economists was constantly expressing and encouraging discontent with levels of employment in the 1950s and 1960s. Perhaps, in the long run, social and political forces were bound to take over and destroy this prosperity. Indeed, according to Professor Hayek's later views, nothing less than fundamental constitutional restraints on the power of democratic majorities, and the removal from political authorities of any power or influence over the money supply, could prove effective bulwarks against inflation. These views may well seem to possess some valid basis in the 1970s. But it seems difficult to blame Keynes for not taking such a very fundamental, political line in the 1930s, since Professor Hayek himself, apparently no longer believing in the efficacy of the policies he was proposing in the 1930s, only took to this fundamental line some 20 or 30 years after Keynes's death.

Inadequacies and dangers can certainly be discerned in Keynes's doctrines (as, indeed they were at the time by Pigou, Robertson and Henderson). A more cautious and modest view on the part of his followers on the gains achieved by the Keynesian 'revolution', especially in terms of generality, might have been in order. The dependence of Keynes's doctrines on the special conditions of the time should have received much more emphasis, as should the liability to rapid obsolescence, from which most economic doctrines are liable to suffer. Basically the most serious weakness was political: that is, an over-optimism, perhaps even naïveté, regarding the possibility of enlightened management of the economy by popularly elected governments (Skidelsky, 1976 (a), p. 9). From time to time, throughout his career, Keynes would castigate politicians in the most scathing terms. But he always rapidly recovered his optimistic belief that, under his tutelage, governments would muster a sufficiency of enlightened altruism to implement his latest proposals for economic management.[5] Nevertheless, in spite of this fundamental political question-mark, we do not accept that because by the 1970s so-called 'Keynesian' doctrines in Britain had run into a 'crisis', or at least into profoundly serious difficulties, *therefore* Keynes's own proposals were originally fundamentally unjustifiable and invalid. For two crucial allowances, or adjustments, have to be made in respect of:

(a) historical changes in conditions and institutions, as compared with those which confronted Keynes; and

(b) the serious alterations made in 'Keynesian' doctrines since his death.

This latter process is what we are centrally concerned with here.

In any event, before a judgement on this issue can be finally passed, what Keynes himself proposed in the last ten years of his life must be disinterred and stripped of the distorting accretions of myth and propaganda behind which it has become concealed in the decades since his death.

III

Most of Keynes's writings on domestic economic policies and policy objectives were, of course, concerned with conditions extremely different from those in Britain in the 1950s and 1960s. Nevertheless, in various writings in the last ten years of his life, following the publication of *The General Theory*, Keynes gave strong indications of his views on peacetime policies on employment targets and the avoidance of inflation, which contrast widely with those which became associated with his name in the fifties and sixties.

Let us begin with some articles written in 1937, one year after *The General Theory* (but not yet made available in his *Collected Writings*).[6] (I discussed these articles in the Appendix to Hutchison, 1968, pp. 295–8, which contains most of the passages from

Keynes's letters and articles quoted here.) 1937 was a peak year, and unemployment was back around 12 per cent. These articles are probably Keynes's only, or much his most significant, contribution regarding current policies for dealing with the upper turning-point of the cycle, as contrasted with the depths of the depression. Moreover they were his last pronouncements on current domestic policy problems under peacetime assumptions and it is very remarkable that they have not received more attention. The first of them was entitled 'How to Avoid a Slump' (*The Times*, 12 Jan. 1937).

Keynes begins by remarking that we have 'climbed out of the slump'. There was not 'a precarious boom'. There was 'nothing wrong', but the time had come to level off activity and above all to take precautions against a descent into another slump. Keynes maintained: 'We are in more need today of a rightly distributed demand than of greater aggregate demand.'[7] He insisted that economists were 'faced with a scientific problem which we have never tried to solve before'. He claimed – emphasizing broad agreement on policy questions, as contrasted with the pressing of extreme disagreements in *The General Theory* – that 'we have entirely freed ourselves – *this applies to every party and every quarter –* from the philosophy of the *laissez-faire* state'. He added somewhat modestly and tentatively: 'Perhaps we know more'.

Keynes went on:

Three years ago it was important to use public policy to increase investment. *It may soon be equally important to retard certain types of investment, so as to keep our most easily available ammunition in hand for when it is more required.* . . . Just as it was advisable for the Government to incur debt during the slump, so for the same reasons *it is now advisable that they should incline to the opposite policy.* . . . Just as it was advisable for local authorities to press on with capital expenditure during the slump, so *it is now advisable that they should postpone whatever new enterprises can reasonably be held back.*

Keynes then admitted that it might be considered premature to abate efforts to increase employment so long as the figures of unemployment remained so high – i.e. around 11–12 per cent. He explained, however:

I believe that *we are approaching, or have reached, the point where there is not much advantage in applying a further general stimulus at the centre.* So long as surplus resources were widely diffused between industries and localities it was no great matter at what point in the economic structure the impulse of an increased demand was applied. But the evidence grows that – for several reasons into which there is no space to enter here – *the economic structure is unfortunately rigid*, and that (for example) building activity in the home counties is less effective than one might have hoped in decreasing unemployment in the distressed areas. *It follows that the later stages of recovery require a different technique. . . .*

We are in more need today of a rightly distributed demand than of a greater aggregate demand; and the Treasury would be entitled to economise elsewhere to compensate for the cost of special assistance to the distressed areas.

It should be noted that Keynes specifically and explicitly took account of rearmament expenditure (14 Jan. 1937): 'sooner or later the building activity will relax; and *the cost of rearmament is neither permanent nor large enough while it lasts to sustain prosperity by itself* (in 1936 at least 7 or 8 times as much was spent on new building as on rearmament).' Let us repeat that what Keynes was concerned with was not rearmament, but, as the title of his articles indicated, 'How to Avoid a Slump'. In a speech on 25 February 1937, Keynes again stressed the damping down of aggregate demand. But although the government was now proposing to borrow £80 million per annum for defence purposes for five years, Keynes emphasized:

I feel no doubt that the sums which the Chancellor of the Exchequer proposes to borrow are well within our capacity; *particularly if as much of the expenditure as possible is directed to bringing into employment the unused resources of the special areas. It is incumbent on the Government to have a concerted policy for retarding other postponable capital expenditure, particularly in the near future, if temporary congestion is to be avoided.*

By 11 March, in an article headed 'Borrowing for Defence', Keynes was maintaining: 'The Chancellor's loan expenditure *need* not be inflationary. But . . . *it may be rather near the limit.*[8] *. . . In two years' time, or less, rearmament loans may be positively helpful in warding off a depression. On the other hand, the War Departments may not succeed – they seldom do – in spending up to their time-table.*' Keynes added: '*It is most important that we should avoid war-time controls, rationing and the like.*'
He went on:

The number of insured persons who are still unemployed is, indeed, as high as 12½ per cent. . . . But though the new demand will be widely spread . . . we cannot safely regard even half of these unemployed insured persons as being available to satisfy home demand. For we have to subtract the unemployables, those seasonally unemployed, etc., and those who cannot readily be employed except in producing for export.

It should be emphasized that Keynes's proposals again amounted largely to the medicine as before, that is, counter-cyclical public works. He wanted a Board of Public Investment to prepare detailed schemes which could be put immediately into operation as required – a proposal which had appeared in the Liberal Yellow Book of 1928 and which Winston Churchill had advocated in 1908.

That Keynes's concern throughout 1937 was avoiding a slump is made absolutely clear in a letter to *The Times* of 28 December, in which he supported proposals for preparing schemes of public works against the next downturn, when unemployment would be liable to rise again from the 11–12 per cent at which it then stood. He was engaged in attacking the arguments of those who were still clinging to the traditional Ricardian case against public works. Keynes asked whether it was being argued that:

e.g. slum clearance and the improvement of transport facilities do not increase employment? Or that they are of no public benefit when made? Does he [Sir Charles Mallet, to whose letter of 18 December Keynes was replying] believe that the present rearmament expenditure, partly financed out of loans, has no effect on employment? Or is he supposing that there is some special virtue in instruments of destruction, so that expenditure on them helps employment, whereas an equal expenditure on, let us say, objects of public health would be of no use?

If he disputes the view that public loan expenditure helps employment he is *running counter to the almost unanimous opinion of contemporary economists.*

Keynes conceded that 'public loan expenditure is not, of course, the only way, *and not necessarily the best way to increase employment.*' Again, however, he argued: 'It is very generally held today that there is a good deal of advantage in retarding expenditure by such bodies when other sources of demand are strong. . . . This is probably a reason for *not pushing such expenditure at present.*'

On 3 January 1938 Keynes again emphasized the overwhelming weight of opinion in favour of public works against unemployment, which policy, he maintained, was bound to be adopted when the next depression came: 'The weight both of authority and of public opinion in favour of meeting a recession in employment by organised loan expenditure is now so great that *this policy is practically certain to be adopted when the time comes.'*

By March 1938, with Hitler's reorganization of his high command and the annexation of Austria, the international situation had clearly moved into a new and much grimmer phase. But what emerges clearly from these writings of Keynes in 1937, his last under fully peacetime assumptions, is that his ideas about how far unemployment could or should be reduced simply by additional government spending, and about the dangers of inflation, differed vastly from the doctrines on these subjects on behalf of which his magic name came to be invoked, or which came to be described and advocated as 'Keynesian', or 'neo-Keynesian', in the 1950s and 1960s. For in 1937 Keynes was clearly concerned with the *possible dangers of inflation when unemployment was still around 11–12 per cent*. From that level downwards Keynes insisted that unemployment must be dealt with, *not by the general expansion of aggregate demand by government (or by 'a further general stimulus at the centre'), but by 'a different technique'*: that is, by specific measures in the depressed areas.

With unemployment still at 11–12 per cent, Keynes was urging the damping down of extra public borrowing and deficits. *This does not, of course, imply that Keynes did not think that unemployment would and should come down to a lower level*, but that he was relying on the further impetus of the boom in the private sector and on the adoption of the 'different technique'.[9]

In fact, Keynes can be said to have suggested a similar concept to that now called – following Professor Milton Friedman – a 'natural rate' of unemployment in that he stressed 'the unfortunately rigid' elements in the British economy which made it undesirable to try to reduce unemployment further by the expansion of central government demand. It is not, of course, maintained that Keynes held to a clear and consistent concept of the natural rate, or that these articles spell out the doctrine of a natural rate of unemployment as clearly as it came to be understood in the 1970s[10] But Keynes's writings of 1937 clearly suggest that attempts to bring unemployment down below a certain level by more and more of what he called a 'general stimulus at the centre', may constitute a disastrous mistake.[11]

During the war, when unemployment had been reduced to below one per cent, Keynes was apparently prepared to suggest about 4½ per cent unemployment as an equilibrium level for peacetime. But he was sceptical about the feasibility of the Beveridge target of three per cent.[12] Anyhow, these estimates were all obviously based on the fundamental principle which he firmly proclaimed in the House of Lords (in May 1944) that: '*We intend to prevent inflation at home.*'

Moreover, it must be emphasized that during the war, in discussing figures like 4½ or three per cent, Keynes was simply speculating about general, more or less hypothetical, target figures. His last operational peacetime policy proposals regarding a current employment target were those of 1937.

We would conclude this section by noting that we have not been calling attention simply to a single paragraph, nor even to a single article, which might represent an aberration, but to views expressed over a period of a year in a number of articles and letters. Furthermore, we would emphasize still further that we are not, of course, suggesting that Keynes, had he lived, would have necessarily held to exactly the same views in 1957 or 1967 as he expressed in 1937. We are simply insisting that it is quite unjustifiable to proclaim as 'Keynesian', or 'neo-Keynesian', views which conflict seriously with those which Keynes expressed in some of his last relevant pronouncements.[13]

IV

The doctrines of Keynes set out in his articles of 1937 obviously conflict very seriously with the Pseudo-Keynesian views regarding employment policy and its objectives developed in the 1950s and 1960s. Anyhow, his attention having been called to these statements of Keynes, Lord Kahn seems to have regarded them as requiring some kind of explanation, since a perfectly clear and straightforward interpretation of them was so completely unacceptable to the new 'Keynesian' orthodoxy (Kahn, 1974; also 1976b).

Lord Kahn found that Keynes's articles 'convey a curious impression', and indeed constitute a 'mystery', which, however, he claimed, 'was soon cleared up' by the explanations he offered. He began by stating that Keynes 'did not in these articles mention the needs of rearmament.' *This statement is quite incorrect.* We have just quoted two or three explicit references by Keynes to rearmament and could have quoted more. One of his articles (11 March) was headed 'Borrowing for Defence'. Keynes was explicitly taking the needs of rearmament into account. Lord Kahn then goes on to explain the non-fact of Keynes's omission to mention rearmament as:

prompted by political strategy. The time was not quite ripe.
    It is my belief that Keynes was anxious that a considerable reserve army of unemployed be maintained to meet the demands of the drastic stepping up of the rearmament programme . . . as well as the highly probable demand for recruits into the armed forces.

What Lord Kahn is inviting his readers, including admirers of Keynes, to believe is, first, that Keynes was guilty of duplicity towards the British public in that he *pretended* that he was concerned with avoiding the next slump, and the unemployment it would bring, when really *he was anxious to maintain 'a considerable reserve army of unemployed'*. Obviously anyone who sees Keynes as a man who believed above all in open, frank, and rational debate is, according to Lord Kahn, profoundly mistaken in this case.

    Secondly, admirers of Keynes are invited by Lord Kahn to believe that Keynes was 'anxious' to maintain 'a considerable reserve army of unemployed', *for an indefinite period*; since it must be remembered that in 1937 it was very unclear when, whether, or how many armament workers and recruits for the forces would be required. But Keynes intended, according to Lord Kahn, that 'considerable' numbers of men should be kept out of work for an indefinite period, *who otherwise could readily have been put into jobs* – although if military exigencies later became pressing these men could have moved, or even been conscripted, into defence work or the services.[14]

    It is quite extraordinary, both to attribute to Keynes concealment of motives on some theory of 'political strategy' and 'unripe time', as well as to ascribe to him an anxiety to maintain a reserve army of unemployed *for an indefinite period and for no economic reason*.

    Also completely unexplained by Lord Kahn are Keynes's repeated warnings in 1937 regarding a forthcoming slump and unemployment – *in spite of rearmament* – and his repeated demands for the preparation of plans for *civilian* public works, such as '*slum clearance and the improvement of transport facilities*' (28 Dec. 1937). It is not clear why Keynes was so repeatedly expressing these worries about combating unemployment *in the next slump*, when 'we shall be hard put to it, in my opinion, to develop useful activities on an adequate scale', if what he was really concerned with was *the maintenance, for no economic reason, of 'a considerable reserve army of unemployed'.* That it was all, throughout a whole year, an elaborate public deception, 'prompted by political strategy', is simply not credible. In fact Keynes was claiming that 'in two years' time, or less, rearmament loans may be positively helpful *in warding off a depression'* and that the War Department would not 'spend up to their time-table'.

Perhaps it may appear that all that Lord Kahn's 'explanation' of Keynes's writing in 1939 does really explain, are the extreme lengths to which 'Keynesians' are prepared to proceed in trying to explain away the wide divergence between Keynes's views on employment policies and objectives and the Pseudo-Keynesian orthodoxies which became the conventional unwisdom of the 1950s and 1960s.[15] The perfectly clear and straightforward meaning of Keynes's articles of 1937 – not to mention the parallel recommendations of the Committee on Economic Information of which he was a leading member – demonstrates that this divergence is very wide indeed.

Lord Kahn concluded his account entitled 'What Keynes Really Said' with the assertion that: 'Had Keynes survived for some considerable number of years, I believe that in the light of post-war experience he would have aimed at an appreciably more ambitious full employment target, but would have regarded . . . 2·2 per cent unemployed . . . as unduly low.' All that should be said is: 'Perhaps so, perhaps not'. But it is certainly unjustifiable to imply that the views on employment targets and policies which came to be described as 'Keynesian' in the 1950s and 1960s were those held by Keynes, or that they would have been approved by Keynes had he lived. Moreover, Lord Kahn is here certainly not telling us 'What Keynes Really Said'; while his assertion also conflicts with his cautious statement elsewhere that: 'The question what Keynes would be advocating today is, of course, a nonsense question' (1975a, p. 32).

However, as we shall see, Lord Kahn himself, together with Sir Roy Harrod and Joan (Lady) Robinson, had, for years past, been laying down the answers to just such 'nonsense' questions with the utmost confidence.

V

For an appreciation of the general principles of economic policy with which, at the time of his death, Keynes was approaching the problems of the postwar world, his last, posthumously published article, 'The Balance of Payments of the United States' (1946), is obviously of major interest and importance.

In this article Keynes came to the conclusion that, although he was prepared to resort to 'exchange variation and overall import controls', we *'would need such expedients less if the classical medicine is also at work'*. In fact Keynes did not regard it as necessary or desirable to rely primarily or predominantly on government controls, which must be used, as he puts it, 'not to defeat but to implement the wisdom of Adam Smith'. He maintained:

I find myself moved, not for the first time, to remind contemporary economists that the classical teaching embodied some permanent truths of great significance. . . .

There are in these matters deep undercurrents at work, natural forces, one can call them, or even the invisible hand, which are operating towards equilibrium. . . . If we reject the medicine from our systems altogether, we may just drift on from expedient to expedient and never get really fit again.

Finally, Keynes deplored how much 'modernist stuff, gone wrong and turned sour and silly, is circulating'. The proclamation of these guidelines, or principles, of wide generality, were virtually Keynes's final words as an economist. It seems difficult to deny how profoundly and acutely distasteful they must have been to some of the Keynesian entourage.[16]

Lord Kahn subsequently (1956) complained that this last article of Keynes was written in a 'more than usually optimistic vein, and also in a strangely complacent vein' (1972, p. 123). This may have referred to Keynes's excessive short-run optimism regarding dollar-shortage.[17] But surely Keynes was much less wide of the mark regarding long-run dollar prospects, on which policies should have been based, than the various enthusiasts for government regulation who went on predicting a disastrous dollar shortage as a chronic, *permanent*, world problem right up to when the 'shortage' was becoming a massive surplus.[18] Anyhow, Keynes certainly did not show himself in the least optimistic or complacent about the effectiveness of government controls over trade or wages, regarding which Pseudo-Keynesians were to be so persistently over-optimistic in the ensuing decades.

However, by 1974 Lord Kahn was prepared to admit that

Keynes 'did display prophetic instincts' in this last article. But Lord Kahn went on:

It is less obvious that Keynes was justified in his remarkable belief in the efficacy of 'deep undercurrents at work, natural forces, one can call them, or even the invisible hand, which are operating towards equilibrium'. Keynes, a sick man, was displaying a natural irritation over 'modernist stuff gone wrong and turned sour and silly'.

But who can Keynes have been getting at in these famous words? Anyhow, it is perhaps permissible to suggest that in subsequent decades it would have been only 'a sick man' who would *not* very frequently have felt irritated over 'modernist stuff, gone wrong and turned sour and silly' – surely one of Keynes's truly prophetic phrases.[19] However, at the time, Keynes was so incensed as to express himself, in private, in a highly deplorable manner. He wrote to Lord Halifax regarding the opposition to the Loan Agreement with the US, in the Labour Party and among that party's economist supporters: 'The doctrine of non-discrimination does commit us to abjure Schachtian methods, which their Jewish economic advisers (who, like so many Jews are either Nazi or Communist at heart and have no notion how the British Commonwealth was founded or is sustained) were hankering after' (1979, vol. 24, p. 626; for similar expressions by Keynes, see his essay on Einstein, 1972, pp. 383–4; and also 1979, vol. 23, p. 107).

Certainly it is very easy to understand, from the passages we have quoted from Keynes's last article, the complaint of Joan Robinson that some 'Keynesians' 'sometimes had some trouble getting Maynard to see what the point of his revolution really was' (1975, p. 125). No wonder Keynes is reported, in the last year of his life, as saying: 'I am not a Keynesian' (cited in Colin Clark, 1970, p. 53). In fact it might appear that Keynes himself was rather a 'bastard Keynesian' – to apply the genealogical certification so magisterially proclaimed by Joan Robinson. For, as we have seen, on the broad principles of international, or *external*, economic policy, Keynes, in his last article, came down in favour of relying, to a significant extent, on the 'natural forces' of the price mechanism, and on the classical 'medicine'. Correspondingly, in the economy *internally*, Keynes, in the *The General Theory* was quite emphatic about how 'the classical theory comes into its own again', as he put it:

If we suppose the volume of output to be given . . . then there is no
objection to be raised against the classical analysis of the manner in which
private self interest will determine what in particular is produced, in
what proportions the factors of production will be combined to produce
it, and how the value of the final product will be distributed between
them. (1936, pp. 378–9)

These clear and emphatic statements are alleged by Professor
Robinson to be 'ill-considered', and 'quite contrary to his main
argument' (1979, p. 127). Similarly, of course, Keynes's equally
clear and emphatic statements about the broad principles of
international economic policy were described by Lord Kahn and
Professor Robinson as those of 'a sick man', into which he
'lapsed', 'against his better judgement'. Keynes should be defended against this kind of attack. On these broad issues of
principle he was not guilty of any ill-considered inconsistency, or
of some kind of intellectual weakness or decay. Keynes simply
happens to have stood for fundamentally different politicoeconomic principles from those of his 'Keynesian' followers.

VI

We turn now to the emergence, in the two decades after Keynes's
death, of Pseudo-Keynesian doctrines, drastically differing from
those of Keynes, regarding employment objectives and the
dangers of inflation.[20]
    With the proclamation in 1944 of 'a high and stable level of
employment' (HMSO, 1944) as an agreed objective of economic
policy, there was, for a very short time, a notable measure of
caution and moderation regarding the level of employment which
it was sensible, feasible or desirable to aim at. There seemed, very
briefly, to be some realization of the dangers of pushing policies
directed against the social injustice of unemployment so far as to
incur the serious risk of releasing other acute sources of social
injustice, such as inflation or the restriction of freedoms. Pigou,
for example, had observed that the result of maintaining a very
high level of employment might be that 'a spiralling movement of
inflation is allowed to develop' (1944, p. 72).
    Lord Kaldor in 1944 went so far as to assert that Beveridge's full
employment objective of three per cent would (and should) be
combined *with price stability*. He assumed 'that post-war govern-

ments will pursue a monetary and wage policy which maintains the prices of final commodities constant'. Lord Kaldor then cautiously added: 'A policy of a rising price level might be incompatible with the maintenance of stability in the long run' (1944, p. 398). Also among the assumptions of Beveridge's three per cent target was not only the pursuit of price stability, but compulsory arbitration, and that: 'In peace in a free society, men should not be imprisoned for striking, though they may rightly be deprived of all support if the strike is contrary to a collective bargain or an agreed arbitration' (*ibid*, p. 200).

But the dangers of the pursuit of the full employment objective creating injustices, or loss of freedom in other directions, were, perhaps, most incisively insisted upon by Joan Robinson. In a paper of 1946 she argued:

Nor is completely full employment desirable. The attainment of full employment, in this absolute sense, would require strict controls, including direction of labour. To raise the average of employment from 86 per cent (the average for Great Britain 1921–38) to, say, 95 per cent would be compatible with a greater amount of individual liberty than to raise it from 95 per cent to 98 per cent. To *raise it from 95 per cent to 98 per cent (not momentarily – but on the average) would involve great sacrifices of liberty, and to raise it from 98 per cent to 100 per cent would involve complete conscription of labour. No-one regards 100 per cent employment as a desirable objective.* (1951, p. 106, italics added)[21]

One may not today agree with the precise estimate of the trade-offs as they were envisaged in the 1940s by Joan Robinson, and it is not clear whose – or what kinds of – 'liberty' she held to be threatened by reducing unemployment to two or even five per cent. But one must certainly admire her cautious and discerning insistence on the serious costs, or the various forms of injustice, or loss of freedom, which the pursuit of very high levels of employment might entail.

Thus when, in the 1940s, the revolutionary attempt was launched at 'full employment' in peacetime, three conditions in particular were set out by people claiming to be followers of Keynes regarding:
    (1) trade unions and the right to strike (Beveridge);
    (2) the importance of price stability (Kaldor); and
    (3) the preservation of freedom (J. Robinson).
When Keynes remarked that there was 'no harm in trying' for Beveridge's three per cent target (though he doubted whether it

was attainable), it must be assumed that Keynes placed at least as much weight on the conditions regarding strikes and price stability as had Beveridge and Kaldor. Nor is it reasonable to assume that Keynes would have rejected less firmly than Joan Robinson any great 'sacrifices of liberty'. One can also surely be confident that Keynes would not have forgotten or surrendered on these conditions because they began to run counter to fashionable opinion or were unpalatable to the trade union leaders.

For after Keynes's death all this caution and moderation turned out to be very short-lived. By the early or middle 1950s the trend of public taste for bursts of very high employment, and the politicians' eagerness to meet these tastes – *regardless of losses or dangers in other directions* – had become clear. One could not hope to keep one's place on the trendy political bandwagon if one nagged away about price stability and the dangers to freedom of over-full employment. Keynes himself would surely have had to endure the most appalling vituperation in 1957 if he had then repeated the kind of views about employment targets which he had expressed in 1937. (But one may assume that Keynes would not have been concerned about his popularity with politicians of one stripe or another.) 'Growthmanship' also was beginning to emerge at this stage, and a body of doctrine began to achieve a dominating influence which may be described as 'Pseudo-Keynesian'. For, while the Master's magic name was frequently invoked on behalf of the new conventional unwisdom, *it is impossible to find statements of these new doctrines in Keynes's writings.*

Four main Pseudo-Keynesian doctrines may be distinguished; there are no grounds for supposing that Keynes would have supported any of them:

(1) *The first was that by expanding aggregate demand the unemployment percentage should be pushed down to levels well below those that had been regarded by Keynes as safely attainable.*

Lord Kahn, for example, in 1956, simply proclaimed the Beveridge target of three per cent as 'obsolete' (1972, p. 102); while Joan Robinson (1966) stated that any target above two per cent was 'cold-blooded' and 'out of the question' (1966, p. 20). The great sacrifices of liberty which had been discerned in 1946 as required by such low levels of unemployment were now left unmentioned. Sir Roy Harrod wanted a *zero* target for unemployment. In an article in the *New Statesman* (1969), entitled 'The Arrested Revolution', Sir Roy claimed *absolutely certain knowledge* about Keynes's views on employment targets:

People sometimes say to me that what worried Keynes was the massive unemployment of pre-war days. Surely he would not object to raising unemployment from 1·5 to 2·5 per cent in this country or from 3·3 per cent to 4 per cent in the USA if, as so many are now urging, that cured the external deficits of those countries? . . . *He certainly would object.* (p. 809)

There is no doubt about the popularity of such arguments with politicians and public. But the possibility that by pushing down unemployment in the short term, by government expansion of aggregate demand, one was likely only to *increase* it seriously in the long term – or to bring about totalitarianism – was something which Sir Roy was unable or unwilling to contemplate. Nor can it easily be explained how the views of Sir Roy, which he attributed to Keynes, are compatible with the proposals which Keynes put forward in his articles of 1937, either as interpreted straightforwardly or even according to the 'explanation' of Lord Kahn. Indeed by 1977 Lord Kahn was admitting that, since the end of the war: 'There have been periods in which employment has been *considerably above the level which Keynes would have advocated*' (1977, p. 3, italics added).

Precisely. But surely, then, the genuine 'Keynesians' must have been those who, from time to time, have had the courage, as Keynes presumably would have had, to attack over-full employment – like Sir Dennis Robertson, Lord Robbins and others; while the 'Pseudo'-Keynesians have been those who in 30 years have repeatedly called for higher and higher employment percentages and have at no time come out against the pushing up of employment 'considerably above the level which Keynes would have advocated'.

(2) *On the top of the full employment objective, pushed much further than Keynes approved, the objective of 'full growth', or 'growth in accordance with maximum potential', was to be adopted.*

Sir Roy Harrod asserted that this new objective was 'supported by many economists who would claim to have drawn their inspiration from Keynes. . . . *I have no doubt at all that Keynes himself, were he alive . . . would be an ardent apostle of growth policies.*' (1964, p. 47, italics added) Lord Kaldor (1963) proclaimed that the rate of growth of the British economy could and should be raised by 'comprehensive planning' and 'purposive direction' (1963, p. 63, and 1964, p. 199). Joan Robinson maintained: 'We could evidently quickly work up to 6 or 7 per cent [rate of growth] if

Britain abandoned her defence effort.' (1965, p. 146).

Of course, hardly a vestige can be found in the later, rather stagnationist, writings of Keynes of this kind of Pseudo-Keynesian growthmanship (in spite of Sir Roy Harrod, in 1964, having 'no doubt at all' of Keynes's 'ardent' support).

(3) *The third Pseudo-Keynesian policy doctrine was that price stability must have a minor or reduced priority as an objective.*

After a decade in which prices in Britain had already risen almost unprecedentedly fast by fully peacetime standards, Lord Kaldor warned the Radcliffe Committee (1959) of 'The Dangers of a Regime of Stable Prices' (1964, p. 137). Apparently Lord Kaldor had dismissed as 'obsolete' his emphasis of 1944 on how a policy of a rising price level might be incompatible with economic stability in the long run. Lord Kahn also affirmed to the Radcliffe Committee that even advocating the merits of absolute price stability was 'highly prejudicial to the country's interests'. He also asserted:

> In the absence of anything like what might be called a wages policy it would, I am convinced, be economically expedient, as well as politically inevitable, *to abandon any idea of stability of the price level.* (1960, p. 143, italics added)[22]

The contrast is striking between such views as these and Keynes's own statement:

> I am not yet converted, taking everything into account, from a preference for a policy today which, whilst avoiding deflation at all costs, aims at the stability of purchasing power as its ideal objective. (1930, vol. 2, p. 163, quoted in Haberler, 1974, p. 245)

Thus, with a nice sense of timing, it was just at the historical juncture when in Britain, creeping inflation was about to pass into cantering inflation, with expectations delicately poised, that neo-Keynesian exponents of growthmanship chose to dismiss price stability as a 'dangerous' objective.

(4) *Fourthly, it was maintained that any tendencies to inflation could and should be countered mainly or entirely by wages or incomes policies.*

Lord Kahn informed the Radcliffe Committee:

> It would, I submit, be a grave mistake for the Committee to accept the view that it is the proper function of monetary and budgetary policy to secure a tolerable behaviour of prices. One can readily admit the

advantages of a stable price level taken in isolation. It does not follow – very far from it – that the right aim of monetary policy is to secure a stable price level. The real solution lies elsewhere. It lies in the realm of wage negotiations. (1960, p. 143)[23]

In practice, according to Joan Robinson, stating what she described as 'A Neo-Keynesian View': '*Incomes policy is the only real remedy*' (1974, p. 488, italics added). There is very little justification, in the writings of Keynes himself, for such exclusive emphasis on 'incomes policy', or extensive central controls in peacetime.

However, there seemed to be wide disagreements among Keynesians, as we shall see (section VII, pp. 130–5), on what the role of trade unions had been, or might be, or as to how they might be expected to play their part – vital questions if sole reliance for averting inflation was being placed on 'incomes policy'. We may simply note that the growthmanship doctrines of how the growth-rate in Britain could and should be significantly raised, or doubled, by 'purposive planning' etc., combined with the advocacy of a rising price level and the abandonment of price stability, were obviously calculated to encourage the militant stepping-up of wage claims, and thus, on Keynesian views of the causal process, constituted a direct encouragement of rampant inflation.

Pseudo-Keynesian doctrines, explicitly invoking the name of Keynes, were also widely disseminated in non-specialist political journalism. In particular was this so with what could be regarded as a further Pseudo-Keynesian doctrine which maintained that because, in the 1930s, Keynes had advocated public expenditure against unemployment, therefore *any cuts in public expenditure, in virtually any circumstances, must be anti-Keynesian, or a betrayal of Keynes's teachings.* For example, when in February 1976, with a public sector deficit of around £10,000 million, and a heavy adverse balance of payments, the Labour government was putting forward some (partly illusory) public expenditure 'cuts', the *New Statesman* proclaimed: 'It is exactly 40 years since Keynes produced *The General Theory* and half a century since he wrote *The End of Laissez-Faire*. . . . The Government's White Paper reads as if . . . [they] had never been written.'

Ten years previously, in July 1966, with unemployment at a record peacetime 'low' of about 1·1 per cent, a Labour government had also engaged in 'cuts', regarding which the columnist of

Encounter enquired whether it was not the case 'that the Government, and the Labour Party, have now flung Keynes to the winds and that, in the advanced enconomic thought of today, Keynes has been superseded by Callaghan, with his eternal Micawber verity that a country in the red is necessarily ruined?' (1967, p. 53).

Regarding the 1966 crisis, the diaries of the Rt Hon. R. H. S. Crossman provide an interesting example of Pseudo-Keynesian doctrines being pressed upon ministers as expert 'briefing'. Shortly after the crisis, Mr Crossman describes how he sought advice from the economic staff of the Prime Minister's 'kitchen cabinet':

> I've been thinking of a speech in which I could suggest that the thirties' crisis was a Keynesian crisis of demand failure whereas the crisis of the sixties was caused by full employment and the resulting excess demand and inflation. Michael taught me in a severe tutorial that *it's politically dangerous to talk about inflation in this way as a disease of the economy.* The real contrast, he says, is between the 'demand–pull' failure in consumer demand in the 1930s which could have been solved by Keynesian methods of stimulating expenditure and the new crisis of 'cost–push' and stunted economic growth in the 1960s. If I stress the notion of inflation I'm failing to realise that inflation is not a disease comparable to mass unemployment; *indeed inflation has certain advantages as part of a process of economic growth.* (1976, p. 41, italics added; 'Michael' is Mr Michael Stewart, author of the Pelican textbook, *Keynes and After.*)

It is obviously not fair to put all the blame on the politicians for the neglect of the dangers of inflation, when what was being impressed on them by their 'Keynesian' advisers was not the dangers of inflation but *the dangers of talking about inflation as a disease.* Anyhow, in the production of this crucially influential climate of opinion among politicians and public, in the 1960s and early 1970s, the invocation of the charismatic name of Keynes was a persistent leitmotif.

VII

Regarding the role of trade unions, the spirit of Keynes must often have felt like the Almighty in wartime, being invoked, or appealed to, by all the warring parties. It is, therefore, first desirable to recall the strongly 'classical' (or neoclassical) component in Keynes's treatment of real wages and unemployment. As Professor G. W. Maynard has observed:

Keynes put far more emphasis on the relationship between real wages and the level of employment than subsequent expositions of his theory make clear. . . .

What is often overlooked in current discussion of present-day unemployment and the relevance of Keynesian policies for its solution is Keynes's explicit acceptance in *The General Theory*, which he did not later modify, of the classical postulate that the level of employment cannot be such (or at any rate cannot remain such) that the marginal product of labour is less than the marginal disutility of labour or *a fortiori* less than the real wage being demanded, for in that case employers would be making a loss on marginal units of labour employed which they would seek to avoid by dismissing labour. (1978, pp. 3, 8)

Professor Maynard goes on to conclude, with regard to the level of unemployment in Britain in the 1970s, that it would have been seen by Keynes as having contained a considerable 'voluntary' element.

This explicit neoclassical component in Keynes's ideas is obviously of central importance for policy and has been rejected by 'Keynesians'. As Mr Trevithick has said:

To this extent, Keynes, unlike many Keynesians, had his feet firmly planted in classical ground. Keynes's endorsement of the classical theory of labour demand has profound implications which have been largely overlooked by economists who would broadly describe themselves as Keynesians. Of pivotal importance is the proposition that a decline in the real wage rate is a *sine qua non* for the attainment of full employment. Unless some means can be found for depressing the real wage rate to its market clearing level all attempts at stimulating employment will prove to be sterile. (1980, pp. 50–1)

Keynes's argument has been disregarded in discussion on the role of trade unions, a subject of much importance because of the emergence in the 1960s and 1970s of the trade union leaders as the new baronial elite. Indeed, a prominent brand of Pseudo-Keynesianism has furnished the unions and their economic spokesmen with a complete outfit of doctrines to support their vested interests, including unlimited public spending, unlimited 'job protection', excessive employment targets, and a far-reaching disregard of the costs of inflation. Some versions of Pseudo-

Keynesian conventional wisdom invoke Keynes's name for a comprehensive apologia on behalf of the trade union leaders, denying in the strongest terms that they have any responsibility for unemployment.[24] At the first Keynes Seminar held at the University of Kent, Mr R. Opie proclaimed:

Keynes exonerated the trade unions. Unemployment is not high because wages are too high. . . . Wage cuts alone will not cure unemployment nor do wage increases cause it. In passing, one might note an extraordinary revival of the wage-cut doctrine in the pronouncements of Her Majesty's present Ministers. We have been told frequently that the record levels of unemployment were due to the record rate of price inflation, and that in turn is due to the record rate of wage inflation. The implication was not that wage cuts would restore full employment. That would no doubt be a little too crude – but a more subtle 'first derivative' argument, viz. that a cut in the rate of wage *increases* will do the trick. We have, fortunately, heard less of this antediluvian argument since Mr Barber's latest expansionary budget, and *I expect we shall now hear no more of it at all.* (1974, pp. 80–1, italics added)

In fact, very much more was soon heard, in most emphatic, or even 'antediluvian', terms from the supreme 'Keynesian' authority, Lord Kahn, who insisted, with much indignation, on the gross culpability of the unions and their leaders and on the disastrous results of their policies: 'The result has been a crazily high rate of increase of money wages. *Unemployment results partly directly and partly because the Governor of the Bank of England feels compelled to adopt restrictive measures*. . . . Trade union leaders must accept responsibility for this. . . . They carry on their shoulders responsibility for a tragic situation.'

In a further contribution Lord Kahn referred to 'the astonishing stupidity of our trade union leaders', and to 'their complete failure to take a long-sighted view'. The men who run the TUC, Lord Kahn asserted, 'are sadly lacking in intelligence' (1975b, p. 142; 1976b, pp. 4–5).[25]

Lord Kahn did not volunteer to explain how he had come to entertain either the hopes he had indulged in for so long regarding the prospects for negotiating agreements on incomes policies with people of such 'astonishing stupidity', or the visions which in 1958 he had commended to the Radcliffe Committee regarding 'a considerable improvement in the state of awareness of the importance of restraint over wage increase' (1960, p. 143). In 1976, however, Lord Kahn went on to contrast the English unions with those of the German Federal Republic: 'Western Germany provides the best example of trade-union leaders who are long-sighted and who, as a result of modesty in the size of their claims for wage increases . . . have secured an economic climate conducive to productive investment and the growth of productivity.' (1976a, p. 5). This is an especially interesting comparison because, as long ago as 1950, when Dr Erhard was launching out on free-market policies, Lord Balogh castigated the 'obsolete' and 'iniquitous' policies of Dr Erhard's 'satellite economists' who were, he alleged, trying to discredit 'enlightened Keynesian economic policy'. Lord Balogh maintained: 'The currency reform helped to weaken the trade unions. They cannot and do not press with decisive force for more decent working and social conditions. Their weakness may even inhibit increases in productivity.' (1950, p. 7)[26]

Leading 'Keynesians', of different political inclinations, have tended to protest vehemently that the Keynesian 'revolution' was never properly completed. Joan Robinson, for example, asked 'What has become of the Keynesian Revolution?'; while Sir Roy Harrod referred to 'The Arrested Revolution' (J. Robinson, 1975; Harrod, 1969, p. 808). What seems to have been meant was that Joan Robinson and Sir Roy had not always been one hundred per cent successful in selling as 'Keynesian' the particular nostrums they favoured. *Moreover, 'Keynesian' economists, through the fifties and sixties, constantly expressed and encouraged discontent with employment levels in Britain.*

On the whole, however, what Lord Balogh called 'enlightened Keynesian economic policy' was carried to very considerable lengths in Britain – in marked contrast with the German Federal Republic. Certainly Lord Balogh, Lord Kaldor and Lord Kahn could enjoy the full satisfaction of knowing how amply their grave warnings of the 1950s and 1960s had apparently been heeded by governments in Britain. Nobody in Britain could complain that they had been led astray by the 'obsolete' and 'iniquitous' system which Dr Erhard – flouting 'enlightened *Keynesian* economic policy' – had launched in the German Federal Republic.[27] Nobody in Britain could complain that the 'weakness' of trade unions had inhibited the increase of productivity – as in the German Federal Republic. Surely, as regards the perilous 'dangers of a regime of stable prices', it could justly be claimed that governments in Britain had come to avoid them like the plague. Certainly, again, through all the vagaries of 'wages policies', the 'economic expediency' of abandoning 'any idea of the stability of the price-level' has been meticulously respected.

The very familiar closing words of Keynes's *General Theory* may well exaggerate somewhat the influence of the ideas of economists.[28] But if, in practice, economic doctrines have exercised *any* influence on the course of economic policies between, say, 1946 and 1976, the doctrines of Pseudo-Keynesian economics would seem in Britain to have been more influential than any others.[29]

In 1967 Sir Austin Robinson. proclaimed: 'I think we can honestly say that the world today is a different place from what it was in the 1930s in very large measure as a result of the economic thinking that began in this Faculty in Cambridge in those exciting years of the 1930s'. (1967, p. 43). This is a rather spacious claim. If we may leave the world as a whole out of account, we might presume, however, that the claim might also be thought to have some validity for Britain's position in the 'exciting years' of the 1970s.

We would emphasize, however, that we are not here primarily concerned with the question as to *how far* 'Neo-' or Pseudo-Keynesian doctrines actually influenced British economic policy, nor with the question whether such effects as they did have – if any – were beneficial, or catastrophically damaging for the British economy and for the morale and standards of living of the British people. *We are mainly and primarily concerned with an episode in the history of economic thought, that is, with the change and contrast between the views expressed by Keynes on employment targets and inflation, and the views propagated in his name by his self-styled followers in the 1950s and 1960s.* Professor Moggridge who, as editor of the Keynes papers, has something of the role of an official spokesman, has written: 'It is clear . . . from Keynes's war-time discussions of the implications of working the economy at "full employment" that he, for one, had before his death not come to any firm policy conclusions.' (1975; see also Hutchison, 1977b)

But, as we have seen, Lord Kahn, Sir Roy Harrod, Joan Robinson, Lord Balogh and others (not including Lord Kaldor) were repeatedly proclaiming, in the fifties and sixties, what the 'Keynesian', or 'Neo-Keynesian' views were, or what Keynes would have been advocating, decades after his death, regarding the problem of the day – which, oddly enough, usually turned out to coincide precisely with their own particular nostrums, and to diverge very widely from what Keynes had said in some of his latest relevant writings. Only belatedly, in the 1970s when the problems of the British economy had indeed become baffling, were Lord Kahn and Sir Roy Harrod sometimes to be found dismissing the matter of what Keynes would be advocating today as 'a nonsense question' to which it would be 'most inappropriate' for them to provide an answer.[30] We would agree with Mr Tim Congdon's conclusion:

It is important, therefore, to examine carefully the credentials of any group which calls itself 'Keynesian'. . . . The Keynesians . . . have freedom to propound their own views as those of Keynes – and it amounts to a licence to counterfeit his intellectual coinage. . . .
    They have propagated an influential, but spurious, oral tradition. (1975, pp. 23–4)

VIII

Regarding economists generally in the fifties and sixties, Dr Gunnar Myrdal has complained of their

slowness to recognise what had become and was to remain the main post-war problem, namely inflation. . . . Few economists made an early move to analyse the problem in any depth. Some of them even invented reasons why a measure of inflation was needed to speed up economic growth and stabilise economic development. Practically nobody tried seriously to spell out the thesis . . . that inflation has arbitrary, unintended and therefore undesirable effects on resource allocation and the distribution of incomes and wealth. (1973, pp. 19–21)

One may certainly doubt whether Dr Myrdal's accusations would ever have been valid against Keynes himself, had he lived. But they obviously apply to the prevailing Pseudo-Keynesian body of opinion in Britain, where inflation, since the early 1950s, had remained, for the most part, more serious than in most other similar countries. Outstanding among those economists in Britain who warned against the dangers of inflation in the fifties had been Sir Dennis Robertson, who had generally supported Keynes's policy proposals in the interwar years and who emphasized (1955) that 'both the admitted inequities and the long-term economic and social dangers generated by even a slow inflationary process are so apparent that some of those who accept it as inevitable, and even on balance desirable, have felt moved to make suggestions for modifying the incidence of its impact.'

But, as Sir Dennis went on to point out, regarding attempts at 'modifying the incidence' of inflation at an earlier, not intolerable stage:

> The rush for the band-wagon would set the wagon itself smartly rolling foward, and there would always be somebody left lagging behind. But what that means is that the planned orderly fall in the value of money would be in danger of turning into a landslide, generating not a comfortable condition of 'full employment' but a hectic and disorderly muddle, which could only be checked, at the cost of much disemployment and distress, by the re-establishment of drastic monetary discipline. (1966, pp. 251–2)

But, then, Sir Dennis was an outmoded, 'neoclassical' economist.

Alongside those of Sir Dennis Robertson, the warnings of Lord Robbins should be cited, as imparted particularly in his paper, 'Full Employment as an Objective' (1949).[31] Together with the dangers of inflation and economic authoritarianism, Lord Robbins emphasized the implications of an open-ended commitment by government to the trade unions to the effect that 'whatever rate of wages you call for, we are prepared to inflate sufficiently to prevent unemployment'. Lord Robbins concluded: 'To frame policy with an eye *inter alia* to the maintenance of high levels of employment is wisdom. To frame it with regard to full employment *only* is likely to lead to disappointment and even, perhaps, to something worse than disappointment.'

On the other hand, Pseudo-Keynesian doctrines followed the tastes of public and politicians in abandoning the caution and moderation evident in Keynes's own writings, and in far-reachingly neglecting the dangers and injustices of inflation and probable losses of freedom; unlike Keynes who, on the one peacetime occasion (1920) when an outburst of inflation threatened the British economy during his lifetime, proposed thoroughly drastic measures. (See Howson, 1973; Congdon, 1975.) There are no grounds for arguing that Keynes would have abandoned his previous caution, or employment targets, because of pressure from, or unpopularity with, politicians and public.[32] In fact, there are no valid grounds for assuming that in the fifties Keynes would have *dis*agreed with Sir Dennis Robertson and Lord Robbins, rather than with Lord Kahn, Joan Robinson and Sir Roy Harrod.

It is important to emphasize the connection between inflation and government intervention in and regulation of the economy. Although Pseudo-Keynesian economists did not, of course, *want* inflation, some of them – quite unlike Keynes – wanted very much indeed its usual fruits and consequences in the form of wage and price controls, regulation of profits, widespread subsidization, import controls, etc., for which inflation provides a pretext. Some of the more extreme Pseudo-Keynesians were certainly strongly in favour of destroying the mixed economy and replacing it by a regime of 'purposive direction' and 'comprehensive planning'. A permissive attitude to the money supply is well calculated to promote such objectives, and sophisticated defences for such permissiveness were devised.[33]

Those ready to take risks with inflation were certainly not unprepared for, and indeed strongly in favour of, comprehensive government intervention, even, in some cases, in accordance with the Soviet model.[34] In fact, 'Pseudo-Keynesian' economics consisted, to a large extent, of urging politicians on to over-full employment and growthmanship, while claiming that the latest Wage Restraint or Prices and Incomes Policy, Statement of Intent, or the Planned Growth of Incomes, or Social Compact or Contract, etc., etc., etc., not merely *might eventually* restrain (it was nice to believe) but *was already* restraining and keeping inflation down to a harmless level – all accompanied by constant invocations of the magic name of Keynes.[35]

There can be no doubt that Pseudo-Keynesian economists in Britain rejected what Keynes advocated as the 'attempt to use what we have learnt from modern experience and modern analysis, not to defeat, but to implement the wisdom of Adam Smith.' In practice, Pseudo-Keynesian economics amounted to a wholesale rejection, in the domestic field, of that kind of 'classical medicine' of which Keynes wrote at the end of his last article (1946): 'If we reject the medicine from our systems altogether, we may just drift on from expedient to expedient and never get really fit again' (p. 186).

Anyhow, though regarding the quantitative details of feasible economic objectives Keynes might well have altered his views over the years, it is surely improbable that he would have retreated significantly on his fundamental political commitments, such as his commitment to freedom. This commitment was demonstrated in 1940 – with Hitler at the gates – when he denounced rationing:

If the community's aggregate rate of spending can be regulated, the way in which personal incomes are spent and the means by which demand is satisfied can be safely left free and individual. . . . *This is the only way to avoid the destruction of choice, and initiative, whether by consumers or producers, through the complex tyranny of all-round rationing.* This is the one kind of compulsion of which the effect is to enlarge liberty. (1940, quoted in Skidelsky, 1979a, p. 34; italics added)

Professor Skidelsky points out that the issue of freedom was one 'on which he differed strongly' from Lord Kahn – who, of course, not only supported rationing in wartime but has advocated extensive controls in peacetime (see, for example, Kahn, 1949). This 'strong' difference is fundamental, and certainly was so for Keynes, who described it as one '*marking the line of division between the totalitarian and the free economy*' (op. cit., italics added). Mr Walter Eltis has found it 'puzzling why so many Keynesians wish to run the British economy in an essentially East-European or at any rate Crippsian way' (1977, p. 38). It is even more puzzling that economists should be called 'Keynesian' who differ 'strongly' from Keynes regarding what he himself maintained was the fundamental political division between totalitarianism and freedom.

IX

We have not been concerned here with basic criticisms of Keynes's more 'general' theories, or of the more general aspects of his theories, which are not subject to the kind of obsolescence, or irrelevance, due to historical and institutional change. In this field, shelves-full of literature have long existed. We are, however, to some extent, though not primarily, concerned with the extent to which Keynes's doctrines were based on empirical propositions or assumptions for which there may have been much justification in his own day, but which have been rendered seriously invalid or irrelevant by historical and institutional changes. This is a kind of obsolescence, or source of anomaly, to which theories in economics are seriously liable, and which is sometimes not recognized, or sufficiently allowed for, by economists who overconfidently assume a kind of epistemological parity with the natural sciences.

It is obvious enough, to start with, that whereas Keynes's *General Theory* assumed deflation, stagnation, and heavy unemployment, within about four years of its publication inflation and very high levels of employment had generally become, and have since remained, the rule. Much more specifically, both Mr Colin Clark and Professor Milton Friedman, for example, have emphasized (from contrasting points of view) the obsolescence of Keynes's basic assumption about money and real wages and the 'money illusion' of workers.[36] Another major contrast between the conditions of the thirties and those of the postwar British economy has been emphasized by Professor R. C. O. Mathews: it is what he calls 'the trend increase in the scarcity of labour relative to capital' (1968, p. 568).

However, our primary concern here is not with this kind of historical or institutional obsolescence, to which virtually all empirically significant economic theories may be more or less liable. We are concerned primarily with the distortion or alteration of Keynes's tentative policy doctrines and objectives, and with the unjustifiable invocation of his name on behalf of doctrines which there are no good grounds for supposing he would have supported.

It should be emphasized that the alterations to Keynes's doctrines did not amount simply to normative changes in policy preferences, or in objectives, or values, regarding the trade-off between unemployment and inflation. The alterations we have cited amounted to a fundamental change in positive theory, regarding how the economy worked. Keynes, in 1937, was ready to step up public investment or public works to bring down unemployment to somewhere in the region of 10–12 per cent. He then pointed to the 'rigidity' of the British economy, which necessitated what he called 'a different technique' from that of 'a further general stimulus at the centre' by additional government spending.[37] Of course Keynes *might*, quite possibly or probably, have revised what seemed subsequently a high estimate of the natural rate, or the level of unemployment at which to break off the stimulus to aggregate demand by increased central government spending. But he clearly thought that there was some *quite significant* level of unemployment at which the policy of stimulating general government spending should be curbed. Therefore, what Professor David Laidler maintains about 'Keynesian' economics may unfortunately be true enough; but it is not true about the writings of Keynes (with which, of course 'Keynesian' economics has had only incidental similarites):

The whole intellectual basis of post-war 'demand management' by government is undermined if the natural unemployment rate hypothesis is true. Policy is based on the assumption that Keynesian economics tells us how we may attain *any* level of unemployment we think desirable simply by manipulating monetary and fiscal policy. (1975, p. 45, italics added)

Keynes's most relevant writings showed that he at least strongly suspected that something like what Professor Laidler calls 'the natural rate hypothesis' *was true in 1937 – the last fully peacetime year Keynes experienced.* Keynes himself clearly did *not* 'tell us how [or that] we may attain *any* level of unemployment we think desirable simply by manipulating monetary and fiscal policy'.

It must be remembered that the unemployment problem in Britain, and the intensive study of it, did not begin with Keynes, but well before World War I. It was in 1905, for example, that Joseph Chamberlain proclaimed: 'The question of employment, believe me, has now become the most important question of our time' (see Skidelsky, 1976b, p. 542). The pioneer works appeared in the decade before the war with the contributions of Beveridge, Pigou, and the Royal Commission on the Poor Laws. Before the emergence and dominance of the Keynesian theory of deficiencies in aggregate effective demand, the analysis of unemployment was in terms of its different types – frictional, seasonal, cyclical, etc. Policy proposals were in terms of specific measures appropriate to these different types, and can be said, to a significant or large extent, to have consisted of measures designed to reduce the 'natural rate'. This was most obviously the case with measures to reduce 'frictional' unemployment by creating labour exchanges (as carried out by Churchill, with Beveridge as his *aide*, before World War I). Keynes was well aware of these differing types of unemployment even if 'Keynesians' were, or are, not. But his own main contribution was directed to the extremely high levels of unemployment in the interwar years, which seem to have been persistently above any 'natural' rate, however precisely defined (as were, possibly or probably, also the levels reached in the deeper depressions of the nineteenth-century business cycle).

As Mr Colin Clark has observed:

Even now we are still standing too close to make a real assessment of Keynes's contributions to economics, how far they represented permanent additions to our methods of analysis, to what extent they were *ad hoc* proposals to put right the tragic and unnecessary unemployment and depression of the 1930s, *which would have been valuable if applied at the time but which may have become irrelevant or positively misleading later.* (1970, p. 53, italics added)

Keynes's proposals in the 1930s for reducing unemployment had a specially important role for fiscal policy and public works – though we have seen that he stated clearly that 'public loan expenditure' was *'not necessarily the best way to increase employment'*. By the time of Keynes's death the nature and magnitude of the unemployment problem had obviously begun to change fundamentally from what it had been in the thirties. Whatever precise role remained for 'demand management', or in particular for 'the general stimulus at the centre', by public loan expenditure, of aggregate demand, a relatively much more important role emerged for the 'different technique' which Keynes had called for in 1937 in view of the 'unfortunately rigid' structure of the British economy. It seems clear that this 'different technique' to deal with rigidity would have broadly corresponded, in *some* important respects, with the kind of proposals to reduce 'frictional' and other forms of unemployment put forward by the pre-Keynesian pioneers before 1914. It seems equally clear that Keynes's 'different technique' would also have broadly corresponded, in *some* important respects, with what today, following Professor Friedman, is described as reducing the 'natural' rate of unemployment.

Pseudo-Keynesians have not recognized the various and changing aspects of the unemployment problem and thereby have propagated different policies and objectives from those of Keynes himself. But it would be quite unjust, especially in view of his explicit and open-minded recognition of the different types and aspects of unemployment and the different policies it requires, to attribute any kind of dogmatic blindness, or mystique, to Keynes. However, the Pseudo-Keynesians have certainly supplied an excellent example for Professor Bronfenbrenner's general account (quoted above, p. 109) of how it may come about that a once-triumphant theory, 'thesis', or 'paradigm' 'hardens from doctrine to dogma', and how 'the thesis turns apologetic, repetitive, and lifeless . . . because problems arise for which the answers stemming from orthodox paradigms are either lacking or unacceptable.'

But just as mistaken as a failure to recognize its subsequent decline would be a denial of the original achievements of the 'revolution' in, and for, its own time.

Our main and primary concern in this chapter has been with the history of economic thought, that is, with contributing to the formation of a less inaccurate record, which is an important task from the point of view of intellectual standards, and also one not devoid of practical and political significance. We are also concerned with the clarification of the extent and limits of knowledge and ignorance in economics. In its heyday 'the Keynesian revolution' helped to build up generally over-optimistic notions about economic knowledge, and more specifically about how far methods had been discovered for maintaining any desired levels of employment at negligible cost with the support of incomes policies; while simultaneously, and on top of that, it was suggested that 'purposive' neo-Keynesian growth policies would (about) double British rates of growth. In fact, 'the Keynesian revolution' was carried far beyond anything contemplated in the writings of Keynes. Disillusion has been politically dangerous. Though unfortunately belated, it is surely better late than never to attempt to disperse illusions and seek to attain a less inaccurate and more realistic grasp of the extent and limits of economic knowledge.[38]

Notes

1   The fairly sudden decline and fall of English classical political economy, and the nature and processes of 'revolutions' in the history of economic thought, are discussed in Hutchison, 1978.
2   It may be noted that Professor Johnson subsequently changed fundamentally his ideas regarding exchange-rate theory and policy (see Hutchison, 1977, p. 180, and Johnson, 1976, p. 17).
3   See the letters in *The Times* 17 and 19 Oct. 1932, the first signed by Keynes (and others) and the second by Hayek (and others).
4   As evidence we may cite, for example, Fisher's famous pronouncement (15 Oct. 1929) that 'stock prices have reached what looks like a permanently high plateau. . . . I expect to see the stock market a good deal higher than it is to-day within a few months' (quoted in Galbraith, 1961, pp. 95, 116). Professor Friedman and Anna Schwartz write on the American literature at this time:

Contemporary economic comment was hardly distinguished by the
correctness or profundity of understanding of the economic forces at
work. . . . Many professional economists as well as others viewed the
depression as a desirable and necessary economic development required
to eliminate inefficiency and weakness, took for granted that the appropriate cure was belt-tightening by both private individuals and the
result rather than a contributing cause. . . . One can read through
the annual *Proceedings* of the American Economic Association or the
Academy of Political Science and find only an occasional sign that
the academic world even knew about the unprecedented banking
collapse in process, let alone that it understood the cause and
remedy. (1965, pp. 113–5)

It might be asked where this complacent disregard of 'The Great Contraction' had come down from. Whence else than from an unconcern with
the money supply of Smithian origin? But Professor Friedman and Anna
Schwartz are disregarding the considerable body of opinion which
supported proposals of a Keynesian type for countering 'the Great
Contraction' (Stein, 1969, especially chapters 1–7).

5   Hutchison, 1973, p. 142. The kind of political assumption on which
Keynes tended to rely, that the management of the economy would be in
the hands of a mandarin elite of high civil servants, stemmed from his
own early days in the India Office in 1906–8 (see above, pp. 70–8).
The criticisms of such elitist assumptions by Professors Buchanan and
Wagner, in respect of the decades following World War II (and Keynes's
death) in Britain and the US, clearly have much justification. But
Professors Buchanan and Wagner do not recognize that the Employment
Act of 1946, which they regard as inspired by the ideas of Keynes, was
followed by about two decades of almost unprecedented prosperity and
stability. It seems rather one-sided *both* to deny Keynes any credit for this
success, *and* to heap the blame on him for what began to go wrong two
decades after his death. Professors Buchanan and Wagner also make no
distinction between the actual doctrines of Keynes, and the ideas
propagated as 'Keynesian' by those seeking to exploit the charisma of his
name. (See Buchanan and Wagner, 1977.)

6   The revision of this chapter was completed before, the appearance of
vol. XXVII of Keynes's Writings which covers the subject of post-
World-War II employment policies. However, Professor Allan Meltzer
has had a preview of this volume and has kindly let me see his article,
'Keynes's General Theory: a Different Perspective', to be published
shortly. Professor Meltzer expresses his agreement with the main
arguments of our first edition (1977) and regards vol. XXVII as
providing additional evidence for them: 'Keynes did not accept the
postwar policies called Keynesian. He described them as "modernist
stuff, gone wrong and turned sour and silly" ' (see Meltzer, 1981).

7   All references in this section, unless otherwise stated, are to *The
Times* of 1937. Italics have been added.

8   Sir John Hicks has written (1974, p. 61): 'The view which emerges from *The General Theory* is more radical than "full employment without inflation"; it is nothing less than the view that inflation does not matter. . . . The extreme position which he takes by implication in *The General Theory* is surely to be explained by the circumstances of its time. Inflation in 1936, seemed far from being a danger.' If inflation seemed far from being a danger in 1936, *by 1937 it was, for Keynes, by no means remote.* Keynes was doubtless much more flexible and quick on his feet than most of his followers.

9   In a letter written soon after the publication of *The General Theory* (of 30 Apr. 1936) Keynes predicted: 'Our methods of control are unlikely to be sufficiently delicate or powerful to maintain continuous full employment. I should be quite content with a reasonable approximation to it' (1979, vol. 29, p. 235). This is an example of the new material which has become available since much of this chapter was first published, and which generally seems to support, rather than to run counter to its main thesis, as is further confirmed by Professor Allan Meltzer who has seen the not-yet-published evidence in vol. XXVII of Keynes's writings. (See Meltzer, 1981).

10   See, however, Professor William Fellner's criticisms of both the natural rate concept and of Keynes's concepts of 'voluntary' and 'involuntary' unemployment (1976, pp. 54–5).

11   Keynes's views in his *Times* articles of January 1937 were the same as those of the Committee on Economic Information (of which he was a leading member) in its report of February 1937. The Committee maintained:

> 'We can no longer anticipate that the stimulus to economic activity generally associated with an increase in investment will make any substantial impression on the remaining volume of unemployment. . . . Apart from the special areas *the postponement of such investment activity as is not of an urgent character would, on balance, prove beneficial to the average level of employment over a period of years*. . . . Our first recommendation is therefore that the government should take what steps are possible to postpone work upon investment projects which are not of an urgent character.' (Howson and Winch, 1977, p. 346).

It is not clear whether Lord Kahn would apply his explanation of Keynes's views to the simultaneous recommendations of the Committee on Economic Information. (See next section.)

12   By the middle of 1939 Keynes was maintaining that 'the end of abnormal unemployment was in sight', with the total at about 1½ million and a further reduction of at least half a million forecast for the end of the year. But then it was a twilight period of mobilization between peace and impending war, so that conclusions about Keynes's views on peacetime normality cannot be drawn. (*The Times*, 17 Apr. and

24–25 July 1939, and *The Listener,* 1 June; also Hutchison, 1968, p. 298.)

13 According to Meltzer (1981), when discussing post-war employment policy in 1942–3, 'Keynes's opinion was that if 5% unemployment rate is the "minimum practicable rate of unemployment" . . . tax rates should not decline until unemployment reaches 8%'.

14 Even Winston Churchill was proclaiming, on 15 September 1937: 'I declare my belief that a major war is not imminent, and I still believe there is a good chance of no major war taking place in our time': quoted in Taylor, 1972, p. 375. Mr Taylor adds: 'Nowadays it is too easily believed that there was a steady slide towards war from 1931 to 1939'.

15 Professor Moggridge, the leading authority on the Keynes papers, has remarked that he has 'not as yet come across sufficient evidence to support' Lord Kahn's 'construction' (1976, p. 177). But there is much more than sufficient evidence to *refute* Lord Kahn's 'construction', if one assumes that there has always been much more than sufficient evidence to refute the proposition that Keynes was a purveyor of elaborate and self-contradictory public deceptions.

16 According to Professor Meltzer (1981, n.33): Keynes expected the transition from war to peace 'to last about five years', and he believed that controls would ease the transition. If a crisis occurred, he was prepared to accept autarky as a "last resort" (XXVII, p. 404, n. 18). But he supported forcefully Lionel Robbins' statement on the importance of preserving 'the liberty, the initiative and . . . the idiosyncracy of the individual in a framework serving the public good' (XXVII, p. 369).

17 On this point, too, Keynes's views have been distorted. Lord Balogh has asserted: 'Keynes wrote in his last article that . . . the Americans would prove a high-living and high-spending country and that the balance of world trade would be restored in the next two years.' There is no mention whatsoever of 'the next two years' in Keynes's article, and his justified prediction that 'the United States is becoming a high-living, high-cost country beyond any previous experience' referred specifically to 'the long run'. (See Thirlwall, ed., 1976, p. 98, and Keynes, 1946, p. 185.)

18 Opinions on the dollar 'shortage' in the 1940s and 1950s are quoted in Hutchison, 1968, pp. 44–9, 96–8, 161–5. Lord Balogh continued periodically to proclaim a dollar 'shortage' throughout the fifties down, at least, until 1958 (1958, p. 235).

19 Regarding the last, posthumously published article of Keynes, Jacob Viner, perhaps the greatest economist-scholar of his day, remarked how it 'startled his disciples by its optimistic tone, and there was serious consideration of the desirability of suppressing it' (1964, p. 265). This is an extraordinary suggestion. But, according to Per Jacobsson, regarding this last article, Lord Kahn explained that 'the trustees had a long and serious debate about whether or not to publish it. They thought that Keynes had written it while he was ill, that he had not really meant what he had written.' (E. Jacobsson, 1979, p. 212) Certainly this is just what

Joan Robinson was thinking more than thirty years after Keynes's death, when she attributed the same thought to Lord Kahn (see Kahn, 1976c). According to Mrs Robinson: 'At the end of his life, feeling obliged to defend the Bretton Woods agreement against his better judgement (Kahn, 1976c), he lapsed into arguing that, *in the long run*, market forces would tend to establish equilibrium in international trade' (Robinson and Wilkinson, 1977, p. 10). Lord Kahn, in fact, refers to Keynes as 'a sick man' when writing this article – as presumably he had been for years (Kahn, 1976c). On the other hand, Sir Roy Harrod, Joint Editor of the *Economic Journal*, explains how this article reached him two days after Keynes's death 'in an envelope addressed in his own handwriting', and how they had 'agreed that he would have to defer publication until the British Loan was through Congress' (1951, p. 621). The article was in fact published in the next number of the *Economic Journal*, immediately following Keynes's death and his sending in of the final version. Sir Roy also explains how, just previously, Keynes had heartily approved of Harrod's pamphlet vigorously supporting Bretton Woods (*A Page of British Folly*, 1946), in which Harrod maintained, against 'critics and cavillers' that: 'We are forced to suppose that . . . there are some resolute minds who for reasons of power politics do not fancy the harmonious and close accord of the United States and the United Kingdom'. Sir Roy was undoubtedly justified in this supposition. See also 1951, p. 609.

I am indebted to Professor Robert Skidelsky for calling my attention to the Life of Per Jacobsson by his daughter: *A Life for Sound Money* (1979). See his review (1979b), where he concludes: 'During and immediately after the war, the Keynesian position was captured by left-wing economists who used his ideas to push political (and economic) causes which were not necessarily his own.'

20   An earlier and shorter version of the following paragraphs may be found in the latter part of my paper to Section F of the British Association, 1975 (Hutchison, 1976).

21   See also J. Robinson, 1947, p. 26: 'In general it may be said that *something appreciably short of full employment must be regarded as the optimum*' (italics added).

22   Lord Kahn has subsequently referred to the fifties as 'a period of very modest inflation' (1977, p. 11). On the other hand, as the Radcliffe Committee prudently warned at the time:

> Nobody has lost sight of – indeed nobody has been allowed to lose sight of – the disadvantages of instability in the internal and external value of money. *The rise in the cost of living has been a constant embarrassment to Governments and by 1957 the more ominous phrase 'falling value of money' was constantly used.* (1959, p. 18, italics added)

23   As Mr Eltis has noticed, Lord Kahn also advised the Radcliffe Committee regarding budgetary policy: 'To my mind, the "overall" deficit is

of no significance' (Kahn, 1960, p. 145; Eltis, 1976, p. 18).

24   We agree with Mr Tim Congdon that generally speaking 'the Keynesians are somewhat ambivalent in their attitude to the union move-ment', but not that 'an insistence on the villainy of trade unions is, how-ever, common to all the Keynesians' (1975, p. 34). Anyhow, 'Keynesians' have tended to support strongly the various restrictionist demands of the trade union leaders for import controls and for staying out of the Euro-pean Economic Community.

25   It is interesting to contrast Lord Kahn's pronouncements on the trade union leaders with his fellow 'Keynesian', Sir Roy Harrod's, confidence that a national wage agreement could be reached 'given a guarantee of price stability', because 'many trade union leaders are good economists' (*The Times*, 21 July 1976). Lord Kahn also leaves unexplained his doctrine that monetary policy must always be so permissively framed as to exclude *any* unemployment, however 'crazily' high wages are pushed by leaders of such 'astonishing stupidity'.

26   Though he has been quite prepared, when it has suited him, to invoke the magic name of Keynes for polemical purposes, Lord Balogh should not, of course, be described as 'Keynesian', or 'neo-Keynesian'. In fact, Lord Balogh has rightly insisted that the 'revolution' was 'never fully accepted by Keynes', who later became an advocate of 'what really amounts to . . . something like *laissez-faire*'. In other words, in Joan Robinson's terms, Keynes *was* 'a bastard Keynesian' (see Thirlwall, ed., 1976, p. 66). It is surely a reasonable speculation that Keynes, had he lived, would have approved enthusiastically of Dr Erhard's policies and there are few, or no, grounds for supposing that he would have condemned them. Incidentally, by the later 1970s some Labour Party economists were actually trying to claim that Federal Germany's economic successes were due to *their* kind of policies.

27   In 1976 Heinrich Dräger (who in 1932, in his *Arbeitsbeschaftung durch produktive Kreditschöpfung*, had put forward proposals against unemploy-ment very like those of Keynes) made the interesting claim that 'today, in 1976, the Federal Republic of Germany is the leading country in respect of *rightly understood* Keynesian policies' (see Dräger, 1976). Dr Dräger's claim may be much less unjustifiable than those of English 'neo-Keynesians', which must be among the most dubious in intellectual history. Certainly it would seem to show a much more serious concern for Keynes's reputation to seek to associate genuinely Keynesian policies with the outstanding economic success of the German Federal Republic than with the failures of British policies, especially after 1964. We would, however, be inclined to accept the description of the policies of the GFR as 'neoclassical' (see Roberts, 1979). But it is difficult not to agree with Professor M. Cranston: 'It is indeed arguable that, of all people, the English have understood Keynes least, and profited least from what he had to offer.' The sources of this misunderstanding seem obvious. Professor Cranston continues: 'Two of Keynes's most important critics –

von Hayek and von Mises – held that Keynes's mixture of liberty and state guidance simply will not work, that you have to settle for one or the other. The experience of several countries suggests that Keynes was right; that his mixture, does work. It is unfortunate that Great Britain is not one of them.' (1977, p. 114) Responsibility for this tragedy may be divided between British institutions and the 'neo-Keynesians'.

28   In recent history surely no more valid (or less invalid) illustration of Keynes's assertions could be found than the dash for growth of 1971–73 'distilled' from the fashionable academic growthmanship of 10–15 years previously.

29   'The key point to note is that eighteen years ago three of the greatest Keynesians offered their countrymen monetary expansion, indifference to inflation, and the irrelevance of deficits' (Eltis, 1976, p. 18). We would add that this 'Keynesian conventional wisdom' had little basis in, or affinity with, the writings of Keynes.

30   See Kahn, 1975a, p. 33; and Keynes, 1972, p. 8, where Sir Roy Harrod inquired regarding the problem of inflation in the 1970s: 'What do we do? What is the remedy? It would be most inappropriate for me to stand up here and tell you what Keynes would have thought'. But in the 1970s, as we have seen, Sir Roy knew 'certainly', and had 'no doubt at all', about 'what Keynes would have thought' – at least when this coincided with Sir Roy's ideas. Again, as late as 13 January 1977, Sir Roy was proclaiming in a letter to *The Times*, 'how furious Keynes, joint founder of the IMF, would have been' at the conditions under which Britain was borrowing; although the rate of inflation and the magnitudes of the external payments, and budgetary deficits were at levels unprecedented in peacetime.

31   Reprinted in Robbins, 1949, pp. 18–40. We might add, however, that we are certainly not among those who would suggest that Lord Robbins should, in the seventies, retract his retraction (made in the late thirties and forties) of his fundamental opposition to the public works policies of Keynes and the majority of English economists in the early thirties (Jay 1977).

32   We do not agree with all Professor Hayek's judgements on Keynes, but the following seems completely convincing:

'I have little doubt that we owe much of the postwar inflation to the great influence of such over-simplified Keynesianism. Not that Keynes himself would have approved of this. Indeed, I am fairly certain that if he had lived he would in that period have been one of the most determined fighters against inflation. About the last time I saw him, a few weeks before his death, he more or less plainly told me so. As his remark on that occasion is illuminating in other respects, it is worth reporting. I had asked whether he was not getting alarmed about the use to which some of his disciples were putting his theories. His reply was that these theories had been greatly needed in the 1930s, but if these theories should ever become harmful, I could be assured that he would quickly bring about a change in public opinon.' (1973, p. 103)

33 It was not that the deliberate and explicit wrecking of the mixed economy by the encouragement of inflation was propagated by *all* Pseudo-Keynesians in the name of Keynes. However, such a policy was explicitly advocated by two Oxford economists, Messrs A. Glyn and B. Sutcliffe, who claimed: 'We have shown that capitalism will be unable to continue accepting the rate of wage increase which has prevailed in the recent past without jeopardising its own existence'. The controversial normative or political message was then proclaimed: 'This means that the working-class leaders must adopt a new attitude to wage demands: they must realise that wage claims are becoming political weapons in a battle in which the existence of capitalism is at stake. *By abolishing the private ownership of capital and redistributing income a socialist system could almost immediately provide a decent standard of life for everyone.*' However, unlike Joan Robinson and others, Messrs Glyn and Sutcliffe did not describe their views as 'neo-' or 'post-Keynesian' (1972, pp. 10, 202, 215, italics added.)

34 'I am confident that in the end we shall find that full employment can be obtained only by aiming high, and if the investment target is over-shot, by controlling cumulative movements directly and by fiscal measures. This was the way the Soviet obtained its results and I doubt whether we can do better.' (Lord Balogh, 1963, p. 23)

35 For example, as early as 1956 Sir Roy Harrod was claiming: 'Some hold that wage-earners are greedy, not to say insatiable, and that, with full-employment, they will persistently bid up their wage demands more than the rise in productivity and that we are thereby doomed to a régime of chronic inflation. I regard this as unduly pessimistic' (Harrod, 1956). In 1958, as we have noticed, Lord Kahn was referring to the 'considerable improvements in the state of awareness of the importance of restraint over wage increases'. Lord Balogh, after proclaiming in 1964 that 'the greater equality implied by tax reform will provide the basis for a national incomes policy', was announcing that the Labour government had 'obtained support of the trade unions for a well-conceived plan for an incomes policy'. (See Hutchison, 1968, p. 225.)

36 Mr Clark emphasizes that the assumption of workers' money illusion 'was an important but purely temporary truth from the 1930s', and that 'even as a theory only valid for a short period, in a time of heavy unemployment, the doctrine of labour's "money illusion" was applicable only in the advanced industrial countries' (1970, pp. 54–5). Milton Friedman also questioned more fundamentally the 'money illusion' assumption (1975, p. 17). Mr Walter Eltis suggests two further institutional changes in the role of the British economy which have undermined the relevance or feasibility of Keynes's doctrines:

First, relatively smaller economies cannot pursue Keynesian methods of raising employment as can more powerful countries.

> . . . it is the great and powerful that must follow Keynesian deficit-financing policies. It is they whom Keynes addressed in 1936 (when he addressed the powerful by addressing his own countrymen). . . . But the weaknesses in these policies have not been understood, so small countries like Britain in the 1960s and 1970s, advised by Keynesian fine-tuners, have accelerated domestic inflation and destroyed the international values of their currencies, either deliberately or accidentally, under the mistaken belief that they were pursuing full employment.

At this point we may note the contrast with Mr H. D. Henderson in 1933 insisting: 'World recovery can indeed only be brought about if the stronger financial countries lead the way and we belong to this category' (Howson and Winch, 1977, p. 129).

Secondly, Mr Eltis maintains, regarding the rate of interest and international complications.

> Keynes's assumptions that the British interest rate is independent of foreign interest rates and that government bonds are a typical portfolio asset are comprehensible in the context of the Britain of the 1930s. London was then a great financial centre, so if he believed that world interest rates were determined in London, with sterling the *numéraire* against which other currencies were at a premium or discount, this would not have been absurd . . . in 1936 it might have been reasonable to regard bonds as a typical portfolio asset.

(The two quotations from Mr Eltis are from his trenchant article, 'The Failure of the Keynesian Conventional Wisdom', 1976, pp. 8, 12.)

37   Mr G. C. Peden (1980) has denied that Keynes's ideas in 1937 about unemployment targets and government spending 'differed vastly' from those of 'Keynesians' or 'neo-Keynesians' in the fifties and sixties. He bases this denial on the assertion that the elasticity of supply was *much* smaller in 1937 than in subsequent decades, and that the economic structure was then *particularly and peculiarly* rigid. But he gives no evidence for any 'peculiar' rigidity at that particular date, when unemployment was 12–13 per cent, as contrasted with subsequent levels of 2–3 per cent when 'Keynesians' (like Harrod and Prof. Robinson) were demanding more expansionist spending measures. Doubtless in 1937 there were shortages of some kinds of skilled labour – *as always*. But Mr Peden gives no evidence for his rejection of the view he cites (p. 157), of A. J. Brown and E. M. Burrows, that generally 'there was little shortage of labour anywhere in the UK between 1928 and 1938'.

38   This subject is discussed more fully in the author's *Knowledge and Ignorance in Economics*, Blackwell, 1977.

Complaints may be, and have been, made that a study such as this involves 'tracking down quotations' or 'lifting them out of context'. (See the '*Comment*' by Lord Kahn published with the original edition of this paper, 1977.) Such reactions might be taken to indicate a desire to ward off criticism. *Any* critical examination must require 'tracking down quotations', and one cannot quote, at less than virtually infinite length without, to some extent 'lifting' passages 'out of context'. Of course, quotations, like statistics, or any other kind of empirical evidence, can, intentionally or unintentionally, be misrepresentative or misleading. If this is the case with regard to any of the quotations in this chapter or volume, let it be shown. But to object to 'tracking down quotations', *as such*, or to 'lifting them out of context', is sheer obscurantism.

References

Balogh, T. (1950), *Germany: an Experiment in 'Planning' by the 'Free' Price Mechanism.*
   (1958), 'Productivity and Inflation', *Oxford Economic Papers*, N.S., vol. 10, pp. 220ff.
   (1963), *Planning for Progress*, Fabian Society.
   (1976), 'Keynes and the I.M.F.', in Thirlwall (ed.), 1976.
Bronfenbrenner, M. (1971), 'The "Structure of Revolutions" in Economic Thought', *History of Political Economy*, vol. 3, pp. 139ff.
Buchanan, J. M. and Wagner, R. (1977), *Democracy in Deficit.*
Clark, C. G. (1970), *Taxmanship*, IEA, 2nd ed.
Congdon, T. (1975), 'Are We Really All Keynesians Now?', *Encounter*, Apr., pp. 23ff.
Cranston, M. (1978), 'Keynes: His Political Ideas and their Influence', in Thirlwall (ed.), 1978.
Crossman, R. H. S. (1976), *Diaries of a Cabinet Minister*, vol. 2.
Dräger, H. (1932), *Arbeitsbeschaffung durch produktive Kreditschöpfung.*
   (1976), in G. Bombach *et al.* (ed.), *Der Keynesianismus*, vol. 2.
Eltis, W. (1976), 'The Failure of the Keynesian Conventional Wisdom', *Lloyds Bank Review*, Oct., pp. 1ff.
   (1977), 'The Keynesian Conventional Wisdom', *Lloyds Bank Review*, July, pp. 38ff.
Encounter (1967), column by 'R', Jan., p. 53.
Fellner, W. J. (1976), *Towards a Reconstruction of Macroeconomics.*
Friedman, M. (1975), *Unemployment versus Inflation*, IEA.
Friedman, M. and Schwartz, A. (1965), *The Great Contraction 1929–1933.*
Galbraith, J. K. (1961), *The Great Crash 1929.*
Glyn, A. and Sutcliffe, B. (1972), *British Capitalism, Workers and the Profits Squeeze.*
Haberler, G. (1974), *Economic Growth and Stability.*
Harrod, R. F. (1946), *A Page of British Folly.*
   (1951), *The Life of J. M. Keynes.*

(1956), *Time and Tide*, 28 July, p. 900.

(1964), 'Are We Really All Keynesians Now?', *Encounter*, Jan., pp. 47ff.

(1969), 'The Arrested Revolution', *New Statesman*, 5 Dec.

(1976), letter in *The Times*, 21 July.

(1977), letter in *The Times*, 13 Jan.

Hayek, F. A. (1932), letter in *The Times*, 19 Oct.

(1935), *Prices and Production*, 2nd ed.

(1939), *Profits, Interest and Investment*.

(1973), *A Tiger by the Tail*, IEA, 2nd impression.

(1975), *Full Employment at Any Price?* IEA.

(1976), *Choice in Currency*, IEA.

Hicks, Sir John (1974), *The Crisis in Keynesian Economics*.

HMSO (1944), *White Paper on Employment Policy*, Cmd. 6527.

(1959), *Report of the Committee on the Workings of the Monetary System*.

(1960), *Committee on the Working of the Monetary System, Principal Memoranda of Evidence*.

Howson, S. (1973), 'A Dear Money Man? Keynes on Monetary Policy 1920', *Economic Journal*, June, vol. 83, pp. 456ff.

Howson, S. and Winch, D. (1977), *The Economic Advisory Council 1930–1939*.

Hutchison, T. W. (1968), *Economics and Economic Policy in Britain 1946–1966*.

(1973), 'The Collected Writings of J. M. Keynes' *Economic History Review*, Feb., pp. 142ff.

(1976), 'Economists and Social Justice in the History of Economic Thought', in A. Jones (ed.), *Economics and Equality*, pp. 58–63.

(1977a), *Knowledge and Ignorance in Economics*.

(1977b), letter in *Encounter*, Mar., p. 92.

(1978), *On Revolutions and Progress in Economic Knowledge*.

Jacobsson, E. (1979), *A Life for Sound Money*.

Jay, P. (1977), in *The Times*, 17 Feb.

Johnson, E. and Johnson, H. G. (1974), 'The Social and Intellectual Origins of the General Theory vol. 6,' *History of Political Economy*, Fall, pp. 261ff.

(1975), 'Keynes and British Economics', in M. Keynes (ed.), *Essays on John Maynard Keynes*, pp. 110ff.

(1976), 'Money and the Balance of Payments', *Banca Nazionale del Lavoro Quarterly Review*, pp. 3ff.

Kahn, Lord (1949), 'Professor Meade on Planning' *Economic Journal*, Mar., pp. 1ff.

(1960), Evidence in *Committee on the Working of the Monetary System, Principal Memoranda of Evidence*, pp. 143ff.

(1972), *Selected Essays on Employment and Growth*.

(1974), 'What Keynes Really Said', *Sunday Telegraph*, 22 Sept.

(1975a), *On Re-Reading Keynes*, British Academy.

(1975b), letter in *New Statesman*, 1 Aug., p. 142.

(1976a), 'Thoughts on the Behaviour of Wages and Monetarism', *Lloyds Bank Review*, Jan. pp. 4ff.

(1976b), 'Unemployment as Seen by the Keynesians', in G. D. N. Worswick (ed.), *The Concept and Measurement of Involuntary Unemployment*, pp. 27ff.

(1976c), 'Keynes and the Historical Origins of the I.M.F.', in Thirlwall (ed.), 1976.

(1977), 'Mr Eltis and the Keynesians', *Lloyds Bank Review*, Apr., pp. 3ff.

Kaldor, Lord (1944), Appendix C to W. Beveridge, *Full Employment in a Free Society*.

(1963), 'Going into Europe', *Encounter*, Mar., pp. 63ff.

(1964), *Essays on Economic Policy*, vol. 1, pp. 199ff.

Keynes, J. M. (1930), *Treatise on Money*, 2 vols.

(1936), *The General Theory of Employment, Interest and Money*.

(1937), articles in *The Times*, 12, 13 and 14 Jan. and 11 Mar.; and letter, 28 Dec.

(1939a), in *The Times*, 17 Apr. and 24–25 July.

(1939b), in *The Listener*, 1 June.

(1940), letter in *The Times*, 10 Apr.

(1946), 'The Balance of Payments of the U.S.' *Economic Journal*, vol. 56, June, pp. 172ff.

(1972), *Collected Writings*, vol. 10, ed. D. E. Moggridge and E. Johnson.

(1973), *Collected Writings*, vol. 14, ed. D. E. Moggridge and E. Johnson.

(1979–80), *Collected Writings*, vols. 23, 24 and 29, ed. D. E. Moggridge.

Laidler, D. (1975), 'The End of Demand Management', in *How to Reduce Unemployment in the 1970s*, IEA, pp. 45ff.

Mathews, R. C. O. (1968), 'Why has Britain had Full Employment since the War?', *Economic Journal*, Sept., vol. 78, pp. 568ff.

Maynard, G. W. (1978), 'Keynes and Unemployment Today', *Three Banks Review*, Dec.

Meltzer, A. (1981), 'Keynes's General Theory: a Different Perspective', *Journal of Economic Literature*, March.

Moggridge, D. E. (1975), letter in *Encounter*, Sept., p. 89.

(1976), *Keynes*.

Myrdal, G. (1973), *Against the Stream*.

New Statesman (1976), editorial, 20 Feb., p. 211.

Opie, R. G. (1974), 'The Political Consequences of Lord Keynes', in D. E. Moggridge, (ed.), *Keynes: Aspects of the Man and his Work*, pp. 75ff.

Peden, G. C. (1980), 'Unemployment in the Later Nineteen-Thirties', *Oxford Economic Papers*, March, pp. 1ff.

Pigou, A. C. (1944), *Lapses from Full Employment.*

Radcliffe, Lord (1959), *Report of the Committee on the Working of Monetary System.*

Robbins, Lord (1949), 'Full Employment as an Objective', in *The Economist in the Twentieth Century*, pp. 18ff.

Roberts, C. C. (1979), 'Economic Theory and Policy Making in West Germany', *Cambridge Journal of Economics*, vol. 3, no. 1, pp. 83ff.

Robertson, D. H. (1966), 'Creeping Inflation', in *Essays in Money and Interest*. pp. 245ff.

Robinson, Sir Austin (1967), *Economic Planning in the United Kingdom.*

Robinson, J. (1947), *Essays in the Theory of Employment*, 2nd ed.

    (1951), *Collected Economic Papers*, vol. 1.

    (1965), *Collected Economic Papers*, vol. 3.

    (1966), *Economics: an Awkward Corner.*

    (1974), 'Inflation and Stabilisation, a Neo-Keynesian View', *The Spectator*, 19 Oct., p. 488.

    (1975), 'What has Become of the Keynesian Revolution?' Presidential Address to Section F of the British Association, 1972, in M. Keynes (ed.), *Essays on John Maynard Keynes*, pp. 125ff.

Robinson, J. and Eatwell, J. (1973), *An Introduction to Modern Economics.*

Robinson, J. and Wilkinson, F. (1977), 'What has Become of Employment Policy?', *Cambridge Journal of Political Economy*, Mar., pp. 10ff.

Schumpeter, J. A. (1972), *Ten Great Economists.*

Skidelsky, R. (1976a), 'The Political Meaning of the Keynesian Revolution', *The Spectator*, 7 Aug., p. 9.

    (1976b), 'Where Import Controls Come In', *New Statesman*, 22 Oct., p. 542.

    (1979a), 'Is Keynes Still Relevant?', *Encounter*, Apr., pp. 29ff.

    (1979b), Review of E. Jacobsson, *A Life for Sound Money, Spectator*, 19 May, p. 26.

Stein, H. (1969), *The Fiscal Revolution in America.*

Stewart, M. (1967), *Keynes and After* (2nd ed., 1972).

Taylor, A. J. P. (1972), *Beaverbrook.*

Thirlwall, A. P., ed. (1976), *Keynes and International Monetary Relations.*
(1978), *Keynes and Laissez-Faire.*

Trevithick, J. A. (1980), *Inflation*, 2nd ed.

Viner, J. (1964), 'Comment', in R. Lekachman (ed.), *Keynes' General Theory: Reports of Three Decades*, pp. 253ff.

5

Walter Eucken and the German Social-Market Economy

I

No short and simple, non-trivial generalization will stand up to much critical examination regarding the complex subject of the effects on economic policies of the theories, doctrines and ideas of economists. Nevertheless, striking generalizations have from time to time been attempted, as notably in the famous, now somewhat hackneyed, concluding paragraph of Keynes's *General Theory*. In those so-often-quoted words Keynes described the world as being 'ruled by little else' than 'the ideas of economists and political philosophers, both when they are right and when they are wrong' (1936, p. 383). Certainly economists have been prepared to claim credit for phases of outstanding economic success. For example, in the middle of the nineteenth century, when the English economy was approaching the peak, relatively, of its economic power, and when England was justifiably coming to be known as 'the workshop of the world', Nassau Senior triumphantly claimed credit for the ideas of his fellow classical political economists. In 1853 he asserted to a Frenchman regarding England's economic success: 'It is the triumph of theory. We are governed by philosophers and political economists and you see the results.' (1878, p. 169).

Moving forward about a century we find Keynes's Cambridge successors claiming credit, on behalf of Keynes's ideas, for the historically almost unprecedented economic success, in terms of such usual indicators as levels of growth and unemployment, which much of the Western world enjoyed in the two decades or so after World War II. As Sir Austin Robinson maintained:

In the year 1947–8 we began to use in peacetime the principles that

Maynard Keynes had worked out for war finance. We began to plan the use of national resources. If we are looking to the credit side I think we can honestly say that the world today is a different place from what it was in the 1930s in very large measure as a result of the economic thinking that began in this Faculty in Cambridge in those exciting years of the 1930s. (1967, p. 43)[1]

Later Professor Hayek also agreed in attributing a very powerful and pervasive influence to Keynes's ideas. But he analyses and evaluates their effects rather differently, in that he holds them to be responsible for what he calls 'Keynesian inflation' and maintains that the widespread and extremely serious problems of the 1970s should, to a large extent, be regarded as 'the economic consequences of Lord Keynes' (Hayek, 1978, pp. 191–2). Though Keynes, in his much-quoted passage, acknowledged that economists were liable to be as influential when they were 'wrong' as when they were 'right', naturally one does not find economists claiming a powerful influence in periods of policy failure, though, as we see, they may then ascribe great influence to their intellectual and political opponents. But, in any case, there may be some exaggeration here. According to John Stuart Mill it is an illusion for economists to attribute great influence to their ideas alone, at any rate in the short run, either for good or for ill. As Mill insisted: 'Ideas, unless outward circumstances conspire with them, have in general no very rapid or immediate efficacy in human affairs' (1845, p. 503).

Since World War II there has been one outstanding national politicoeconomic success in the Western or North Atlantic world: that is, of course, the success of what is widely called the '*Soziale Marktwirtschaft*' in the German Federal Republic. How far does this example refute Mill's warning? Perhaps not, in so far as 'outward circumstances' may be held to have 'conspired' significantly in support of whatever power ideas may have wielded at the crucial juncture in Germany after World War II. But rapid and lasting economic success, at least in terms of the usual quantitative indicators, can certainly be claimed, and a cogent, clear-cut system of politicoeconomic ideas was certainly at work. However, no attempt is being made here to ascribe any particular effect to these ideas, or to account for their precise *modus operandi*, or to trace out the precise channels, personal, intellectual or political, through which they bore fruit in policies and institutions. We would simply declare our own belief, or prejudice, that although cases could be pointed to where the ideas of economists have had damaging rather than beneficial effects, or no effects at all, or where their beneficent effects have been much exaggerated, *in this case*, of the German Federal Republic after 1948, we have an unusually unambiguous example of the beneficent effects of economists' ideas on economic policies.

In the following notes we shall: (1) seek to indicate briefly the German forerunners, and some of the special features of the *kind* of free-market ideas which made for economic success; (2) briefly point to some of the 'outward circumstances' which 'conspired' with these ideas in bringing about this economic success; and (3) note how the free-market ideas in Germany at this time ran counter to fashions prevalent elsewhere.

II

It was maintained by Professor Hayek in his well-known book *The Road to Serfdom* that after about 1870 Germany became the great source of ideas favourable to socialism and economic planning, and that it was pre-eminently German economists, belonging to the Historical School, or the *Verein für Sozialpolitik,* who, in the later decades of the 19th century turned the tide of ideas against the free-market economy, the case for which had earlier been developed by English thinkers. After 'about 1870', Professor Hayek writes:

for the next sixty years Germany became the center from which the ideas destined to govern the world in the twentieth century spread east and west. Whether it was Hegel or Marx, List or Schmoller, Sombart or Mannheim, whether it was socialism in its more radical form or merely organization or planning of a less radical kind, German ideas were everywhere readily imported and German institutions imitated. (1944–1962, p. 21)

Professor Hayek went on to emphasize 'how very considerable was the lead which Germany had in the development of the theory and practice of socialism', and how 'by the time Hitler came to power liberalism was to all intents and purposes dead in Germany' (pp. 22, 30).

Though certainly there is some degree of truth in these national generalizations, there may also be some exaggeration. English

socialism and English ideas in favour of economic intervention-
ism, or 'planning', developed mostly under their own steam, as in
much of the rest of the world, in large part as a reaction to
instability, inequality and war, and especially during the great
slump after 1929. Moreover, the economic ideas of Marx,
uninfluential in Britain until the late 1960s, had a partly British
ancestry – including a British place of birth or conception in
Manchester in the 1840s. However, what we wish to emphasize
here is that *it was German economists, inclined towards the Historical
School or the Verein für Sozialpolitik, who first developed an effective,
fundamental critique of socialist economic planning, a critique subsequently taken over by economists in other schools.* For one can find in the
writings of Schäffle, Brentano and Nasse, back in the 1870s, the
main arguments of the modern liberal critique of socialist
economics.[2] (In fact, far from neoclassical theories representing, as
is often alleged, a reaction against Marxist ideas, the more
effective critical reaction came from the fundamental methodological opponents of neoclassicism, the German historicals.) Their
arguments were taken up in the 1920s by Mises and his followers,
who had the recent war and postwar experiences of socialism and
'planning' to draw upon, and who added a certain dogmatic
extremism.

   To point out that those who in the 1940s in Germany developed
a telling critique of centrally-administered, socialist planning had
this earlier tradition behind them, does not in the least detract
from their originality and achievement. In particular, of course, in
1945–48, it was possible to point directly at a centrally administered economy in a state of total breakdown, and to dissect and
pinpoint the fatal defects, and the politicoeconomic interconnections, which had led to disaster. This is just what Walter Eucken
did in his article, published in the decisive year of 1948, 'On the
Theory of the Centrally Administered Economy: an Analysis of
the German Experiment' (Eucken, 1948).

                                    III

In the leading democratic industrialized countries, over the past
half-century or century, free-market economies have been subject
to an ever-increasing degree of intervention or regulation, often
highly distorting or frustrating, by elected governments. The
prime, classical example of a successful market economy, in its

day was that established, in a *comparatively* pure and unrestricted form, in Britain in the 1830s and 1840s. The political basis was an electorate, after 1832, consisting approximately of the wealthiest 14–15 per cent of the male population. But after 1867, as electoral power was extended down to lower levels of the wealth pyramid, the role of government in the economy was extended, at first gradually, and then, in the 20th century, especially during major wars, much more rapidly and widely. Moreover, democratic governments have tended to concede very much greater powers to trade unions, as, for example, in Britain from as early as the 1870s onwards. In other words, democratic governments, as electorates came to include larger percentages of the poorer members of society, have felt compelled to respond to demands from electoral majorities, or from significant pressure groups, for mitigations of the economic insecurities and inequalities manifested by market economies in their purer or pristine forms. Thus market forces have usually been very much softened and restricted, and their efficiency blunted and undermined. This kind of development has been obvious in many or most of the leading Western democratic countries.

In Britain the market economy, based on the principle of private property, had been introduced and shaped in a framework of massive inherited inequalities, going back to the feudal order, with the majority of the working population lacking almost any political or economic power. This was the kind of 'capitalism' which Engels and Marx were concerned with. In fact, the inequality of power in the labour market was pointed out by Adam Smith in *The Wealth of Nations*.

On the other hand, in the USA and other 'newer' countries, with no feudal inheritance behind them, it was possible to sustain the notion, at least in the early decades of the 19th century, 'that those who engaged in market transactions possessed relatively equal bargaining power. . . . The market was thought to be the most powerful institutional expression of the ideal of equality of opportunity' (Horwitz, 1976, p. 629). Nevertheless, even in the USA, in the twentieth century, in response to persisting inequalities, insecurities and instabilities, especially during the great depression of the 1930s, the long-term trend of the role of government as a consequence of electoral pressures has been towards a wider and wider extension. In the 1950s and early sixties it seemed in some leading countries that a balance between market forces and the role of government might have been reached in the kind of 'mixed' economies then enjoying almost unprecedented success in terms of growth rates, levels of employment, and price stability. But in the late sixties any balance previously obtaining was, in a number of countries, seriously upset in the direction of a still more extensive role for government in the economy.

Indeed so persistent, and seemingly ineluctable, has been the extension of the role of government in so many economically advanced, democratic countries, that it is difficult to cite any case from such countries where a significant rolling back of the interventionist tide has been achieved, *except after major wars*. Even here, the role of government in the economy has usually only been reduced as compared with the all-pervasive central regulation of wartime, and not nearly pushed back to the previous peacetime level.

To these generalizations the Social-Market Economy of the German Federal Republic has provided the outstanding exception among leading Western democratic countries. The role of government in the German economy was, and has remained over thirty years, reduced to well below the previous peacetime levels of the 1930s. (Italy might be suggested as another such case. But the Italian economy of the 1950s and sixties did not embody market principles to the same extent as did the Social-Market Economy in Germany, and, of course, has not enjoyed, over the decades, a comparable lasting success in terms of the conventional indicators.) Moreover, the Social-Market Economy of Germany has so far retained its essential conformity with market principles through changes of the party in power. It has retained an unprecedentedly high level of success over thirty years, an exceptional record in view of the rapid fluctuations of the twentieth century; and at the end of the seventies it is *relatively* stronger than ever in Western Europe and the world.

If one seeks an explanation of this, in many important respects remarkable case, one must surely examine both of the two main types of factors responsible: (1) the 'outward circumstances' which have 'conspired' in Mill's words to promote the success of the particular kinds of policies pursued; and (2) the nature or quality of the particular ideas from which these successful policies were derived.

IV

(1) One would have to go much more deeply than is possible here

into recent German economic and political history, and into the related climate of opinion, to explain adequately how outward conditions conspired to promote the successful launching of a market economy in Germany in the late 1940s. However, an obvious striking difference may be noted between the relevant history and opinion in Germany, over the last half-century or so, and that in England, and, to a lesser extent, in the United States. This contrast suggests how recent economic and political experiences, and the currents and climates of opinion, and of expectations, which they create, are of crucial significance with regard to what kinds of policies are politically feasible for governments, or easier to implement, in a particular country at a particular time.

In Germany in 1948 experience of economic 'planning' and a centrally administered economy was immediately and directly associated with political dictatorship, defeat in war, followed by complete economic breakdown. The crippling inefficiency of the comprehensive controls, as they were operating in 1948, together with the stark obviousness of the interrelation between total economic control and total political dictatorship, were inescapable. These experiences obliterated memories of the insecurities and mass unemployment in the late twenties and early thirties under the more-or-less market economy of the Weimar Republic. Another economic lesson, the learning of which was to prove of great value in the second half of this century, was that of the dire costs, wastes and insecurities stemming from inflation, whether open or suppressed – a lesson which, except in wartime, never seriously had to be confronted in Britain until the mid-seventies.

The extremely different, almost opposite, experiences and memories in Britain (and, to a lesser extent in the USA) had promoted almost exactly opposite attitudes and expectations, which made very different policies feasible or attractive. After 1945 there was, of course, in Britain a strong desire for the dismantling of wartime rationing and controls. But this was not accompanied by any general rejection of economic planning and government regulation of the economy. The centrally administered war economy, in the running of which Keynes and other economists had played a significant part, was seen as having promoted full employment, some measure of social reform, and a 'fairer' distribution of income, at the same time as providing the foundations for a successful war effort (see Addison, 1975). After 1945 the great fear in Britain, and also in the United States, was not political dictatorship and inflation, but a return to the unemployment and deflation of the more or less market economies of the 1930s. This fear went very deep indeed in Britain, and it was stimulated by the erroneous predictions of economists, especially in the USA, of another great world slump after the war. The widespread and powerful postwar influence of 'Keynesian' economics in Britain, and, to a lesser extent in the USA, was based on this fear and the experiences which inspired it.

(2) Together with the right historical conjuncture, or 'outward circumstances', favouring the launching of a market economy, there was, of course, the nature and quality of the ideas themselves as a factor in promoting their success. Free-market policies, and the ideas behind them, have been formulated and advocated in significantly, though sometimes subtly, different modes, both in the more distant past and more recently. A vital broad distinction here might be described as that between the 'Smithian' and the 'Ricardian' modes of argument for free market policies.

The kind of case based on Ricardo's methodology, followed also by some 'neoclassicals', is conceived in narrowly economic terms and derived from an abstract, purely economic model of competitive equilibrium presented as achieving some kind of Utopian 'maximum' or 'optimum'. This kind of case involves highly abstract assumptions, or even an *a priori* methodology, including the often question-begging assumption of perfect knowledge, and it is liable to be formulated in dogmatic and extreme terms. This mode of argument is now, probably, relied upon much less than it used to be.

The other kind of case for the competitive market economy is formulated in much broader terms, comprehending the political and social order, and especially the legal foundations and framework of the economic order. This 'Smithian' mode, starting out from a realistic view of man and his psychology, and recognizing the all-pervasiveness of ignorance in human affairs, gives as important a place in its objectives to freedom and the rule of law as it does to the attainment of some ideal, optimal economic efficiency. The ideas behind the launching of the Social-Market Economy, coming down, as they did, in part from the Historical School, followed this 'Smithian' mode. For example, Walter Eucken laid great emphasis on the 'interdependence between the economic order and all other forms of order' (i.e. legal, social and political) (1952, p. 21). For Eucken the essential basis for successful economic policies was a sound legal and institutional framework: that is, economic policy-making must begin with

'*Ordnungspolitik*'. Technical policy issues (or '*Prozesspolitik*' relating to questions of monetary versus fiscal policy, or employment policy, must be subordinated to the requirements of the economic framework (or '*Ordnung*'). This approach of Eucken's, deriving in part from the Historical School, is in marked contrast with that prevailing in the dominant versions of Anglo-American economics. Moreover, while various tributaries to the broad flow of ideas about economic individualism and free markets have, over the decades, come down from Manchester, Vienna, London, Chicago, Virginia and elsewhere, the distinctive Freiburg contribution, with its concern for the legal and institutional order, is much closest, methodologically, to the original Glasgow source of Adam Smith.

Eucken condemned the policy of *laissez-faire* as incompatible with the maintenance of a legal order based on the idea of a *Rechtsstaat*, because such a policy conceded too much power to monopolies and partial monopolies. Similarly an economic order based on central direction will threaten the rule of law (p. 91). Eucken recognized, too, the past failures of market economies and admitted, in one of his last lectures: 'We still have no answer to the problem of how to organize an industrialized economy humanely and efficiently' (1951, p. 28). He emphasized that an economic system which combined a reasonable or viable degree of efficiency, while providing for human freedom, 'requires the framing of an economic constitution. The problem will not solve itself simply by our letting economic systems grow up spontaneously. The history of the last century has shown this plainly enough. The economic system has to be consciously shaped.' (1950, p. 314)

This rejection of a reliance on spontaneous forces in the modern world contrasts, at least superficially, with Hayek's appeal to supposedly beneficent spontaneity and his condemnation of deliberate 'constructivism' (1978, pp. 3–22). According to Eucken the launching of the Social-Market Economy was and had to be an explicitly 'contructivist' act. In any case, as Henry Wallich emphasized, those 'whose principle is "the freer the better" and who reject any admixture of control as an adulteration cannot claim Germany's success as a proof of their doctrine' (1955, p. 18).

Eucken specially emphasized the duty of the state to combat cartels, which had earlier been allowed much too much scope in Germany. He did not specifically mention trade unions in this connection, but would certainly have opposed the unrestricted powers which labour cartels came to acquire in Britain. Regarding

monetary and stabilization policy Eucken was critical of Keynesian ideas and of full employment as a policy objective, though not
dogmatically so, as (unlike the Austrian economists) he had
supported proposals for government employment policies and
credit expansion in the desperate situation of 1931.

Others, besides Eucken and the Freiburg circle, notably
Professor Alfred Müller-Armack, worked out and fought for the
ideas on which the Social-Market Economy was based. Furthermore, in the ensuing years, the economic policies pursued in the
German Federal Republic by no means in all respects followed
Eucken's ideas.[3] But, as Professors Stolper and Roskamp put it,
Walter Eucken 'is justly considered the intellectual godfather of
the postwar German economic policy' (1979, p. 377). It seems
difficult to deny what the Swiss economist W. A. Jöhr affirmed just
after Eucken's death: 'Certainly very few economists have, on a
similar scale, achieved such immediate success with regard to
economic policy' (1950, p. 277).

Thus, if the ideas of economists contributed significantly to the
economic success of the German Federal Republic after 1948,
then, surely, among the essential components of this contribution
were the breadth of vision and the undogmatic quality which
inspired the work of Eucken, Müller-Armack, and their colleagues. In turn these drew, to a significant extent, on the ideas
and approach of the historical school. For though Eucken
criticized severely and discerningly the defects and excesses of
'*Historismus*', he ascribed a much fuller role to the historical and
institutional aspects of economic problems than for the most part
(except for Alfred Marshall and one or two others) did those who
followed the main lines of Anglo-American orthodoxy. For his
idea of the '*Wirtschaftsordnung*' and his concern with different kinds
of 'economic order', Eucken was much indebted to historical
economists.[4]

V

Little interest seems to have been shown by American and British
economists in the economic experiment in Germany in and after
1948. Hardly a handful of articles are to be found on the subject of
the German economy in the leading British and American journals
in the late 1940s and early fifties. In Britain and, to a lesser extent,
in the United States, the most widely propagated doctrines on

economic policy contrasted sharply with those which inspired the infant Social-Market Economy in Germany. Therefore, most of the comment forthcoming in Britain and the USA tended to be suspicious, disapproving, pessimistic, or outright condemnatory. Policies in Germany, it was suggested, were based on obsolete, outmoded economic ideas which had been superseded by those prevailing in enlightened circles in Britain and America.

Among leading economists writing in the leading journals in Britain and America only Professors Friedrich Lutz and Gottfried Haberler seem to have expressed enthusiasm for the remarkable initial economic success in Germany in 1948–9 (and, of course Lutz was a product of the Freiburg school). Lutz maintained regarding the current reform:

Germany is thus returning to the classical methods of monetary policy. As she is also returning as far as possible to a free market economy, we witness the remarkable spectacle of a country whose economy had been paralysed by a lost war and its aftermath, attempting reconstruction by organising its economy according to the 'old fashioned' precepts of the classical economists, and doing so on the whole with marked success. (1949, p. 131)

Gottfried Haberler, a month or two later, was even more enthusiastic:

A truly spectacular example of what can be achieved by liberal economic policies is the amazing improvement that has taken place in Germany since June 1948. . . . The potency of liberal policies, of what Lord Keynes has called 'the classical medicine' has once again been dramatically demonstrated by the recent German events. This is the more important because this test was made under most difficult circumstances. (1949, p. 437)

However, the majority of economists in Britain and America who discussed the subject advocated very different policies from the 'out-of-date' ones pursued in Germany after June 1948. For example, F. A. Burchardt and K. Martin of the Oxford University Institute of Statistics had recommended (Dec. 1947) a much more extensive apparatus of controls to deal with suppressed inflation:

The most promising alternative approach would probably be for public authorities to lay their hands on as large a part of current industrial output as is possible and so to prevent production from being absorbed outside official channels. That is, public trading agencies might be set up which would buy part of the output of certain industries and sell it in the controlled market. (1947, p. 414)

According to these Oxford economists shortages of manpower would not present a problem in setting up a much vaster bureaucratic apparatus, which, in fact, would contribute to reducing the unemployment problem: 'In view of the surplus of clerical labour in Germany the difficulties of introducing such a scheme should not be exaggerated' (p. 413).

According to Messrs Burchardt and Martin, a stronger central government was the first essential for more successful economic policy-making in Germany. Their recipe against suppressed inflation was reinforced controls: 'There should be more scope than there is now for new measures to stimulate output for direct attacks on costs once the controls – both physical and fiscal – are reinforced in a reformed price system' (p. 416).

A year after the currency reform a notable analysis of the problems of the German economy was given in the *American Economic Review* by Dr H. Mendershausen. Dr Mendershausen recognized the remarkable results of the currency reform: 'The effect of the monetary and economic measures was impressive. If the Rentenmark of 1923 performed a miracle, the Deutsche Mark of 1948 may be said to have wrought a revolution.' (1949, p. 646) But he was highly critical and pessimistic regarding the future. First the 'rigid approach to fiscal policy appears like the ghost that Keynes laid' and showed 'an extreme distrust of public authorities'. Secondly a sharpening of economic inequalities in 1948–49 'put the stamp of inequity on the recovery process and invited irresponsibility and conflict' (pp. 661–2). Dr Mendershausen recognized that it was Professor Erhard's policy 'to make the new markets the vehicle of recovery and to wait for a larger aggregate of income to soften the impact of growing inequality' (p. 662). But Dr Mendershausen was not prepared to wait. (In fact, it is surely extremely doubtful whether any rapid, general upsurge of production can reasonably be expected, starting from abysmally low levels, if *no* increase in inequality whatsoever, even a quite temporary one, is permitted.)

A symposium on economic policy in Germany was held at the meeting of the American Economic Association in December 1949. None of the speakers expressed any optimism or approval regarding the policies then being pursued in the Federal Republic. Professor Walter Heller (subsequently to become Chairman of the Council of Economic Advisers under President Kennedy) criticized the absence of fiscal policies and the inequalities that had emerged, and quoted Dr Mendershausen on the latter point. Regarding fiscal policy he foresaw that a 'greater risk of persistent deflation' might discourage investment and production. Professor Heller concluded: 'The positive use of fiscal and monetary measures to which the foregoing analysis points is, to be sure, not in full harmony with the orthodox, free-market policies espoused by the current administration of the West German Federal Republic' (1950, p. 547).

One of the most significant passages in the symposium came from one of the discussants, Dr D. D. Humphrey, who stated, in terms of broad principle, the case against the German experiment:

It was the failure of the market to limit the growth of inequality which led to its undoing. The phenomenal increase in wealth which the system created was eclipsed by the growth of inequality. Man's sense of well-being is measured by comparison with his contemporaries rather than his ancestors. The result of the extension of democracy from politics to economics is the socialism of the welfare state. But equality stops at the frontier with the inevitable result that socialism within the nation has produced nationalism between nations. This is the period of social nationalism. (1950, p. 571)

Though Dr Humphrey's statement provided a plausible and profound analysis of the apparently irresistible forces and tides opposed to a revival of market economies, he seemed to be implying an over-pessimistic estimate of the power of the German Social-Market Economy to overcome those forces and tides.

The most remarkable denunciation of the infant Social-Market Economy came in an article and pamphlet, both published in 1950, by Dr T. Balogh of Oxford – later, after 1964, to become Economic Adviser to the government of Sir Harold Wilson, and to be ennobled as Lord Balogh. Dr Balogh began by pointing to the extreme contrast between the economic ideas and policies which were prevailing in the German Federal Republic and the policies and ideas dominant in Britain. He denounced the British authorities in Germany for 'having given birth to an iniquitous new German economic and social system. . . . They were apparently completely unaware of the fact that this policy was certainly contrary to the spirit of the domestic policy of the Government they represented.' (1950b, pp. 8, 72) According to Dr Balogh 'the currency was reformed according to a wicked formula'. Moreover, the reform 'helped to weaken the Trade Unions. . . . Their weakness may even inhibit increases in productivity, since large scale investment at high interest does not pay at the present low relative level of wages.' (pp. 6–7)

According to Dr Balogh, these policies could not be sustained, because production was geared to a particular distribution of income: 'In the long run this income pattern will become intolerable and this productive pattern unsafe. Both will have to be readjusted. When the attempt is made to recreate mass demand and to wrench the productive system into another shape, a serious crisis and terrible social costs will be inevitable.' (pp. 6–7) 'In order to enforce efficiency', statutory controls and 'some physical control of investment will also prove inevitable' (pp. 62–3). Meanwhile, Dr Erhard and his 'satellite economists' and 'experts' are trying to discredit 'enlightened Keynesian economic policy' (p. 68). In fact, according to Dr Balogh, the German government had been relying on completely outmoded and erroneous economic theories. It had 'tried to apply to real life an abstract, obsolescent and internally inconsistent economic theory and certainly did not succeed' (1950a, p. 95).

Above all, Dr Balogh emphasized the alarming political consequences which would result from the free-market policies then being pursued in Germany: 'The danger of present policy is that it will first provoke dangerous extremes of political temper and will then be abandoned for internal or international reasons' (1950a, p. 97).

According to Dr Balogh: 'Nothing but fast reform by free men can prevent the Western Germans from deserting political moderation for the militant extremes of right and left. Time, and a near example, are working against the West if nothing changes' (1950b, p. 65).

Dr Balogh pointed to 'a final warning in the gain which the Soviet Zone of Germany has been able to record'. According to Dr Balogh, the Allied authorities 'in this appalling repetition of history' had made the same mistakes as their predecessors when faced by Hitler in the thirties: 'As in the 1930s the Allies are about to vindicate those Germans who believe that "firmness" and the insatiability of demands towards foreigners pays handsomely' (1950b, pp. 65–70). (Presumably Dr Balogh was referring here to

Professors Eucken and Müller–Armack as well as Dr Erhard.)[5]

Finally an example may be cited of English views regarding some of the leading ideas behind the Social-Market Economy as expressed in an anonymous review of Walter Eucken's, *Foundations* in the typical 'Establishment' weekly, *The Times Literary Supplement*. In a discussion of Eucken's work under the heading 'Economics under the Nazis',[6] it was observed, with questionable accuracy, that Eucken was:

the leader of the neo-liberal (though not wholly *laissez-faire*) school of economics in Germany. As the most influential member of the Economic Advisory Council of the Western German Government he bore a considerable share of the responsibility for the policy of decontrol and deflation pursued in that country which resulted in mass unemployment and a degree of social inequality unparalleled even under the Nazis. (Anon., 1950)

The expert in *The Times Literary Supplement* concluded that no one in England had anything to learn from Eucken and that his book 'completely falls to the ground for use at British universities'. Obviously, the ideas that were helping to provide the theoretical foundations for the German Social-Market Economy had nothing to contribute, as far as English economists were concerned, to any problems which *their* economy might have to face.

Fortunately we need not end this chapter on such a depressed and depressing level. Mention should certainly be made, in conclusion, of Egon Sohmen's discerning account of the progress of the Social-Market Economy, nearly a decade later, by which time a significant measure of success could be claimed for it. Sohmen noted that 'West Germany's impressive recovery took place under policies that were in many respects the direct antithesis of post-Keynesian prescriptions for rapid economic growth' (1959, p. 989).[7] He emphasized that 'few other countries have pursued a hard-money policy with similar determination' (p. 989), observing that the level of unemployment in the early years was seriously raised by the influx of ten million refugees, together with the destruction of equipment on a larger scale than in other countries. He pointed to the important lesson: 'The constancy of the employment level precisely during those years when West Germany's national product was rising most rapidly also illustrates how relatively unimportant for the level of production full employment of the labour force may occasionally be as compared to its efficient allocation.'

Sohmen also indicated another lesson (of special significance for the English economy) with regard to the harmful activities of trade unions: 'A thoroughgoing re-examination of the economic role of unions in a full-employment economy is long overdue. . . . To accommodate union pressure by permitting creeping inflation does not seem to help matters' (p. 998). Finally, with regard to the current orthodoxies Sohmen presciently maintained:

We may tend to smugness about the progress economics has made during the past few decades. If performance in the real world is a criterion, the success of a country whose government has systematically disregarded some of the most widely accepted doctrines of recent vintage should give us pause. . . .

By and large, few signs of revolt against the entrenched authority of post-Keynesian thinking can as yet be detected among economists in the Anglo-Saxon countries in spite of the incontrovertible evidence of something rotten in the body of doctrine that constitutes the orthodoxy of today. (pp. 1000, 1002)

It is noteworthy that just as policy in Germany never suffered from the more extreme and dogmatic forms of 'Keynesian' fiscalism – as Britain has – so, subsequently, it has not been affected by the more extreme and oversimplified forms of monetarism.

VI

At the launching of the Social-Market Economy its opponents, or critics, representative of a broad spectrum of the conventional wisdom among British and American economists of the day, had maintained that this experiment, running against the tide of opinion and history, would fail both in terms of production and distribution, in particular with regard to social welfare and the standard of living of the lower paid. As we have seen, it was even asserted that the East German planned economy might forge ahead. (We are not concerned here with political implications, but these would certainly have been catastrophic for the whole Western World, if the Social-Market Economy had failed.) When, however, the economic success, in terms of the usual quantitative indicators, of the German Federal Republic became obviously undeniable, both in relation to any previous performance, and in relation to the contemporary performances of other comparable countries, then the Social-Market Economy was accused of fostering 'materialism' and the new vice of 'consumerism'. Let us repeat that we are simply concerned here with 'success' in terms of the usual economic indicators.

We quoted earlier J. S. Mill's statement that ideas have 'in general no very rapid or immediate efficacy in human affairs' unless 'outward circumstances conspire with them'. However, Mill added that 'the most favourable outward circumstances may pass by, or remain inoperative, for want of ideas suitable to the conjuncture. But when the right circumstances and the right ideas meet, the effect is seldom slow in manifesting itself.' (1845, p. 503) We would conclude that in 1948 there were German economists who ensured that 'the right ideas' were on hand to meet 'the right circumstances', and that the 'effect' was not 'slow in manifesting itself'.[8]

Notes

1   One anonymous authority maintained regarding Keynes's *General Theory*: 'It is a direct result of his apparently remote and theoretical reflections that governments since the war have known how, by influencing the level of demand in an economy, to abolish the spectre of mass unemployment' (*Everyman's Encyclopaedia*, 1967).

2   As Schäffle asked and argued:

How would the requirements for different kinds of goods be ascertained under the closed and unified system of production of the socialists? . . . The freedom to decide on one's own needs is surely the fundamental basis of all freedom. . . . We must point out that, as at present formulated, socialism still does not indicate how such an immense collective quantity of labour and capital would be organised so as to bring all the units into useful employment. . . . What are the criteria according to which labour is to be distributed throughout the broad field of production? Will it consent to be moved around, resettled, and retrained by economic bureaucrats? . . . Any advantages will turn into their opposites in a mechanically organised system of forced labour, if freedom of individual movement is not fully preserved. . . . If every one had their needs laid down by a central authority then such a state would represent the apogee of slavery and boredom.'

Lujo Brentano, one of the founders of the *Verein für Sozialpolitik*, deployed similar arguments to those of Schäffle:

Errors of calculation will occur just as much under "a planned direction of production" as they would under free private enterprise. Indeed, if human nature did not undergo a radical change, these errors in calculation under a planned direction of production, would be far more frequent. For however large the number of officials one may conceive a country to be covered with, whose sole duty it would be to ascertain quantitatively and qualitatively the different requirements at different points, such 'consumers' councils' will never have the same interest in directing production in accordance with consumers' tastes as would the free private entrepreneur whose whole economic existence depends on fulfilling this function correctly.

Erwin Nasse was still more emphatic:

A planned direction of production *without* free choice of goods and jobs would not be inconceivable, but would bring with it a destruction of culture and everything that makes life worth living. To combine a planned direction of all economic activity *with* free choice of goods and jobs is a problem which can only be compared with that of the squaring of the circle. For if everyone is allowed to decide freely the direction and nature of his economic activities and his consumption, then the direction of the economy as a whole is lost.

These quotations from Schäffle, Brentano and Nasse are taken from Hutchison, 1953, pp. 294–8, where much lengthier extracts are given. See Schäffle (1875), English translation 1889 pp. 90–5; and Schäffle (1881), vol. 3, pp. 469ff. See also Brentano, 1878, p. 119; Nasse, 1879, p. 164.

3 See Blum, 1969, on the contrasts between '*Neoliberalismus*' and '*Ordoliberalismus*'.

4 As Friedrich Lutz has observed regarding Eucken: 'His academic training followed, in the first instance, the lines of the historical school. These years were very far from wasted for him. What was best in the historical school he absorbed as part of his intellectual make-up: that is, the urgent concern with the real world.' (See Eucken, 1952, pp. 192–3.)

5 Professor Haberler has called attention to a further example of 'conventional wisdom', from J. K. Galbraith who concluded: 'There never has been the slightest possibility of getting German recovery by the wholesale repeal' [of controls, regulations and bureaucracy] (1948, p. 95).

6 For a scholarly account of some aspects of 'Economics under the Nazis' see Blumenberg-Lampe, 1973. See also Wallich, 1955, p. 114–5, who writes of Eucken and the Freiburg school: 'During the Nazi period the school represented a kind of intellectual resistance movement, requiring great personal courage as well as independence of mind'.

7   Sohmen added as a footnote the entirely justified explanation:

The use of the term 'post-Keynesian' rather than 'Keynesian' throughout this essay was prompted by our conviction that Keynes would not have been too eager to identify himself with some of the ideas for which the authority of his name has been appropriated. The disregard of resource allocation, the neglect of international repercussions of domestic policies, the acceptance or even advocacy of creeping inflation, to name only a few characteristics of an important segment of the post-Keynesian school seem anathema to Keynes' economic philosophy. (p. 1000 n)

In fact Heinrich Dräger, who, in Germany in 1932, had put forward employment policies like those of Keynes in his *Arbeitsbeschaffung durch produktive Kreditschöpfung*, may well have been much nearer the mark than English 'Keynesians' when he claimed in 1976: 'Today the Federal Republic of Germany is the leading country in respect of rightly understood Keynesian policies. Certainly this is a new form of Keynesianism, less concerned with the regulation of the business cycle and with fighting business crises. Today it is growth and structural problems which are important.' (See Bombach *et al.*, ed., 1976, vol. 2, p. 321; and also our preceding chapter.)

8   In the *Cambridge Journal of Economics*, March 1979, in an article on 'Economic Theory and Policy Making in West Germany', Mr C. C. Roberts points out that considerable influence on policy in the German Federal Republic has been exercised by the Council of Economic Experts, constituted in 1963, and that 'the policy advocated by the C.E.E. is based on the neoclassical theory of price determination and resource allocation', and on the view that 'the role of the state is thus to ensure the smooth operation of market forces', with 'some contribution in certain circumstances from Keynesian measures' (pp. 83–4). It would be difficult to draw up a better founded or more glowing testimonial to the 'Neoclassical Synthesis' and 'Bastard Keynesianism'. However, Mr Roberts concentrates on showing that from 1974 to 1977 the neoclassical advice of the C.E.E. was followed by a serious fall in the rate of growth and a rise in unemployment to four per cent. The world oil crisis (a special difficulty for the G.F.R.) is not mentioned, nor the fact that even in these difficult years, the West German economy was performing much better than the British economy, with its neo-Keynesian advisers *and* North Sea oil.

References

Addison, P. (1975), *The Road to 1945*.
Anon. (1950), 'Economics under the Nazis', in *Times Literary Supplement*, vol. 49, p. 729.

Balogh, T. (1950a), 'Germany, an Experiment in "Planning" by the "Free" Price Mechanism', *Banca Nazionale di Lavoro Quarterly Review*, no. 3, pp. 71–102.

(1950b), *Germany: an Experiment in 'Planning' by the 'Free' Price Mechanism*.

Blum, R. (1969), *Soziale Marktwirtschaft*.

Blumenberg-Lampe, C. (1973), *Das Wirtschaftpolitische Programm der Freiburger Kreise*.

Bombach, G. *et al.*, ed. (1976), *Der Keynesianismus,* 2 vols.

Brentano, L. (1878), 'Die Arbeiter und die Produktionskrisen', *Jahrbuch für Gesetzgebung, Verwaltung und Volkswirtschaft im Deutschen Reich*, Zweiter Jahrgang, Drittes Heft, pp. 109–76.

Burchardt, F. A. and Martin, K. (1947), 'Western Germany and Reconstruction', *Bulletin of the Oxford University Institute of Statistics*, no. 9, pp. 405–16.

Dräger, H. (1976), in Bombach *et al.* (ed.), 1976, vol. 2.

Eucken, W. (1948), 'On the Theory of the Centrally Administered Economy: An Analysis of the German Experiment', translated by T. W. Hutchison, *Economica*, vol. 15, pp. 79–100, 173–93.

(1950), *The Foundations of Economics*, translated by T. W. Hutchison.

(1951), *This Unsuccessful Age*.

(1952), *Grundsätze der Wirtschaftspolitik,* ed. E. Eucken-Erdsiek and K. P. Hensel.

Everyman's Encyclopaedia (1967), 'Economic Thought, History of'.

Galbraith, J. K. (1948), 'The German Economy', in S. E. Harris (ed.), *Foreign Economic Policy for the US*, pp. 91ff.

Haberler, G. (1949), 'Economic Aspects of a European Union', *World Politics*, vol. 1, pp. 431–41.

Hayek, F. A. (1944 and 1962), *The Road to Serfdom*, Phoenix edition, 1962.

(1978), *New Studies in Philosophy, Politics, Economics and the History of Ideas*.

Heller, W. W. (1950), 'The Role of Fiscal-Monetary Policy in German Economic Recovery', *American Economic Review, Papers and Proceedings*, vol. 40, pp. 531–47.

Horwitz, M. J. (1976), 'The Legacy of 1776 in Legal and Economic Thought', *Journal of Law and Economics*, vol. 19, Oct., pp. 621ff.

Humphrey, D. D. (1950), in Discussion on 'Economic Policy in Germany', *American Economic Review, Papers and Proceedings*, vol. 40, pp. 569–72.

Hutchison, T. W. (1953), *A Review of Economic Doctrines 1870–1929*.

(1968), *Economists and Economic Policy in Britain 1946–1966*.

(1977), *Knowledge and Ignorance in Economics*.

(1978a), 'Friedrich Engels and Marxist Economic Theory', *Journal of Political Economy*, vol. 86, pp. 303–19.

(1978b), *Revolutions and Progress in Economic Knowledge*.

Jöhr, W. A. (1950), 'Walter Euckens Lebenswerk', *Kyklos*, vol. 4, pp. 257–78.

Keynes, J. M. (1936), *The General Theory of Employment, Interest and Money*.

Lutz, F. A. (1949), 'The German Currency Reform and the Revival of the German Economy', *Economica*, vol. 16, pp. 122–42.

Mendershausen, H. (1949), 'Prices, Money and the Distribution of Goods in Postwar Germany', *American Economic Review*, vol. 39, pp. 646–72.

(1950), 'Fitting Germany into a Network of World Trade', *American Economic Review, Papers and Proceedings*, vol. 40, pp. 548–67.

Mill, J. S. (1845), 'The Claims of Labour', *Edinburgh Review*, vol. 81, no. 164, pp. 498–525.

(1909), *The Principles of Political Economy*, ed. W. J. Ashley.

Nasse, E. (1879), 'Uber die Verhütung der Produktionskrisen durch staatliche Fürsorge', *Jahrbuch für Gesetzgebund, Verwaltung und Volkswirtschaft im Deutschen Reich*, Dritter Jahrgang, Erstes Heft, pp. 145–89.

Roberts, C. C. (1979), 'Economic Theory and Policy Making in West Germany', *Cambridge Journal of Economics*, vol. 3, no. 1, Mar., pp. 83ff.

Robinson, E. A. G. (1967), *Economic Planning in the United Kingdom*.

Schäffle, A. (1875), *Die Quintessenz des Sozialismus*; English translation, 1889.

(1881), *Bau und Leben des Sozialen Körpers*.

Senior, N. W. (1878), *Conversations with M. Thiers, M. Guizot and Other Distinguished Persons During the Second Empire*, ed. M. C. M. Simpson.

Sohmen, E. (1959), 'Competition and Growth: the Lesson of West Germany', *American Economic Review*, vol. 49, pp. 986–1003.

Stolper, W. F. and Roskamp, K. W. (1979), 'Planning a Free Economy', *Zeitschrift für die gesamte Staatswissenschaft*, vol. 135, part 3, Sept., pp. 373–404.

Wallich, H. C. (1955), *The Mainsprings of the German Revival*.

6

Carl Menger on Philosophy
and Method

I

Menger's *Untersuchungen über die Methode*, translated (1963) as *Problems of Economics and Sociology*,[1] appeared in 1883, twelve years after the *Grundsätze*. It is a book of a very different kind.[2] Whereas the *Principles* have a classic, definitive (or relatively definitive) quality, the '*Problems*', though containing arguments of the widest general significance, are mainly related to a particular intellectual controversy which had been raging in Germany and Austria during the intervening years.

The *Problems* have two aspects: First they are a critique of, or a polemic against, the aims and methods of historical economics in Germany, as these had developed between the 1840s and the 1870s. This theme or purpose is forcefully announced in the Preface and it recurs throughout the volume, providing the principal unifying thread which holds together the wide and varied range of philosophical and methodological ideas and arguments developed in the four 'books' and thirteen appendices. In fact, in histories of economic thought the place often ascribed to the *Problems* is that of constituting the opening barrage in the *Methodenstreit*.

On the other hand, however, there is in the *Problems* this wide and varied range of ideas and arguments, which, though pointed by Menger more or less directly towards his primary polemical theme, can be discussed, and discussed with some advantage, separately and in detachment from their original controversial setting. Accordingly this account begins by looking at one or two of Menger's most important ideas, before turning briefly later to their controversial setting. We, therefore, take first the ideas in book I about the nature of economic theory and economic laws, and then his ideas in book III about 'organic' social phenomena or processes, whereby individual actions bring about unintended or unforeseen social consequences. Account must also be taken of important arguments on philosophy and method which are to be found in other writings of Menger, both before and after the *Problems*, which seem to indicate some changes of view (for example, with regard to the work of Wilhelm Roscher, the leader of the older historical school).

II

Menger devotes the first 'book' of his *Problems* to explaining and justifying his conception of political economy as a theoretical subject. He starts by distinguishing between 'two great classes of scientific knowledge', the 'individual' and the 'general' (or theoretical). This distinction is, of course, essential. But rather than simply to distinguish, Menger seems sometimes to suggest the *separation* of the two types of knowledge, whereas surely the more important methodological questions relate rather to how general and individual propositions are in different ways *combined*, in historical explanations on the one hand, and in the application of 'general' theories to particular cases, on the other.

As to Menger's conception of 'general' theoretical knowledge, two points may be made.

The first concerns the role that Menger sees for it in prediction and control. He emphasizes that: 'All human prediction and, indirectly, all arbitrary shaping of things depends on that knowledge which we have previously called *general*' (1963, p. 36). Menger is thus putting a significant stress on prediction as an (or the) aim of the theoretical economist, in so far as this aim consists in contributing to policy-making, and it would have been most interesting if he had gone further into the question of predictions in economics, and of just how they can be, and are, arrived at. Menger rightly emphasizes the essential role of general propositions in propounding disciplined predictions. But crucial questions about the validity and reliability of predictions arise out of the nature and content of the general propositions from which they can be derived in economics and the social sciences.

The second point, on the other hand, which may be noticed, is that Menger's conception of economic theory *seems* to be highly anti-nominalist, or even 'essentialist', a conception which would not probably be widely held today. But it may be noted that Menger rejects *a priori* axioms and theorems deduced from them:

Theoretical economics has the task of studying the *general nature* (*das generelle Wesen*) and the *general inter-connections* of economic phenomena, not of analyzing economic *concepts* and of drawing the logical conclusions resulting from this analysis. The phenomena, or certain aspects of them, and not their linguistic image, the concepts, are the object of theoretical research in the field of economics. . . . It is a sign of the slight understanding, which individual representatives of the historical school in particular have for the aims of theoretical research, when they see only *analyses of concepts* in investigations into the nature of the commodity, into the nature of economy, the nature of value, of price and the like, and when they see 'the setting up of a system of concepts and judgements' in the striving for an exact theory of economic phenomena. A number of French economists fall into a similar error when, with an erroneous view of the concepts 'theory' and 'system', they understand by these terms nothing more than theorems obtained deductively from a priori axioms, or systems of these. (1963, p. 37n)[3]

It is here that what has been described as the basic Aristotelianism of Menger's philosophy seems to show itself, which seems to resemble closely what Sir Karl Popper calls 'methodological essentialism'.[4] As Sir Karl describes it:

The school of thinkers whom I propose to call *methodological essentialists* was founded by Aristotle, who taught that scientific research must penetrate to the essence of things in order to explain them. Methodological essentialists are inclined to formulate scientific questions in such terms as 'what is matter?' or 'what is force?' or 'what is justice?' and they believe that a penetrating answer to such questions, revealing the real or essential meaning of these terms and thereby the real or true nature of the essences denoted by them, is at least a necessary prerequisite of scientific research, if not its main task. (1961, pp. 28–9)

Paradoxically, Popper is concerned with 'essentialism' because be believes that 'it furnishes in its turn some of the most powerful arguments in support of the doctrine that the social sciences must adopt a historical method; that is to say, in support of the doctrine of historicism' (1961, p. 34). But Menger apparently holds that *general* theoretical inquiry is, or should be, concerned with *das Wesen* of economic phenomena, as are his 'exact' method and laws. His rejection of mutual interdependence and of mathematical methods seems to have been rooted in the same classical philosophical attitude. It has been suggested that there is some logical or psychological connection between individualism and philosophical nominalism on the one hand, and, on the other hand, between collectivism and philosophical essentialism. This pattern hardly seems to hold in the case of Carl Menger (cf. Hayek, 1949, p. 6n).

The question of the nature of economic laws, if there are any propositions that really deserve this name, is central to all questions of what economists do, can do, should try to do, or of how they should try to do it, and we therefore turn to Menger's conception of economic laws. This is based on a distinction between what he calls laws of nature, which he renames 'exact' laws, and, on the other hand, 'empirical' laws. Again the distinction is vital and fundamental, and still often not kept sufficiently clear, between analytical propositions of 'pure theory', not testable empirically, and, on the other hand, testable or falsifiable empirical generalizations. But serious questions arise regarding each type and, in particular, as to whether *either* type of proposition, as described by Menger, can suitably be regarded as a 'law', or provide the basis for 'scientific' predictions.

Menger's 'exact' laws do not merely state regularities to which there are in fact no exceptions: they are in principle unfalsifiable. They are laws 'which are not only without exceptions (*ausnahmslos*), but according to our laws of thinking *simply cannot be thought of in any other way but as without exceptions*' (1963, p. 61, italics added).

In fact, it is irrelevant and misconceived to attempt to test 'exact' laws empirically (and, of course, theoretical economics is an 'exact science'):

Testing the exact theory of economy by the full empirical method is simply a methodological absurdity, a failure to recognize the bases and presuppositions of exact research. At the same time it is a failure to recognize the particular aims which the exact sciences serve. To want to test the pure theory of economy by experience in its full reality is a process analogous to that of the mathematician who wants to correct the principles of geometry by measuring real objects. . . . (p. 69)

On the other hand, *empirical* laws are laws to which exceptions are possible or may actually exist: in fact, exceptions *must* be 'possible' in respect of laws about human activities, Menger later explains, because of freedom of the will:

We admit quite unreservedly that *real* human phenomena are not strictly typical. We admit that just for this reason, and also as a result of the freedom of the human will – and we, of course, have no intention of denying this as a practical category – *empirical laws of absolute strictness* are out of the question in the realm of the phenomena of human activity. (p. 214)

On the other hand, freedom of the will does not apparently detract from the 'exactness' of 'exact' laws, and while these are not empirically testable, Menger's Aristotelian essentialism, as we have seen, precludes the possibility of their consisting simply of conceptual analysis. While 'exact' laws follow logically, by deduction, from conditions or assumptions, 'empirical' laws are stated unconditionally.

As an example we may take Menger's treatment of the relationship between an increase in demand and a rise in price, that is, 'the law of demand', as it is often called. For Menger there are two analogous laws of demand: an 'exact' law of demand and an 'empirical' law. He writes:

The law that a rise in the need (*Bedarf*) for a good results in a rise in price, and indeed that a rise in the need for a particular quantity also results in a rise in price determined according to this quantity, is not true – is unempirical, when tested by reality in its full complexity. But what else does this prove than that the results of exact research do not find their criterion in experience in the above sense? The above law is, in spite of everything, true, completely true, and of the highest significance for the theoretical understanding of price phenomena, if one regards it from the standpoint which is appropriate for exact research. . . . (1963, pp. 71–2)

'Exact' laws, Menger goes on, are fundamentally different from 'empirical' laws and the difference is too easily overlooked because of 'a superficial similarity':

The exact law states that, on definite assumptions, an increase in demand, of a definite quantity, must be followed by an increase in prices of just as definite a quantity. The empirical law states that an increase in demand, *as a rule*, is actually followed by a rise in *real* prices. . . . The first law holds true for all times and for all nations when goods are exchanged; the latter is subject to exceptions, even within a particular nation, while the *size* of the effects of demand on prices differs widely, and can only be discovered by observations. (p. 72)

It must be emphasized that, for Menger, his 'exact' laws are not tautological, or purely logical, or mathematical. They possess *some* kind of essential, or even empirical content, but are not to be tested empirically – nor by purely logical or mathematical criteria. It is not clear how they can be tested at all, or how any conflicts or divergences arising between 'exact', essentialist laws or theories could be resolved, if both empirical and logical mathematical testing are ruled out as inadequate.

Now perhaps what is called 'the law of demand' has a better claim to the title of 'law' than any other pretender among the propositions of economics. But, if so, the law of demand can certainly not be regarded either as an 'exact' law, or as an 'empirical' law as *conceived by Menger*. A genuine 'law of demand', if we admit the term, must be somewhere between the two. A genuine law of demand, unlike Menger's 'exact' laws, must be testable or falsifiable, and it cannot be one that 'our laws of thought prevent us from thinking of in any other way but as absolute and with no exceptions'. On the other hand, unlike Menger's 'empirical' laws, a genuine law of demand will not be simply an unconditional generalization. Indeed, as Sir Karl Popper has said, the term empirical law 'is somewhat misleading' (1961, p. 120). In fact, today it seems desirable to recognize that there are *almost* no, and perhaps *absolutely* no, generalizations in economics that are safely and suitably, in the interests of clarity, to be described as 'laws'. This is, of course, not simply a verbal point. The term 'law' is misleading in economics not merely because it suggests a stricter and (in Popper's sense) more 'forbidding' proposition than almost any economic generalization can claim to be, but still more because it is applied indiscriminately to a varied range of propositions of differing types, some of which are themselves, individually, highly ambiguous, or varyingly inter-preted, such as Say's Law, Walras's Law, Engel's Law, the Law of Diminishing Returns, the Law of Demand, and so on. It has been said, not unjustifiably, that:

A typical law in the physical sciences is stated precisely, usually in mathematical terms, and is quite free of ambiguity. It has been tested repeatedly and has withstood the tests. The usual law in the social sciences, on the other hand, is ordinarily couched in Big Words and a great deal of ambiguity. (Kemeny, 1959, p. 244, quoted in Hutchison, 1964, p. 94)

In fact, Professor Hayek has come to reject the conception of law in the social sciences and doubts 'whether we know of any "laws" which social phenomena obey' (1967, p. 42). Moreover, for the purposes of prediction, recognized by Menger in his Preface, economic 'laws', in any reasonably precise sense, provide very little in the way of a basis, and economists and social scientists in fact predict, and necessarily so – if they are to attempt prediction – predominantly on the basis of extrapolating trends, or tendencies, or loose generalizations in terms of vague or subjective degrees of probability.

Mention should be made here of a very significant point regarding the fundamental assumptions of price theory to which Menger was one of the first theoretical economists to give some of the great emphasis that it deserves. It amounts to the most serious and fundamental of all the abstractions widely resorted to in microeconomic theorizing, the abstraction from ignorance and uncertainty. As Menger puts it:

Here we should like above all to point to a gap in the above line of argument which catches the eye of anyone to any extent familiar with psychological investigations. The circumstance that people are not guided exclusively by self-interest prohibits, in the above sense, the strict regularity of human action in general, and of economic action in particular – and thereby eliminates the possibility of a rigorous economic theory. But there is another factor, equally important, that does the same thing. I mean *error*, a factor which surely can be separated still less from human action than custom, public spirit, feeling for justice, and love of one's fellow man can be separated from the economy. Even if economic men always and everywhere let themselves be guided exclusively by their self-interest, the strict regularity of economic phenomena would none the less have to be considered impossible because of the fact, given by experience, that in innumerable cases they are in error about their economic interest, or in ignorance of economic conditions. Our historians are too lenient towards their scholarly opponents. The presupposition of a strict regularity in economic phenomena, and with this of a theoretical economics in the full meaning of the word, includes not only the dogma of ever-constant self-interest, but also the dogma of the 'infallibility' and 'omniscience' of men in economic matters. (1963, p. 84)

Later, in his Appendix VI, which has the rather challenging title: 'That the starting-point and final objective of all human economizing is strictly determined', Menger emphasizes further that 'exact' laws are limited in applicability to a special kind of infallible human behaviour:

Volition, error, and other influences can, on the contrary, and actually do, bring it about that human agents take different roads from a strictly given starting-point to a just as strictly determined goal of their action. On the other hand, it is certain that, under the above presuppositions, only *one* road can be the *most suitable*. . . . (p. 217)

The assumption of self-interest has, since Menger's day, been reduced to one of consistency. But the exclusion of ignorance and error largely remains as a vast simplification and limitation. In emphasizing this assumption of correct knowledge, and the exclusion of ignorance and error, Menger was taking the first step towards the opening up of the analysis of expectations – correct or fulfilled, or incorrect and disappointed – and their relation to equilibrium and disequilibrium, that is, he was attempting a step towards a kind of dynamic analysis. *But in doing so he was admitting that his 'exact' laws had a very limited applicability to actual economic behaviour and its prediction.* Menger seemed to restrict 'exact' laws, or the very possibility of such laws, explicitly to a kind of optimizing or maximizing calculus and he seemed to admit the seriously restrictive nature of the abstraction involved here when he implied that the historical critics had been too forbearing regarding the limitations of economic theory.[5]

III

Book III of the *Problems* is about 'The Organic Understanding of Social Phenomena', and is devoted to Menger's discussion of how some social institutions have developed in a spontaneous, unplanned way, and have come unintentionally, but none the less effectively and beneficently, to serve important social functions. (Incidentally, it was particularly because of its contribution to this subject that the recent English translation of the *Problems* was undertaken.)

Menger argues that as with processes of nature:

Similarly we can observe in numerous social institutions a strikingly apparent functionality with respect to the whole. But on closer examination they nevertheless do not prove to result from an *intention aimed at this purpose*, i.e., the result of an agreement by members of society, or of positive legislation. They, too, present themselves to us as 'natural' products (in a certain sense), as *unintended results of historical development*. One needs, for example, only to think of the phenómenon of money, an institution which to so great an extent serves the welfare of society, and yet in by far the majority of nations is by no means the result of an agreement directed at establishing it as a social institution, or of positive legislation, but is the unintended product of historical development. One needs only to think of law, of language, of the origin of markets, the origin of communities and of states, etc. (1963, p. 130)

Menger asks: 'How can it be that institutions which serve the common welfare, and are extremely significant for its development, come into being without a common will directed towards establishing them?' (p. 163)

What Menger seems to be envisaging partly coincides with Adam Smith's 'hidden hand', by the operation of which, individuals narrowly pursuing their own self-interest, unconsciously and unintentionally promote the wider social welfare. But Menger includes a much broader range of institutions and processes than those simply of competitive markets. Three points about Menger's arguments may be added here:

(1) First, Menger links closely the explanation of this kind of 'organic' social institution with his emphasis on what has come to be called 'methodological individualism', or 'the compositive method', as he himself called it: that is, on the need for explaining human behaviour and institutions in terms of individual motives and actions. Menger regards this as 'the most important task of the exact method of theoretical research':

Whoever wants to understand theoretically the phenomena of a 'national economy' and those complicated human phenomena which we are accustomed to designate with this expression, must for this reason attempt to go back to their *true* elements, to the *individual economies in the nation*, and to investigate the laws by which the former are built up from the latter. But whoever takes the opposite road fails to recognize the nature of 'national economy'. He starts off on the foundation of a fiction, but at the same time he fails to recognize the most important problem of the exact orientation of theoretical research, the problem of reducing complicated phenomena to their *elements*. (p. 93)

More recently the concept of 'methodological individualism' has been much argued over, but what Menger himself seems to have meant by his 'compositive' method contains a very relevant warning, today, regarding the explanatory value and validity of much 'positive' or pseudo-positive macroeconomic and macro-econometric model-building.

(2) Secondly, Menger's emphasis on the importance of the unintended consequences of individual actions obviously recognizes the extent of ignorance in human actions and even of error, though of what might be called errors of *o*mission rather than *com*mission. For Menger is concerned with consequences which were not consciously envisaged at all, and were outside the expectations or horizons of the actors altogether. He was not concerned with, or not so much with, particular consequences which have turned out differently from those explicitly envisaged or anticipated in people's *conscious* expectations or horizons. It is the ignorance of unawareness, or of unconsciousness, rather than of conscious explicit error, that Menger is here concerned with, and it is not simply that the particular individual actors are not aware of the consequences of their own and their fellow individuals' actions: nobody, including the rulers, or would-be rulers, is aware of what is happening or of the consequences.

But this unawareness to a considerable extent fades and dissolves with the growth of social and economic awareness in more selfconscious societies – whether they can be regarded as more informed or more misinformed. There has been not simply the growth of formal knowledge in the field of economics, but the beginnings of economic journalism, market reports, basic statistical series, etc. For better or for worse, there is less and less scope for unawareness (while there is more scope for knowledge and more scope for error). But there is certainly less and less scope for the kind of 'organic', unselfconscious behaviour and institutions, as social and economic knowledge, and its communication, grows and spreads; and these were growing rapidly in Menger's time. In fact it would seem that these 'organic' institutions cannot survive very long in the selfconscious 'electronic village' in which we live today. They, and the study of them, remain of importance for earlier societies, or those less developed in respect of social and economic awareness. But once this awareness and study has come into existence, however erroneous it may be, about any kind of social phenomena, decisions will be subject to deliberate, conscious, or 'planned' intervention.[6] To a large extent today, for a government, or other kind of decision-making body, consciously to leave alone and do nothing about some kind of social or economic phenomenon or institution, involves just as, or almost as, deliberate and purposive a decision as to intervene and regulate. Examples could be cited from the economic policies of British governments in both the early and late 1970s. But the point is most clearly demonstrated in the case of the major economic success story, in the Western world, of the decades after World War II, that of the 'Social-Market' Economy of the German Federal Republic. As Walter Eucken, one of the most influential of its intellectual founders, insisted, a free-market economy must today be just as consciously and deliberately constructed or 'planned' as some socialist experiment: 'The problem will not solve itself simply by our letting economic systems grow up spontaneously. . . . The economic system has to be consciously shaped' (1950, p. 31).

We would add, incidentally, that the assumption of a kind of passive ignorance essentially underlies the existence and operation of this kind of 'organic', unselfconscious behaviour or institution, and that Menger does not make it clear how this kind of ignorance is compatible with the assumption of 'omniscience', or 'infallibility', on which the use of his 'exact' method rests.

(3) The third point is that although Menger was critical of would-be reformers who failed to perceive or appreciate the possibly, or even frequently, beneficent workings of some originally spontaneous, unplanned social institutions, he was also critical of the unqualified conservative defence or exaltation, which he attributed to Burke, Savigny, and their followers, of such 'natural' institutions and processes. On the one hand, it is noteworthy that Menger is ready to sympathize with Burke and Savigny in their attacks on some forms of classical liberalism, but on the other hand, he is not prepared to join them in an attitude 'of simply maintaining that what had developed "organically" was unassailable, as if it were the higher wisdom in human affairs, as opposed to the deliberate ordering of social conditions' (1963, p. 233; see also 1935, p. 84). In fact Menger quotes these sentences of his in *Die Irrthümer des Historismus* when he rejects Schmoller's charges *both* on the one side, of what was then called '*Manchestertum*', or a kind of extreme economic liberalism, *and*, on the other side, of conservative 'mysticism'.

Menger goes on to praise, by way of contrast with Burke and Savigny, those German legal historians who had avoided:

that one-sidedness which we have seen as characterizing Burke's and Savigny's opposition to the rationalism and pragmatism of the French Age of Enlightenment. . . . Nowhere do they, like Burke, defend what already exists, what has developed historically, simply in opposition to the efforts at reform of their contemporaries. Nowhere, like Savigny, do they think that the wisdom in social institutions which have come about organically is *a priori*, and without sufficient proof, higher than human wisdom, i.e. higher than the judgement of the present. (1963, p. 181)

Menger later concludes:

But never, and this is the essential point in the question under review, may science dispense with testing for their suitability those institutions which have come about 'organically'. It must, when careful investigation so requires, change and better them according to the measure of scientific insight and the practical experience at hand. No era may renounce this duty. (1963, p. 234, italics added)

IV

It is in book III, 'On the Organic Understanding of Social Phenomena', that Menger compares the methods and materials of the natural and social sciences. But on this subject Menger's remarks in the Preface to this *Principles* must first be noted, where he goes a long way towards insisting on the similarity of methods. Regarding what he calls 'the empirical method' Menger maintains:

This method of research, attaining universal acceptance in the natural sciences, led to very great results, and on this account came mistakenly to be called the natural–scientific method. It is, in reality, a method common to all fields of empirical knowledge, and should properly be called the empirical method. (1950, p. 47)

However, as an Aristotelian, Menger goes on to insist that:

Every method of investigation acquires its own specific character from the nature of the field of knowledge to which it is applied. It would be improper, accordingly, to attempt a natural–scientific orientation of our science.

Past attempts to carry over the peculiarities of the natural–scientific method of investigation uncritically into economics have led to most serious methodological errors, and to idle play with external analogies between the phenomena of economics and those of nature. (p. 47)

Menger insists on the existence of economic laws: 'I wish to contest the opinion of those who question the existence of laws of economic behaviour by referring to human free will, since their argument would deny economics altogether the status of an exact science' (p. 48). Moreover he asserted a very close parallel between the relation of theory to practice in chemistry and in economics respectively: 'Economic theory is related to the practical activities of economizing men in much the same way that chemistry is related to the operations of the practical chemist' (p. 48).

In his *Problems* Menger continued to insist on fundamental similarities between the methods of the natural and social sciences, while retaining certain important qualifications arising out of the differences in material as between the two groups of sciences. According to Menger, natural and social sciences are alike dependent on the two 'methods' which he calls 'the empirical-realistic' and 'the exact'. But here Menger significantly emphasizes that the two must be *combined*:

> All theoretical understanding of phenomena can be the result of a double orientation of research, the *empirical-realistic* and the exact. . . . Only their combination can procure for us the deepest theoretical understanding of the phenomena considered here which is attainable in our age. (1963, p. 140)

In fact, Menger compares the methodological individualism, which he insists on for the social sciences, with the 'atomism' of the physical sciences. But at this point Menger does, in passing, put forward the claim for a great advantage of the social over the natural sciences, which was subsequently taken very much further, and developed much more pretentiously, by Wieser and other Austrians. Menger asserts, surely very questionably, that 'atoms' and 'forces' are not 'of an empirical nature' and goes on:

> From this there arise ultimately quite extraordinary difficulties for the exact interpretation of natural phenomena. It is otherwise in the exact social sciences. Here the human *individuals* and their *efforts*, the final elements of our analysis, are of empirical nature, and thus the exact theoretical social sciences have a great advantage over the exact natural sciences. The 'limits to the knowledge of nature' and the difficulties resulting from this for the theoretical understanding of natural phenomena do not really exist for exact research in the realm of social phenomena. (1963, p. 142n)

However, this rather pretentious claim only appears in a footnote. Subsequently in an appendix entitled 'In the Realm of Human Phenomena Exact Laws (So-called "Laws of Nature") can be Established under the Same Formal Presuppositions as in the Realm of Natural Phenomena', Menger concludes:

It is a pecularity of the exact social sciences that exact research in the realm of the phenomena of human activity starts with the assumption of a definite volitional orientation of the acting subjects. *This does not, however, establish an essential distinction between exact research in nature and exact social research, for the former starts with presuppositions which exhibit a formal analogy to the one under discussion here.* (p. 215n, italics added)

Carl Menger's emphasis on the similarities between the methods and criteria of the social and natural sciences differs profoundly from that of Wieser, Mises, and other Austrians, whose approach was much closer to that of German historical economists, such as Sombart, who insisted on the wide and profound *dis*similarities between the social and natural sciences.[7]

V

There is nothing, or very little, in the writings of previous economists to compare with Menger's discussion of 'organic' social phenomena and their unintended, unplanned, unconsciously arrived-at consequences. But as regards the nature of economic theorizing, or of theoretical political economy, Menger's account, some key points of which we have discussed already, is mostly in fairly close agreement with the conclusions that had been arrived at by Senior, or by Mill in his early essay 'On the Definition of Political Economy', or by Cairnes in his *Character and Logical Method of Political Economy.* (Nor do later expositors of the deductive method in economics, for example Mises and Robbins, depart *very* fundamentally from the general conceptions outlined in book I of Menger's *Problems.*) Of course, there are various interesting departures on secondary points. Certainly Menger's Aristotelian philosophical framework is not to be found in the English writers (however precisely this is to be interpreted, or however important or unimportant it is for his economic theories). There are also terminological differences, for example Menger's use of the term 'exact'. On the other hand, there is also Menger's profoundly important recognition of the assumption of *Unfehlbarkeit,* or *Allwissenheit,* which is, as we have noted, hardly to be found in the classical writers or, indeed in many writers after Menger, until comparatively recently.

However, in some respects Menger was very critical of the English classical economists. Anyhow, it was to a wrong-headed reaction to the intellectual position that the English classicals bequeathed, that Menger, in his Preface, traces back the confusions and errors of the German historical economists. Here is Menger's account:

The conflict of views about the nature of our science, its problems, and its limits, especially the effort to set new goals for research in the field of political economy, did not originally develop from the interest of economists in epistemological problems. It begins with the recognition, becoming more and more clear, that the theory of economics as it left the hands of Adam Smith and his followers lacks any assured basis, that even its most elementary problems have found no solution, and especially that it provides an insufficient basis for the practical sciences of political economy, and thus also for practical policies in this field. Even before the appearance of the historical school of German economists the conviction grew more and more that the previously prevailing belief in the perfection of our science was false, and that, on the contrary, the science needed a fundamental reconstruction. (1963, p. 27–8)

Menger goes on:

The theory of political economy, as in the main, the so-called classical school of English political economists formed it, has not been able to solve in a satisfactory way the problem of a science of the laws of economy. But the authority of its doctrine is a burden on us all and hinders progress in those directions on which the minds of researchers, long before the appearance of A. Smith, sought the solution of the great problem of establishing the foundations of the theoretical social sciences. (p. 29)

Later, in book IV, Menger sharply criticizes Adam Smith and his followers, as well as the conservative critics of English liberal ideas, such as Savigny, and he actually applies to both the identical critical adjective 'one-sided' (*einseitig*). Eleven years later again, in his obituary of Roscher, Menger writes approvingly of 'the historical-empirical reaction against the abstract, unempirical schematism (*Schematismus*) of particular disciples of A. Smith, as well as against the scientific representatives of 'Manchester liberalism' (*Manchestertums*) in the field of theoretical and practical economics in German' (1935, p. 276). Here Menger shows the considerable extent of the common political–philosophical ground he shared with the Germans.

Though he maintains that Smith and his followers had recognized the importance of the historical study of political economy, Menger sharply criticizes what he calls their *Pragmatismus,*[8]

which in the main had only an understanding for the *positive* creations of public authorities. It was, therefore, unable to understand and to value the significance of 'organic' social structures for society in general and for economic life in particular, and hence was nowhere concerned to *conserve* them. What characterises the theories of A. Smith and his followers is the one-sided rationalistic liberalism, the often impetuous drive to do away with what exists, or with what is not always sufficiently understood, and the equally impetuous pressure to create something new, frequently without adequate knowledge and experience.

Organically developed economic institutions had usually provided so wisely for the living, for what already existed, for what was close and immediate. 'Pragmatism' (*Pragmatismus*) in economics was concerned with the welfare of man in the abstract, with the remote, with what did not exist, with the future. In this striving, the living, and the justified interests of the present, were all too often overlooked. (1963, p. 177)

Menger concludes that this kind of 'pragmatism', as he calls it, 'against the intentions of its representatives, leads inevitably to socialism'. Certainly Menger's words have their relevance today for some of the more grandiose experiments of recent times in 'growth' planning. It is right also to emphasize, as Menger seems to suggest, that the creation of the classical market economy, as, for example, it was set up in Britain in the middle third of the 19th century, was a rational, large-scale reform, put through by political power (*öffentliche Gewalt*, or *positive Gesetzgebung*). But in the previous passage his criticism is hardly on target, as regards Adam Smith, at any rate, especially when he apparently sets him against Burke;[9] and Menger also seems to miss the mark when he goes on: 'In this one-sidedly pragmatic view of the nature of social institutions Adam Smith's ideas, and those of his closest disciples, are near to those of the writers of the French enlightenment and to those of the French Physiocrats in particular.' (1963, p. 172). Certainly this would apply to James Mill and Ricardo.

In passages like this Menger seems to be aligning himself with such critics of English classical political economy as Coleridge,

Sismondi (whom he approvingly mentions) and the German romantics. Anyhow, it is clear that Menger would have agreed with Jevons, rather than with Marshall, that the new analysis of value in 1871 was a necessary, fundamental and revolutionary departure, not merely an evolutionary shift of emphasis, as compared with the theory of the English classicals. But Menger's attitude to the English classicals is a finely balanced one, by no means 'one-sided', and it probably fluctuated over time. In his later essay of 1891 on 'The Social Theories of Classical Political Economy and Modern Economic Policy', Menger vigorously defends Smith and the classicals against charges of extreme *laissez-faire* and against the hostile attitude of contemporary historical economists and policy-makers in Germany (1935, pp. 219ff).

Finally, in the *Problems* Menger maintains that the reaction in Germany against the doctrines of the English classicals had been exaggerated and misconceived, in that it was thought and claimed that a completely new method had been discovered, or that a new direction (or *Richtung*) for political economy had been found in the historical method, which had been borrowed by a superficial analogy from the study of law and languages. He justifiably complained that this had had the result that theoretical research fell more and more into a decline with those who claimed a predominant, or even exclusive, position for the historical approach. This verdict has certainly been confirmed by such subsequent authorities as Wicksell, Schumpeter and Erich Schneider, who have examined the consequences of the German historical school and of the *Methodenstreit*.

VI

We come now to some more general aspects of the *Problems* and of the '*Methodenstreit*', as whose opening shot the book is often described in histories of economic thought.

As has been revealed by Professor Kauder (1962) from Menger's papers in Tokyo, the philosophy and method of economics and the social sciences was one of Carl Menger's earliest and deepest interests, from before the publication of the *Principles*, and from some time before his decision – whenever precisely he made it – to launch a fundamental and comprehensive attack on the methods of the historical school. In fact, Menger's economic theories and concepts in the *Principles* were deeply rooted in, and to some extent grew out of, and were shaped by, his philosophical and methodological ideas. But although some of the leading methodological ideas in the *Problems* can be discerned in the *Principles* there was certainly no inkling revealed in 1871 of the onslaught to be made twelve years later. On the contrary, Menger dedicated his first great work to Wilhelm Roscher, 'with respectful esteem', without the slightest hint of what, at the end of the *Problems*, he was to refer to as 'the methodological errors of the founder of the historical school of German economists which have done such harm to the development of our science and especially its theoretical side' (1963, p. 189; also 1935, p. 3).

Moreover, at the end of his Preface to the *Principles* Menger had gone so far as to claim:

It was a special pleasure for me that the general theories of the science, on which we have been working, have been to no small extent the product of recent developments in German political economy, and that the reform attempted here of the most general principles of our subject is therefore built on a foundation which has been laid almost entirely by the efforts of German researchers. (1950, p. xlviii)

In fact, in the extensive footnotes to the *Principles* it is German historical economists (and Aristotle) who are generally most frequently and most approvingly cited, though the great German contributors to economic analysis are very little mentioned, von Thünen not at all, and Mangoldt only very fleetingly. As we have mentioned, in the last chapter, on Money, Menger himself followed a historical method by tracing the origins of money from, or in, 'the earliest periods of economic development'. Here Menger complains that earlier economists had shown little interest in historical research so that the question he was concerned with was lost sight of until taken up by, among others, Roscher, Hildebrand and Knies (1950, pp. 259, 261). In his later article on Money (1892 and 1909, included in 1936, pp. 1 ff) the historical method is taken further by Menger in terms of a 'law' and 'stages' of development (*Entwicklungsgesetz* and *Entwicklungsstufen*) and in a section 'On the Type of Money Suitable for each People and Period' (1936, p. 4).

In his Preface to the *Problems* Menger draws a completely contrasting picture – as compared with the *Principles* – of the condition of political economy in Germany, with misconceived objectives being pursued by confused and erroneous methods. In the absence of fuller biographical information one can only speculate as to exactly how, why and when Menger's attitude to the German historical economists, and their concepts and methods, went through its great transformation between the publication of the *Principles* and that of the *Problems*. Presumably the extreme lack of interest and understanding shown in Germany, not only for Menger's own answers but for the central theoretical questions he had examined so profoundly in the *Principles*, was what stirred him, along with the increasingly exclusivist and dismissive attitude assumed by German historical economists. As Wicksell put it: 'That Menger should feel offended by this lack of understanding is not surprising, although rather regrettable' (1958, p. 190). But, above all, Menger was concerned to resist an exclusivism, or what he repeatedly called 'one-sidedness' in research priorities and interests which he rightly foresaw would have narrowing and impoverishing results for economics and economic policy.

It is sometimes suggested that Menger's quarrel was rather with the 'younger' historical school led by Schmoller than with the 'older' school which had been led by Roscher. In so far as Menger's protest was ultimately against the narrowing, 'one-sided' exclusivism of his German contemporaries, of whom Schmoller was the main leader, this suggestion is valid. Nevertheless, in the text of the *Problems* Roscher comes under much more frequent and explicit attack than Schmoller, who receives very little actual mention. Indeed, at one point early in the book (1963, p. 14n), Menger expresses support for criticisms of Roscher made by Schmoller and others,[10] and he more than once insists, as in the opening words of the Foreword to *Die Irrthümer des Historismus*, that: 'The lack of clarity of "the historical school of German economists" regarding the aims and methods of research in political economy was a fault clearly apparent on the original foundation of this school, and this has not been removed in the course of almost five decades' (1935, p. 3).

In fact, though less aggressive and exclusivist in manner than Schmoller, Roscher and the older historicals were, in some ways, more pretentious in substance, that is in their ambitions or claims to establish laws of development, about which Schmoller himself expressed scepticism.

Menger's criticism of the historical economists and the historical method is preponderantly and ultimately defensive in substance, though hardly defensive in tone. It is not the pursuit of historical researches that Menger attacks but the 'one-sided' and exclusive importance then attached to them in Germany. He was not questioning fundamentally the significance or methods of historical economics, except the kind of naïve inductivism that assumes that explanations and predictions would somehow emerge from the amassing of descriptive material in historical monographs. Menger does not even oppose fundamentally the search for laws of development; he claims simply that this is a subsidiary aim:

Theoretical economics is the science of the general nature or the forms of phenomena (*Erscheinungsformen*), and general connections (the laws) of economy. In contrast to this comprehensive and significant task of our science the establishment of 'laws of development' of the economy . . . must, though by no means unjustified, seem still quite secondary. It must seem to be a task which should by no means be neglected by theoretical research. . . . But its results constitute only a very small part of theoretical economics. (1963, p. 119)

As Schumpeter said of the *Methodenstreit* (not entirely adequately, but with much justification): 'Neither party really did question its opponent's position *outright*. The quarrel was about precedence and relative importance and might have been settled by allowing every type of work to find the place to which its weight entitled it.' (1954, p. 814)

For Menger, what the historical economists were concentrating on so exclusively was 'secondary'. As he put it in *Die Irrthümer des Historismus*, they were 'porters', or 'carriers' (*Kärrner*), who brought the bricks and sand to the building site but imagined they were the architects (1935, p. 46). For Schmoller, the theory which Menger championed was simply a small corner of the subject as a whole, *eine Eckchen*, as he called it, which Menger mistook for the whole building.

The apparent differences in 'methods' to which the two parties wished to give primary or exclusive place, corresponded with, and were shaped and determined by, the two very different major questions, or fields or branches of the subject, in which they were interested. The working out of the elements of microeconomics, which Menger saw, justifiably, as the immediate central task, required mainly deductive analysis, or a 'theoretical' method, as he called it. For tracing the changes, development or 'growth' of national economies, or of industries or sectors therein, the overriding concern of the historicals – and one in which interest seems to have increased throughout the world in the last couple of decades – a predominantly historical method was obviously more suited. In fact the *Methodenstreit* was, to a large extent, not a quarrel about methods so much as a clash of interests regarding what was the most important and interesting subject to study: pricing and allocation analysis, or the broad development and change of national economies and industries. As Menger himself agreed in his very generous obituary tribute to Roscher in 1894:

The differences which have arisen between the Austrian school and some of the German historical economists were by no means ones of method in the proper sense of the word. If the German historical economists were often described – even in scientific works – as representatives of the inductive method, and the Austrian economists of the deductive method, this does not correspond with the facts. The true contrast between these schools is not even remotely characterised as that between an empirical and a rationalist approach or an inductive and deductive one. Both recognise that the necessary basis for the study of real phenomena and their laws is that of experience. Both recognise – I may well assume – that induction and deduction are closely related, mutually supporting, and complementary means to knowledge. The real foundation of the differences, which are still not completely bridged, between the two schools is something much more important: it relates to the different view regarding the *objectives* of research, and about the set of tasks, which a science of economics has to solve. (1935, p. 279)

Though he complains of their 'one-sidedness', Menger went on to recognize the achievements of Roscher and the historical economists, and he applauds their reaction against 'the abstract, unempirical schematization (*'Schematismus'*) of some of Adam Smith's followers'. He concluded: 'The Austrian school has never denied the value and significance of historical research, and even the philosophy of history, as Roscher understood it' (1935, p. 280).[11]

In fact, like most economists throughout the history of the subject, with their conceptual or analytical novelties, both parties in the *Methodenstreit* were over-ambitious as to what could be achieved, *solely* by their own particular new devices, in respect of useful and valid contributions to policy: the historicals in so far as they aimed at setting out 'laws', or necessary 'stages', of development; and Menger with regard to the content and predictive capacity of his 'exact' laws based on abstraction from ignorance, error and uncertainty. On either side there was initially an insufficient readiness to admit that for adequate answers to most significant economic questions, of almost any kind, the two methods would have to be combined. As Schumpeter wrote of the founders of neoclassical price theory:

They naturally exaggerated the importance of their central achievement. They saw more in it than do we, that is, more than a logical schema that is useful for clearing up certain equilibrium relations but is not in itself directly applicable to the given processes of real life. They did not realise how many and how important the phenomena are that escape this logical schema and loved to believe that they had got hold of what was essential and 'normal'. (1954, p. 1132)[12]

One might speculate as to just how Menger would have assessed recent applications of deductive analysis to problems of growth and to macroeconomic analysis generally, in relation to the criteria of his individualist, or microeconomic, 'compositive' method, and 'exact' laws.

The most eminent economists who have examined and pronounced judgement on the *Methodenstreit*, Wicksell and Schneider, for example, while deploring the influence of the German historical school, regard the long and acrimonious battle largely as a waste of time and effort (Wicksell, 1958, pp. 190ff; Schneider, 1962, pp. 301ff). It is difficult to resist such a verdict. Among its various unfortunate consequences, the *Methodenstreit* got what is called 'methodology' a bad name, largely because of the tactics of the protagonists. But if one means by 'methodology' the critical examination of the assumptions, concepts and theories of economists, and the policy conclusions that they claim to base on, and derive from their theories, then 'methodology' is seldom, if ever, a waste of time or effort, and frequently, in the interests of intellectual clarity and integrity – especially in policy debates – it is a vitally necessary task. There is a kind of would-be hard-headed dismissal of 'methodology' as 'a waste of time' compared with what is called 'constructive' work, which in economics is quite unjustified and too often a pretext for complacency and pretentiousness.[13] Menger was certainly well justified in launching a thorough criticism of the historical method, showing up with precision the limitations of any conclusions obtained or obtainable by it. Equally, on the other hand, a critical examination of the deductive method, its basic assumptions, the testability thereof, and their predictive value, would have been a highly justifiable work of critical clarification. But the battle became much too much concerned with what sort of questions should have priority, and with the prestige and influence of particular groups or schools.

In conclusion, there is another unfortunate consequence of the *Methodenstreit*. This is that its sound and fury tended to obscure one of Carl Menger's most notable intellectual characteristics: and that is the essential balance and moderation of the positions he ultimately adopted on substantial issues of method and policy, as contrasted with the temperamental vehemence with which he sometimes expressed himself. As we have seen, *Einseitigkeit*, on whatever side or in whatever direction, was the intellectual sin that Menger was specially and constantly concerned to condemn; and on most of the broad controversial questions that he discussed, he himself never resorted to an extreme or exclusivist position, on issues as to which economists' views have often become unreasonably polarized. Regarding the classical economists Menger was concerned to defend them vigorously but certainly not to abandon the duty of criticism. Again, while prepared to go some way with the conservative champions of unplanned, organically evolved institutions, he was not prepared to reliquish in their defence his critical duties. Then again, on the question of the similarities and dissimilarities between the natural and social sciences, a question which involves many of the main issues in the methodology of economics, Menger went to neither one extreme nor the other, neither insisting on a complete disparity, or wide gulf, between the two, nor concentrating only on the similarity or identity of criteria and methods in the two groups of sciences. He was aware of, and insisted upon, both similarities and dissimilarities, each of which were important in particular contexts.

This then is the emphasis with which one should conclude. For Menger, as an Aristotelian, intellectual virtue was usually to be found in a kind of mean position. He may sometimes have written *fortiter in modo*, but generally and substantially he is to be found *suaviter in re* in the positions he finally adopted: that is, Carl Menger can be seen as essentially a critical, anti-extremist, anti-exclusivist moderate, seeking a balance on those principal issues that he so profoundly examined in his *Problems*.[14]

Notes

1   The page references will be to this English edition. The problems of translating Menger into English are often very difficult. I am much indebted to this excellent translation, but have not followed it at all points. It is by F. J. Nock, with an introduction by L. Schneider.

2   And one on which it is by no means easy to comment. There is a great deal that is obscure regarding Carl Menger's intellectual biography, the early influences that affected his work, his philosophical presuppositions and intellectual objectives. These obscurities are not serious for the understanding of the *Principles*, but they make the interpretation of the *Problems* much more difficult.

3   Menger emphasized this idea very strongly in one of the two substantial letters he wrote to Walras: 'We do not simply study quantitative relationships but also the NATURE (das WESEN) of economic phenomena. How can we attain to the knowledge of this latter (e.g. the nature of value, rent, profit, the division of labour, bimetallism, etc.), by mathematical methods?' (Walras, 1965, vol. 2, p. 3)

4   See Kauder, 1958, pp. 411ff; Hansen, 1968. These Aristotelian influences on Menger (which also seem to be at work in his monocausal approach and his rejection of interdependence and mathematics) do not necessarily seem *very* important for the interpretation of his economic theories in the *Principles*. But they constituted something of a barrier to mutual understanding with those – like Walras – who did not share these presuppositions. It would be an interesting task, but one too lengthy and difficult to attempt here, to try to trace the relationships between Menger's conception of the 'exact' method and the a priorism of L. von Mises. See also Bostaph, 1978.

5   See also Menger's references to error and ignorance in his *Principles*, where he writes: 'Of course, error and imperfect knowledge may give rise to aberrations, but these are the pathological phenomena of social economy and prove as little against the laws of economics as do the symptoms of a sick body against the laws of physiology' (1950, p. 216; see also p. 224). According to Menger, imperfect knowledge is 'pathological'!

6   It is certainly *not* being maintained here that heightened awareness or social selfconsciousness has always been, or is generally, accompanied by sufficiently reliable knowledge on which more successful economic planning and intervention can be based. In some cases, in particular fields, increased knowledge *may* help to provide the less inaccurate predictions necessary for less unsuccessful policies or plans; but often it is not forthcoming, since policy ambitions constantly tend to outrun, sometimes disastrously, advances in knowledge and improvements in predictions.

7   Professor L. M. Lachmann, a leading contemporary Austrian (though a pupil of Sombart in Berlin), remarks that Sombart 'appears to

be correct' in characterizing the *Problems* as the 'most significant methodological work dealing with economics in the manner of the natural sciences' (1977, p. 48). For Sombart and Lachmann this represents profound error – though, in turn, Sombart was denounced by Hayek as a 'historicist', along with Marx and Spengler (1952, p. 199). Lachmann maintains that: 'The real theoretical work of the Austrian school had scarcely begun in 1883. . . . What later on became the characteristic method of the school had scarcely made an impact in 1883.' In particular Professor Lachmann emphasizes the idea of '*Verstehen*' ('Understanding') which came in later from German writers such as Dilthey. It may be noted that Professor Hayek in his introduction to Menger's works held that Menger's 'interest in the natural sciences is beyond doubt, and a strong bias in favour of their methods is evident throughout his work' (1934, p. ix); 'throughout' perhaps goes too far.

8   By *Pragmatismus* Menger does not seem to mean what is usually meant by 'pragmatism' in English so much as an eagerness, or over-eagerness, for the practical reformist application of inadequate economic theorizing.

9   The suggestion might be ventured that Menger would have gained much from reading Professor F. A. Hayek's essay 'Individualism: True and False' (1949, pp. 1ff).

10   Unfortunately a precise examination of the treatment of Roscher on the one hand, as compared with Schmoller on the other, is rendered more difficult by the fact that neither in the original, nor in the translation, is an index provided. I have so far traced only four references to Schmoller in the *Problems*, two of which (p. 14n and p. 279n) are favourable, one quite trivial (p. 61n), and only one of which is critical and important, though defensive (p. 74n), regarding abstraction and 'the dogma of self-interest'. Perhaps Schmoller only came to be seen as the prime antagonist *after* his famous review. In the *Problems* the references to Roscher are much more numerous and much more severe.

11   Professor Bostaph (1978) has emphasized the differences in epistemology between Menger and the German historicals, which undoubtedly constituted a part of the wide range of differences between the two sides. But they were also divided by differences in the nature of the problems in which they were centrally interested.

12   Schumpeter has sometimes been described as a neoclassical economist, prejudiced against the English classicals. Would that historians of economics from the English classical, Keynesian, and Marxian viewpoints had always been as coolly critical as Schumpeter of the schools they championed. See Hutchison, 1978, p. 237.

13   Menger, perhaps rightly, asserted that the greatest achievements have been made by those uninterested in 'methodology', which is, however, of the greatest importance for 'secondary' work. Certainly, for a Smith, Menger, Cournot or Keynes, 'methodology' may be a waste of time, but it provides an indispensable discipline for lesser mortals.

14   Mr Max Alter has discerningly emphasized the German romantic-historicist influences in Menger's work, which exist side by side with his 'positivist' postulates and his 'emphasis on law-like behaviour, a static conception of human nature and compartmentalisation of scientific disciplines'. Mr Alter maintains that Menger did not perceive any incompatibility or contradictions between these contrasting sets of ideas or postulates. Certainly in any strong, exclusivist form such ideas *are* contradictory. However, if, for Menger, '*Einseitigkeit*' was a major intellectual sin, then he would have sought to blend and balance contrasting ideas, or postulates, by rejecting exclusivist, or 'one-sided' formulations of them – even if this meant reducing some of them to platitudes (of which wisdom often consists). Menger's contrasting influences and postulates have persisted, in modified forms, in the methodological doctrines of Menger's Austrian successors. But there they have sometimes been asserted (as we shall see in the next chapter) in such extreme and dogmatic terms as to be quite irreconcilable and contradictory. I am much indebted to an unpublished paper by Mr Alter (1980).

References

Alter, M. (1980), 'On the Intellectual Background of the Older Austrian School', unpublished.

Bostaph, S. (1978), 'The Methodological Debate between Carl Menger and the German Historicists', *Atlantic Economic Journal*, vol. 6, no. 3, pp. 3–16.

Eucken, W. (1950), *The Foundations of Economics*, translated by T. W. Hutchison.

Hansen, R. (1968), 'Der Methodenstreit in den Sozialwissenschaften zwischen Gustav Schmoller und Carl Menger', in A. Diemer (ed.), *Beiträge zur Entwicklung der Wissenschaftstheorie im 19. Jahrhundert*, pp. 162–5.

Hayek, F. A. (1934), Introduction to *Collected Works of Carl Menger*, vol. 1.

(1949), *Individualism and Economic Order*.

(1952), *The Counter-Revolution of Science*.

(1967), *Studies in Philosophy, Politics and Economics*.

Hutchison, T. W. (1964), *'Positive' Economics and Policy Objectives*.

Kauder, E. (1958), 'Intellectual and Political Roots of the Older Austrian School', *Zeitschrift für Nationalökonomie*, vol. 17.

(1962), 'Aus Mengers nachgelassenen Papieren', *Weltwirtschaftliches Archiv*, vol. 89, pp. 1ff.

Kemeny, J. G. (1959), *A Philosopher Looks at Science*.

Lachmann, L. M. (1977), *Capital, Expectations and the Market Process*.

Menger, C. (1935), *Collected Works*, vol. 3.

(1936), *Collected Works*, vol. 4.

7

Austrians on Philosophy and Method (since Menger)

I

It may be worth observing at the outset that not even the simplest or most obvious observations about 'Austrian' economists, theories or doctrines have recently passed without dispute. Moreover, what one must get used to is that what much later have been described by 'Austrians' as the most characteristic and important of their ideas were historically of German, rather than Austrian, origin: while some of the most fundamental ideas of two of the great original Austrian founders, Menger and Böhm-Bawerk, have been dismissed as fundamentally erroneous and non-'Austrian'. For example, as we have seen in chapter 6, the assumption that 'Austrian' ideas on philosophy and method in economics derive significantly from, or originate, with Menger's *Problems* has been rejected by a distinguished exponent of neo-'Austrianism'. The same kind of question as to what is truly 'Austrian', and what is not, could be raised with regard to the second member of the great original triumvirate, Böhm-Bawerk.[1] Böhm-Bawerk hardly made a major, distinctive contribution to methodological ideas. Rather than Menger's adjective 'exact', Böhm-Bawerk preferred the description 'isolating', or 'abstract-deductive', for the method of economics. But he insisted most emphatically that the methods and criteria of economics were closely parallel with those of the natural sciences. He rejected, very sensibly, both Baconian induction, at one extreme, and a priorism at the other. According to Böhm-Bawerk:

The abstract-deductive method . . . has no fancy *a priori* axioms as a basis for its inferences, nor does it confine itself to inferences and deductions. On the contrary, it starts exactly as the historical school would have it start, with observations of actual conditions and endeavours from this empirical material to build general laws. . . .

The best-known among the doctrines of the abstract-deductive school is the theory of value based on final utility. How did they arrive at it? By some soaring *a priori* speculation? Not at all. In the first place they simply observed how men practically regard property. (1924, pp. 263–4)[2]

In fact, Böhm-Bawerk's critique of Marx and of Marx's theory of value was explicitly based on empiricist principles and on the methods and criteria of the natural sciences:

> Herein lies, I believe, the alpha and omega of all that is fallacious, contradictory, and vague in his treatment of his subject by Marx. His system is not in close touch with facts. Marx has not deduced from facts the fundamental principles of his system. . . .
>
> In the domain of natural science such a work as Marx's would even now be impossible. In the very young social sciences it was able to attain influence, a great influence. (1896/1949, pp. 101, 117)

Böhm-Bawerk's briefly stated methodological ideas had (unfortunately perhaps) little influence, and would certainly be rejected by modern Austrians, who at some points seem to owe much more to German than to Austrian philosophical traditions.[3] In fact, the Austrian philosophical tradition in so far as it may have been represented by Mach, Wittgenstein, Schlick and Popper, has been comprehensively rejected by some modern Austrian economists, sometimes in terms of the philosophical Boo-adjective 'Positivist'. For example, that great economist of Austrian origin, Joseph Schumpeter (characteristically Viennese in spirit), whose remarkable *Jugendwerk* of 1908, *Das Wesen und Hauptinhalt der theoretischen Nationalökonomie*, could be said to have followed the Austrian philosophical tradition, was sternly and fundamentally criticized by Wieser, and was later described by Hayek as one of 'those economists who approach economic phenomena in the light of a certain branch of positivism' (1949, p. 90). Certainly Schumpeter displayed an enthusiastic regard for the theories of Walras, and criticized the ideas of Ludwig von Mises on socialism. Anyhow, Schumpeter cannot certainly be counted as an 'Austrian' economist and will not be included in this review.

Some common tendencies in their methodological doctrines are indeed apparent among some of the older Austrians, and, to some extent, these tendencies have descended to modern Austrians. But as we shall see (in section VII below) very profound divergences of view on the methodology and philosophy of economics can be discerned among modern 'Austrians'.

II *Wieser*

Since Böhm-Bawerk did not write any really important, original work on methodology, and Schumpeter is not counted as an 'Austrian', after Carl Menger the next – and in some ways the most influential and distinctive – contribution to Austrian ideas on the philosophy and methodology of economics came from Böhm-Bawerk's brother-in-law, Friedrich von Wieser (1851– 1926).

Wieser certainly maintained, or elevated even further, the considerable epistemological pretensions for economics suggested in Menger's claims regarding 'exact laws'. But above all, it was Wieser, possibly influenced by German ideas picked up during his studies at Heidelberg, who developed among the Austrians the emphasis on the fundamentally distinct characteristics, and the more certain foundations, of economics and the other social sciences, as compared with the natural sciences. If Menger's ideas show a strain of Aristotelian essentialism, Wieser develops a more Cartesian, or perhaps (as Lakatos called it) Euclidean, concept of political economy, which had come down from J. B. Say, via Senior and Cairnes:[4] that is, the idea that political economy is based on a few fundamental assumptions which should not only be regarded as self-evident and beyond dispute, but which also possess sufficient content to yield, by deduction, an array of significant conclusions. Moreover, Wieser ascribes a kind of inner necessity to these propositions. But he insists that these assumptions are, and must be, 'empirical', and he rejects any suggestion of a priorism.

Wieser expounded his methodological standpoint in a review article (included by Hayek in Wieser's *Gesammelte Abhandlungen*) in which he vigorously and fundamentally rejected the ideas of Schumpeter, accusing him of being 'blinded by the success of the exact natural sciences' (1929, p. 12). Schumpeter is accused of neglecting the rich insights made available by 'inner observation' ('*innere Beobachtung*') which, according to Wieser, by means of 'the psychological method', provides, for economists and other social scientists – such as sociologists – 'a huge advantage' over natural scientists. Wieser claimed:

We can observe natural phenomena only from outside but ourselves from within. . . . This psychological method chooses the most advantageous position for observation. It finds that certain acts take place in our consciousness with a feeling of necessity. What a huge advantage for the natural scientist if the organic and inorganic world clearly informed him of its laws, and why should we neglect such assistance? (1929, p. 17)

Subsequently Wieser maintained:

The theoretical economist need never deplore a lack of the instruments which are employed in the exact natural sciences. . . . Let their instruments be infinitely refined, still they must be content to describe a succession of happenings, abandoning the hope of showing how the effect springs from its cause. The group of practical sciences, of which economic theory is one, can accomplish more. (1928, p. 8)

As Wieser explains:

For all actions which are accompanied by a consciousness of necessity, economic theory need never strive to establish a law in a long series of inductions. In these cases we, each of us, hear the law pronounced by an unmistakable inner voice. (*ibid.*)

It may, of course, be professionally highly reassuring for some economists and sociologists to be told of their huge advantage over natural scientists, and of how an infallible inner voice informs them of the laws of social economics. Quite a number of economists at one time supported the doctrine of Wieser – e.g. F. H. Knight, who held it to be 'essentially sound' (1956, p. 163). However, one may object to Wieser's claims both in principle, as fostering an overconfident 'pretence of knowledge', dogmatically protected against testing; and in practice, on the grounds that these important propositions, proceeding from an 'inner voice', have never been specified with sufficient lucidity and precision to render them susceptible to critical appraisal, or to demonstrate that significant conclusions can, in fact, logically be derived from them. Only Senior, long ago, attempted, reasonably lucidly, to specify four such 'Elementary Propositions' of the Science of Political Economy, only one of which could have been derived from introspection, that is, his first proposition that 'every man desires to obtain additional Wealth with as little sacrifice as possible.'[5] This leaves the question begged, which continued to be so often left begged for the greater part of a century, as to the constantly shifting and often inadequate knowledge with which 'every man' is equipped in his decision in pursuit of his desire for wealth.[6]

In Wieser's writings (unlike, briefly, in Menger's *Problems*) there seems to be very little recognition of the significance, and ubiquity, of ignorance and uncertainty, which are especially relevant with regard to his opportunity-cost doctrine. Anyhow, it seems quite erroneous and misleading to suggest that the general propositions of economists and sociologists can derive some kind of greater necessity or reliability from the use of introspection, and that they are somehow, in this way, more securely and authoritatively based than the natural sciences. But it may be noted that the political tendency which Wieser represented, on this vaguely formulated and somewhat pretentious methodological basis, lay in a very different direction from that taken up so vigorously by many subsequent Austrians. For, rightly or wrongly, Wieser was highly critical of free-market capitalism, attached great importance to the growth of monopoly, and was highly sympathetic to social democratic and reformist ideas – in complete contrast with his classical and methodological predecessors, J. B. Say, Senior and Cairnes, and even more so with regard to some of his Austrian followers (see Wieser, 1928, *passim*).

III *Mises*

A fuller survey than this would have to include the contributions of Richard Strigl and Hans Mayer. Strigl's work, *Die ökonomischen Kategorien und die Organisation der Wirtschaft* (1923), treats economics as a narrowly deductive subject, concerned simply with the logic of allocation formulae, while everything empirical, relating to tastes, technology, knowledge, and virtually everything else, are, according to Strigl, simply to be regarded as the 'data' for economists' deductions.[7] Hans Mayer's ideas follow in important respects those of Menger. His first publication (1911) was concerned with criticizing Schumpeter's methodological ideas. Later, in his lengthy essay 'Der Erkenntiswert der funktionellen Preistheorien' (1932), Mayer criticized the non-Austrian price theories of Cournot, Jevons, Walras, Pareto and Cassel, in terms similar to Menger's criticism of Walras. He rejected the use of mathematics in formulating economic theories in that it can simply express functional relationships and not get at real causes.

The next major distinctive development in Austrian ideas on the philosophy and method of economics can be said to have come from Ludwig von Mises (1881–1973), a pupil of Wieser. It is not easy to assess the place of Mises in the history of economic thought. Some Austrian enthusiasts would seem to place him among the two or three most important economists of the 20th century. Others would assess him very differently. Certainly Schumpeter and others have given a noteworthy place to Mises's *Theory of Money and Credit* (1911). Perhaps he is best known for his robust and comprehensive criticisms of socialist economics, for which he probably deserves much credit. But his main point about the 'impossibility' of allocating resources rationally under socialism was not as original with Mises as his admirers have suggested. German historical economists, and others associated with the *Verein für Sozialpolitik*, such as Nasse, Brentano, and especially Schaeffle, had discerned the main critical point decades before – and this had even been briefly but clearly glimpsed by Friedrich Engels (see above, Chapter 1, p. 14).

However, it is the very forthright methodological views of Mises with which we are concerned here, which for a time in the thirties had a very powerful influence in London and elsewhere, and which in some Marxist quarters may be in for something of a revival today. Mises's views owe something to Menger's notions regarding 'exact laws', but more to the epistemological pretensions of Wieser regarding the reliability and advantages of introspection. But Mises certainly added his own particular emphasis.

He starts by claiming the epistemological uniqueness of economics as a part of the study of human action (or 'praxeology'). The nature of human action provides economics with an *a priori* basis.[8] In fact:

one must not take one's cue from geometry, mechanics, *or any other science*. . . .
The starting point of praxeology is a self-evident truth, the cognition of action, that is, the cognition of the fact that there is such a thing as consciously aiming at ends. (1962, pp. 5–6, italics added)

Again:

Praxeology is *a priori*. It starts from the *a priori* category of action and develops out of it all that it contains. . . .

The question whether the judgements of praxeology are to be called analytic or synthetic and whether or not its procedure is to be qualified as 'merely' tautological are of verbal interest only.

Every theorem of praxeology is deduced by logical reasoning from the category of action. It partakes of the apodictic certainty provided by logical reasoning that starts from an *a priori* category. (p. 44)[9]

An essential element in Mises's *a priori* praxeology is the dogma that all 'action is by definition rational' (1960, p. 35). Whether underlying this axiom of 'rational' action there is the assumption (made by so many economists since Ricardo) of '*Allwissenheit*', as Menger put it, or what assumptions, if any, are being made as to the extent of knowledge or ignorance, or the nature of shifting expectations, does not seem to matter. On this specific, vital point, chapter 6 of Mises's *Human Action*, on 'Uncertainty', sheds little or no light. It is not very illuminating for him to insist, for example, that 'action is always speculation. . . . In any real and living economy every actor is always an entrepreneur and speculator' (1949, p. 253), when he fails to spell out just how it is possible, from his *a priori* axioms regarding such speculative actions, that non-trivial conclusions of 'apodictic certainty' can be obtained, which relate to real-world conditions of uncertainty and ignorance. Nor, incidentally, is it at all clear how far the insistence of Mises on the assumption of rational action implies the assumption of 'rational expectations' – however precisely these are to be defined. It might appear that Mises is *not* concerned to assume rational expectations when he insists: 'The laws of catallactics which economics expounds are valid for every exchange regardless of whether those involved in it have acted wisely or unwisely or whether they were actuated by economic or non-economic motives' (1960, p. 34).

Where precisely this leaves the equilibrium concept, and the equilibrating mechanism, of such special significance to many of those who advocate free markets, is also left unclear. But the precise and lucid use of language, as a means of communication, which might be regarded as specially incumbent on academics disporting themselves in this particular intellectual area, cannot be counted among Mises's more obvious intellectual virtues. For example, his supporters have had to explain that when Mises wrote that socialism is 'impossible', he 'obviously meant that the proposed methods of socialism could not achieve what they were supposed to do' (Hayek, 1978, p. 297).[10]

It may be noticed, in particular, how Mises completely rejects Sir Karl Popper's proposed demarcation 'between what we may accept as scientific and what not' (as Hayek puts it 1978, p. 31). According to Mises:

> If one accepts the terminology of logical positivism and especially also that of Popper, a theory or hypothesis is 'unscientific' if *in principle* it cannot be refuted by experience. Consequently, all *a priori* theories, including mathematics and praxeology, are 'unscientific'. This is merely a verbal quibble. No serious man wastes his time in discussing such a terminological question. Praxeology and economics will retain their paramount significance for human life and action however people may classify and describe them. (1962, p. 70)

In fact, Mises insists very emphatically, like Wieser, on the fundamental differences between natural and human sciences, and traces the impossibility of questioning *a priori* judgements back to introspection:

> What we know about our own actions and about those of other people is conditioned by our familiarity with the category of action that we owe to a process of self-examination and introspection as well as of understanding of other people's conduct. To question their insight is no less impossible than to question the fact that we are alive. (p. 71)

We shall be proceeding next to discuss the doctrines of Mises's pupil Hayek. We shall see how, in their first phase, or what we call Hayek I, his ideas on the methodology of economics, have marked similarities with those of Mises; but we shall also see how subsequently Hayek II diverges in the most important and fundamental respects from Mises – regarding economic laws, Popper's falsifiability principle, the similarities between the natural and social sciences, and on other important points.

IV *Hayek I (–1936)*

Through the multifarious experiences and upheavals of the middle decades of the twentieth century Hayek's long intellectual career has shown much constancy of view. Moreover, his criticisms of socialism in the thirties and forties can be seen, in the seventies, to have deserved much more serious concern from many economists (including the present writer) than they received when first published. But, on some quite fundamental and very important points of methodology and philosophy, vital and critical changes in Hayek's views can be discerned – as also, incidentally, on money and on some issues of employment policy – which have not received the attention and appreciation which they deserve.

Hayek's first book, *Monetary Theory and the Trade Cycle* (1933), which originally appeared when he was Director of the Austrian Institut für Konjunkturforschung, is to an important extent a methodological work, concerned primarily with the methods and criteria according to which an explanation of aggregate economic fluctuations (or the trade cycle) should be sought. Affinities with the ideas of Austrian predecessors, notably with those of his 'mentor' Mises,[11] are apparent, but the methodology of the trade cycle represented a new problem. Let us note first the strong claims for prediction and forecasting which Hayek made, perhaps to some extent following Menger, as an essential task of theoretical economics:

> Every economic theory, and indeed all theory of whatever sort, aims exclusively at foretelling the necessary consequences of a given situation, event or measure. The subject-matter of trade cycle theory being what it is, it follows that ideally it should result in a collective forecast showing the total development from a given situation under given conditions. In practice, such forecasts are attempted in too unconditional a form, and on an inadmissibly over-simplified basis; and, consequently the very possibility of scientific judgements about future economic trends to-day appears problematical, and cautious thinkers are apt to disparage any attempt at such forecasting. In contrast to this view, *we have to emphasize very strongly that statistical research in this field is meaningless except in so far as it leads to a forecast. . . . In particular any measures aimed at alleviating the Trade Cycle (and necessarily based on statistical research) must be conceived in the light of certain assumptions as to the future trend to be expected in the absence of such measures.* (1933, p. 36n, italics added)

This represents a fundamentally different methodological view, regarding prediction, from that of some modern Austrians.

Hayek goes on to claim, following Wieser, that 'we can deduce from general insight how the majority of people will behave under certain conditions'. But, of course, if these certain conditions are, and have to be, grossly oversimplified in order to yield deductions, then, as Hayek concedes, deduction will not be enough: 'The actual behaviour of these masses at a given moment, and therefore the conditions to which our theoretical conclusions must be applied, can only be ascertained by the use of complicated statistical methods' (p. 37).

Hayek is especially concerned to insist on the indispensability of the equilibrium, self-adjusting model in trade cycle research as in all economic theorizing:

We can gain a theoretically unexceptional explanation of complex phenomena only by first assuming the full activity of the elementary economic interconnections as shown by the equilibrium theory, and then introducing consciously and successively just those elements which are capable of relaxing these rigid interrelationships. (1935, pp. 95–6, italics in original)
Only in this way is it possible to incorporate Trade Cycle theory into the static system *which is the basis of all theoretical economics.* (p. 98, italics added)

As regards this 'static system' Hayek insists: 'The essential means of explanation in static theory . . . is the assumption that prices supply an automatic mechanism for equilibrating supply and demand'. (p. 43)[12] Thus he apparently maintains that 'the basis of all theoretical economics' is 'the assumption that prices supply an automatic mechanism for equilibrating supply and demand.'

Hayek went on to explain that by 'equilibrium theory' was understood a theory of both micro- and macroeconomic equilibrium, that is,

we have primarily understood the modern theory of the general interdependence of all economic quantities, which has been most perfectly expressed by the Lausanne School of theoretical economics. The significant basic concept of this theory was contained in James Mill's and J. B. Say's *Théories des Débouchés.* (p. 42n)

The 'automatic mechanism for equilibrating supply and demand' depends on an assumption of full knowledge – or what Menger called the essential assumption of '*Allwissenheit*'. This '*Allwissenheit*' had somehow to be reconciled, according to Hayek, with the ignorance and uncertainty entering through the monetary framework. All the other multifarious and ubiquitous sources of ignorance and uncertainty have apparently to be excluded by assumption. For 'exact' theories simply cannot yield their conclusions deductively except (as Menger had clearly recognized) on the assumption of '*Allwissenheit*'. Ignorance may bring in a fatal 'indeterminacy' (however exactly 'indeterminacy' is to be interpreted):

In place of such a theoretical deduction, we often find an assertion, unfounded on any system, of a far-reaching indeterminacy in the economy. Paradoxically stated as it is, *this thesis is bound to have a devastating effect on theory; for it involves the sacrifice of any exact theoretical deduction, and the very possibility of a theoretical explanation of economic phenomena is rendered problematic.* (p. 96, italics added)

It would seem, therefore, that assumptions of ignorance *must* be ruled out (unless, possibly, when ignorance arose through the monetary framework; though how methodologically this was to be accommodated was unclear):

At one point or another, all theories which start to explain cyclical fluctuations by miscalculations or ignorance as regards the economic situation fall into the same error as those naïve explanations which base themselves on the 'planlessness' of the economic system. They overlook the fact that, in the exchange economy, production is governed by prices. . . . Within the framework of a system of explanations in which, as in all modern economic theory, *prices are merely expressions of a necessary tendency towards a state of equilibrium*, it is not permissible to reintroduce the old Sismondian idea of the misleading effect of prices on production without first bringing it into line with the fundamental system of explanation. (pp. 84–5, italics added)

To some extent, in the context of the problem of the trade cycle, Hayek seems to have been expressing a somewhat similar fundamental methodological aperçu to that of J. S. Mill and F. Y. Edgeworth[13] regarding the dependence of the deductive method on the assumption of competition (which includes in turn, *and is necessary for the inclusion of*, the vital '*Allwissenheit*' assumption).

However, there seems to be in Hayek's methodological principles in his first book, in this attempt to base an explanation of the trade cycle on the retention of static assumptions, a strenuous effort to square an epistemological circle.

Another expression of Hayek's earlier methodological views came in a discussion of economic calculation in a socialist economy. Here the influences of Wieser (whose essays Hayek edited) and of Hayek's 'mentor' Mises are apparent. A very fundamental contrast is drawn between the natural and social sciences:

The essential basic facts which we need for the explanation of social phenomena are part of common experience, part of the stuff of our thinking. In the social sciences it is the elements of the complex phenomena *which are known beyond the possibility of dispute*. In the natural sciences they can be at best surmised. The existence of these elements is so much more certain than any regularities in the complex phenomena to which they give rise that it is they which constitute the truly empirical factor in the social sciences. (1935 and 1949, p. 126, italics added)

Hayek is especially concerned to insist that in the social sciences, that is, economics, sociology, etc., on the basis of these foundations (which are 'beyond the possibility of dispute', rather than 'at best surmised' as in the natural sciences) 'general laws' can be established, that is, 'inherent necessities determined by the permanent nature of the constituent elements'. The erroneous methods of historical economists had led to the disastrous conclusion that 'there were no laws of social life other than those made by men' (1935 and 1949, p. 127).

Hayek thus went beyond the pretensions of Ricardo and James Mill, who claimed parity for the laws of their new Science of Political Economy with the laws of Newton and Euclid. But he did not specify precisely any examples of these propositions which were to be regarded as both empirical and 'beyond the possibility of dispute'. So it was impossible to appraise them critically or to assess how far they operate effectively as postulates.[14] It may well be possible, of course, to formulate some such propositions. But, first, no special 'indisputability' should be claimed for them on the basis of introspection; and second it would need to be shown that these propositions are necessary for the reaching of interesting conclusions. *We would emphasize that these ideas of Hayek I are still cited by modern Austrians as an embodiment of Austrian methodology.*

V *Hayek II (1937–)*

If 1936 is a famous date in the history of economics for *hoi polloi*, 1937 must be regarded as a special year by those connoisseurs who, surely justifiably, regard as fundamentally important the recognition of the significance for economic theorizing of uncertainty, ignorance, and shifting, erring expectations; and who realize also the extent to which orthodox theories, since Ricardo, have been based on, and so narrowly limited by, the assumption of what Menger called '*Allwissenheit*'.[15] In 1937 several fundamental contributions appeared on this subject. In his article of that year in *The Quarterly Journal of Economics*, Keynes then made the main point of his attack on classical economic theory that it 'tries to deal with the present by abstracting from the fact that we know very little about the future'; and that 'the hypothesis of a calculable future leads to a wrong interpretation of the principles of behaviour' (1937, pp. 186, 192).[16]

Also in 1937 Hayek published his paper 'Economics and Knowledge', which may be his most important article on economics. It certainly marks a vital turning-point, or even U-turn, in Hayek's methodological ideas, *and ought to be, but has not been, recognized as marking a fundamental shift in Austrian ideas.* The main insights of this article are quite incompatible – except, possibly, at a level of extreme triviality – with the methodological ideas in his previous writings. We are not, of course suggesting that there was an absolutely clean break in Hayek's views from one year, or publication, to the next. Premonitions of a major change are discernible in parts of two articles published in 1935.[17] But it might be regarded as highly significant that this pathbreaking paper of 1937 opens with what seems to be the first reference in Hayek's writings to Karl Popper, though the influence of Popper is not obvious in the subsequent pages.[18] Anyhow, Hayek begins by stating that his main contention will be:

that the tautologies, of which formal equilibrium analysis in economics essentially consists, can be turned into propositions which tell us anything about causation in the real world only in so far as we are able to fill those formal propositions with definite statements about how knowledge is acquired and communicated. (1937 and 1949, p. 33)[19]

Observing that correct foresight is 'the defining characteristic of a state of equilibrium' (1937 and 1949, p. 42), Hayek then explains that 'the only justification' for the concern of economists with 'the admittedly fictitious state of equilibrium', is 'the supposed existence of a tendency toward equilibrium. It is only by this assertion that such a tendency exists that economics ceases to be an exercise in pure logic and becomes an empirical science.' (p. 44) He then goes on to attack what Keynes was calling 'orthodoxy', or 'classical theory':

In the usual presentation of equilibrium analysis it is generally made to appear as if these questions of how equilibrium comes about were solved. But if we look closer, it soon becomes evident that *these apparent demonstrations amount to no more than the apparent proof of what is already assumed.* (p. 45, italics added)

Certainly this complaint of Hayek II would seem to have some relevance for the methodological treatment of equilibrium analysis by Hayek I (1933).

Hayek II then recognized that the necessary assumptions about the actual acquisition of the knowledge necessary for the attainment of equilibrium will 'be of a hypothetical character' and obviously cannot be established *a priori* (1937 and 1949, p. 46). But he then confessed:

I am afraid that I am now getting to a state where it becomes exceedingly difficult to say what exactly are the assumptions on the basis of which we assert that there will be a tendency toward equilibrium and to claim that our analysis has an application to the real world. (p. 48)

Hayek II's analysis of the equilibrium postulate certainly gives a very dubious look to that 'system of explanation', as Hayek I had called it, in which, 'as in all modern economic theory, prices are merely expressions of a necessary tendency towards equilibrium'. One can only wonder, too, what had happened to those 'essential basic facts' which we need for the explanation of social phenomena, which 'are known beyond the possibility of dispute', and which were 'so much more certain' than the basic facts of the natural sciences. As regards the axioms of Mises, with their 'apodictic certainty', it would seem that these can only find relevance in some hyperabstract world of '*Allwissenheit*'.

However there is *some* significant continuity between Hayek I and Hayek II with regard to prediction. Unless one assumes some measure of predictability, and the power to predict, equilibrium theorizing, or indeed any economic theorizing, will be frustrated. So it is necessary to assume 'that there must be some discernible regularity in the world which makes it possible to predict events correctly' (p. 49).[20] This conclusion certainly conflicts with some subsequent Austrian doctrines regarding the impossibility of predicting human actions.

After 1937 Hayek's methodological ideas were advanced in a series of papers of which we would mention three in particular: 'Degrees of Explanation' (1955), 'The Theory of Complex Phenomena' (1964), with its highly significant addendum of 1967, and 'The Pretence of Knowledge', Hayek's Nobel Lecture of 1974. We shall not designate these as representative of Hayek III, IV or V, because they represent progressive developments quite compatible with Hayek II (while the 1937 'Economics and Knowledge' is quite incompatible with Hayek I).

These three papers all show a marked Popperian influence, insignificant before 1937. Indeed the papers of 1955 and 1964 were reprinted in a volume dedicated to Sir Karl (1967). This influence is apparent in Hayek's renewed emphasis on prediction: 'Prediction and explanation are merely two aspects of the same process' (1955 and 1967, p. 9); so that to the extent that human action is unpredictable it is inexplicable. Hayek also puts great emphasis on falsifiability: 'It is certainly desirable to make our theories as falsifiable as possible' (1964 and 1967, p. 29).[21]

Testing '*at every step*' is also recommended (1955 and 1967, p. 6). Moreover, the Popperian influence was especially clear in Hayek II's abandonment of the radical rejection, upheld by leading Austrians before and since, of the idea of common methods and procedures as between natural and social sciences. Hayek II agreed that what he had been attacking as 'scientism', and rejecting for the social sciences, was not really the method of the natural sciences, and that 'the difference between the two groups of disciplines has . . . been greatly narrowed' (1967, p. viii).[22] The differences between sciences were now seen to turn on degrees of the complexity of their subject matter rather than on whether they were 'natural' or 'social' (or human).

Finally, and not stemming from any Popperian influence, Hayek II displays a very changed attitude to economic and social laws. Hayek I had followed previous economists, including both the English classicals and Menger, in a belief in economic and social laws, as existing apparently in a similar sense to that in other sciences. Hayek II rejects the existence of laws in the social and economic world: 'The conception of law in the usual sense has little application to the theory of complex phenomena. . . . I rather doubt whether we know of any "laws" which social phenomena obey.' (1967, pp. 41–2) However, though believing that economists can predict, Hayek does not explain how they can do this without knowing any 'laws'; that is, he does not envisage that in economics and the social sciences predictions have to be based on trends (a procedure condemned by Popper).

We come, in conclusion, to Hayek's Nobel Lecture 'The Pretence of Knowledge'. Here Hayek claims that economists 'have made a mess of things' because they have pretended to be able to predict with the accuracy of natural scientists. We have now come a long way from Hayek I's claims of 1935 (see above, pp. 210–14). In fact, in terms of prediction, which Hayek always has seen as an important and to some extent attainable aim, the social sciences can only manage 'a second best' as compared with some of the natural sciences (1975 and 1978, p. 33).

Nevertheless, Hayek, surely justifiably, goes on: 'Yet, as I am anxious to repeat, we will still achieve predictions which can be falsified and which therefore are of empirical significance' (*ibid.*). He reiterates, in the most emphatic general terms, the demarcation principle of Popper: 'We cannot be grateful enough to such modern philosophers of science as Sir Karl Popper for giving us a test by which we can distinguish between what we may accept as scientific and what not' (p. 31).

Of course such a demarcation principle sweeps out of court the introspective and 'apodictic' certainties of Wieser and Mises, as well as Hayek I's basic facts 'beyond the possibility of dispute'. For this demarcation principle is common to natural and social sciences and it implies common criteria to be upheld by both natural and social scientists. Certainly it has always been vital, in view of pretensions to knowledge, ancient and modern, to emphasize how the study of economics simply has not provided laws on a par with those of some natural sciences; and it is only epistemologically realistic to recognize how unlikely it is that the material with which the economist deals ever will yield 'laws' on a par epistemologically with those of physics. In view of the modern pretensions of mathematical and quantitative economists, it has been specially desirable, if unpopular, to insist in recent years on these limitations, and on the dissimilarities between the material of the natural and social sciences. But it would be disastrous to collapse into the kind of obscurantism which refuses to recognize, or to try to uphold, *any* common epistemological criteria or standards which should be shared by natural and social scientists alike (as Popper has always insisted). That way lies the permissive chaos in which the principle that 'anything goes' will ripen into the dogmas of mob rule, and so usher in the dictatorship of some genocidal popular or 'proletarian' boss, such as 'the great scientist', Stalin.

There is no reprehensible 'pretence of knowledge' in *trying* to follow the criteria, and uphold the standards, of the natural sciences, as far as the material allows. Pretentiousness cannot lie in simply trying critically to see how far the material permits one to go – which in economics has not been a completely negligible distance. 'The Pretence of Knowledge' lies rather in claiming for economics a precision and reliability similar to or even greater than those of the natural sciences, and in claiming the power to which such success would entitle one – if it ever were even approximately achieved.

VI *Dilemmas of Modern Austrians*

We have sketched the development of Hayek's methodological ideas from their initial phase, in which the influence of Wieser and Mises was preponderant, to their subsequent blossoming, increasingly under the influence of Popper, from Hayek II's 1937 paper 'Economics and Knowledge', and in subsequent articles. We have emphasized that, on a whole series of basic philosophical or methodological issues, Hayek II's views are quite incompatible with Hayek I's. Therefore, to try to cling to the doctrines of Wieser, Mises and Hayek I, while seeking to exploit the insights and Popperian influences of Hayek II, can only lead – and, in fact, has led – to fundamental dilemmas. Mr Barry has maintained that Hayek has been responsible for an 'attempt to combine two rather different philosophies of social science' (though we would say, rather, that he moved from one (I) to the other (II) without ever bringing out explicitly the magnitude of the transition). Anyhow, according to Mr Barry:

The difficulty, I think, lies in Hayek's attempt to combine two rather different philosophies of social science; the Austrian praxeological school with its subjectivism and rejection of testability in favour of axiomatic reasoning, and the hypothetico–deductive approach of contemporary science with its emphasis on falsifiability and empirical content. This was not really a problem for Mises since he did not endorse the Popperian approach but it is something of a problem for Hayek. (1979, p. 40)

No matter whether, or how far, it is 'something of a problem' for Hayek, there is certainly the problem, or 'dilemma', for later Austrians of having to decide between two fundamentally incompatible philosophies. Certainly a dilemma is clearly apparent in adjacent essays by two American neo–Austrians, Professors

Rothbard and Kirzner. Not that anything of a problem, or any dilemmas, were recognized by Professor Rothbard, who holds fast to the doctrines of Wieser, Mises and Hayek I. Indeed, in his essay 'Praxeology, the Methodology of Austrian Economics', Rothbard reproduces (1976, p. 26) the passage from Hayek I cited above, regarding how, 'in the social sciences it is the elements of the complex phenomena which are known beyond the possibility of dispute. In the natural sciences they can be at best surmised.' Rothbard maintains, quite justifiably, that in this passage 'Friedrich A. Hayek trenchantly described the praxeological method in contrast to the methodology of the physical sciences'. Having noted how 'the praxeological method' had come down from J. B. Say, Senior and Cairnes, Professor Rothbard describes how this method starts from 'self-evident propositions marked by their strong and evident truth rather than by being testable hypotheses, that are, in the current fashion considered to be "falsifiable" ' (p. 27).

As usual, apart from issues of principle, the difficulty emerges as to the kind of knowledge, ignorance, and expectations, which shape people's actions. In fact, Rothbard entirely disregards Hayek II's insistence, in his 'Economics and Knowledge', on the vital importance of the expectations and the kind of knowledge with which people are assumed to act.

But if Professor Rothbard largely disregards the message of Hayek II, Professor Israel Kirzner, in the next essay 'On the Method of Austrian Economics', reacts in what seems a rather excessive way and may be in danger of conceding too much to a kind of nihilist obscurantism.

Professor Kirzner actually begins with the remarkable claim: 'One of the areas in which disagreement among Austrian economists may seem to be non-existent is that of methodology' (1976, p. 40).[23] Certainly disagreements, or indeed fundamental contradictions, have been completely disregarded. But they have plainly existed since 1937 at least (and perhaps much earlier). However, Kirzner goes on to admit that in fact 'even with respect to method there are differences of opinion among individual [Austrian] thinkers' (p. 40). Kirzner then propounds 'a dilemma' – though the differences seem much wider and the dilemmas much deeper than Kirzner envisages. Professor Kirzner starts from Hayek II, and does not mention Hayek I (thus reversing Professor Rothbard's procedure). Kirzner quotes Hayek II (1937), as we have above, as holding that to assert the applicability of equilibrium theory one needs to assume a certain amount and kind of knowledge, predictability, and ability to predict, and that this assumption cannot be *a priori*, or derived from introspection, but must be 'of a hypothetical character'. But Professor Kirzner then asserts, as a 'basic Austrian tenet', that *there is an indeterminacy and unpredictability inherent in human preferences, human expectations and human knowledge*' (p. 42, italics in original).[24] Of course it might be held that though preferences, expectations and knowledge are unpredictable, actions *are* predictable. But this view can hardly be held by 'Austrians'.[25]

In the first place, it is difficult to discern where this allegedly basic Austrian 'tenet' has come from. Neither Menger nor Hayek (I or II) would seem to have accepted such a proposition. The only possible Austrian source would seem to lie in the ambiguities regarding prediction of Mises. Anyhow, though, of course, preferences, expectations and knowledge are not at all precisely predictable, and though they are not nearly as precisely predictable as many physical phenomena, *they are, to some extent, imprecisely predictable*. For no ordered or civilized human society or social activity would have been possible if human preferences, expectations and knowledge were completely unpredictable. This is not necessarily to claim that economists have been, or ever will be able to improve the accuracy of economic predictions very significantly beyond what is possible without their efforts (though in some cases they seem to have been able to do this). Economic predictions will never be sufficiently accurate to enable markets to come precisely into equilibrium with the speed and perfection depicted by economists' models which abstract from human ignorance. Far less will economic prediction ever be accurate enough to enable the more optimistic dreams and ambitions of socialist planners to be fulfilled (though, of course, to create a Gulag involves creating a lot of predictable activity regarding death-rates, for example). But there is certainly a 'dilemma' regarding prediction which Austrian economists need to resolve. Such a resolution would not be difficult if the Popperian insights of Hayek II are followed out and the a priorist tenets of Wieser, Mises and Hayek I are eliminated.[26]

Another Austrian dilemma can be discerned on the subject of *Wertfreiheit*, on which some Austrians have laid great emphasis. There would seem to be a considerable contrast, not to say contradiction, between the following two statements of Mises (see Hutchison, 1964, p. 42 n. 2):

What is impermissible, however, is the obliteration of the boundary between scientific explanation and political value judgement.

Two pages later Mises maintains:

To the man who adopts the scientific method in reflecting upon the problems of human action, liberalism must appear as the only policy that can lead to lasting well-being for himself, his friends, and his loved ones, and, indeed, for all others as well. Only one who does not want to achieve such ends as life, health, and prosperity for himself, his friends, and those he loves, only one who prefers sickness, misery and suffering may reject the reasoning of liberalism on the ground that it is not neutral with regard to value judgements. (1960, pp. 37, 39)

But Professor Kirzner holds that these two statements are quite reconcilable, though he concedes that, in Mises's writings, 'one may on occasion find language superficially implying that a certain policy is simply wrong or bad' (1976, p. 82). But apparently Mises was not asserting *his own* value judgements. His criticisms are to be understood as to 'reflect only his opinions concerning the degree of success with which others are pursuing *their* purposes'. (Kirzner, 1976)

It seems doubtful whether this is all that Mises's words can reasonably be understood as implying (even allowing, as one must, for a fair margin of imprecision in his writing). But, in any case, Professor Rothbard rejects such an interpretation and denies Mises's entitlement to it:

Mises often states that interventionary measures in the market, e.g., price controls, will have consequences that even the government officials administering the plans would consider bad. But the problem is that we do not *know* what the government officials' ends are – *except* that they demonstrably *do* like the power they have acquired. . . . We therefore cannot say that government officials would invariably concede, after learning all the consequences, that their actions were mistaken. (1970, p. 293)

If Professor Rothbard's interpretation is correct – and it certainly seems plausible – then Mises was *not* simply reflecting other people's value judgements but asserting his own. Of course, there is nothing necessarily wrong with such assertions. But the significance seems questionable of Mises's previous assertion that it is impermissible to obliterate the boundary between scientific explanation and political value judgement.

What, however, stands out are the deep contradictions pervading Austrian methodological views as between those deriving from Wieser, Mises and Hayek I, on the one hand, and those following Hayek II, on the other. These differences cover such crucial issues not only as prediction and predictability, but as testing and falsifiability and the similarities in criteria and methods as between economics and the natural sciences.

What needs to be emphasized is the desirability of discarding the remaining residues of the a priorist 'Pretence of Knowledge', which came down from Wieser, Mises and Hayek I. For claims to establish *a priori* judgements of 'apodictic certainty' or 'beyond the possibility of dispute', together with comprehensive denunciations as 'Positivist' and 'Empiricist' of the criteria of testability and falsifiability, may serve to support infallibilist, authoritarian and anti-libertarian attitudes and to play into the hands of the enemies of freedom. It is very dangerous for *any* individual or group to claim access to significant *a priori* and infallible politicoeconomic judgements, beyond the possibility of dispute and testing. Obviously anyone who *did* dispute them would be a kind of psychiatric case.

One of Professor Hayek's most important and illuminating papers on political and social philosophy is his 'Individualism: True and False' (1945). True individualism is linked with the empiricism of the English philosophers, and notably with Locke, Mandeville, Hume, Smith and Burke, and in the nineteenth century is represented by historians such as Acton and De Tocqueville rather than by the English 'classical economists, or at least the Benthamites or philosophical radicals among them' (e.g. James Mill and Ricardo). The false individualist is 'the rationalistic pseudo-individualist' who intellectually paves the way for the dominance of quite opposite philosophies. Unfortunately, Hayek does not follow the story of his distinction beyond the middle of the last century. Certainly 'false individualism' did not then disappear, but may still be discerned around us. Nor does Hayek give more than one or two hints regarding the epistemological and methodological aspects of true and false individualist philosophies, though there certainly are complementary and fundamentally contrasting epistemological and methodological ideas corresponding with Hayek's vital distinction. But Hayek's hints do provide a significant clue. He traces the relationship of true individualism with philosophical nominalism, as opposed to what Popper calls 'essentialism', and in contrast with the rationalism of 'the Cartesian school', Hayek observes:

The antirationalistic approach, which regards man not as a highly rational and intelligent but as a very irrational and fallible being, whose individual errors are corrected only in the course of a social process, and which aims at making the best of very imperfect material, is probably the most characteristic feature of English individualism. (1949, pp. 8–9)

Surely Hayek would have included a 'rationalist utilitarian' among 'false individualists'. Indeed, in what seems to be his first explicit disclaimer with regard to Mises, Hayek states: 'Mises was, of course, a rationalist utilitarian in which direction, for reasons given, I cannot follow him' (1979, p. 205). For surely no '*true* individualist' will lay claim to knowledge of significant *a priori* propositions of 'apodictic certainty', which are 'beyond the possibility of dispute'. We would suggest that a further exploration of the complementary methodological and epistemological aspects of Hayek's vital and fundamental distinction would suggest that 'False', as well as 'True' Individualism has been very much present among modern Austrian views on the philosophy and method of economics. It may simply be added that the more highly one esteems what may be regarded as the essential Austrian message of individualism and subjectivism, the more desirable it should seem that its philosophical and epistemological foundations should be soundly and consistently formulated. The Austrians, with their concern for individualism, subjectivism and liberty, possess a general message ultimately far more valid and valuable than the Keynesians and the Marxians. But it is important that their methodology, or epistemology, should be clearly, logically and explicitly compatible with their political principles. As well as its ethics, politics, and economics, freedom has its epistemology, which must surely be one of its most fundamental aspects and requirements.

Notes

1   The Austrian theory of capital is often regarded as Böhm-Bawerk's, and a distinguishing feature of the Austrian over-investment theory of the trade cycle was held to be its reliance on his capital theory (see Hayek, 1931, p. 22). But Carl Menger told Schumpeter that 'Böhm-Bawerk's theory is one of the greatest errors ever committed' – and 'not for nothing' according to Professor L. M. Lachmann, who criticizes Böhm-Bawerk as an aggregative Ricardian. (See Schumpeter, 1954, p. 847; Lachmann, 1977, pp. 27, 261.)

2   Regarding his own theory of capital, Böhm-Bawerk insisted:

Ich kann darum auch versichern, dass ich meine Meinung von dem – bisher wenigstens universellen Auftreten der Zinsercheinung gewiss nicht aus einer aprioristischen Überzeugung von der Richtigkeit meiner Zinstheorie und ihrer, "drei Gründe" sondern einfach aus einer Betrachtung der aus dem Augenschein, der Geschichte und Statistik zugänglichen Tatsachen geschöpft habe. (1924, p. xi)

Regarding parallels with the methods of physics, Böhm-Bawerk maintained:

Aber – so wird man vielleicht einwenden wollen – der Naturforscher deduziert auch die Grösse und Geschwindigkeit der $\propto$ – und β – Partikel doch nur aus Prämissen, die er zuvor induktiv festgestellt hat; er fusst also auch in seinen deduktiven Zwischenoperationen doch immer wieder auf der Erfahrung. Ganz wahr und natürlich! Aber der deduktiv operierende Nationalökonom von heutzutage macht es ja auch nicht anders. Es ist eines der bösesten Missverständnisse, die Zeitweise die Methodenkontroverse vergiftet haben, wenn man die abstrahierenden Deduktionen moderner Sozialtheoretiker auf gleichen Fuss mit den aprioristischen Spekulationen mittelalterlicher Scholastiker stellte. (1924, p. 192)

3   I am indebted on this point to Mr Max Alter, who is working on Menger's philosophical ideas, and who emphasizes the influence on them of Savigny, Droysen and other German historians and historical philosophers.

4   Three different versions can be identified of the long-standing, classical and neoclassical conception of the subject as entirely, or almost entirely, deductive, based on a very few basic postulates. According to (1) these very few postulates, though obvious to elementary common sense, are not necessarily derived from introspection, but 'from observation or consciousness' (Senior). According to (2) these postulates are derived from introspection, and are endowed thereby with much greater certainty than can be obtained in the natural sciences, thus giving the social sciences a great advantage. But, at the same time, these postulates remain in some sense or other 'empirical' (Wieser). According to (3) these postulates consist of *a priori* judgements, of 'apodictic certainty', which they bestow on the conclusions deduced from them, though these are not analytic or tautological (Mises).

5   See Senior 1836/1951, p. 26. Senior's second Elementary Proposition is a vacuous version of the Malthusian population doctrine, the precise cash value of which remains obscure: 'That the Population of the world, or, in other words, the number of persons inhabiting it, is limited only by moral or physical evil, or by fear of a deficiency of those articles of wealth which the habits of the individuals of each class of the inhabitants lead them to require.'

6   John Stuart Mill in his early essay does remark that Political

Economy is concerned with man 'as a being who desires to possess wealth, *and who is capable of judging of the comparative efficacy of means for obtaining that end*' (1844, p. 137, italics added). But Mill shows no sign of realizing the magnitude of this additional qualification, or abstraction, regarding knowledge.

7   This work of Strigl's seems to have had a considerable influence on Robbins's *Essay on the Nature and Significance of Economic Science* (1932 and 1935), and is several times cited therein.

8   The absolutely fundamental contrast should be noted between Mises's conception of the rationality principle and that of Sir Karl Popper who states that, in his view, *those who assert that this principle is valid, or true,* a priori *are certainly mistaken.* Sir Karl maintains that the principle is certainly false, empirically, though it is a useful approximation to reality, and that it is testable and should be tested. See Popper, 1967, pp. 145–8.

9   See also Mises, 1949, p. 39: 'The theorems attained by praxeological reasoning are not only perfectly certain and incontestable, like correct mathematical theorems. They refer, moreover, with the full rigidity of their apodictic certainty and its incontestability to the reality of action as it appears in life and history. Praxeology conveys exact and precise knowledge of real things'. (Quoted in Grunberg, 1978, pp. 544–5.)

10   Another example of lack of clarity is with regard to Mises's claims regarding prediction. He writes: 'Praxeological knowledge makes it possible to predict with apodictic certainty the outcome of various modes of action. But, of course, such predictions can never imply anything regarding quantitative matters.' (1949, p. 117) Elsewhere Mises points out with regard to predictions that: 'even if they are "qualitatively correct" . . . they may bring disaster if they are "quantitatively" wrong' (1962, p. 66). Objections may be raised to 'apodictic certainty' being claimed for *any* genuine predictions, as well as regarding the distinction between 'qualitative' and 'quantitative'. It is unclear, for example, how this distinction applies to cost-benefit estimates. Two different such assessments might be quantitatively very near together (around zero) and differ qualitatively; or they might agree qualitatively but be wide apart, and conflict vitally in quantitative terms.

11   See O'Driscoll, 1977, p. 34; also Barry, 1979: 'Much of Hayek's early writings on methodology are elaborations of Mises's position' (p. 20).

12   Hayek repeated this point most emphatically in *Preise und Produktion*, 1931, pp. 34–5: '*Ich glaube, dass, wenn wir überhaupt versuchen wollen, wirtschaftliche Erscheinungen zu erklären, uns dazu kein anderer Weg zur Verfügung steht als der, auf der Grundlage fortzubauen, die uns statische Theorie bietet*'.

13   'Only through the principle of competition has political economy any pretension to the character of a science' (Mill, 1909, II, IV, I). According to Edgeworth if monopoly replaced competition 'abstract

economists . . . would be deprived of their occupation. . . . There would survive only the empirical school, flourishing in a chaos congenial to their mentality.' (1925, vol. 1, pp. 138–9) As Sir John Hicks later put the point: 'It has to be recognised that a general abandonment of the assumption of perfect competition . . . must have very destructive consequences for economic theory. . . . The basis on which economic laws can be constructed is therefore shorn away.' (1946, pp. 83–4) The point is that only so long as one can retain the assumption of competition can one retain the essential assumption of '*Allwissenheit*' – at least with regard to any significant kind of case. In this connection, Oskar Morgenstern made an especially illuminating contribution in his article 'Vollkommene Voraussicht und wirtschaftliches Gleichgewicht' (1935), in which he showed very clearly how the assumption of knowledge required for equilibrium models is incompatible with conditions of oligopoly.

14 Of course one can kill sheep by incantations *plus* a little arsenic. So one can claim that economic theories rest on a number of self-evident postulates, 'beyond the possibility of dispute', which can easily be formulated, but which, by themselves, can do no effective work without 'a great multitude of subsidiary postulates' as Lord Robbins put it (1932 and 1935, p. 79). Robbins agreed with Hayek in claiming that economic theories were somehow more securely founded than those of the natural sciences:

'In Economics, as we have seen, the ultimate constituents of our fundamental generalisations are known to us by immediate acquaintance. In the natural sciences they are known only inferentially. There is much less reason to doubt the counterpart in reality of the assumption of individual preferences than that of the assumption of the electron.' (p. 105)

15 cf Lachmann, 1956, p. xv:

'The fact remains that the two greatest achievements of our science within the last hundred years, subjective value and the introduction of expectations, became possible only when it was realized that the causes of certain phenomena do not lie in the "facts of the situation" but in the appraisal of such a situation by active minds.'

One may agree with Professor Lachmann's historical judgement regarding the significance of expectations, while disagreeing that a realization of their importance is at all incompatible with what Làchmann calls 'the rigid canons of Logical Empiricism' (any more than was the abandonment of Newtonian theory and the introduction of relativity in physics). 'Appraisals' by 'active minds' are, of course, part of 'the facts' of a more complex kind of situation.

16 Professor Shackle (1967, p. 135) refers to Keynes's paper of 1937 as 'that apotheosis of his thought'. But that was hardly how it was treated by most 'Keynesians' in the ensuing decades. Shackle held that Keynes

here was concerned 'to deny the orderliness of economic society and economic life and to deny this life the attribute of orderliness was to seem to deny the study of it the attributes of science' (p. 134). Most Keynesians would have strongly disagreed with this conclusion, though it is similar to one propounded regarding the assumptions of competition by J. S. Mill and Edgeworth.

17   See the papers 'The Maintenance of Capital' and 'Price Expecta-tions, Monetary Disturbances and Malinvestments', republished in 1939. There are even some hints in an article of 1928 on 'intertemporal equilibrium'. Later, in 1965, Hayek explained 'why though at one time a very pure and narrow economic theorist, I was led from technical economics into all kinds of questions usually regarded as philosophical. When I look back, it seems to have all begun nearly thirty years ago, with an essay on Economics and Knowledge.' (1967, p. 91) Hayek's approach to fundamental problems of policy broadened out from what might be described as a narrowly 'Ricardian' to a comprehensively 'Smithian' approach.

18   Mr N. Barry (1979, p. 27) recognizes that 'the acceptance of the Popperian methodology does indicate a departure from the praxeological approach characteristic of the Austrians and their followers.' But we certainly would not agree with Mr Barry when he suggests that Hayek has *not* 'made drastic revisions'; and to say that 'there is nothing of crucial importance that he has consciously abandoned' is surely refuted by the recognition by Mr Barry just quoted, *which is of crucial importance*.

19   For Mises, of course, Hayek II's problem of turning the tautologies of equilibrium analysis into propositions which tell us something about causation in the real world is solved by a priorism.

Another distinguished Austrian, closely associated with the Vienna Circle, who asserted the importance of empirical testing, was Karl Menger, son of the founder. He took up and countered the claim of Mises 'that certain propositions of economics can be proved', for example, the law of diminishing returns. In his paper on that subject (originally published in 1936) Menger maintained:

> We emphasize that we attach little importance to the rather subtle logical relationships among the various laws about returns. We believe the crucial issue for economics to be whether or not these laws are empirically confirmable, while we regard it as a secondary issue whether or not they follow from certain other propositions. It is, rather, some outstanding economists who have raised this issue by claiming to prove the law of diminishing returns on land logically, and thereby to make empirical tests superfluous. (K. Menger, 1979, pp. 279–80)

20   Hayek went so far as to remark that in a significant sense 'all knowledge is capacity to predict' (1937 and 1949, p. 51n). Also, surely quite validly, he noted how 'the preoccupation with pure analysis'

creates 'a peculiar blindness to the role played in real life by . . .
institutions' (p. 55). This is obviously and especially the case when the
'pure analysis' is concerned with conditions of '*Allwissenheit*, while
'institutions' arise inevitably from ignorance and uncertainty.
21   Contrast Mises: 'What assigns economics its peculiar and unique
position in the orbit both of pure knowledge and of the practical
utilization of knowledge is the fact that its particular theorems are not
open to any verification or falsification on the grounds of experience'
(1949, p. 858).
22   Hayek's *Counter-Revolution of Science* (1952) is a fascinating and most
learned piece of intellectual history, but cannot be understood as
contributing to the analysis of differences between the natural and social
sciences. See Popper (1979, p. 185), who maintains that 'labouring the
difference between science and the humanities has long been a fashion
and has become a bore. The method of problem solving, the method of
conjecture and refutation, is practised by both'. However – though it is
indeed rather a 'bore' having to do so – in the face of the extravagant
pretensions of mathematicians and quantifiers in recent decades, it has
been necessary to stress the wide differences in the feasible aims and
actual achievements as between economics and the most advanced
natural sciences, and to emphasize the much greater significance of the
historical dimension, and of changing institutions, in the social sciences.
23   Subsequently (1979, p. 24) Professor Kirzner wrote:

'We note *what at least superficially appears* to be an important
disagreement between Hayek and Mises concerning the character of
economics. Hayek is often coupled with Mises as espousing the
view of economics as a completely a prioristic body of thought. We
have seen, on the contrary, that Hayek took great pains to
emphasize his perception of economic science as being, with the
exception of equilibrium analysis, empirical science.' (italics added)

The phrase we have italicized seems to amount to an exquisite
understatement. There is here an absolutely fundamental philosophical
clash.
24   This 'basic Austrian tenet', or the view so eloquently propounded
by Professor Shackle, of the unpredictability of human preferences,
expectations and knowledge, 'leads only to total despair' (as Professor
Kenneth Boulding, 1973, so rightly insisted) – that is, if one assumes the
traditional aim of economists as being to provide more rational
recommendations about economic policies. But it seems an equally basic
'tenet' of Austrians that they can put forward most confident recommendations about economic policies with respect to the effective
workings of free markets. Here again there is a fundamental dilemma or
contradiction to be resolved. For while Professor Shackle with his
extremely agnostic, or even nihilistic, views, does not seem concerned
with the traditional aim of economists in respect of policy recommenda-

tions, most Austrians certainly *have* shown themselves thus concerned.
25 The other 'basic Austrian tenet' is simply that 'human action is
purposeful'. Professor Kirzner considers this aperçu so significant
that he insists that it 'needs to be stated and restated, emphasized and reemphasized' (1976, p. 47). How much can logically be
deduced simply from such a generalization that 'man is a purposeful
animal' (or the other kind of general slogan that 'man is a social animal',
much emphasized by Marxians) is not at all clear. But no 'empiricist'
would wish to question in the slightest that – as Kirzner puts it – 'making
reference to human plans and motivations is an essential part of the
economist's scientific task' (p. 47). As Sir Karl Popper has said (1979,
pp. 183–5):

> I am quite prepared to accept the thesis that understanding is the aim
> of the humanities. . . . It must be admitted that, in the sense here
> indicated, we can understand men and their actions and products
> while we cannot understand 'nature' – solar systems, molecules, or
> elementary particles. Yet there is no sharp division here. We can
> learn to understand the expressive movements of higher animals in a
> sense very similar to that in which we understand men. . . . Thus I
> oppose the attempt to proclaim the method of understanding as the
> characteristic of the humanities, the mark by which we may
> distinguish them from the natural sciences. And when its supporters
> denounce a view like mine as 'positivistic' or 'scientistic', then I may
> perhaps answer that they themselves seem to accept *implicitly and
> uncritically*, that positivism or scientism is *the only philosophy
> appropriate to natural sciences*.

26 A further Austrian dilemma in need of elucidation is indicated by
Professor Kirzner's rejection of what he calls 'the Robbinsian concept of
economizing, that is, allocative decision making' (1976, p. 118). This
concept is the central basis of Robbins's *Essay on the Nature and
Significance of Economic Science* (1932 and 1935). But according to
Professor Rothbard (1970, p. 28) when he wrote the *Essay*, 'Robbins
was, at that time, a decidedly "Misesian" economist'. According to
Professor O'Driscoll 'the earlier Austrians in part contributed to the
development of a theoretical edifice they later came to reject' (1977,
p. 32). But the trouble is, and the dilemmas arise, because some
Austrians today, far from rejecting the earlier 'edifice', are strenuously
and even dogmatically upholding it, while very little in the way of
explicit 'rejection' has taken place.

References

Alter, M. (1980), 'On the Intellectual Background of the Older Austrian
    School' (unpublished).
Barry, N. (1979), *Hayek's Social and Economic Philosophy*.

Böhm-Bawerk, E. (1896), *Karl Marx and the Close of his System*, ed. P. M. Sweezy, 1949.

(1924), *Gesammelte Schriften*, ed. F. X. Weiss.

Boulding, K. (1973), review of G. L. S. Shackle, *Epistemics and Economics, Journal of Economic Literature*, vol. 11, no. 4, p. 1374.

Edgeworth, F. Y. (1925), *Papers Relating to Political Economy*, 3 vols.

Grunberg, E. (1978), 'Complexity and Open Systems in Economic Discourse', *Journal of Economic Issues*, vol. 12, no. 3, pp. 541ff.

Hayek, F. A. (1928), 'Das intertemporale Gleichgewichtsystem der Preise und die Bewegungen des Geldwertes', *Weltwirtschaftliches Archiv*, vol. 28, no. 2, pp. 36–76.

(1931), *Preise und Producktion*.

(1933), *Monetary Theory and the Trade Cycle*, translated by N. Kaldor and H. M. Croome from the German of 1929.

(1937), 'Economics and Knowledge', *Economica*, N. S., vol. 4, pp. 33–54.

(1939), *Profits, Interest and Investment*.

(1949), *Individualism and Economic Order*.

(1952), *The Counter-Revolution of Science*.

(1967), *Studies in Philosophy, Politics and Economics*.

(1978), *New Studies in Philosophy, Politics, Economics and the History of Ideas*.

(1979), *Law, Legislation and Liberty*, vol. 3.

Hayek, F. A., ed. (1935), *Collectivist Economic Planning*.

Hicks, J. R. (1946), *Value and Capital*, 2nd ed.

Hutchison, T. W. (1964), *'Positive' Economics and Policy Objectives*.

Keynes, J. M. (1937), 'The General Theory of Employment', *Quarterly Journal of Economics*, vol. 51, pp. 209ff; reprinted in S. Harris (ed.), *The New Economics*, 1947, pp. 181–93.

Kirzner, I. (1976), 'On the Method of Austrian Economics', in E. G. Dolan (ed.), *The Foundations of Modern Austrian Economics*, pp. 40ff.

(1979), *Perception, Opportunity and Profit*.

Knight, F. H. (1956), *On the History and Method of Economics*.

Korsch, A. (1976), 'Der Stand der beschäftigungspolitischen Diskussion zur Zeit der Wirtschaftskrise in Deutschland', in G. Bombach *et al.* (ed.), *Der Keynesianismus*, vol. 1.

Lachmann, L. M. (1956), *Capital and its Structure*.

(1977), *Capital, Expectations and the Market Process*.

Mayer, H. (1911), 'Eine neue Grundlegung der theoretischen Nationalökonomie', *Zeitschrift für Volkswirtschaft, Sozialpolitik und Verwaltung*.

(1932), 'Der Erkenntniswert der funktionellen Preistheorien' in H. Mayer (ed.), *Wirtschaftstheorie der Gegenwart*.

Menger, C. (1963), *Problems of Economics and Sociology*, ed. L. Schneider, translated by F. J. Nock from the German *Untersuchungen über die Methode der Sozialwissenschaften und der politischen Ökonomie insbesonder*, 1883.

Menger, K. (1979), *Selected Papers in Logic and Foundations, Didactics, Economics*.
Mill, J. S. (1844), *Essays On Some Unsettled Questions of Political Economy*.
Mises, L. (1949), *Human Action*.
  (1960), *Epistemological Problems in Economics*.
  (1962), *The Ultimate Foundations of Economic Science*.
Morgenstern, O. (1935), 'Vollkommene Voraussicht und wirtschaft-liches Gleichgewicht', *Zeitschrift für Nationalökonomie*, vol. 6, pp. 337–57.
O'Driscoll, G. P. (1977), *Economics as a Coordination Problem*.
Popper, Sir Karl (1967) 'La Rationalité et le Statut du Principe de Rationalité, in *Les Fondements Philosophiques des Systèmes Econom-iques*, ed. E. M. Claassen.
Popper, Sir Karl (1979), *Objective Knowledge*, revised ed.
Robbins, L. C. (1932 and 1935), *An Essay on the Nature and Significance of Economic Science*, 1st and 2nd eds.
Rothbard, M. (1970), *Power and Market*.
  (1976), 'Praxeology: the Methodology of Austrian Economics', in E. G. Dolan (ed.), *The Foundations of Modern Austrian Economics*, pp. 19ff.
Schumpeter, J. A. (1954), *History of Economic Analysis*.
Senior, N. W. (1936), *An Outline of the Science of Political Economy* (reprinted 1951).
Shackle, G. L. S. (1967), *The Years of High Theory*.
Strigl, R. (1923), *Die ökonomischen Kategorien und die Organisation der Wirtschaaft*.
Wieser, F. (1928), *Social Economics*, translated by A. F. Hinrichs.
  (1929), *Gesammelte Abhandlungen*, ed. F. A. Hayek.

8

The Limitations of General
Theories in Macro Economics

I

In the seventies much interest was shown in the thirties. Especially in respect of their economic problems, comparisons and parallels have often been drawn between the two decades, the earlier of which can be said to have been heralded by the Wall Street crash of October 1929. As regards the history of economic thought, the main consequences of the great depression, which dominated much of the ensuing decade of the thirties, was the development, or some might claim the creation, of modern macroeconomics. But by the end of the seventies, this macroeconomic 'revolution' of the thirties, long believed by many economists to have constituted such a major and definitive advance, was under fundamental reconsideration. For example, in a German work of 1976 on *Der Keynesianismus*, it was observed:

> In view of the fact that the world economy finds itself in a crisis of worldwide dimensions, the question at once arises as to how far certain parallels can be demonstrated with the thirties. It would be interesting to establish to what extent there is a similarity in the forces at work which at that time brought about the economic collapse. . . . Above all this would be essential for answering the question as to how far the solutions put forward then, 45–50 years ago, still possess validity, and should be applied as a means of countering the present recession. In this connection the question has to be examined as to whether demands for an employment policy, financed out of budget deficits (as was demanded by the German reformers . . . and later by J. M. Keynes), should be upheld today in a situation in which inflation has still not been overcome. (Korsch, 1976, vol. 2, p. 11)

As regards parallels, one might mention that in Britain, 1929, like 1979, was an election year in which employment policies were an important issue. The 1929 election marked an important stage in the development of Keynes's ideas, when his proposals for public works against unemployment conflicted with what came to be called 'The Treasury View'. At the 1979 election there was also a clash between those supporting measures of what has come to be called 'job creation' or 'job saving' (who often quite misleadingly compared levels of unemployment in the seventies with those of the thirties) and those proposing to cut down on such measures.

Let it be emphasized, at this point, that when comparing the thirties and the seventies it is the profound contrasts, and not some superficial similarities, which are significant; and moreover that, to some extent, the comparisons favour the inflationary seventies as against the deflationary thirties. Whatever deterioration in the state of world politics took place in the seventies, it does not seem to have stemmed originally, appreciably, or directly, from the severe economic instabilities of the decade (apart from the oil problems on the supply side), while, on the other hand, the deflation of the thirties at once claimed a political casualty of appalling dimensions and consequences in the destruction of the Weimar Republic.[1]

But what should be noticed here is how the similarities between the two decades have been stressed by those clinging to what are claimed to be 'general theories' – which in fact are seriously lacking in generality. According to the argument of this chapter, too many economists were (and are) superficially 'consistent' in holding either (perhaps, in Britain at any rate, with a majority) that Keynesian measures were right in and after 1929, and that similar measures may have been right to counter unemployment in 1979; or, alternatively, with the minority (including notably Professor Hayek), that the seventies have proved the vital error in Keynesian policies, which were always, in the thirties too, fundamentally misconceived.[2] Behind this kind of superficial consistency there would seem to lie, whether or not it is explicitly formulated, a methodological assumption that macroeconomic policies are to be derived from a *general* macroeconomic theory, valid both in 1929 and 1979, and, presumably, at all other dates: that is, a kind of consistency in macroeconomic policies, which seems to be widely maintained (in one direction or another), follows from a methodological programme of *general* macroeconomic theorizing.

The limitations of general macroeconomic theories, which we are emphasizing, do not arise simply from such an obvious transformation or contrast in historical conditions as that between the deflation of the thirties and the inflation of the seventies. Institutions, expectations, and reactions, change historically and crucially. In particular, the ways in which expectations change, and the forces shaping these processes, or what Professor Fellner (1976, p. 50) has called 'the expectational system', and the institutions which form it, shift significantly, to an extent which puts severe limitations on attempts at general macroeconomic theories.

II

When a system of general economic theory began to emerge in the late seventeenth and early eighteenth centuries it comprised a mixture of what in recent decades have come to be called macroeconomic and microeconomic elements. The great intellectual ambition was to produce a comprehensive general theory of the economy (and to some extent of the whole society) – that is, to 'do a Newton', or do for the social and economic world what Sir Isaac had done for the physical world. The system was to be built around general assumptions regarding the individual's pursuit of self-interest in a beneficently self-adjusting system.

In *The Wealth of Nations* the idea of self-adjustment was applied microeconomically, that is to the allocation, valuation and exchange of particular resources, as well as macroeconomically, to the aggregate level of activity and the rate of growth of the economy. Indeed, it was the self-adjusting macroeconomics, rather than the microeconomic component, which was the more revolutionary element in *The Wealth of Nations*, supplanting the 'mercantilists'' doctrine regarding the need for constant government action to maintain and promote employment and growth, in the assumed absence of effective and beneficent self-equilibrating forces.

According to Smithian, or 'classical', macroeconomics, a competitive economy would be macroeconomically self-adjusting through its effectively equilibrating saving and investment processes, together with flexible wages. Self-adjusting processes would work themselves out just as effectively, in the two major markets central to macroeconomics, as they would in 'ordinary' markets:

wages and employment in the labour market, and savings, investment and interest rates in the capital market, would adjust as smoothly and beneficently – indeed 'immediately', as Smith at one point suggested – to equilibrium levels, as the supply, demand and price of, say, wine, would in the wine market. This is what Schumpeter called 'the Turgot-Smith' theory of saving and investment. In fact Smith maintained that, even for the money supply, the operation of market forces could and should be relied upon as confidently as they could for the wine supply.[3]

However, neither by Smith, nor by his classical successors, was the vital question of the monetary framework ever precisely answered. The emergence of cyclical fluctuations came to be recognized, but the more orthodox and influential 'classicals' did not regard instability and unemployment as profoundly or fundamentally serious problems. While the unorthodox Malthus asserted the seriousness of periodic fluctuations, especially for the poor; and while Marx so exaggerated the instability of capitalism as to proclaim, every few years, through the middle decades of the 19th century, that each new downswing in the economy would bring the revolutionary overthrow of the system; John Stuart Mill, on the other hand, overwhelmingly the most influential economist in the middle decades of the 19th century, continued to regard the problem of cyclical fluctuations as relatively unimportant, and prolonged involuntary unemployment as impossible.[4]

When, around 1870, the general theories of the English classicals lost their hold, it was the value and distribution theories which were then abandoned, including notably the Malthusian natural wage doctrine – to a considerable extent for reasons of historical obsolescence and lack of generality. The self-equilibrating macroeconomics for a short time survived unscathed. Moreover, the more fundamental criticisms then being launched by historical economists regarding the limitations of *all* general theories in economics were, on balance justifiably at that time, rejected.

The new body of neoclassical theory was narrowly microeconomic, and aimed at and claimed – not invalidly – the widest generality. Its theories of value, allocation, choice, or exchange, were, much more tightly than in the classical system, built around the completely general fact of scarcity; and they assumed, again, individual self-interest, or at least consistency, together with such general principles as diminishing returns and diminishing utility. These fundamental assumptions, though sometimes expressed as tautologies, *could* be formulated to possess some empirical content or predictive potential. Around this nucleus a strictly microeconomic system of theory was built, for the central core of which very wide generality could be claimed. The nucleus of the theory had relevance for virtually all times, places and situations where scarcity existed, for Robinson Crusoe as well as for a socialist planner, and its generality was largely unaffected by obsolescence due to historical or institutional change. Certainly, the empirical or predictive content was rather thin, and for most applications a range of subsidiary assumptions was needed about the market setting, or other institutional conditions. Some assumption was also necessary regarding the stability of the macroeconomic framework, such as that, made by Marshall in his *Principles*, of a constant purchasing power of money.

These epistemological characteristics of microeconomics have persisted, at least until recently. As Professor Lancaster has observed:

Microeconomics remains primarily concerned with economics in general. . . . Thus simplification in microeconomics will often be of the kind that rejects some special relationship that holds only for one time and place, and concentrates on features common to many times and many places. . . . Simplification in macroeconomics is likely to take an opposite course . . . rejecting general possibilities in favour of known behaviour here and now. (1969, p. 2, quoted by Loasby, 1976, p. 13)[5]

But the fullest and most elaborate applications of this body of microeconomic theory were restricted to competitive markets, and the assumption about competition was essentially interconnected with the vital fundamental assumption of adequate knowledge, or even '*Allwissenheit*' (or '*Unfehlbarkeit*'), as Carl Menger described it (1963, p. 84). It was the need for this assumption about knowledge which entailed the competitive assumption: because only with large numbers of 'small' units in a market process can one dispense with rather arbitrary special assumptions about the expectations of the units involved regarding the reactions, to their own actions, of other units. Certainly, as F. H. Knight observed, it was with regard to knowledge and uncertainty that there existed 'the most important underlying difference between the conditions which theory is compelled to assume and those which exist in fact' (1921 and 1933, p. 51).

Now for the theory of narrowly microeconomic decisions

(regarding, for example, the allocation of consumption spending by small household units) in a reasonably stable macroeconomic environment, the adequate knowledge, or '*Allwissenheit*', postulate did not constitute a *very* serious limitation – provided, of course, that oligopolistic situations are ruled out. But as one approaches macroeconomic, or monetary, questions this assumption soon ceases to look like a justifiable simplification and looks more like a distorting oversimplification. It is not only that uncertainty and erroneous expectations are almost inevitably much more crucially involved in long-term investment decisions than in short-term consumption decisions. As was long ago pointed out, the very existence of money implies something less than '*Allwissenheit*' on the part of those using it, and therefore the possibility of erroneous expectations. In fact there is a sense in which it may be said, regarding traditional microeconomic theorizing on the one hand, and, on the other hand, the macroeconomic theorizing of Keynes and of the business cycle theorists before him, that microeconomics has been about knowledge and macroeconomics about ignorance. But it should be emphasized that quite apart from the significance of uncertainty, ignorance, and expectations, the relationships between, in particular, saving and interest rates, and between the supply of labour and wage rates, cannot, as is well known, be assumed to hold as predictably to the regular patterns as they can with 'normal' goods. That is, of course, just why a separate 'macro' theory of 'employment, interest, and money' was held to be necessary by Keynes, to put alongside the self-adjusting 'neoclassical' microeconomics which he broadly upheld.

Anyhow, as Professor Patinkin has put it, in perhaps rather alarming terms: 'Once the Pandora box of expectations and price uncertainty is opened upon the world of economic analysis, *anything can happen*' (1956, p. 180n, quoted by Shackle, 1961, p. 211, italics added). At least until comparatively recently it seemed rather easier to keep the lid on Pandora's box with regard to microeconomics than it has been, at least in the last hundred years, with regard to macroeconomics. But a 'new microeconomics' may be emerging which attempts a kind of controlled opening of Pandora's box, in the face of the increasing impact of oligopolies and bilateral monopolies which have often supplanted the competitive conditions which general price theory has to some extent necessarily assumed.[6] So this contrast between micro- and macroeconomics should not be pressed in extreme black-and-white terms, but rather as one between shades of grey – which may, however, be highly significant. But while the 'micro' foundations of microeconomics are broadly defensible to the extent that one accepts the simplification of the adequate knowledge postulate, the 'micro' foundations of macroeconomics are by no means so defensible, or unambiguous, in particular with regard to the vital cases of capital markets and labour markets. In any case, the methodological lesson seems to be that, to the extent that Pandora's box is opened up, what can be expected – from either micro- or macroeconomic theorizing – will consist much more of case-studies than general theories.

III

It could be, and has been, argued that for the nineteenth century, and indeed down to 1914, in spite of increasing concern with instability and unemployment towards the end of the century, the classical self-adjusting model provided a reasonable approximation. In fact, Pigou (1949, pp. 85–98) produced some figures as evidence of this. But it is very difficult to quantify accurately the cyclical, and other, unemployment of the nineteenth century, and still more difficult to assess its seriousness socially as an aggravation of the poverty problem, and therefore how far the orthodox leading classicals were justified in so largely disregarding it, to the extent they did.

Anyhow, after 1870, there was, at first, no explicit repudiation or abandonment of the Smithian-Ricardian self-adjusting macroeconomics, as there was, in such revolutionary terms by Jevons, of the Ricardo-Mill value and distribution theory. A self-adjusting 'macro' model based on an effective, self-adjusting mechanism of saving, investment, and interest rates, together with flexible wages, continued a somewhat ambiguous existence, and sometimes was actually applied to real world problems of instability and unemployment. There was, however, some renewed discussion of the desirable monetary framework, and of general price stability, or of a gently rising or falling price level, as a desirable objective.

However, in Britain, at any rate from about the mid-eighties, a considerable change gradually began to gather momentum with regard to problems of instability and unemployment. There was no single dramatic revolutionary break comparable with that with classical microeconomics by Jevons in 1871. Moreover, it is not at all easy to decide just how far in the real world (1) there actually was a quantitative increase in unemployment; (2) there was simply widely *thought* to have been a quantitative increase (though Marshall denied it); or (3) there was a change rather in social preferences, or policy priorities, in favour of attempts to reduce instability, unemployment and poverty. There was certainly to some extent, in Britain, an important move in social and political priorities as part of a broad programme for the reduction of poverty, inspired politically by the extension of the franchise down the wealth scale. The year 1886 might be taken as marking a turning-point. In that year Foxwell published his *Irregularity of Employment and Fluctuations of Prices*, in which, exactly 50 years before Keynes's *General Theory*, he took up the challenge to Smithian-Ricardian orthodoxy which had been bequeathed by Malthus (1836), exactly 50 years previously, and insisted on the seriousness of the unemployment problem: 'It is my most rooted and settled conviction that, of all the many claims of labour, the most grave, the most pressing, and the most just, is the claim . . . to more regular employment' (1886, p. 96).[7]

Furthermore, in 1886, marking the waning influence of the classical macroeconomics as regards policy-making, Joseph Chamberlain enacted an instruction to local authorities to finance relief works during depressions. Practically and quantitatively the results of this measure were negligible. But it was a significant first step, as a break with Ricardian doctrines, and was cautiously approved by Marshall. Subsequently, in 1905, Chamberlain, perhaps the most influential political leader of his day, proclaimed that the problem of unemployment had 'now become the most important question of our time' (see Skidelsky, 1976, p. 542). In fact an impressive study of *Unemployment and Politics* concludes, regarding Britain: 'By 1914 fatalistic acceptance of the inevitability of the trade cycle and doctrinaire prejudice against the relief of unemployment seemed to have largely passed away' (Harris, 1972, p. 5).

Around the turn of the century, therefore, instability, unemployment and the trade cycle had begun to re-emerge as problems of increasing importance for economists. Previous to that, much of the early work on cyclical fluctuations had come from writers outside the orthodox classical and neoclassical traditions, either from historical economists, or Marxists, or what Keynes called 'the underworld'. The attitude to the mainstream neoclassical theories of those economists who first established the main facts and statistics about cyclical fluctuations – such as Juglar and later Mitchell – was one of detachment or scepticism. Before the first and second decades of this century, and the arrival of the second generation of Austrian and Cambridge economists, apart from Wicksell, there was little attempt to bring together the treatment of the problem of cyclical fluctuations with the theories of neoclassical economics. Indeed, some of the more eclectic writers, or those influenced by the historical school, rejected general economic theories of any kind. It was also argued that each particular cycle was to be explained mainly, or entirely, by its own special historical characteristics; and also that several of the contrasting theories of the cycle, then being advocated in general terms, might each have been valid in particular cases.

In particular and of fundamental significance, psychological fluctuations and changes in expectations were invoked as explanatory factors by some theorists. Indeed the role of errors in bringing about malinvestment and depression had been emphasized by Sismondi. Such explanations were based on assumptions which conflicted crucially with those on which equilibrium theories of value and price rested. Indeed it was logically difficult to arrive at an explanation of instabilities and fluctuations, inevitably involving erroneous shifts in expectations, which could be incorporated in a body of microeconomic theory firmly anchored to the assumption of correct expectations and '*Allwissenheit*'. However, as, after World War I, more attention came to be devoted to the problems of cyclical fluctuations by economists who accepted orthodox microeconomic theories, attempts to square this logical circle were undertaken.

IV

World War I brought institutional changes of major importance for economic theorizing, such as, in Britain, a significant increase in the bargaining strength of trade unions, resulting from larger numbers and the development of unemployment insurance, together with a marked growth in their political influence with the rise of the Labour Party. Wages came to be much less flexible downwards both in real and monetary terms. Professor Kindleberger has noted as a turning-point that in the first great postwar

slump in Britain, of 1921, money wages fell by 38 per cent –
though real wages rose because the cost of living had fallen by 50
per cent (January 1921–December 1922). But this was the last time
that money wages could be reduced so far and so fast. According
to Kindleberger: 'For the first time on any substantial scale, the
economic system developed an asymmetry: with expansion from
full employment, one encountered price and wage increases in the
manufacturing sector; with contraction, stubborn resistance of
prices and wages and unemployment' (1973, pp. 32–3). (See also
Moggridge, 1977, p. 110 and Haberler, 1974, pp. 5–6.)

But although World War I brought, or immensely speeded up,
fundamental institutional changes, it did not at first bring any
rapid or profound changes in economic ideas. A variety of
conflicting or complementary business cycle theories continued to
be debated, while postwar governments seemed rather more
concerned than previously, in a confused way, to take responsibility, of some kind or another, for economic instability and
unemployment, and for policies to counter them. In Britain the
policy of counter-cyclical public works to combat unemployment
was by now widely accepted by economists. Keynes was probably
justified in 1929 when he claimed that the majority of economists
supported his proposals and rejected the classical Treasury
arguments against them. Moreover, by 1929, in Britain at any
rate, opposition to money wage cuts as a counter to unemployment had increased, and was opposed by the alleged chief
spokesman for 'classical' economics, Pigou. By 1931 Keynes
himself was claiming, not without some justification, that
'scarcely one responsible person in Great Britain' disagreed with
his opposition to wage cuts (Keynes, 1931).

However, another work on cyclical fluctuations, published in
German in 1929, can be said to constitute the most strenuous
attempt to construct a theory of the trade cycle, while retaining, as
far as possible, the equilibrium assumptions of classical theory,
and seeking to incorporate such a macroeconomic theory of
fluctuations into the corpus of orthodox, self-equilibrating microeconomics. This work was Hayek's *Monetary Theory and the Trade
Cycle* (1932a).

Hayek maintained that the pricing process, presumably including all wages and interest rates, was, in a market economy, strictly
self-equilibrating, unless it was upset by monetary disturbances.
According to Hayek, 'the basis of all theoretical economics' is the
assumption that prices supply 'an automatic mechanism for

equilibrating supply and demand'. Therefore, explanations of cyclical fluctuations in terms of ignorance or erroneous expectations, such as had been developed from Sismondi onwards, must logically be excluded from any theory which is to be compatible with this 'basis of all theoretical economics' – unless such errors had been brought about by the process of creating money (Hayek, 1932a, pp. 43, 95–8). Thus ignorance brought about by the inflationary creation of money could frustrate the equilibrating forces in the system, but no other kind of ignorance could do so. It would seem that trying to fit together contrasting micro- and macroeconomic theories, one of which assumed knowledge and the other ignorance, was logically a very difficult undertaking. In fact, the contradiction arose from, on the one hand, taking fluctuations or business cycles at all seriously, as amounting to more than fleeting, frictional disequilibria, while, on the other hand, seeking to apply the orthodox model based on the '*Allwissenheit*' assumption.[8]

So strongly did Hayek adhere to the idea of effectively self-equilibrating properties as inherent in the market economies of that time, that he opposed any kind of prompt government action against the downswing of the economy as likely to prevent, or distort, the beneficent equilibrating forces in the system. He denounced both any increase in the quantity of money, and the objective of a stable price level, and, in June 1932, with unemployment in Britain over 20 per cent, he was still opposed to credit expansion or public works policies (1932a, pp. 19–21).[9]

Hayek's was the most thoroughgoing attempt to incorporate classical micro- and macroeconomics into a theory of the business cycle consistent with the 'normal' neoclassical microeconomic models. It has been suggested that in Germany from 1930–32, a strenuous attempt was made to implement policies based on this kind of theory. Certainly the imposition of general, across-the-board wage cuts, attempted by Brüning, did not precisely correspond to the kind of wage flexibility assumed in the classical or neoclassical model. But, as Professor Korsch maintains: 'The economic policy carried out by Brüning had powerful support in neo-classical price theory, according to which a free market economy, left to itself, without state interference, regulates itself and finds its way back to full employment' (1976, vol. 1, p. 14). Professor Korsch goes on to emphasize that the overinvestment theory of Hayek and others 'was widely held in Germany at the time of the economic crisis' (p. 48).[10]

Anyhow, Germany from 1930 to 1932 must have gone through about the most drastic deflationary exercise in attempted flexibility that any leading economy has endured in this century. But the cuts in money wages did not restore profitability, and it was subsequently claimed that the German experience of wage reductions, in a climate of strongly deflationary expectations, lent support to Keynes's thesis 'that (apart from possible effects on the rate of interest) all round reductions of money wages are not likely to result in reductions in real wages, or in lower wage costs relative to the value of output' (Guillebaud, 1939, p. 25).

In the light of the experiences of the thirties perhaps it does not seem very surprising that most economists rejected as – in the circumstances – seriously inadequate the general theory of classical macroeconomics, and the kind of restatement of it put forward as a general theory of the trade cycle.

V

Keynes's *General Theory* was conceived at the bottom of the slump and appeared in a brief interval, four or five years after the most drastic deflation in modern history, and with rearmament proceeding in Britain, about one year or so before the onset of the inflationary process which in different forms has lasted almost uninterruptedly for forty years, with recent disastrous accelerations. Beyond its exposition of a 'theory' which gained wide acceptance, Keynes's *General Theory* seemed to many economists to tidy up a whole area of economics, or even to build up a whole new sector of economic theory. '*The* General Theory', it was said, was 'discovered' by Keynes (or by Keynes's alleged anticipator Kalecki).

But it is, first, essential to distinguish between a 'theory' and what might be called 'a conceptual framework'. *The General Theory* certainly provided a framework of concepts – 'the marginal efficiency of capital', 'the propensity to consume', etc. – and there were also the national income and social accounting concepts developed alongside *The General Theory* by Keynes and others, though they stemmed from the *Treatise* and were hardly advanced by *The General Theory*. 'Conceptual frameworks' such as these, and the taxonomies and statements of definitional relationships between concepts, cannot be falsified in the same sense in which a theory with empirical or predictive content can be falsified. In a sense, conceptual frameworks are valid at all times and places, though they may be more or less interesting or useful according to changing historical and institutional conditions. The utility of Keynes's 'conceptual framework', however – as Keynesians claimed – may not have been seriously affected by the transition from conditions of acute deflation to those of varying types and speeds of inflation in subsequent decades. With conceptual frameworks, the kind of obsolescence due to historical and institutional change, which may undermine economic *theories*, is apt to be much slower and milder. But Keynes did not call his work, nor was he concerned simply with constructing, a 'General Conceptual Framework' (of Employment, Interest and Money); what he enunciated was *The General Theory* – that is, something empirically falsifiable.

About the central generalizations on which Keynes's ('general') theory was based, the following points may be noted:

(1) First, there is the important extent, sometimes overlooked, to which there is a neoclassical component in Keynes's *General Theory*. This occurs especially (as we noted above) with regard to the inverse relationship, which Keynes reasserts, between real wages and employment, which derives from the fundamental microeconomic principle of diminishing marginal productivity. As Professor Geoffrey Maynard has pointed out: 'Keynes in fact put far more emphasis on the relationship between real wages and the level of employment than subsequent expositions of his Theory make clear' (1978, pp. 3, 7).

This general neoclassical proposition incorporated by Keynes may certainly have retained validity in the 1970s, as Professor Maynard shows with regard to the level of unemployment in Britain in the seventies, which therefore would apparently have been held by Keynes to contain a considerable 'voluntary' element.[11] (See also Trevithick, 1980, p. 50.)

(2) On the other hand, the main, stable general relationship which Keynes attempted to establish, with regard to consumption and income, cannot even approximately be held to rank with the central generalizations of microeconomics – insubstantial though these may be. This proposition of Keynes certainly failed to provide a stable, law-like foundation for a 'General Theory' in spite of his claims. Keynes wrote:

The fundamental psychological law upon which we are entitled to depend with great confidence both *a priori* from our knowledge of human nature and from the detailed facts of experience, is that men are disposed as a rule and on the average to increase their consumption as their income increases, but not by as much as the increase in income. (1973, p. 96, italics added)

It could, of course, be maintained that not very much is being said here. But in any case, there simply is no proposition here which begins to deserve the title of a 'law'. Of course, there may be a useful concept, and it may be possible to spot trends which may be depended upon up to a point, for the purpose of putting forward tentative forecasts – though hardly 'with great confidence'. For such trends will shift with historical changes in institutions and expectations. Keynes is attempting here to provide for his general macroeconomic theory some kind of reliable general proposition which will do the work, or bear the load, carried by the central generalizations on which general microeconomic theory depends. But these latter seem both considerably more general and less unreliable than Keynes's so-called 'fundamental psychological law'.

(3) Thirdly, Keynes in his *General Theory*, like Myrdal, Hayek and others in the thirties, was one of those who came to emphasize the importance of expectations, and he criticized the previous orthodoxy for its dependence on the assumption of adequate knowledge. Recently it has been suggested that this was Keynes's most important fundamental contribution. But Keynes, like most of the others who made this very justifiable criticism, did not realize the fundamental methodological conclusion that follows regarding attempts to build general economic theories *without* this classical assumption about adequate knowledge. Keynes emphasized that his *General Theory* had to be based on assumptions about erroneous expectations. But he did not discover any propositions, both richly significant, *and of valid generality*, which could serve as such basic assumptions. They were – and are – simply not available. So he had to base his theory on propositions about particular *ad hoc* trends in expectations, which seemed appropriate in the early thirties in Britain. He could not have done anything else. He *had* to deal with cases, and brought to bear his superb discernment in selecting them. But, of course, he was not constructing a 'General Theory'. Regarding ignorant and erroneous expectations one cannot propound general laws, only tentative patterns or trends, which may well alter in the course of historical and institutional change. As Professor W. H. Meckling

has put it: 'It is one thing to reject the "perfect knowledge" assumption, but it is another entirely different thing to make a case for any given alternative' (1978, p. 103); and it is *especially* difficult to make a case for the *generality* of an alternative.

One often-cited example of an *ad hoc* assumption about expectations from Keynes's *General Theory* is that of his controversial proposition as to the impossibility of reducing real wages by cuts in money wages during a depression. This generalization seems to have depended on the assumption of a kind of deflationary expectation on the part of employers, which may well have been relevant in the early thirties, and indeed which may have been actually confirmed by what happened in Germany from 1930–32, but which certainly might not, and did not, hold under changed conditions. Another example of an important assumption by Keynes, involving a particular kind of ignorance or expectations, was that regarding 'money illusion' in labour markets, or what Professor Fellner calls 'the alleged real wage equilibrating effect of inflation' (1976, p. 44). Such an assumption may well have been relevant in the early thirties at the time of, or just after, a catastrophic and unprecedented fall in prices, so that an inflationary (or as it was then called 'reflationary') rise in prices could be expected simply to restore a status quo and not continue indefinitely. As Professor Brian Loasby has observed: 'The typical Keynesian model is an exercise in institutional ad hocery. Its performance depends crucially on some piece of specific irrationality (such as wage rigidity or money illusion) for which no theoretical justification is given' (1976, p. 14).

It is, in particular, *informational and expectational* 'ad hocery' on which Keynesian, *or any*, macroeconomic, models *must* essentially depend, and it is a *historical* justification which they must look for, because, in actual historical situations, relevant information and expectations must, to a significant extent be *ad hoc*. An example of a historical component of Keynes's *General Theory* which turned out to be quite ungeneral, but which figured very prominently in Keynesian theorizing in the thirties and forties, was the longer-run stagnation thesis. This thesis underlay the Keynesian predictions of a great postwar slump, but was discarded as the 'boom' continued in the fifties.

Finally, just as Keynes's economic theory must be distinguished from his conceptual framework, so it must also be distinguished from the political and social framework he assumed, about which assumptions inevitably have to be made when theories are to be applied to policy. Assumptions about the political and social framework may, in fact, have an even more rapid and more serious rate of obsolescence than do more narrowly economic assumptions. Certainly in the case of the political and social framework which Keynes assumed there was soon very serious obsolescence.

First, Keynes's political assumption that the management of the economy would be controlled by a mandarin elite of high civil servants, proof against the pressures of democratic or demagogic politics, dated back to his own early days in the India Office in 1906–08, where at that time especially, it had much validity. Obviously in Britain since the fifties, when the postwar 'management' of the economy got under way, it has been pathetically invalid.

Second, Keynes made another assumption about world politics, also dating from his own early years, to the effect that his own country held a powerful, even dominating, position in the world economy, and so could effectively lead an expansionist policy – an assumption seriously obsolete within a few years of the publication of *The General Theory*, and perhaps even since the latter part of World War I.

But we are concerned here not so much with the obsolescence of *political* assumptions, vital though these may be for policy applications, as with the lack of generality in the *economic* assumptions regarding expectations, and the institutions which shape them, and how these shift and change. It is the shifting, inconstant, and unstable nature of expectations which makes a 'General (Macroeconomic) Theory' an impossibility or a misnomer, at any rate one that goes beyond tautologies, or near tautologies, and possesses *some* useful predictive potential.

However, there was one sense in which Keynes's claim to generality for his theory, as against the classical theory, seems to have had much validity. He argued that macroeconomic equilibrium, with reasonably 'full' employment, allowing for frictions, had not historically been the general case over the centuries. Instead, he suggested that some kind of fairly chronic unemployment had been endemic. This is the implication of his claims on behalf of the pre-Smithian, or 'mercantilist' writers, who were so concerned with unemployment and deficiencies of effective demand. This kind of unemployment seems to have been pretty widespread through much of the 17th and 18th centuries, just as excesses of effective demand, inspired by democratic governments, seem to have become something of a usual case in the last forty years. Economists have often been prone to assume that the last decade or two of their own experience constitutes a general norm of world history, or that the economies of other countries and other times have worked in just the same way as the economy of their own country and their own time. Of course 'general' does not mean 'universal'. But what are proclaimed as 'exceptions' to a 'general' case ought to be reasonably clearly specified, if the use of the adjective is not to beg the vital question as to whether the 'exceptions' are not more important than the 'general' case, and whether it may not be tendentious to claim generality for any particular case.[12]

VI

Whether it was further developed or criticized, accepted or rejected, Keynes's work was treated as, and indeed largely re-established, *general* macroeconomic theory, as complementary with general microeconomic theory, making up together, according to one influential version, a kind of general 'neoclassical synthesis', replacing the more closely knit general Smithian or 'classical' synthesis.

However, though various attempts were made to revise and solidify the fundamentals of Keynes's edifice, including particularly the consumption function, nothing was established which came near to deserving the description of a fundamental law. Moreover, revisions of Keynes's *General Theory*, or other developments in macroeconomics, such as, for example, the Phillips curve, were asserted or rejected as *general* relationships, indefinitely or widely valid, regardless of significant changes in institutions and expectations. Instead, a generalization such as the Phillips curve should have been asserted, or rejected, as an interesting trend, possibly very useful while it lasted, but liable to go awry in the course of historical and institutional change, as it rather soon did.

But the main development in macroeconomics since Keynes's *General Theory* has been the counter-revolutionary assertion, or reassertion, of the contrasting, and at least at some points, presumably, empirically incompatible, general theory – the Quantity Theory of Money. We are not concerned simply with a Quantity Conceptual Framework. Nor are we concerned with issues of monetarism *versus* fiscalism as policy principles, which are distinct from the strictly theoretical issues. Though quite a number of economists, past and present, would disagree, it might readily be admitted that the Quantity Theory constitutes the most serious qualification to the thesis of the limitations of general macroeconomic theories. It might well seem the least weak candidate for being upheld as a general macroeconomic theory.

The question is whether the Quantity Theory is a sufficiently powerful and comprehensive exception as to nullify the thesis of this paper. Certainly the revival of the quantity theory, in the face of the extremely exclusivist (and in Britain practically disastrous) anti-quantity dogmatism of some versions of the Keynesian 'General Theory', was very much to be welcomed. The question is, however, whether or how far an adequate general macroeconomic theory can be a strictly quantity theory. A number of enthusiastic authorities would probably give an affirmative answer. But it may seem doubtful whether, or how far, the kind of qualified, flexible consensus which has grown up – much more, in Germany and the US than (unfortunately) Britain – can be described as a consensus round the quantity theory – though that theory may play a significant part in the consensus. If the Keynesians have seriously underestimated the potential stability of the economic system, the monetarist quantity theorists may have seriously underestimated certain elements of instability.

In fact, the whole history of monetary theory, for over 200 years, has consisted, to a large extent, of a debate between quantity theorists and the upholders of alternatives and qualifications to the quantity theory as a general theory. Many of the most valuable contributions to monetary theory have surely come in the form of criticisms, or even rejections, of a quantity theory, from Cantillon and Sir James Steuart in the 18th century, to Wicksell, Keynes, and leading Austrians, in the 20th. Unhistoriate contemporaries today sometimes seem to imagine that anyone critical of the quantity theory must be committed to the more dubious propositions of 'Keynesianism'.

What are especially questionable are attempts to establish monocausal explanations of inflation and deflation by dismissing, as 'eclecticism', from the investigation all factors other than the quantity of money – even the question as to *why* fluctuations in the quantity of money may occur. For example, here is the contrast drawn between 'the monetarist and eclectic approach' by an English 'monetarist':

The essence of eclecticism it is maintained is the rejection of mono-causal explanations of inflation and, by implication, the denial of the propriety of relying on a single policy instrument, be it control of the money supply or incomes policy, in any attempt to stabilize or reduce the rate at which prices rise. If prices can rise for a variety of reasons, then the control of inflation requires the simultaneous use of a variety of policy instruments. It follows that eclecticism provides a rationale for discretionary economic policy. . . .

There seems to be here an undesirable fusing (which is sometimes met with in this debate from the monetarist side) of the theoretical or explanatory, with the political or therapeutic. Meanwhile this contrast continues:

The monetarist, in contrast to the eclectic, rejects discretionary economic policy, focuses on long-run relationships, accepts the existence of a stable demand for money function and maintains that the control of the growth of the money supply, combined with a flexible exchange rate, is necessary and sufficient for stabilizing or reducing the rate of price inflation. (Zis, 1977, pp. 55–6)

It seems in this kind of argument that the positive investigation of economic, or socioeconomic causation is to be narrowly restricted, so as to exclude the kind of factors (including questions of why the money supply may fluctuate) on which, as a matter of political principle, it may be considered undesirable to try to operate. Because, justifiably or unjustifiably, one may not wish to go in for 'discretionary' policies, one denies, quite unjustifiably, that any of the factors on which discretionary policies might operate may be among the important 'causes' of inflation. Even if it were conceded that the quantity theory, rightly formulated, contains some of 'the truth', and even 'nothing but the truth', it would not follow that it is 'the whole truth', or even enough of the truth to comprise a 'General Theory'. In particular, it would seem that important historical and institutional questions will always have to be attended to regarding the changing nature and varieties of M, in the course of historical and institutional changes, and, in particular, regarding the changing institutional or expectational factors making for fluctuations in M.

VII

There might seem to be something paradoxical in the claim, long more or less tacitly held on behalf of classical and neoclassical theorizing, that a body of theory based on such a simplified assumption as adequate knowledge, or even '*Allwissenheit*', or '*Unfehlbarkeit*', could be regarded as a 'General Theory'. Surely, in the disturbed politicoeconomic world of much of this century, it should be regarded rather as a special, even extreme case, if ex-post were to equal ex-ante, expectations to turn out correct, and knowledge prove adequate, or even perfect. But the essential '*Allwissenheit*' assumption was for long included only tacitly, or as an ambiguous aside,[13] with no further reference to expectations being regarded as necessary. Expectations, or assumptions about them, hardly figured, and, in a sense, were hardly required to figure, in theories in which the expected and the actual realized events and quantities 'naturally', or 'normally', came out in equilibrium as the same thing.

Expectations only, or almost only, received any attention from those concerned with cyclical fluctuations or disequilibrium. In other words, expectations were only of interest when – quite exceptionally – they were wrong, that is, when disequilibrium was regarded as a serious problem, as, for example, in Sismondi's explanation of depressions and crises in terms of erroneous expectations, or in the psychological explanations of fluctuations in terms of optimistic and pessimistic expectations, as argued by Walter Bagehot, Marshall, Pigou, and Keynes, and in the monetary and business cycle theory of Irving Fisher.

It was during the catastrophic fluctuations of the thirties that much more attention began to be focused on expectations by a number of economists of differing schools, including Myrdal, Keynes, and also Hayek (1937) – who did so in the course of a fundamental revision of the views he had expressed in his earlier work. However, this concern with expectations, and the problems of their errors and changes, did not survive at all vigorously in the period after World War II.

In the first place, the postwar world enjoyed a period of unprecedented stability and economic success for about twenty years (quite a long time in human lives, including the lives of economists), so that the problems of profound disequilibria seemed to be much less serious and more easily preventable, thanks to advances in economic theory.

Secondly, there has been considerable methodological resistance to following up problems of expectations, and of errors and of changes in them, because the admission of such problems, or the opening of Pandora's box (as Professor Patinkin described it), inevitably brings not merely policy implications, but very profound methodological consequences. When errors, ignorance, and uncertainty regarding expectations, are taken to be serious, then there is little in the way of firm and reliable general assumptions on which to build valid general theories of employment, interest and money: the thread of order and predictability, loosely holding economic decisions and actions together, becomes tangled or broken. With some perhaps excusable poetic exaggeration, it can be said regarding the logic of most economic model-building that with the opening of 'Pandora's box', or with the introduction of uncertainty and erroneous expectations: 'Things fall apart; the centre cannot hold' – though it does not necessarily follow that 'mere anarchy is loosed upon the world' (see Yeats, 1934, p. 211); or, as in an apophthegm attributed to Wittgenstein: 'If there were no connection between the act of expectation and reality, you could expect a nonsense'.

There is only one way in which expectations can be correct, but an infinite number of possible ways in which, more or less seriously, they may go wrong. This inevitably has methodological consequences, for it may only be possible to examine the variety of possibilities in terms of case studies. As Professor Herbert Simon has observed, the assumption of ignorance and uncertainty:

requires a basic shift in scientific style, from an emphasis on deductive reasoning within a tight system of axioms to an emphasis on detailed empirical exploration of complex algorithms of thought. Undoubtedly the uncongeniality of the latter style to economists has slowed down the transition. . . .

As economics becomes more and more involved in the study of uncertainty, more and more concerned with the complex actuality of actual decision-making, the shift in programme will become inevitable. Wider and wider areas of economics will replace the over-simplified assumptions of the situationally constrained omniscient decision-maker with a realistic (and psychological) characterization of the limits on Man's rationality, and the consequences of those limits for his economic behaviour. (1976, pp. 147–8; see also Hutchison, 1978, p. 211)

In articles of 1937 both Keynes and Hayek glimpsed this point. But Hayek then largely abandoned the problem of cyclical fluctuations, while in the postwar world the Keynesians, also in part unwilling to face an uncongenial change in scientific style, optimistically believed – initially with some apparent validity –

that the problems of aggregate fluctuations could fairly simply be kept in check by new recipes based on the 'General' Keynesian Theory. But in the seventies serious problems of profound disequilibrium came back again in the form of chronic inflation, accompanied by severe shocks from the supply side, and so, inevitably, did a renewed attention to expectations.

VIII

It might be thought obvious that the kind of inflation which has existed in many countries for the past decade or more has immensely increased the uncertainty and ignorance amid which expectations and decisions have had to be formed. In the first place, particular prices are affected very differently in the course of inflation. Moreover, inflation has not been, of course, at a steady rate. It has soared up, then fallen back to a half or a third of its previous level, and then headed upwards again. Possibly a cycle of higher and lower inflation rates may emerge, linked with cyclical fluctuations. But this has hardly become established yet. Anyhow, to assume a steady rate of inflation is obviously quite a grotesque oversimplification. Meanwhile it would seem that economic expectations of every kind are inevitably fraught with greater error and uncertainty than in a climate of approximate price stability, or in one of a stable rate of inflation, both with regard to the calculations of final consumers regarding relative prices, as well as regards longer term investment decisions.

It hardly seems surprising that some strange, paradoxical reactions have appeared with regard to major aspects of economic behaviour. In Britain, for example, at the beginning of this decade, when inflation was shooting up, real interest rates, for sometime, fell to negative levels, so that one would presumably have expected saving to fall. Quite the contrary. Saving showed a large increase, in spite of rising rates of inflation and negative interest rates. Certainly such a reaction is quite explicable, but hardly in terms of a general theory based on 'normal' reactions to price changes. Moreover, it has been pointed out by Mr Trevithick (1975) how inflationary processes changed in Britain as between the World Wars, and how Keynes recognized that the inflationary technique by which British governments effectively raised a large proportion of war resources in World War I would not have been effective in World War II, because of changes in the institutional and expectational system. Such changes may have significantly affected inflationary (or deflationary) processes, and crucially altered the appropriate policy responses, through much of the twentieth century, as between World War I, the great slump of the thirties, World War II, the creeping inflation of the fifties, and the galloping inflation of the seventies; and such changes will presumably continue.

Though, of course, learning processes of one kind or another take place, the lessons to be learnt are frequently changing, so that new and different lessons have to be mastered before the old ones have been assimilated, especially if massive shocks from the supply side are superimposed on sharply changing rates of inflation. In any case, learning is not always rapid and direct, but may often follow a variety of irregular, zigzag paths (as one might expect university teachers, at any rate, to appreciate).

The rational expectations assumption, which takes a number of different stronger or weaker forms, seems to be a modified extension, or adaptation, of the traditional assumption of adequate knowledge, or '*Allwissenheit*' (introduced explicitly by Ricardo) on which equilibrium models have long depended, and which has certainly long served as an essential building block for equilibrium model builders. When J. F. Muth (1961) introduced the rational expectations assumption he was certainly well justified in complaining about the way in which economists had treated assumptions about expectations, either by devising them *ad hoc* to fit a particular case and then claiming generality, or by simply plucking them out of the air: 'To make dynamic models complete, various expectations formulas have been used. There is, however, little evidence to suggest that the presumed relations bear a resemblance to the way the economy works.' (1961, p. 315)

Methodologically, the rational expectations assumption certainly obviates the need for that uncongenial 'basic shift in scientific style, from an emphasis on deductive reasoning . . . to an emphasis on detailed empirical exploration' which Herbert Simon regards as necessary for dealing with problems involving ignorance and uncertainty. From some points of view, it is an attractive assumption, politically as well as methodologically. Muth went on to maintain that 'expectations, since they are informed predictions of future events, are essentially the same as the predictions of relevant economic theory' (p. 316).

One is entitled to ask, at least in some important cases, just what the agreed predictions of the relevant economic theory are or would be, particularly in situations in which elements of oligopoly, or game-strategic guesswork, may be significant.

As we observed earlier, in his *Monetary Theory and the Trade Cycle* (1932) Hayek, adhering, as far as he could, to the '*Allwissenheit*' assumption of equilibrium models, maintained that one *must* assume that all expectations were correct and that all errors were excluded, *except* for such miscalculations as were introduced by monetary changes. Now the rational expectations hypothesis seems to be designed, more or less, to plug the knowledge gap regarding the ignorance, and consequent disturbances of the equilibrating process, caused by monetary changes.

Certainly the rational expectations assumption started as an attempt to deal with the vital question of the kind of learning processes with which people adapt, or fail to adapt. Certainly also, with regard to inflation, it is realistic to assume that not all the people can be completely fooled all the time. But the RE assumption represents a fairly sweeping simplification; and F. H. Knight's dictum may be worth repeating here regarding the traditional '*Allwissenheit*' assumption as being 'the most important underlying difference between the conditions which theory is compelled to assume and those which exist in fact' (1921 and 1933, p. 51).

Apart from the question of the nature of the 'compulsion' on the theoretical economist to assume a Utopian degree of knowledge, one might ask also, *if* the rational expectations assumption is intended as a first approximation, to what more realistic second or third approximations it could lead on. Perhaps enquiring about the realism of assumptions is regarded as methodologically naïve and unjustified (though it is arguable that a careless disregard for such realism is a dangerous methodological attitude).[14] But if the rational expectations assumption is not to be questioned for its realism, then very thorough tests of the conclusions, and some consensus about their implications, should be forthcoming. Moreover the following questions may be worth pressing:

(1) First, if rational expectations are based on 'the predictions of relevant economic theory', or of expert economic information, surely this should not be regarded as costless; so that the question follows as to how far such information will be acquired, and rationality in expectations achieved, if the cost is considerable.

(2) Secondly, as Professor Fellner has emphasized, it is necessary 'to recognise that the relation of the authorities to the public has an essential game-of-strategy aspect' (1976, p. 2). In such a situation

it hardly seems possible to draw conclusions of *general* validity regarding possible outcomes.

(3) Thirdly, as has been pointed out by Professor Ramser (1978, p. 70), with perfect information, costless information-processing, and flexibility of wages and prices, there would certainly seem to be little or no scope for measures to influence the level of employment, or indeed, any need for them. In any case, as Professor Barro has observed: 'Rational verses nonrational expectations is not *per se* the key division between Keynesian and non-Keynesian models and, accordingly is not the essential basis for a division between activist and non–activist policy conclusions' (1979, p. 56).

Certainly the rational expectations hypothesis has called attention to, and illuminated, the problems of learning and of reactions under persistent inflation. It has also brought out very convincingly the acute dangers of relying on money illusion to restore or maintain an equilibrium or to justify persistent inflationary policies. Under some institutional and expectational settings the RE hypothesis might even constitute a reasonable approximation. But it would appear to represent too much of a simplification to serve as the foundation of a general macroeconomic theory.[15]

IX

General theories require general laws, or substantial reliable generalizations, as a basis. There have, on the whole, for much of the past two hundred years, been rather more in the way of such substantial general propositions to serve as a basis for microeconomics than for macroeconomics, though even for microeconomics the basic generalizations are somewhat tenuous, unless ignorance and uncertainty are ruled out – as they mostly have been until comparatively recently. Though this difference in the structure of macro- and microeconomic theorizing may be regarded as one between different shades of grey, it may help to explain the considerably higher degree of consensus among economists regarding microeconomic policies as contrasted with macroeconomic issues. The much more extensive disagreements on macroeconomic policy issues stem from the more serious lack of agreed and firm generalizations on which macroeconomic theory rests.[16]

The loose macroeconomic theories of the mercantilists, who

perceived little in the way of self-equilibrating forces in the economies of their day, and who therefore advocated constant government activity, were superseded by the General Theory of the Smithian–classical revolution, which denied that instability and unemployment were more than frictional problems. After about a century of domination, the Smithian-Ricardian General Theory began gradually to lose support, and was finally swept aside after the Great Slump by the General Theory of the Keynesian revolution. For some years the Keynesian General Theory has been in decline. One of the challengers for the vacant role of dominant, or even exclusive, General Macroeconomic Theory is a kind of modified version of the Smithian-Ricardian General Theory, based on a combination of the quantity theory and the rational expectations hypothesis. But the argument of this paper is that the progressive programme for macroeconomics is not one of seeking to establish a dominant, or exclusive, General Theory.

On the other hand, it is certainly *not* the argument of this paper that, over the decades or centuries, attempts to build such general theories have not been worth while. In what may, in the nineteenth century, have been in some ways a significantly less oligopolistic and unpredictable world, a reasonably adequate General Theory may have been a more feasible intellectual aim. Nor is it argued here that the critical discussion of general hypotheses, or at any rate general conceptual frameworks, may not continue to prove fruitful. What is being criticized is the debating of macroeconomic problems in terms of confrontations between rival general theories. This obstructs the reaching of a consensus, which may draw on contrasting general theories, and fails to recognize the inevitable limitations of general theories in the social sciences, which are especially serious with regard to macroeconomics.

In Britain (1980) – unlike in Germany and the United States – polarized confrontation is still very apparent. Here are two predictions, from the opposite sides, about the future of economic knowledge.

(1) The first is:

Within five years the standard macroeconomic model will be an equilibrium model in which expectations are formed optimally and contract arrangements respond to economic forces (especially inflation); according to this model, there will be *scope* for output stabilisation policy but its practical role will be a very limited one, and the major potential contribution of 'macro' policy will be in holding the fiscal deficit, and money supply growth to a non-inflationary path. (Minford, 1980, p. 24)

(2) At the other end of the spectrum it was stated (1978):

We now have a much better insight into the problem of managing an economy than we had in the aftermath of the Keynesian revolution. We are on the verge of evolving an integrated theory of inflation which should be capable of forging the tools necessary for securing prosperity combined with price stability, partly through intervention in commodity markets and partly through incomes policies in the industrial countries. (Kaldor, 1978, p. xxxviii)

It is hardly possible that both of these typical predictions by these two distinguished authorities will turn out correct. The safest bet would seem to be that they will both, as general theories, turn out considerably wrong. The interesting question is: what, and how much (if anything), will each contribute to an eventual institutional-relative synthesis, not in the form of a 'general theory', but in that of a set of case studies. Meanwhile, the continuing state of the macroeconomic debate in Britain, in terms of a kind of party–political confrontation between dogmatic general theories, is deplorable intellectually and highly damaging to policy.

Notes

1   See Fellner, 1976, p. 22:

The 1930s were not simply a painful episode in world history. In the interpretation of that period and of its sequels it is proper to place the events in Germany in the center of the story, but there is more to the story than its center. The ending of parliamentary rule in Germany and Hitler's coming to power early in 1933 resulted in very large part from the extraordinarily high German unemployment of that period, even if the expropriation of much of the middle class through the hyperinflation following World War I must also be taken into account in interpreting the German political upheaval. Whatever other circumstances may have played a role in the turn of events in Germany and whatever other mistakes may have acquired importance in shaping the history of the subsequent decades, it remains true that for the 1930s any reasonable observer will be inclined to attribute more than the usual importance to conjectural history: without the Great Depression no Nazi takeover, without the Nazi takeover no World War II, without World War II no iron curtain across Europe and none of the corollaries of the latter in our lifetime.

2   See, for example, Professor Ivor Pearce in 'Confrontation with Keynes', 1978, where Keynes's ideas are alleged to be made up of age-old myths and fallacies, invalid 'in any age' (p. 107). Professor Pearce upholds 'Say's Law' in the sense that 'there has never really been any significant hoarding in any age'. But this was denied by Say himself, who attacked Ricardo by insisting that 'many savings are not invested when it is difficult to find employment for them' (1841, p. 45n). Moreover, the importance of hoarding, throughout the ages, has been emphasized by the vigorously anti-Keynesian authority on 'Mercantilism', Eli Heckscher (1955, vol. 2, p. 349). It may be possible to argue for a 'Say's Trend' or 'Say's Tendency', as operative in a very 'long-run' sense at certain buoyant periods. But as a *general law* Say's rather vague proposition is indefensible and, incidentally, not consistently maintained by Say himself, who advocated public works against unemployment (1841, p. 86n).

3   According to Smith:

   We trust with perfect security that the freedom of trade, without any attention of government, will always supply us with the wine which we have occasion for: and we may trust with equal security that it will always supply us with all the gold and silver which we can afford to purchase, or to employ, either in circulating our commodities, or in other uses. (Smith, 1976, vol. 1, p. 435).

Such assertions by Smith may have provided the original source of that unconcern with the money supply which, intellectually, was behind the unconcern with what Friedman has called 'The Great Contraction' of the early thirties.

4   See Schwartz, 1972, p. 38; Link, 1959, pp. 168, 177–9. According to Professor F. W. Fetter: 'Except for a short period after the Napoleonic Wars, unemployment was not, in the eyes of people who were to the left of centre by the standards of the times, the great economic problem of the nineteenth century. Certainly there was unemployment, and at times it was serious' (1965, p. 138). Professor Fetter adds that other problems 'seemed more important'. This order of importance changed later in the century.

5   Also, Sir John Hicks has pointed out regarding one major component of macroeconomics: 'Monetary theory is less abstract than most economic theory; it cannot avoid a relation to reality, which in other economic theory is sometimes missing. It belongs to monetary history, in a way that economic theory does not always belong to economic history.' (1977, p. 45; 1967, p. 156)

6   As was pointed out by a distinguished critic at the AEI, the price of another vital world commodity – other than labour and capital – has been having a 'macro' impact and has also not been operating with the

smoothly beneficent, self-adjusting effects of standard microeconomic models. Reductions in demand as well as higher oil prices have been followed by cutbacks of supplies by oil producers. In fact, as Marshall assumed, microeconomic theory has to be about 'small' commodities, changes in the supply, demand and prices of which do not generate 'large' effects.

7   As regards Malthus, the last paragraph of the second, posthumously published edition of his *Principles of Political Economy* insists that cyclical fluctuations should not be dismissed simply as frictions: 'Theoretical writers are too apt, in their calculations, to overlook these intervals; but eight or ten years, recurring not unfrequently, are serious spaces in human life' (1836, p. 437).

8   As Sir John Hicks (1979, p. 199) has put it regarding Hayek's *Prices and Production* (1932b): 'Things were allowed to go wrong, but only for monetary reasons; it was only because of monetary disturbances that an exception was allowed to the rule that market forces must tend to establish an equilibrium. If money could only be kept "neutral", all would be well. (An anticipation of latter-day monetarism!)'

9   It should be noticed how *completely* opposed the diagnosis and remedies of Professor Hayek at that time were to those of Chicago economists, both then and subsequently.

10   It seems improbable, however, that Brüning was much influenced by this kind of economic theory. The decisive influence was the desire to end reparation payments, and, in view of German fears about inflation, to maintain the exchange parity of the mark.

11   Certainly Keynes's distinction between 'voluntary' and 'involuntary' unemployment may be regarded as dubious, or unoperational, outside perfectly competitive equilibrium. See Fellner, 1976, pp. 53–5.

12   As Schumpeter said of Keynes's *General Theory*: 'There is one word in the book that cannot be defended on these lines – the word "general". These emphasizing devices – even if quite unexceptionable in other respects – cannot do more than individuate very special cases. Keynesians may hold that these special cases are the actual ones of our age. They cannot hold more than that.' (1952, p. 286) Schumpeter drew a significant parallel between Keynes and Ricardo, who also claimed generality for a theory built on highly special assumptions. On the generality of Keynesian economics see the study of that title by J. Pekkarinen (1979), who (p. 57) also quotes Schumpeter as above. It is strange that in his Preface to the French edition of *The General Theory* Keynes maintains that his theory was 'general' in a quite different sense, that is 'aggregate' or 'macro':

> I have called my theory a *general* theory. I mean by this that I am chiefly concerned with the behaviour of the economic system as a whole – with aggregate incomes, aggregate profits, aggregate output, aggregate employment, aggregate investment, aggregate saving rather than with the incomes, profits, output, employment,

investment and saving of particular industries, firms or individuals.
(1973, p. xxxii).

There is surely, here, a rather misleading suggestion that the distinction between 'partial' (Marshallian) and 'general' (Walrasian) theories is relevant.

On the other hand, in his Preface to the German edition (1936) Keynes claimed the kind of 'generality' which he claimed in the English Preface, in more emphatic terms:

> The theory of output as a whole, which is what the following book purports to provide, is much more easily adapted to the conditions of a totalitarian state, than is the theory of the production and distribution of a given output produced under conditions of free competition and a large measure of laissez-faire. *This is one of the reasons which justifies me in calling my theory a general theory. Since it is based on fewer hypotheses than the orthodox theory, it can accommodate itself all the easier to a wide field of varying conditions.* The theory of the psychological laws relating consumption and saving . . . remain[s] as necessary ingredients in our scheme of thought. (1973, vol. 7 pp. xxvi–xxvii)

The passage in italics above occurs in the original German edition but is omitted from the German Preface in the *Collected Writings*. I am grateful to Mr R. Miller of the Institute of Economic Affairs for calling my attention to this remarkable passage. See also in *Cambridge Journal of Economics*, 1980, vo. 4, no. 3, the note by B. Schefold, 'The General Theory for a Totalitarian State'.

13   See Mill, 1844, p. 137. Mill writes of the fundamental assumption of Political Economy that it is concerned with man 'solely as a being who desires to possess wealth *and who is capable of judging of the comparative efficacy of means for obtaining that end*' (italics added). This is the sole fleeting (but absolutely vital) mention of the '*Allwissenheit*' assumption in Mill's essay.

14   The following criticism seems well justified:

> I regard rationality of expectations . . . as an empirical hypothesis way over at one end of the range of possibilities. The other end of the range is occupied by simple rules of thumb. The *a priori* plausibility of rational expectations does not seem high; the empirical evidence in its favour that I have seen is weak and very indirect, certainly no better than that for rules of thumb. Moreover, the hypothesis of rational expectations has not been able to account, so far as I know, for the wide dispersion of actually reported expectations at any instant of time, except by the undocumented assumption that information sets differ. But the differences in information, would have to be incredibly large to account for the observed dispersion of expectations. (Solow, 1980, p. 257)

15   However, if the RE hypothesis is interpreted simply as providing a positive argument for rules rather than authorities in monetary and macroeconomic policy, then it has much in its favour:

> The main argument turns out to be a positive (as opposed to normative) one: our ability as economists to predict the responses of agents rests, in situations where expectations about the future matter, on our understanding of the stochastic environment agents believe themselves to be operating in. In practice, this limits the class of policies, the consequences of which we can hope to assess in advance, to policies generated by fixed, well understood, relatively permanent rules. (Lucas, 1980, p. 205)

It is quite irrelevant to prove that an enlightened economist could theoretically often provide more successful macroeconomic management than any set of rules. In practice, the management is *not* going to be in the hands of enlightened economists, but in those of unenlightened politicians blown to and fro by conflicting advice, ignorant public opinion, and by electoral pressures and ambitions. A simple set of rules might well be far less disastrously unsuccessful. But then it may be politically very naïve to suppose that politicians could ever be brought to accept constitutional rules restricting their powers and discretion.

16   See the paper 'What Economists Think', which provides a survey of the views of American economists (Kearly *et al.*, 1979, pp. 28ff). One conclusion is that 'consensus tends to centre on micro-economic issues involving the price mechanism while the major areas of disagreement involve macro-economic and normative issues' (p. 36). As regards English economists see Brittan (1973) and Keegan (1979), who observes: 'In fact on the micro-economic matters . . . the economics profession is remarkably united. . . . It is on the bigger, "macro" issues about how to sustain output or employment, or reduce inflation, that the real differences lie.'

References

Barro, R. J. (1979), 'Second Thoughts on Keynesian Economics', *Papers and Proceedings of the American Economic Association*, vol. 69, no. 2.

Brittan, S. (1973), *Is there an Economic Consensus?*

Dobb, M. H. (1937), *Political Economy and Capitalism*.

Fellner, W. J. (1976), *Towards a Reconstruction of Macroeconomics*.

Fetter, F. W. (1965), 'The Relation of the History of Economic Thought to Economic History', *Papers and Proceedings of the American Economic Association*, vol. 55, no. 2.

Foxwell, H. S. (1886), 'Irregularity of Employment and Fluctuations of Prices' in *The Claims of Labour*, by J. Burnett *et al.*

Guillebaud, C. W. (1939), *The Economic Recovery of Germany*.

Haberler, G. (1974), *Economic Growth and Stability*.

(1979), 'Notes on Rational and Irrational Expectations', in *Festschrift for A. Jöhr*.

Harris, J. (1972), *Unemployment and Politics, 1885–1914*.

Hayek, F. A. (1932a), *Monetary Theory and the Trade Cycle*, translated by N. Kaldor and H. M. Croome from the German *Geldtheorie und Konjunktur-theorie*, 1929.

(1932b), *Prices and Production*. (2nd ed., 1935)

(1937), 'Economics and Knowledge', *Economica*, N.S., vol. 4, pp. 33–54.

Heckscher, E. (1955), *Mercantilism*, 2 vols.

Hicks, Sir John (1967), *Critical Essays in Monetary Theory*.

(1977), *Economic Perspectives*.

(1979), 'The Formation of an Economist', *Banca Nazionale del Lavoro Quarterly Review*, no. 130.

Hutchison, T. W. (1978), *Revolutions and Progress in Economic Knowledge*.

Kaldor, Lord, (1978), *Further Essays on Economic Theory*.

Kearly, J. R., *et. al.* (1979), 'What Economists Think', *Papers and Proceedings of the American Economic Association*, vol. 69, no. 2.

Keegan, W. (1979), 'Penalty for Being First', *The Observer*, 16 Sept.

Keynes, J. M. (1931), 'An Economic Analysis of Unemployment', in Q. Wright (ed.), *Unemployment as a World Problem*.

(1973), *The General Theory of Employment, Interest and Money*.

Kindleberger, C. P. (1973), *The World in Depression*.

Knight, F. H. (1921 and 1933), *Risk, Uncertainty and Profit*.

Korsch, A. (1976), 'Der Stand der beschäftigungspolitischen Diskussion zur Zeit der Wirtschaftskrise in Deutschland', in G. Bombach *et al.* (ed.), *Der Keynesianismus*, vol. 1.

Lancaster, K. (1969), *Introduction to Modern Microeconomics*.

Link, R. (1959), *English Theories of Economic Fluctuations, 1815–1848*.

Loasby, B. (1976), *Choice, Complexity and Ignorance*.

Lucas, R. E. (1980), 'Rules, Discretion, and the Role of the Economic Adviser', in S. Fischer (ed.), *Rational Expectations and Economic Policy*, pp. 199–210.

Malthus, T. R. (1836), *Principles of Political Economy*, 2nd ed.

Maynard, G. W. (1978), 'Keynes and Unemployment Today', *Three Banks Review*, Dec.

Meckling, W. H. (1978), 'Comment', in J. M. Buchanan and R. E. Wagner (ed.), *Fiscal Responsibility in Constitutional Democracy*, pp. 101ff.

Menger, C. 1963, *Problems of Economics and Sociology*, ed. L. Schneider, translated by F. J. Nock from the German *Untersuchungen über die Methode der Sozialwissenschaften, und der politischen Ökonomie inbesondere*, 1883.

Mill, J. S. (1844), *Essays on Some Unsettled Questions of Political Economy*.

Minford, P. (1980), 'The Nature and Purpose of UK Macroeconomic Models', *Three Banks Review*, March, pp. 3–24.

Moggridge, D. E. (1977), *British Monetary Policy 1924–1931: the Norman Conquest*.

Muth, J. F. (1961), 'Rational Expectations and the Theory of Price Movements', *Econometrica*, vol. 29.

Patinkin, D. (1956), *Money, Interest and Prices*.

Pearce, I. (1978), 'Confrontation with Keynes', in *Confrontation*, IEA.

Pekkarinen, J. (1979), *On the Generality of Keynesian Economics*.

Pigou, A. C. (1949), *Employment and Equilibrium*, 2nd ed.

Ramser, H. J. (1978), 'Rationale Erwartungen und Wirtschaftspolitik', *Zeitschrift für die gesamte Staatswissenschaft,* vol. 134, part 4, pp. 57ff.

Say, J. B. (1841), *Traité d'économie politique*, 6th ed.

Schefold, B. (1980), 'The General Theory for a Totalitarian State?' *Cambridge Journal of Economics*, vol. 4, no. 5.

Schwartz, P. (1972), *The New Political Economy of J. S. Mill*.

Shackle, G. L. S. (1961), 'Recent Theories Concerning the Nature and Role of Interest', *Economic Journal*, vol. 71, June, pp. 209ff.

Schumpeter, J. A. (1952), *Ten Great Economists*.

Simon, H. (1976), 'From Substantive to Procedural Rationality', in S. J. Latsis (ed.), *Method and Appraisal in Economics*.

Skidelsky, R. (1976), *New Statesman*, 22 Oct.

Smith, A. (1976), *The Wealth of Nations*, ed. R. H. Campbell, A. S. Skinner and W. B. Todd, 2 vols.

Solow, R. (1980), 'What to Do (Macroeconomically) When OPEC Comes', in S. Fischer (ed.), *Rational Expectations and Economic Policy*, pp. 249–68.

Trevithick, J. A. (1975), 'Keynes, Inflation and Money Illusion', *Economic Journal*, vol. 85 Mar. pp. 101ff.

(1980), *Inflation*, 2nd ed.

Yeats, W. B. (1934), *Collected Poems*.

Zis, G. (1977), 'The 1969-70 Wage Explosion in the United Kingdom', *The National Westminster Bank Review*, pp. 55–64.

9

On the Aims and Methods
of Economic Theorizing

I *Aims and Claims*

(1) The 'methods', or criteria, of a subject, or the principles for appraising its results, depend on the aims and claims with which the subject is, or should be, pursued. Regarding the aims of economic theorizing Sir John Hicks has observed:

There is much of economic theory which is pursued for no better reason than its intellectual attraction; it is a good game. We have no reason to be ashamed of that, since the same would hold for many branches of pure mathematics. (1979, p. viii)

No theoretical economist, certainly not one of Sir John's stature, seems previously to have ventured to state this somewhat revealing aperçu in quite such forthright terms. Sir John is denying, as regards 'much of economic theory', that it can reasonably be regarded as promising any significant relevance for serious real-world problems, the possession of which would presumably provide what many might (rightly or wrongly) hold was a better reason for pursuing economic theory than its simply being 'a good game'. Certainly what, according to Sir John, is the best justification for much of economic theory – i.e. that it is a good game – is a perfectly acceptable justification for an academic economist, *if it is, in each case, fully and clearly acknowledged as such.* But in fact, over the decades and centuries, a very different kind of aim and claim has been suggested or proclaimed by many economists, ancient and modern. For example, the Director of the National Institute was, and would still be, quite justified, with regard to academic, as well as government and business economists, in his observation:

There are few contemporary economists who would not claim that their work and their ideas are intended to contribute in some degree, however indirectly, to the improvement of a firm, an industry, a national economy or the world as a whole. (1972, p. 75; see also Hutchison, 1977, p. 144)

If both these observations, that of Mr Worswick and that of Sir John Hicks, are largely correct, as would seem to be the case, then a state of considerable obscurity, or at least of unrealized intentions hardly recognized or admitted as such, would seem to exist. Certainly academic economists, like academic mathematicians, are fully entitled to pursue 'good games'. But what would be intellectually deplorable would be that what can only, or best, be justified as a good game was being sold to students, research foundations, or the public, as contributing 'in some degree, however indirectly, to the improvement of a firm, an industry, a national economy or the world as a whole'. It would seem that there must be some considerable measure of intellectual obscurantism lurking here, which, in the interests of accurate trade descriptions, ought to be dispelled.[1]

(2) However, this chapter is concerned mainly with questions of methodological criteria, critical principles, or what Sir Karl Popper calls a 'demarcation' principle. From this point of view what is relevant is that if, or in so far as, economic theory is pursued simply as a good game, then the questions of criteria, critical principles or demarcation, with which we are here concerned, do not seem so very serious or complex, and do not seem to involve the kind of issues which arise when economic theory is involved, directly or indirectly, with policy-making, that is, with aspects of the 'goodness' not simply of a game, but of an economy and a society.

As regards what are simply 'games', why should not the players devise their own rules or criteria so as to make them 'good games' from their own point of view, or from the point of view of the spectators who finance them? In settling the rules, as contrasted with the observation, or administration, of a particular set of rules, surely 'anything goes', or should be allowed to 'go', which will, in the opinion of players and spectators, contribute to the goodness of the game. Certainly a given, or agreed set of rules must be adhered to, or administered, in the interests of the goodness of particular contests or matches. But in *setting up the rules*, or the set of distinctions between 'fair' and 'unfair' play, what Lakatos called a 'Polanyite consensus', on the part of the players, should be all that is required. Of course distinctions, or 'demarcation' problems, may constantly be arising on the field of play, *within* a set of rules. But the problems of setting up and administering the rules of bridge, chess or even cricket seem to be of a different order of complexity from setting up, or administering, the rules of a subject, or 'science', concerned with the performance of an economy and polity.

(3) However, as Mr Worswick, surely correctly, observed, few economists today, and far fewer in the past, would admit that the best reason for the pursuit of economic theory, or at any rate of the particular economic theories in which they were interested, was that these provided a good game. Certainly the great economists of the past, from the mercantilists onwards, including Smith and Malthus, Ricardo and Mill, Walras, Marshall or Keynes, seem primarily, and quite explicitly, to have been motivated by, and convinced of, the significance of their theories for increasing the wealth and welfare of nations, reducing poverty, inefficiency, or unemployment. They may have been quite mistaken in their aims and claims. The now somewhat hackneyed closing paragraph of Keynes's *General Theory*, regarding the tremendous political influence of the ideas of economists, may, indeed, be something of an exaggeration. But unquestionably, for centuries, real-world significance and influence, relevant to the well-being of firms, industries, nations, or the world as a whole, has been sincerely held by economists as the overriding aim and claim – and even achievement – of the subject. So if it is true, especially in recent decades, with the vast increase in the numbers of academic economists, that much of economic theory is pursued because it is a good game, it is also, and long has been, true that many economists have been, and are, concerned primarily with devising or supporting economic policies which they wish to see adopted through the political process.

(4) 'An advising profession' is how that of economists has been described;[2] and once one is concerned, directly or indirectly, with 'advice' and arguments for and against policies, one is inevitably liable to be involved with issues or processes of political persuasion and power. This concern inevitably raises questions of the possibility and desirability of distinguishing some kinds of arguments relevant to policy-making from others, or possibly with desirable rules for policy debate. Of course, these same distinctions or demarcations exist, and arguably should be

observed or maintained, whether it is simply a question of a game, to the goodness of which such 'rules', or distinctions and demarcations, may be held to contribute, or whether *a fortiori*, there is significant involvement with real-world policy arguments. Naturally, also, on the other hand, it *can* be maintained that 'anything goes', or should go, with regard to the involvement of 'the economics profession' in the area of policy debate, just as when it is simply the goodness of a game that is in question.

However, it is assumed here that a public role of involvement, direct or indirect, with policy arguments, *should* be accompanied by a commitment, at least to clarity, which will imply keeping as clear and distinct as is practicable (if not perfectly, at any rate to a significant extent) such distinctions and demarcations as that, for example, between normative and positive arguments, predictive or persuasive statements, and also the distinctions between tested, not-yet-tested, and untestable theories and propositions. Explicit emphasis on, and observance of, such distinctions may indeed hamper or reduce some kinds of persuasive power, and may, therefore, be rejected by those concerned overridingly with exercising political influence and power, if they are prepared to use *any* stick, including any kind of ideological rhetoric or ambiguity, in arguing against those whom they see as their political opponents, not to mention concealing or falsifying evidence.

(5) The argument of this chapter assumes, or implies, that a distinction can and should be drawn between clarifying the range of choice between policies by trying to improve the predictions about their consequences, and, on the other hand, primarily persuasive arguments regarding whether particular policies ought to be adopted or rejected. It is assumed that, to a significant extent, though not with an absolute ideal perfection, such distinctions can be observed and maintained.

Arguing for the maintenance of such distinctions and criteria, as far as is practicable, almost certainly involves intellectual, and even, to some extent ethical and political value-commitments. As Lakatos observed, regarding scientific knowledge generally: 'The problem of demarcation between science and pseudo-science is not a pseudo-problem of armchair philosophers: it has grave ethical and political implications' (1978, vol. 1, p. 7). This is especially important with regard to economists and political economy. No one has insisted, for example, more emphatically on the widespread value-assumptions of economics than Dr Gunnar Myrdal. (Indeed some might hold that, at times, he has tended to overstate their inevitable ubiquity.) But Dr Myrdal also insists on the desirability and duty, and therefore on the practicability, of conceptual and terminological discipline; that is, of regard for the kind of distinctions and demarcations which will reduce, or immunize against, bias:

> To keep concepts and terms clear, disinfected, logical and adequate to reality is a primary behest of the scientist. In this slippery field only the utmost purism can be accepted. It is apparent that economists as well as other social scientists have in recent decades dangerously lowered their scientific sights and work standards. . . . We should never compromise with our duty to speak the language of strict science. (1973, pp. 157, 165–6; see also Hutchison, 1978, p. 274, and above, chapter 3, pp. 64–5)

It is obviously pointless to proclaim that only 'the utmost purism' is acceptable, if the distinctions and demarcations required for such 'purism' are impossible or impracticable to maintain to any significant extent. Those who pursue economic theorizing simply as a good game – even if reluctant openly to admit this – may reject attempts to uphold such distinctions and criteria as unnecessarily fussy and restrictive: they would claim that they should be allowed to carry on with their game without the interruptions of officious would-be referees constantly and critically blowing their methodological whistles. Similarly, those economists concerned with using 'any kind of stick' to beat political opponents will also reject the observance of such distinctions. Both such parties will argue in terms of *the difficulties* of drawing such demarcations and distinctions. They will think up ambiguous examples in attempts to prove their impracticability and proclaim the liberating message of 'anything goes'.

Certainly there can be no 'legislation', or no enforcement of legislation, in this area beyond that of constant criticism, and the constant pressing of critical distinctions and demarcations as far as they will go, in the first instance in the interests of clarity, and beyond that in the interests of rational public policy debate in a democracy, that is, if one accepts Sir Karl Popper's prescription: 'Aiming at simplicity and lucidity is a moral duty of all intellectuals: lack of clarity is a sin' (1979, p. 44). This value commitment to clarity in communication is very much stressed here and is one which is, and has been, frequently disregarded and even systematically contravened, in and around the fringes of economics, where there is, and has been, much theoretical writing which seems designed to impress by sheer obscurity, complexity and 'profundity' – and, at the same time, to avoid testing and testability. One thinks especially of some work in the areas of management science, econometric and mathematical model-building, and Marxian theorizing.[3]

(6) It might well be maintained that there are 'professional' obligations on those pursuing what Max Weber called '*Wissenschaft als Beruf*', to maintain certain distinctions and demarcations of the kind outlined above (and which will be discussed further below). But the question remains of the particular combination of aims and claims which economists pursue – and we are concerned here with academic economists rather than with business, government, or party-political economists. In recent decades some economists have very cogently argued that politicians and civil servants cannot be assumed to be seeking altruistically to maximize some ideal concept of social welfare, but rather that their maximands should more realistically be seen as including votes, influence, power, jobs, 'empires' or salaries. Economists must turn this kind of realistic critique of maximands on themselves, and examine how far their own maximand is the goodness of a game, political persuasiveness and power, some kind or other of professional prestige, or rather the growth of knowledge in accordance with the criteria and disciplines of a 'scientific' subject.

Some of these maximands or aims may be to some extent complementary or compatible, but not all the way. Some would seem to conflict or compete quite seriously. As regards the growth of knowledge as the overriding maximand of a 'scientist', it seems that an index-number by which the growth of knowledge in economics and the social sciences could be measured reasonably uncontroversially may well be problematic. But only in respect of a particular maximand or value-commitment can a particular set of rules, criteria, distinctions and demarcations be justified.

II *The 'Methods' and Criteria of the Natural Sciences as a Model for Economics*

(1) The 'methods', criteria and principles of appraisal of the natural sciences may be, and often have been, taken to provide a model for economics and the social sciences. Similarities with the more advanced natural sciences have been emphasized by some

economists and econometricians, who have sought to establish a kind of intellectual parity with natural science, not only in terms of aims and criteria, but also in respect of the firmness of the epistemological foundations of their theories and their operational reliability.[4] Alternatively, other economists have emphasized the unsuitability, or inadequacy, for economists and the social sciences, of the 'methods' and criteria of the natural sciences, in some cases because the use of introspection and 'understanding' ('*Verstehen*') provides economics and the social sciences with much more certain and reliable foundations than are available to natural scientists.

It might be objected that there is not sufficient clarity or agreement as to just what the 'methods' and criteria of the natural sciences are, or should be, which would make for much in the way of a model, or guidance, to emerge. Certainly emphasis and fashion change on this subject, and much argument will doubtless continue on points of formulation and drafting. But the more pretentious kinds of infallibilist scientism which flourished in the nineteenth century, though lingering among some Marxians, have largely faded away, and it now seems often to be overlooked how much wide and substantial agreement exists – for example, as between the ideas of Popper, Kuhn and Lakatos – on issues of more fundamental importance for the appraisal of economic theories than are the continuing and sometimes fierce disagreements on some points. For professional philosophers, or specialist philosophers of science, distinctions and differences in emphasis or formulation may be of great significance, which are not always so important for any actual problems in a particular science, and cannot be shown to be of much importance by relevant examples in economics.

(2) Let us consider next the extremely forthright statement of the natural-scientific view of the methods and criteria of economics given in Professor Milton Friedman's Nobel Lecture (1976). Professor Friedman began by observing that there 'doubtless still remains widespread scepticism among both scientists and the broader public about the appropriateness of treating economics as parallel to physics, chemistry and medicine' (1977, pp. 7–8). Professor Friedman then sets out a long list of similarities between the natural sciences, and economics and the social sciences:

In both, there is no 'certain' substantive knowledge; only tentative hypotheses. . . .

In both social and natural sciences, the body of positive knowledge grows by the failure of a tentative hypothesis to predict phenomena the hypothesis professes to explain.

In both, experiment is sometimes possible, sometimes not. . . .

In both, there is no way to have a self-contained closed system or to avoid interaction between the observer and the observed. . . .

Even the difficult problem of separating value-judgements is not unique to the Social Sciences.

None of these comparisons can be rejected outright. Indeed they contain *some* measure of vital fundamental validity. Especially noteworthy is Professor Friedman's rejection of infallible certainties in scientific knowledge. (This marks a fundamental contrast, of the greatest political importance with Engels's and Marx's claim to infallibly certain scientific knowledge. Marx also suggested the epistemological parity of physics and economics.)[5] But Professor Friedman's view is too one-sided and unqualified. Certainly similarities in principle must not be lost sight of; but neither must the dissimilarities in degree which also are crucial. Discrimination, and getting the balance right, are everything in comparisons of the natural and social sciences. What must be rejected are both overconfident claims in terms of similarities, which may suggest parity in quantifiability and in the precision and reliability of predictions, and also an anti-naturalist and anti-'positivist' nihilism, which rejects all comparisons with the natural sciences, in particular with regard to any demarcations or disciplinary implications, in the name of 'anything goes' (and the mob rule, followed by ideological totalitarianism, which it is hoped will succeed).[6]

(3) One way of summing up the similarities and dissimilarities between the natural and social sciences is to regard the latter as simply 'immature' or 'underdeveloped', as contrasted with the 'maturity' of physics and chemistry, thus implying basic similarities in aims, and, eventually, in achievements, when the less 'mature' and developed social sciences have eventually had time to catch up with the more advanced natural sciences. Some philosophers, notably Kuhn, Lakatos and Ravetz, have pointed to significant contrasts between what they call 'mature' or 'developed' sciences, notably physics and chemistry, and 'immature' or 'ineffective' fields, or 'proto-sciences' as Kuhn called them, among which sociology was mentioned as an example. Though Ravetz clearly placed it among 'immature' and 'ineffective' fields,

Kuhn and Lakatos did not explicitly locate economics in terms of 'maturity' and 'immaturity', though they emphasized the general distinction. But what seems especially significant is that both Kuhn and Lakatos as well as Ravetz, suggest that the methodological prescriptions, or the extent to which they should be enforced, which are appropriate for 'mature' and developed sciences, are not the same as those appropriate for 'immature' or underdeveloped fields. They insist that for the *less* mature and developed sciences, stricter and more explicit methodological prescriptions may be appropriate than for more mature and developed subjects like physics.[7]

It may, incidentally, be worth recalling at this point that whether contrasts or comparisons are drawn in terms of 'maturity' and 'immaturity', or in terms of the nature of the material, natural or social, human or non-human, in either case the distinction is one of degree, and not of some clear-cut dividing line or distinct and profound gulf. But contrasts and comparisons between sciences at markedly different points on the spectrum are no less significant because there is continuity, and not some distinct discontinuity, between them (though a one-dimensional spectrum may be an oversimplified analogy).

(4) Sometimes contrasts and comparisons are drawn between the natural and social sciences in terms of 'methods'. But, as this word is usually understood, this does not seem to be an appropriate or significant point of comparison. (In fact, the word 'methodology' has long seemed to be a rather unhappy one.) However, the term 'methods' sometimes seem to be used to cover the criteria or standards by which results are judged. But, if so, then 'criteria', or 'aims', or 'objectives', are surely more appropriate terms in accordance with which to draw comparisons.

Anyhow, as Ravetz has remarked, 'the "methods" of science are a very heterogeneous collection of things' (1971, pp. 173, 410). There is a wide range of 'methods' used in the sciences, and different sciences use different combinations according to the possibilities presented by their material. In particular, it is unjustifiable to conclude that the 'methods' of the most developed or 'mature' natural sciences are necessarily most appropriate (as J. S. Mill assumed) for sciences concerned with a different kind of material, for which such 'methods' simply may not be feasible. On the other hand, 'methods' which may be dismissed as inadequate or unreliable by the standards appropriate for the most developed and 'mature' sciences, and for the material with which these have to deal, simply may be essential, or the only feasible 'methods' for reaching the only kind of conclusions which 'immature' and underdeveloped subjects may be able to reach, or may be aiming at.

However, in terms of 'methods' it may at least be worth repeating that the much greater difficulty, or virtual impossibility, of controlled experiments in the social sciences, though it may be one of degree, is surely more serious than Professor Milton Friedman allows, and is an obvious fundamental difference as compared with the natural sciences, which cannot be overcome or compensated for by abstract model-building or introspection.

(5) It seems that comparisons are likely to be much more illuminating in terms of the *materials* of different sciences, or groups of sciences, or in terms of *criteria* or *aims*.

Regarding the differences between the materials of the natural and social (or human) sciences there are two kinds of comprehensive and very controversial, mainly normative, arguments, which may be mentioned here briefly, only to be somewhat summarily dismissed.

The first argument is that for a scientist to treat people, or to study their actions and problems, as though they were *things*, is both normatively and positively profoundly wrong. Something of this kind has been argued by that outstanding philosopher-economist, the late E. F. Schumacher. It is argued that man occupies, or should be regarded as occupying, a different level of existence as compared with natural objects, and that to treat man's actions in some sense as determinate or predictable fails to recognize a fundamental distinction and somehow denies man's freedom. Of course, the feelings behind this kind of attitude must be respected and are often flouted. Of course, also, the social or human sciences can be, and are, abused just as the natural sciences have been. Indeed some of the abuses of human and social sciences (in psychiatry to take an obvious example) may well seem, and be, more appalling even than the abuses of physical and chemical science. But all that will be said here is that there does not seem to be any fundamental methodological gulf or distinction which it is essential to insist upon.

A second kind of distinction, which may be dealt with very briefly here (we shall be returning to it later) is based on the view that both valuations and biases inevitably play a much more pervasive and ineradicable role in economics and the social sciences than in the natural sciences. We have already mentioned

Dr Myrdal's well-known views on this point. It may be agreed that on the whole as between the natural and social sciences there is a considerable difference of degree in respect of the complex interconnections between facts and values. But this does not seem so profound as to constitute a fundamental or significant gulf between the two kinds of subjects (as suggested by the situation in the science of genetics aptly cited as an example by Professor Milton Friedman, with whom, on this point, it is easy to agree). Certainly it is important to cultivate a consensus regarding the duty of scientific communicators to clarify as far as possible their assumptions and their terminology. Moreover, there may well be a danger of a kind of vicious circle of 'immaturity' in a subject like economics, which is urgently concerned with policy problems – and hence political power – in that difficulties of testing, and the extent of ignorance, leave a vacuum filled by bias and ideology, which in turn makes critical testing more difficult. But it seems that the greater pervasiveness of bias in the social sciences can be regarded as due rather more to the problematic or complex nature of the basic material than the other way round.

(6) When one seeks to focus on the profound differences in *material* as between the natural and the social sciences it becomes apparent that there are various ways of describing these differences, which might well be regarded as constituting a single fundamental difference, though it may be looked at from different angles. Difficulties in quantifiability, heterogeneity, the absence of 'constants', the 'openness' or the 'complexity' of the material of social and economic systems, or what might be called the historical and institutional dimension (which implies the existence only of trends and not laws), these are all different aspects, or ways of describing the different characteristics of the material of the social, as contrasted with the natural sciences. The differences may only be in degree, but amount to such a considerable degree as to constitute a profound contrast.

A brief anthology of quotations will illustrate the various ways in which the differences in material as between the social and natural sciences may be described.

Sir Karl Popper, who has gone a long way in denying the importance of the differences between the natural and social sciences, has noted the absence of constants in economics, as contrasted with physics, and the 'fundamental difficulties' which result:

It cannot be doubted that there are some fundamental difficulties here. In physics, for example, the parameters of our equations can, in principle, be reduced to a small number of natural constants – a reduction which has been successfully carried out in many important cases. This is not so in economics; here the parameters are themselves in the most important cases quickly changing variables. This clearly reduces the significance, interpretability, *and testability* of our measurements. (1961, p. 143, italics added; for a rather different view of Popper on this subject, see Koertge, 1974)

Professors Hayek, Simon, and others have used the concept of 'complexity' as a, or the, main point of contrast as between the less complex natural, and more complex social sciences. As Professor Hayek has put it:

When we consider the question from the angle of the minimum number of distinct variables a formula or model must possess in order to reproduce the characteristic patterns of structures of different fields (or so exhibit the general laws which these structures obey), the increasing complexity as we proceed from the inanimate to the (more highly organized) animate and social phenomena becomes fairly obvious. (1967, p. 26; see also Simon, 1962, and Grunberg, 1978, p. 547)

Professor Grunberg prefers the term 'openness' as characterizing the material of economics, and concludes:

The expressions *open system, complexity*, and *absence of constants*, as used in the methodological literature of economics, are synonymous. Since the usefulness of the term *complexity* is impaired in scientific discourse by its vagueness in colloquial language, it might be well to avoid it. As to the term *absence of constants*, it may be very useful in certain contexts as long as it is kept in mind that it does not refer to a characteristic of a system distinct from that system's openness. (1978, p. 555)

It may be of interest to add Keynes's characterization of crucial differences in material in his critique of econometrics:

Unlike the typical natural science, the material to which it is applied is, in too many respects, not homogeneous through time. . . .
In chemistry and physics and other natural sciences the object of experiment is to fill the actual values of the various quantities and factors appearing in an equation or a formula; and the work when done is once and for all. In economics that is not the case, and to convert a model into

a quantitative formula is to destroy its usefulness as an instrument of thought. . . .

The pseudo-analogy with the physical sciences leads directly counter to the habit of mind which it is most important for an economist to acquire. . . . One has to be constantly on guard against treating the material as constant and homogeneous. (1973, pp. 296–300, italics added)

The differences in material between economics and the natural sciences might also be described in terms of the historical, or institutional, dimension. As Sir John Hicks has put it, economics:

is on the edge of science and on the edge of history. . . .

As economics pushes on beyond 'statics', it becomes less like science, and more like history. (1979, p. xi)

In other words, static analysis in economics involves a simplificatory reduction of the material of economics to the non–historical simplicity of natural science, by abstracting from the historical-institutional dimension.

(7) Main consequences of these fundamental differences in material are the paucity of laws in economics (in spite of the pretentious claims of classicals, Marxians, and others), and hence the much lower reliability and accuracy of predictions (see Hutchison, 1977, chapter 2). It is not necessary to get involved in a largely verbal argument about the suitable coverage of the word 'law'. Nor is it necessary to insist that there are no propositions whatsoever in economics which might reasonably be called 'laws'. But it is remarkable how economists from Ricardo onwards down to the most recent times, including, of course, Marxian economists, have proclaimed the existence of economic 'laws'. For the propositions involved simply do not approximate in precision to the laws of physics and chemistry, and it is extremely misleading to use the same term to cover both. As Professor Hayek has observed: 'I rather doubt whether we know of any "laws" which social phenomena obey' (1967, p. 42).[8]

There are, of course, useful generalizations in economics and the social sciences, which are better described as trends or tendencies, since they are usually not nearly as precise and testable as 'laws' properly so called. Trends, or tendencies, in fact, and not 'laws', are what the material of economics and the social sciences seems mainly to yield, or has yielded so far. Nor does a closer look at the nature of the basic material suggest that the emergence of 'laws', of the same quality as those of physics and chemistry, is at all likely. But although, on the one hand, it is, of course, vital to appreciate that the important generalizations of economics take the form of trends or tendencies, and not 'laws' in any full sense of the term, it also, on the other hand, seems quite misconceived to deplore the inferior quality or reliability of trends, as compared with laws, or to attempt to prohibit or despise predictions made on the basis of trends rather than laws. For, lacking laws, *trends and tendencies are virtually all economists have*, in general empirical terms, and they must make the best of them.

III *Anti-Anti-'Positivist'*

(1) The term 'positivist' in economic literature seems often to imply the upholding, in economics and the social sciences, of the 'methods', criteria, and aims of the natural sciences.[9] But the term has come to be used quite indiscriminately, as a kind of all-purpose pejorative adjective, from contrasting political directions, by epistemological anarchists as well as by dogmatists of all stripes, from Marxians to Misesists. The term 'positivist' seems especially to be directed at those who support a disciplined observance of, or emphasis on, distinctions and demarcations between normative and positive, or between prescriptive, descriptive or predictive propositions, or between definitional and empirical, or analytic, synthetic or other types of proposition. There follows here a brief examination of one or two of the main examples of what are described, or denounced, as 'positivist' ideas or doctrines.

One such doctrine, which often seems to be regarded as 'positivist', which we have already discussed, is that which maintains the importance and, to a reasonable extent, the practicability, of the distinction between positive and normative statements in the social sciences. We would only add that a main purpose of the anti-positivist rejection of such a distinction seems to be to legitimize and validate the propagation of ideology.

(2) Another methodological idea which seems often to be denounced as 'positivist' is concerned with prediction. By anti-'positivists', prediction is, in some sense or other, held to be 'impossible' in economics; and it is condemned as a typically 'positivist' error to set up improved prediction as an aim for

economics, for it is considered not only epistemologically impossible, but also morally dubious (see Hutchison, 1977, chapter 2). Certainly in so far as 'much of economic theory' is pursued as 'a good game', predictive capacity or performance would seem to be more or less completely irrelevant as an intellectual objective. But, on the other hand, as we have noted, it would seem that a considerable majority of economists throughout the history of the subject have, often quite explicitly, proclaimed the pragmatic 'fruit-bearing' aims and objectives of the science of political economy or economics, in terms of increasing the wealth of nations and reducing poverty and unemployment.

What has to be pressed home to economists who deny improved prediction as an objective is that, in so doing, they must, at the same time, be largely denying this major tradition in their subject. It may be that some kinds of illuminating comment regarding the wealth of nations, poverty and unemployment, *may* be thought possible without *any* attempt at improving predictions. But just how this would be done certainly needs to be spelt out precisely – as it seldom has been. Meanwhile, such other kinds of contributions to less unsuccessful policy-making as may be possible, but not dependent on improved predictions (such as diagnosis without prognosis, or elucidating policy preferences), could hardly prove sufficient to substantiate the considerable aims and claims for their subject put forward by economists throughout the last two centuries. In particular, if improved prediction is denied as a scientific objective for economists, it would certainly seem difficult to find a basis for massively increasing claims to financial support and research resources from business and government, or to discern what precisely economists in business and government are being paid to do.

Indeed, it is hardly an edifying spectacle to contemplate some of the combination of dubiously compatible doctrines, or assumptions, often laced‚ with denunciations of 'positivism', which economists collectively, or sometimes individually, can be found to be maintaining, such as: the forthright advocacy of particular economic policies, or the pronouncement of 'critical judgements' in respect of the advantages and disadvantages of 'capitalism' and 'socialism'; denials of the power to predict (e.g. by F. H. Knight, Professors Jewkes, Shackle and others); claims to 'professionalism', or, sometimes, 'expertise' ('when I say expert, I mean expert' – Lord Balogh);[10] together with, at the same time, a rejection of the distinction between normative and positive arguments.

(3) Next there is the epistemological distinction, denounced by both Marxian and Misesist anti-positivists, between definitional and empirical, or between analytic and synthetic propositions. There is a sense in which such classifications or taxonomies cannot be regarded as true or false, but rather as appropriate or useful – or the reverse. To emphasize the usefulness of these distinctions in economics, for the criticism or appraisal of economic theories, is not to argue that they necessarily provide a completely exhaustive, universal dichotomy; nor that there is necessarily 'some fundamental cleavage' (as Professor Quine puts it) between the two types of proposition;[11] nor again that such a distinction must always be useful in all fields or cases, in particular in philosophy. But the definitional-empirical distinction has often been used by economists, often most illuminatingly and tellingly, especially in the field of macroeconomics, with regard to such propositions as the Quantity of Money doctrine, 'Say's Law', and the Keynesian savings and investment propositions. Here it is certainly vital, or often easy, to distinguish between definitional statements and identities, on the one hand, and empirical statements, or equilibrium conditions, on the other hand. As has often been pointed out, much confusion and obscurantism has reigned, and persisted, through failure to observe this distinction, which failure amounts, according to one distinguished authority, to a 'besetting sin' on the part of economists (Hall, 1959).[12]

Whether or not this distinction is to be regarded as exhaustive and universal or marking a completely 'fundamental cleavage', it is quite essential for the interpretation of important propositions not only in macroeconomics but in microeconomics also. Fundamental propositions regarding the assumption of 'rational' or maximizing action, together with the formulation of such assumptions as diminishing returns, have certainly needed clarificatory analysis in the light of this fundamental distinction between definitional and empirical. In particular, what is called the 'rationality' assumption has often been formulated in a very vague way, in that the amount and kind of knowledge and ignorance, perfect or otherwise, or the kind of expectations involved, 'rational' or otherwise, are left unspecified (while the specification of a particular kind of knowledge or expectations would obviously have to be contingent or empirical).

In particular, the definitional-empirical, or the analytic-synthetic distinctions, may be difficult to apply in the sense that arguments and propositions are sometimes so vaguely formulated that, without further elucidation, it is impossible to classify them as definitely in the one or other category. Certainly, if a *third* category is insisted on, that of 'hopelessly vague' statements, in addition to definitional (or analytic) and empirical, this may readily be granted (see Klappholz and Agassi, 1960, p. 161).[13] But a serious offence is here being perpetrated against the overriding requirement of maximum feasible clarity, and it is arguable that the definitional-empirical distinction should be pressed all the more decisively. Alternatively, if it is claimed that some other, third, type of proposition is involved, then its nature must be spelled out all the more precisely: how conflicts between propositions of that type can be resolved should be explained all the more fully, and important examples from economic theorizing should be supplied.

(4) However, the definitional-empirical and analytical-synthetic distinctions have been comprehensively rejected by anti-positivists, who insist on the importance of some other kind, or kinds, of proposition which do not fit into this distinction, and which are apparently not testable, or to be tested by logical or empirical procedures. As we have seen, this rejection disregards the frequent and illuminating use of these distinctions, particularly with regard to fundamental propositions in macroeconomics.

In fact, clear and reasonably precise examples of these other kinds of proposition, with demonstrations of the important role they play in economic theorizing, have not been forthcoming, though all sorts and kinds of loose general descriptions have been offered. Of course, philosophers may well wish to insist, for philosophical purposes or contexts, on the existence and significance of other types of proposition than definitional and empirical, but unfortunately they have been quite unable to specify whether, or how, these other kinds of proposition, or distinction, have any important role to play in interpreting or appraising actual economic theories, or to give any reasonably clear or precise examples *in economics*. Economists' descriptions of such propositions, though characterized by the widest variety, also never give clear and reasonably precise examples, demonstrating their importance. Among the wide range of descriptions of such propositions have been that they are Aristotelian realist-essentialist propositions (Menger); Kantian synthetic *a priori* propositions (Bernadelli);[14] introspective certainties given by

'inner observation' (Wieser *et al.*); *a priori* praxeological propositions (Mises); or necessary but not purely logical truths embody-
ing 'critical judgements' (Hollis and Nell). Questions as to how
such propositions would be tested are liable to be dismissed as
irrelevant.

Finally, it is important to distinguish between assertions of the
importance in economics of propositions which are neither
definitional nor empirical, and which cannot conceivably be tested
by logical or empirical procedures, and, on the other hand,
decisions that a theory or programme will be persisted with, *even if*
certain assumptions involved have not been, and cannot practically be, adequately tested; or that one or other of a theory's
'assumptions' may be 'protected' as part of a 'hard core', not in the
sense that they are to be regarded as unempirical, or not conceivably testable, but in the sense that the theory or programme
would be persisted with, as the least unpromising theory or
programme available, even if falsifications of such an assumption
occurred. There are not necessarily any dogmatist, infallibilist or
obscurantist implications in this latter attitude, which it may often
be reasonable to resort to, especially in economics and the social
sciences, where policy decisions are pressing, and testing often
very difficult or practically impossible. Such decisions may be
quite compatible with a strenuously critical attitude, a readiness to
test, and attempts at falsification wherever practicable. But it must
be noted that in the actual history of economic theorizing it is
often difficult or impossible to identify, among the varying,
loosely formulated versions of a 'research programme', precisely
what the 'hard core' consists or consisted of; so that something
like *carte blanche* might be claimed for disregarding recalcitrant
evidence in respect of quite a range of varying propositions or
assumptions.

On the other hand, upholding one's assumptions, propositions
and theories, and rejecting as irrelevant all tests, logical and
empirical, while refusing to explain any procedure for how
contradictions or conflicts may be resolved, is to take one's stand
on dogmatism and infallibilism. Certainly, in some cases, the
purpose of insisting on the significance in economics of propositions which are neither definitional nor empirical, and which are
not to be, or cannot be, tested or refuted by logical or empirical
procedures or criteria, seems to have been the protection of
particular political dogmas, against which it is the argument of
this chapter that a distinction, or demarcation principle, should be
firmly maintained.[15]

IV *Testing and Testability*

(1) Methodological prescriptions in support of demarcations, distinctions and discipline, as promoted by criteria of testing and testability, are liable to be described or denounced as 'positivist'. But such criteria are especially important in economics and political economy, for reasons arising out of the nature of the material discussed above.

First, because of the 'complexity' or 'openness' of the material, and the paucity of constants, or because of what might be called the historical–institutional dimension, there is the need for repeated testing and retesting of relationships which often cannot be taken as constant, regular, or even 'normal', over long periods. Unlike laws, trends have to be constantly retested in case they are altering, and it is on trends that much or most of economic predictions have to be based. For this kind of reason, relating to the material of the social sciences, philosophers such as Kuhn, Lakatos and Ravetz, as we have seen, have emphasized that demarcation and discipline should be pressed all the more stringently in what they perhaps misleadingly call the 'immature' social sciences.

Second, because economists and political economy are so closely and intensely involved with extra-scientific objectives, such as power and influence, the distinctions, demarcations and discipline which testing and testable formulations can help in promoting may have a significant role to play in policy discussion in a democracy.

A third factor which heightens the need for testing, arising out of the objectives, rather than the material, of economists, is the importance of improved prediction in a subject which has been so heavily engaged in policy guidance.

(2) However, the very characteristics of the material, which make constant testing and retesting so necessary, make the achievement of decisive results often very difficult, or practically impossible (though not inconceivable). But to maintain that because there are so often immense difficulties in the way of anything resembling decisive tests, *therefore* the desirability and obligation, as far as is practicable, of testing and providing testable formulations, should be dismissed as naïve, is a frequent but preposterous line of argument. It is like arguing that because attempting to counter crime is difficult and costly, and because crime will never be wiped out and there will always come a point

when it is not worth devoting further resources to the fight, therefore it is 'naïve' to attempt any serious campaign against crime at all.

Perhaps it should be added that the objective of, or hope from, constant testing and retesting in economics, is not that all theories except one will sooner or later be cleanly and conclusively knocked down, leaving a single, definitive 'orthodoxy' holding the field. If there is any objective or hope in testing and retesting, other than trying to maximize the relevant and recent evidence, it might rather be that the position would be weakened of any theory or programme claiming to represent a dominant ortho-doxy, the influence of which may really be based appreciably on dubious ideological, or external, factors (see Hutchison, 1978).

(3) We have discussed two of the objections to prescriptions in favour of testing and testable formulations. These are, first, that testing is often very difficult and inconclusive. But this seems to make it all the more important to try to resist vagueness and obscurity by seeking to test or falsify as far as is practicable. Prescriptions in favour of testing and testable formulations are implied by the commitment to clarity in communication. Second, we have discussed and rejected various forms of a priorist objections in terms of the self-evident validity or even the 'apodictic certainty' of particular assumptions and theories, based on introspective, essentialist, or synthetic *a priori* foundations. This line of justification, once highly influential in economics, seems to be undergoing something of a revival from extremely contrasting political directions.

A third kind of objection to testability and testing seeks to maintain that the enforcement of such prescriptions will be – and has been – unduly restrictive and damaging. It has been alleged that promising or budding theories or programmes in economics might be, or actually have been, eliminated, rejected, banished or scrapped by the application of such prescriptions. It has even been rather alarmingly suggested that every economic theory what-soever might 'be banished as pseudo-science', or that the whole subject might be 'legislated out of existence' by such prescriptions (Latsis, 1976, p. 1).

Such alarmist arguments, as well as being devoid of historical foundation, involve a fundamental misunderstanding of the nature of methodological prescriptions and their function. In the first place, the analogy of 'legislation' is profoundly misleading. One cannot be said to 'legislate' without any means of, or even desire for, enforcement. Furthermore, neither the logic of theory choice, nor the actual historical record, suggest that such destructive consequences have followed, or need to, or would, follow, or that it would always and necessarily, in all cases, be damaging to the growth of knowledge if they *did* follow. On the contrary, it might be argued that there has been, and will be, much greater damage to promising new programmes and to the growth of knowledge – not to mention to economic policy-making – from the sheltering of prevailing dogmas, or established exclusivist orthodoxies, against testing and falsification, which may crowd out new theories from receiving the recognition they deserve.

Anyhow, this argument fails to distinguish between the question of the desirability of testable formulations and critical testing, and that of the tactics to be adopted with regard to research programmes when a particular proposition or assumption has been falsified in a particular case. As Professor Musgrave has emphasized (1973, p. 403), the results of a test never can, or do, necessarily entail some kind of final elimination, banishment or scrapping of a theory. A theory may be regarded as having performed far from satisfactorily in such tests (if any) as it has had to meet, and it may even have been 'falsified', but it may still be regarded as the least unsatisfactory theory available; or the programme of which it is a part may be held to be the least unpromising available programme – which will always be a question of judgement.

Moreover, such a theory may still be regarded as the least unreliable basis from which urgent or inevitable policy decisions may be derived. This would certainly seem constantly to have been the relation between economic theories and policies. Throughout history, economic policies have constantly had to be based (and perhaps have to be as much as ever today) on inadequately tested theories, against which, or against the applicability of which, some serious adverse evidence could probably be cited – though they could still reasonably be regarded as the least unreliable theories on which inevitable policy choices could be based. But such obvious intellectual facts of life do not justify refusals to admit weaknesses in theories which tests may have suggested, or attempts to discourage, or ward off as 'naïve', the testing of theories on which favourite or orthodox policies are based.[16] Such obscurantism and complacency simply help to clear the way for political dogmatism and authoritarianism.

As contrasted with the principle of 'Anything Goes', or the

methodological anarchism favoured by Professor Feyerabend, which might prove all too conducive to mob rule, or a 'dictatorship of the proletariat', the prescriptions of testing and testability would promote less dogmatic, more tentative and fallibilist attitudes regarding economic knowledge and ignorance. The application of such prescriptions need not have any alarmistically destructive consequences, but could allow for alternative possibilities to be kept in play while not cosseting them against critical testing or allowing any one of them to claim the authority of some professional orthodoxy, without having passed adequate tests. Anyhow there can be no question of seeking to give 'legislative' force to some kind of veto, or censorship, prohibiting any type of conjecture of speculation (see Hutchison, 1938, p. viii). What is being argued, in supporting a methodological prescription of testability and testing, is simply that all would-be theories, claiming relevance in an empirical science (whose leading practitioners have put forward as a main aim and claim the giving of policy guidance) should be examined in terms of their testability and the tests which they have actually undergone, and that it should be regarded as a serious criticism of a theory if it has not been formulated in a falsifiable form or has not withstood any tests.[17]

There does not seem to be anything naïve or hypercritical in insisting on the questionable status of theories which have not been tested in any way, or at all adequately – for example, regarding monetary and fiscal processes – or on emphasizing that untested speculations should be sharply distinguished from, and not passed off as, authoritative professional orthodoxies. Moreover, it seems that the omission to test, or even to formulate in testable terms, should not be complacently shrugged off with a reference to synthetic *a priori* propositions, arbitrarily proclaimed 'hard cores', the superior reliability of introspection, the non-testability of 'assumptions', or the practical difficulties of testing. Such evidence should be regarded as especially serious with regard to a science which, firstly, is claiming, and aiming at, policy relevance in a democracy; and where, secondly, there seems, from the historical record, to have been a serious propensity to excessive and over-optimistic 'scientific' claims, as well as to the encroachments of political dogmatism.[18]

To look for tests or falsifications of a theory is to look for a kind of highly relevant empirical evidence. It is obviously presumptuous to discount in advance such evidence as tests may yield as totally irrelevant, or to dismiss or discourage *a priori* a systematic search for data.

Of course, it is platitudinous that the significance of the data emerging from tests may be highly disputable with regard to the choice or assessment of theories. But it would surely involve a serious, indeed very 'naïve', misunderstanding of methodological prescriptions to imagine that they can ever provide once-and-for-all, automatic solutions of the problems of appraising or selecting theories in economics. The nature and limits of methodological prescriptions have been well described as follows:

Just as practical philosophy shows that moral decisions are not theoretically decidable, methodology shows that there is no algorism for making decisions in scientific research. The demand for such 'meta-rules' is just as unreasonable as the demand for certain knowledge, or for true hypotheses. Thus Kant notes that the 'Anwendung von Regeln überhaupt verlangt Urteilskraft, die nicht durch Regeln gesichert werden kann'. . . . Methodological rules offer the scientist guiding principles, which not only leave him his full freedom of decision and responsibility, but even increase his freedom by allowing him to conceptualize the developments which are possible within certain kinds of research situations. Practical philosophy also shows that there is no non-formal moral principle which is applicable in every situation without regard to specific circumstances, or which has an unconditional priority over all other principles. These two remarks about moral rules indicate that Feyerabend's thesis concerning the restricted validity of methodological rules is fully correct; but also that it is nothing new – and certainly no objection against Popper. (Radnitzky, 1976, pp. 518–9)

V *On Testing 'Assumptions'*

(1) Very ambiguous and confusing arguments have been advanced regarding the testing of 'assumptions' in economics. As Professor Friedman himself observed in his paper which launched these arguments: 'The very concept of the "assumptions" of a theory is surrounded with ambiguity' (1953, p. 23; see also Hutchison, 1960, pp. xii–xvi). The subsequent discussion of the subject did not remove the ambiguity. Friedman went on to write of 'assumptions' in inverted commas and even questioned whether 'a theory can be said to have "assumptions" at all' (p. 14). No one, of course could or would demand the testing of the 'assumptions' of a theory which did not have any such 'assumptions', or which

only had 'assumptions' such as were not necessarily required as part of the theory; just as no one would demand that 'assumptions' had to be 'realistic' about what was insignificant or irrelevant as far as the theory was concerned.

However, Friedman *did* insist that 'full and comprehensive evidence' is vital 'in constructing hypotheses' which must be 'consistent with the evidence at hand' (pp. 12–13). He went on to hold that 'assumptions' have the necessary role of 'specifying the conditions under which a theory is expected to be valid', and that 'the assumptions of a theory' may 'facilitate an indirect test of the hypothesis by its implications' (p. 23). It seems quite impossible to see how these functions of 'assumptions' can be fulfilled if there is no concern for their 'realism' or testing. For if one is interested in any real-world application of one's theory or hypothesis, one must not only specify 'the conditions under which it is expected to be valid', but also test, in any particular case, how far these conditions are 'really' fulfilled.

(2) Professor Friedman's original ambiguous arguments against the testing of assumptions have been eagerly seized upon and elaborated by the a priorist and 'anti-positivist' opponents of testing. More recently, illuminating criticisms have been developed by Professor Alan Musgrave,[19] who begins by finding (with unduly charitable moderation) that 'the whole discussion is hopelessly confused'. Professor Musgrave then goes on to distinguish between three kinds of 'assumptions', which he calls 'negligibility assumptions', 'domain assumptions', and 'heuristic assumptions'.

With regard to 'negligibility assumptions' (for example, whether air resistance is negligible for the behaviour of falling bodies), then it certainly matters whether such an assumption is true or 'realistic'. If a theory involves the 'assumption' that something is negligible, then it is important to try to check by testing whether it is in fact negligible, or whether it is not. An 'assumption' regarding an economic process that, for example, there is no government, may not be fully 'realistic' (if there is, in fact, a government). But, if a 'negligibility assumption' is being made, then it is necessary, when applying the theory, to test how far the effects of government 'really' are negligible. In some cases they might be negligible and in some cases not negligible.

Professor Musgrave then observes that 'domain assumptions' specify the domain of applicability of the theory (or, as Friedman put it, assumptions may specify 'the conditions under which a theory is expected to be valid). 'Domain assumptions' may be introduced, either initially, or, as an *ad hoc*, immunizing adjustment, possibly justifiably, when a negligibility assumption has been falsified. For example, if there is a government, and its effects on the economic process in question are in some cases not negligible, then the 'domain' assumption' has to be tested directly or indirectly in any particular case to ascertain whether the theory applies to that case or not.

Thirdly, there are simplifying or 'heuristic' assumptions, which do not require (for example) either that there is no government, or that its effects are negligible. A simplifying or 'heuristic' assumption may be used to break down the treatment of a complex process by taking, as 'a first approximation', one factor in the process at a time: that is, by examining the process, first, 'as if' there was no government, then subsequently introducing the effects of government. In economics and other relatively 'complex' or 'open' subjects, this procedure of successive approximations usually does not work out very effectively, in contrast, as Professor Musgrave shows, to Newton's working out of his theory of the solar system. Heuristic assumptions, and 'first approximations', are more fruitful with regard to 'simple', closed material – that is with regard to the solar system rather than the social system. This is because, with regard to simplified 'first approximations' in 'complex' subjects, either there is no one significant second approximation, or the two, or more, kinds of effects of the processes, separated by 'simplifying assumptions', often cannot simply be summed together. But certainly, with regard to 'heuristic' assumptions, it is beside the point to object that they, or their logical consequences, have been falsified. However, simplifying or 'heuristic' assumptions in economics are apt to make for thinner and more inconclusive theories (or simply for taxonomies) than are 'negligibility assumptions', or even 'domain assumptions'. 'Heuristic assumptions' are liable, though not inevitably, to become the resort of those who pursue economic theorizing as 'a good game'.

As Professor Musgrave observes, what may have started life as a 'negligibility assumption' may be pared down to a 'domain assumption', and eventually end up as a 'heuristic assumption', and as part of a taxonomy, or near-taxonomy. It should be noted that there is a large and crucial change of content between the three kinds of assumption (that there is no government, for example) and that they are very different 'assumptions' in their implications.

That is why ambiguities and obscurities as to whether an 'assumption' is concerned with 'negligibility', 'domain' or 'heuristic' simplification may promote such serious confusions or exaggerated claims. As Professor Musgrave concludes:

> Criticism may change the status of an assumption: what in youth was a bold and adventurous negligibility assumption, may be reduced in middle age to a sedate domain assumption, and decline in old-age into a mere heuristic assumption. Such changes can be almost imperceptible if the same form of words is employed for all three 'assumptions'. It is an interesting *historical* question whether this has actually happened in the development of economic theory, and in particular, whether it has happened in the development of the theories which Friedman invokes his methodology to defend. I have the *impression* that it has sometimes happened and that this has gone unnoticed in the debate. If this is correct, then perhaps economists would do well to try to make it clear exactly which sort of assumption they are making at any point in their investigations. (1981, p. 8)

This ambiguity in fundamental 'assumptions' goes back to Ricardo, the great pioneer abstractionist, fundamentally contradictory interpretations of whose famous writings derive from just these fundamental ambiguities.

(3) Such ambiguities and confusions have arisen, especially with regard to the most ubiquitous and uniquely important 'assumption' in the history of economics, ancient and modern, that is, the so-called 'rationality' assumption, in its multifarious forms. First, it has often been far from clear whether this assumption, or some profit-maximizing version of it, is being made as a 'negligibility', 'domain', or 'heuristic assumption'. But on top of this there is a further ambiguity which is just as fundamental and serious. When it is assumed, for example, that people are 'maximizing profits' it has often not been specified with what kind of knowledge or expectations they are being assumed to act. Often, perfect or adequate knowledge has been assumed on the basis of what has been claimed to be a 'general' theory, without this vital (and quite 'unrealistic') component of the 'assumption' being clearly specified. As a 'negligibility assumption' the implication of the perfect (or adequate) knowledge 'assumption' would be that ignorance, error, and the effects thereof, are negligible; as a 'domain assumption' that, ignorance and error may not in some cases be negligible, but that the theory only applies to cases where there are no significant effects from ignorance and error; while as a 'heuristic assumption' the implication is that, in the real world, the

effects of ignorance and error may well seldom or never be negligible, but will be analysed subsequently, while, as 'a first approximation', a process is being studied from which ignorance, error, and the effects therefore, are excluded. From a 'model' dependent on such a simplifying or heuristic assumption, no predictions valid for the complex real world can be derived, until the real world is 'approximated' to more closely.

The difficulty with regard to this fundamental and ubiquitous 'rationality assumption' as a simplifying, 'first approximation' (when it includes the component of perfect or adequate knowledge) is that there is no second approximation to go on to, but only an almost unlimited variety of possible cases. For ignorance and erroneous expectations may, and do, take on an immense variety of forms, and are constantly changing their forms in the course of history. Only through the study of history and institutions may one be able to discuss the shifting trends and patterns which knowledge, ignorance and expectations take on in the real world. Only thus may it be possible to check how far, in the real world, a theory is valid which depends on a particular 'negligibility', or 'domain' assumption about knowledge and expectations.

The fog of ambiguity which has surrounded this unique example of a 'fundamental assumption' in economic theory was well exemplified by Professor Machlup, who observed regarding such 'rationality assumptions':

> Their logical nature has been characterized in various ways: they are regarded as 'self-evident propositions', 'axioms', '*a priori* truths', 'truisms', 'tautologies', 'definitions', 'rigid laws', 'rules of procedure', 'resolutions', 'working hypotheses', 'useful fictions', 'ideal types', 'heuristic mental constructs', 'indisputable facts of experience', 'facts of immediate experience', 'data of introspective observation', 'private empirical data', 'typical behaviour patterns', and so forth. (1955, p. 16)[20]

It can hardly be claimed that the profound ambiguities regarding the 'fundamental assumption' have been removed in the decades since Professor Machlup's observation. When it is borne in mind that such an assumption, or assumptions, underlie a very large part of economic theory, such a degree of ambiguity regarding its logical or epistemological nature seems highly criticizable. Moreover, in so far as this fundamental rationality assumption seems to have long been a central part of economists' 'hard cores', it shows how shifting and ambiguous these cores are liable to be, and how wary any critics should be who are considering granting claims, or a *carte blanche*, for special protection or privileges to such ambiguous 'cores' in economic theorizing.

But, as we have seen, not only has there been profound ambiguity in respect of the fundamental 'rationality assumption' – as to whether, for example, it is definitional or empirical, or as to whether it is a 'negligibility', 'domain', or 'heuristic' assumption that is being made – there has *also* been much fundamental ambiguity, or inexplicitness, with regard to content, or to the kind of knowledge, ignorance and expectations which are being assumed, and which certainly cannot be regarded as given *a priori* or intuitively. If *no* assumption is being made regarding knowledge, ignorance and expectations, then nothing can be deduced regarding how people will act or decide, in a particular case, simply from an assumption that they *would* maximize something *if* they knew how to. Writing on the 'complexity' or 'openness' of the material of economics, Professor Grunberg quite justifiably concluded:

These peculiarities of the vineyard in which economists labour have given a distinctive role in economic theory to the 'rational principle' (in whatever form and disguise it may appear) and an *Alice-in-Wonderland* flavour to much of the recent discussion of the role of assumptions in economics. Early writers on economics apparently had little doubt that the behavioural assumptions of their theories had *some* observable empirical content. I share this conviction. What precisely this content is remains one of the major problems of economics. (1978, p. 555)

Certainly the ambiguities are serious. A first step towards dispelling some of this obscurity would be to set out the 'rationality assumption' (or 'assumptions') in a directly or indirectly testable form, and to clarify (a) whether a 'negligibility', 'domain', or 'heuristic' assumption was being made; and (b) what kind of knowledge, ignorance and expectations were being assumed. The actual testing of the assumption, directly or indirectly, might then be necessary in so far as a 'negligibility' or 'domain' assumption was involved, or a particular kind of knowledge or expectations was being assumed in a particular case. Of course, none of these ambiguities, or the resolution thereof, might matter very much, in so far as simply 'having a good game' was the object of the exercise. But obviously they are very serious if real-world applications, predictions and policies are involved.

VI *Anti-A Priorism and Anti-Infallibilism*

(1) The late Imre Lakatos, referring to what he called the 'Euclidean a priorism' at one time represented in economics by Mises and Robbins, maintained that this was 'today a futile venture' (1978, vol. 2, pp. 10, 90).[21] But Lakatos was prematurely optimistic. Today a kind of 'Euclidean', a priorist rationalism is still being upheld, not only by followers of Mises, but also to justify Marxian economic theories. Perhaps it is surprising that Marxians, until recently, have made such little use, in defending their economic theories, of a priorist claims to 'apodictic certainty', which have, in spirit, such obvious affiliations with their one-party politics (and the sometimes intolerant political methods so long defended by some Marxian economists).

Recently Professors Hollis and Nell (1975, *passim*) have developed their arguments in terms of unhistorical cardboard stereotypes of 'Positivism' and 'Neoclassicism', presenting 'Positivism' as the methodological counterpart of a caricatured 'Neo-Classical Economics'. In their chapter 6, entitled 'A Priori Knowledge', Hollis and Nell, as self-proclaimed 'Rationalists', insist in general terms that 'there can be *a priori* knowledge of matters of fact', conveyed in 'necessary but not purely logical truths' (pp. 140, 170). As usual, no procedures are specified for adjudicating conflicts between such necessary, but not purely logical, statements of *a priori* facts. But Professors Hollis and Nell are quite frank as to why they want the criteria of 'Positivism' and 'Empiricism' to be rejected. This is because, according to 'Positivist' and 'Empiricist' criteria (as Böhm-Bawerk long ago pointed out), the labour theory of value, and other Marxian theories, obviously come off badly. In fact, Hollis and Nell propagate a kind of epistemological anarchism seeking to undermine epistemological standards generally:

After all, why not allow *a priori* knowledge of matters of fact? For that matter, why bother whether a truth is established by logical reasoning or by empirical observation. . . . The epistemologist can perhaps usefully tidy and codify the economist's methods and remove from economics philosophic litter deposited by other philosophers. But what entitles him to impose his view of economic theory? (p. 140)

What, indeed, it may well be asked, entitles Professors Hollis and Nell to deposit their own 'philosophic litter', in terms of *a priori* knowledge of matters of fact, with regard, for example, to interpreting the fundamental propositions of macroeconomics, when working economists (such as Sir Robert Hall already quoted) operate perfectly effectively with the definitional-empirical distinction?

Anyhow, a priorist Austrians might especially ponder the objection of Hollis and Nell that:

> Positivism has done more than package what economists would have thought in any case. It provides neo-Classicism not only with crucial defences but also with methodological ammunition against such basic Classical-Marxian notions as the distinction between productive and unproductive labour (for violating the fact-value distinction), the labour theory of value (for failure to predict). (p. 141)

Of course, the denunciations of 'Empiricism' and 'Positivism' by Austrian a priorists are in just the same terms as those of Marxian a priorists, as when Professor Rothbard claims that 'the methodology of modern positivism and empiricism comes a cropper even in the physical sciences' (1976, p. 29). Again, Marxian and Austrian a priorists alike denounce, in the same terms, the analytic-synthetic distinction, with its link with testability and falsifiability, as when Messrs Hollis and Nell maintain, regarding the doctrines of 'neoclassicism':

> Defence and attack both rely ultimately on the analytic-synthetic distinction. So do the Positivist interpretations of the hypothetico-deductive method and its attendant idols of prediction and confirmation. (p. 141)

According to an Austrian a priorist, Professor Rothbard:

> Sometimes it seems that the empiricists use the fashionable analytic-synthetic dichotomy . . . to dispose of theories they find difficult to refute by dismissing them as necessarily *either* disguised definitions *or* debatable and uncertain hypotheses. (Rothbard, 1976, p. 27)

Messrs Hollis and Nell indicate in general terms the kind of politicoeconomic ideas they aim at establishing, without, of course, formulating any reasonably specific propositions, and without spelling out any precise route by which these might be arrived at:

Neo-Classicism finally falls foul of necessary but not purely logical truths. And it is such truths which make it possible for the economist both to provide explanations, even where his predictions have failed, and to act as a critic and judge of the economic aspects of society, the role we proffer in place of the positivists' passive and neutral observer. (1975, p. 241)

No doubt other economists, as well as Marxians, will enthusiastically support the claims of Messrs Hollis and Nell to provide 'explanations' even when their predictions have failed, and to assume the role of 'critics' and 'judges' of the economic aspects of society. But the whole point of 'ridding ourselves' of positivist distinctions and of not 'bothering' about logical and empirical criteria, as frankly explained by Professors Hollis and Nell, is that we shall then be able to agree with the political 'judgements' of Professor Joan Robinson (presumably including her judgements about Stalin, Mao and the Cultural Revolution):

We hope our arguments will lead the reader to agree with Joan Robinson: 'The success of modern capitalism for the last twenty-five years has been clearly bound up with the armaments race and the trade in arms (not to mention wars when they are used); it has not succeeded in overcoming poverty in its own countries and has not succeeded in helping (to say the least) to promote development in the Third World. Now we are told that it is in the course of making the planet uninhabitable even in peacetime (p. 241, quoting Robinson, 1971, pp. 143–4)[22]

However, doubtless with the aid of their '*a priori* knowledge of matters of fact', Professors Hollis and Nell will be able to re-establish their Marxian economic doctrines so tendentiously called in question by 'positivist' and 'empiricist' criteria. With such criteria eliminated, in an intellectual jungle where 'anything goes', there is, as Professor Musgrave has observed, '*carte blanche* to any group who wants to erect their pet notion into a dogma' (1973, p. 400).[23]

Meanwhile, however, Marxian a priorists might ponder how the most extreme defence of free markets, and the most thoroughgoing attack on socialist economics, was mounted on the basis of an a priorist methodology, not using, but rejecting, 'positivist' and 'empiricist' criteria; while, at the same time, Austrian or libertarian a priorists might ponder how a priorism (not 'positivism' or 'empiricism') is being invoked to validate the labour theory of value, and other Marxian doctrines as to how 'modern capitalism' has depended for its success on the arms race (while making the planet uninhabitable even in peacetime).

It might be regarded as naïve to enquire how total contradictions regarding *a priori* matters of fact, or regarding the 'correct line' of 'apodictic certainties', could ever be resolved or adjudicated, by any intellectual process, as between Marxian and Austrian a priorists, with 'empiricist' and 'positivist' criteria eliminated. Perhaps each side holds that conflicts cannot arise with regard to *their a priori* 'critical judgements', or 'apodictic certainties', because of the infallibility of those who pronounce them. But what happens, epistemologically, when an infallible a priorist force meets an infallible a priorist object? A priorist Austrians might be warned that Marxian 'scientific communities' have their own effective methods of establishing a consensus – as in Cuba, Kampuchea and Afghanistan – which certainly have no regard to 'positivist' and 'empiricist' criteria, but which libertarians might find, in other respects, unattractive.

VII

As Professor Koertge (1979) has emphasized: 'To avoid dogmatism we must always keep the Tested/Not Yet Tested/Untestable trichotomy clearly in mind.' The difficulties, especially in the social sciences, mount up under the middle of these three categories, that is, regarding theories which are not untestable in principle, and of which some kind of tests may have been attempted, though these have been too inadequate or inconclusive to have resulted in any reasonably satisfactory measure of agreement. Moreover, in the social sciences, because of what may be called the historical-institutional dimension, or because the material is not homogeneous through time, *theories constantly need to be re-tested.* As the distinguished Marxian-Neoclassical economist Oskar Lange rather optimistically put it, if tests are inconclusive, or there is 'disagreement about facts', then: 'The conclusion that the issue cannot be settled with the data available has interpersonal validity. Agreement is reached to withhold judgement.'[24] Would that this were so and that judgement was regularly withheld in such cases – especially by Marxians! Unfortunately it seems, at present, rather over-optimistic to assume that this kind of prescription would always be followed, even by academics.

Of course, the man of action may not, in any case, be able completely to 'withhold judgement', in that he may be compelled to act in one way or another, and in so doing explicitly or implicitly commit himself to a choice between theories based on conflicting factual assumptions or predictions. It would be Utopian to expect that politicians, when compelled to choose between untested or inadequately tested theories, might be found proceeding so tentatively, experimentally and undogmatically. But, in any case, we are only concerned with methodological prescriptions for *academics*, for whom explicit agnosticism, or the 'withholding of judgement', is perfectly possible, and might easily be much more prevalent than it is (though, of course, in economics and the social sciences there is a tremendous lot to withold judgement and to be agnostic about).

All methodological prescriptions are inevitably based on some kind of ethical or political presuppositions or valuations, and we are assuming as one of the presuppositions or purposes of our prescriptions that an opposition to dogmatism must be the intellectual foundation of a pluralist or 'open' society, where there are no privileged or protected positions. Certainly prescriptions in favour of testability and testing, and criticisms based on such prescriptions, may strike at the political influence of some kinds of economic theorizing. Certainly, also, a confident dogmatism, together with the protection of those theories which support the favourite dogmas and policies of political orthodoxies, may be calculated to promote economists' political influence or power. Indeed, for those caught up in the bureaucratic or party-political process, or in power conflicts, a confident dogmatism may well seem a desirable or essential attitude.

Just how far academic economists and social scientists are able, as they have largely aimed and claimed to be throughout history, to contribute to more successful policy-making by democratic governments, is obviously somewhat debatable. But a valuable public function which the academic economist *could* undoubtedly perform, if he wished to do so, would be the raising of standards of rational discussion and debate in a pluralist democracy (assuming, of course, the desirability of this kind of political order). Supporting the methodological prescriptions of critical testing and testability will promote more widely an attitude of fallibilism and the critical rejection of the kind of dogmas on which authoritarianism and dictatorships, of one colour or another, are based. This will in turn promote a healthy awareness of the limited possibilities of successful policy-making by governments and business, which will therefore help to prevent Utopian expectations, with the dangers of subsequent excessive political disillusionments.[25]

Such methodological prescriptions, though relevant also in earlier centuries in physics and astronomy, may well be regarded, as they were by Lakatos, as unnecessary, and even 'hubristic', for such subjects today. 'Polanyite autonomy', as Lakatos called it, or even the principle of 'Anything Goes', may well be appropriate, or at least harmless, for such well-developed or 'mature' subjects, without close political involvements – as also for that body of economic theorizing which is pursued as 'a good game'. What, however, is profoundly dangerous is to conclude or allow that the permissive prescriptions relevant for the most developed, 'mature' or 'successful' sciences are appropriate for other subjects dealing with a very different kind of material, and possessing a very different political relationship and involvement. Today, it seems at least as important, and perhaps more important, to emphasize these distinctions between different sciences, or groups of sciences, and their methods, aims and criteria, than it is to emphasize what all sciences have in common.

Notes

1   By all means may students pursue *'Economics for Pleasure'* (as Professor Shackle aptly entitled one of his books). But it may be an optimistic delusion to imagine that such 'pleasure' can equip one for dealing with real-world problems.

It is reasonable to enquire how much of higher education in economics is concerned with proficiency in games playing, and how clearly and explicitly this is brought home to students. On this question the judgement of Sir Henry Phelps Brown is notable:

One economist who had held the highest responsibilities as an adviser told me that when an able young man who had taken honours in economics at the university joined his staff, he had to begin by unlearning his advanced theory. Another adviser whose responsibilities had been no less high told me that an entrant whose graduate work had been wholly in economic history would be as eligible as one who had been drilled in economic theory and econometrics.

Professor Phelps Brown concludes:

> The insights yielded by economic analysis are essential but they are those of quite elementary analysis. My contention is that the economist who is best equipped to understand the working of the economy around him, and to advise on policy, needs in point of analysis the equipment that is needed by the economic historian. (1980, pp. 5, 13; see also Phelps Brown, 1972)

2   See Lucas, 1980, p. 207: 'As an advising profession we are in way over our heads.'

3   See the report on the researches of Dr Scott Armstrong on 'the Fox phenomenon'. Dr Fox delivered, on three occasions, a deliberate nonsense lecture to audiences of psychologists and social workers. All said it was a comprehensible and stimulating lecture. Dr Armstrong concludes: 'Researchers who want to impress their colleagues should write less intelligible papers. . . . Academic meetings should feature speakers who make little sense'. See *The Times*, June 9, 1980 , p. 14.

4   See, for example, the textbook of R. G. Lipsey (1963–1979), where, in the Introduction on 'Scope and Method', predictions of chemistry (with regard to H_2O) are compared with the predictions of macroeconomics (with regard to public deficits and unemployment).

5   See Marx's comparison of his method with that of physics and his reference to his 'natural laws of capitalist production . . . *working with iron necessity towards inevitable results*' in the Preface to the first edition of *Das Kapital* (1867, italics added).

6   See Hutchison, 1938 and 1960. This book expressed a highly 'naturalistic' view, rejecting the idea of a profound and significant gulf, or contrast, between the natural and social sciences in aims and 'methods'. But it was concerned not with exalting claims on behalf of economics and the social sciences, but with questioning some of the rather high-faluting notions as to how introspection and 'understanding' provided them with *more realistic material, or a more profound insight into it*. A rather questionable nationalistic note (not so questionable then) was introduced with the assertion that writers in the English tradition of philosophy and scientific method had generally taken the 'naturalist' view, while German philosophers and historians (such as Sombart) had more often insisted on some fundamental contrast between '*Naturwissenschaft*' and '*Geisteswissenschaft*' – which the book was concerned to reject.

For two recent works which restate a moderate 'naturalistic' view, see Papineau, 1978, and Thomas, 1979. Though disagreeing with Papineau on some tactical points I would support his strategic argument that the social sciences ought to *try* 'to conform to the standards set by the natural sciences. This is not a popular view nowadays. The "positivist" tradition in the social sciences is currently held in extremely low repute. . . . I agree that much social scientific work aimed at emulating the natural sciences has been both unproductive and fundamentally misguided. But I would not attribute these failures to the intended aim as such. That is, I think there is nothing wrong in itself with the idea that the social sciences ought to emulate their natural counterparts. The real trouble has been that those social scientists who have aimed at being "scientific" have characteristically suffered from one misconception or another about exactly what is involved in being scientific' (op. cit., p. 1).

7   See Hutchison, 1977, pp. 35–57. It should be noted, for example that Kuhn insists on 'Sir Karl's demarcation criterion without which no field is potentially a science' and that 'predictive success must be consistently achieved' (see Kuhn, 1970, pp. 244–5). Lakatos also favoured the application of strict falsificationist criteria in the social sciences and himself applied them to Marxian theories (see Lakatos, 1971, pp. 121–3, and above chapter 1). Because Kuhn and Lakatos sought to modify Popperian discipline and criteria at some points, they have been eagerly taken up by those advocating 'anything goes' and the champions of infallibilist dogmas. This is a gross misrepresentation.

8   Marshall asserted that 'the term "law" means then nothing more than a general proposition or statement of tendencies, more or less certain, more or less definite' (1920, p. 33). But this is very vague, especially in view of the ambiguity of the term 'tendency'. It is important and valid that, as Barrington Moore has stated: 'Social science, after some two hundred years, has not yet discovered any universal propositions comparable in scope or intellectual significance to those in the natural sciences.' Professor Moore adds, perhaps more controversially: 'Classical economics managed to erect at one time a comprehensive and elegant theory to organise its subject matter in a scientific manner. Somehow the facts have changed since the formulation of the theory'. (1958, pp. 127–8) According, for example to J. R. McCulloch: 'The relations between rent and profit – between profit and wages and the various general laws which regulate and connect the apparently clashing, but really harmonious interests of every different order in society, have been discovered and established with all the certainty of demonstrative evidence' (1824, p. 75).

9   The vagueness of the term 'positivist' is well illustrated with regard to Sir Karl Popper. As he complains, his views have often been described as 'positivistic' (1979, p. 185). But Popper himself used the term in a perhaps rather narrow sense, in remarking that 'positivists, in their anxiety to annihilate metaphysics, annihilate natural science along with it' (1959, p. 36). Popper is here applying the term 'positivist' to Wittgenstein and Schlick for their treatment of natural laws.

10   See Balogh, 1963, p. 31n; Hutchison, 1968, p. 268.

11   Professor Quine (1953, p. 20) has denied that there is 'some fundamental cleavage between truths which are *analytic*, or grounded in meanings independent of matters of fact, and truths which are *synthetic*, or grounded in fact'. This is to insist that the distinction is one of shades

of grey, as real-world distinctions usually are, rather than black and white. But distinctions between shades of grey may be of vital importance and quite easy to reach agreement on – as they often are in economics. Professor Quine prefers a classification of statements in terms of those which are 'more a question of the convenient conceptual scheme', and those which are 'more a question of fact' (p. 46). But it should be noted that Professor Quine states that 'as an empiricist I continue to think of the conceptual scheme of science as a tool, ultimately for predicting future experience in the light of past experience' (p. 46). Therefore, with prediction as a major aim and criterion, the requirement of constant testing of one's statements, or systems of statements, seems to be implied, along with the need to accommodate 'recalcitrant experience'. This is in complete opposition to a priorism. It becomes essential to make clear in each case – and often there will be no problem – which kind of test, empirical or logical, is appropriate. It therefore seems misleading and exaggerated to claim that Quine's argument implies the 'abandonment' or 'rejection' of the analytic-synthetic distinction.

12   See Klappholz and Agassi (1962) who interpreted economic models in terms of a sharp distinction between 'identities' ('necessarily true by virtue of the meaning we give to certain words') and 'independent empirical statements'. They convincingly accused a number of distinguished authorities (including Lord Robbins) of a failure to appreciate this distinction and of thus promoting confusion. My enthusiastic agreement with Messrs Klappholz and Agassi's argument was tempered by some bewilderment at their just previously (1960) having rather severely criticized my own (no doubt clumsy) attempts to develop virtually the same criticism based on virtually the same sharp distinction. See also Sir Robert Hall (1959) who stated that 'a besetting sin of economists' was that of 'enumerating purely definitional relationships when they purport to be making statements about reality' (p. 651).

13   I would like to emphasize at this point that I have *never* held that all statements with unspecified *ceteris paribus* clauses, or that all propositions of economic theory, are tautological – simply all propositions of 'pure theory' (see Hutchison, 1938 and 1960).

14   See Kaufmann, 1937. Kaufmann maintained: 'If we understand by the phrase "synthetic propositions *a priori*" principles which, without being based upon experience, can lay down certain rules about experience, then there are no such propositions' (p. 339). Kaufmann went on to deny that, for example, 'the marginal utility principle is an *a priori* proposition which all the same could make some statement about reality' (p. 341), and concluded by emphasizing the importance of 'a clear distinction between definitions and empirical statements', in order to avoid such ambiguities and confusions.

15   One may agree, very nearly, with the conclusion of Professor Bruce Caldwell's critique:

Most formulations within the current philosophy of science broaden the categories once so painstakingly delimited by positivist analysts. . . . Such a broadening can aid insight, but there are dangers. History tells us that positivism was (in part) a response to the speculative excesses of nineteenth-century idealistic philosophy. *The pendulum must not be allowed to swing back; such speculative abuses must not be allowed to reenter science if future work in such fields as the methodology of economics is to have any meaning.* (1980, p. 7, italics added)

But the probability is that this kind of 'broadening' *will* lead straight to such 'speculative excesses', of which there are noxiously many in economics. In some cases, the legitimation of 'speculative excesses' seems to be the prime aim of the recommended 'broadening'.

16 The author of Hutchison, 1938, was a kind of 'falsificationist', and, as a 25-year-old intellectual, was probably, *ipso facto* 'naïve'. But there does not seem to be much telling documentary evidence that he was a 'naïve falsificationist' in the technical sense introduced by Lakatos.

17 As Professor Koertge has remarked: 'It is extraordinary that people who would not dream of taking a medicine which had not been thoroughly tested are quite willing to swallow educational, psychological or political theories which not only have not been tested but which, as actually formulated, are not even in principle testable' (1979, p. 79). Certainly this also is the case with regard to economic policies.

18 See, for example, the severe falsificationist treatment of Marxian theories by Imre Lakatos, who showed, in this case, no inclination towards a forbearing, patient treatment of a 'budding' research programme (see above, chapter 1, p. 21).

19 I am very much indebted to Professor Musgrave for showing me his then unpublished paper and allowing me to quote and summarize from it. See Musgrave, 1981.

20 Our own interpretation of the rationality principle coincides with that of Sir Karl Popper (1967, pp. 145–8): 'Those who argue that the rationality principle is *a priori* wish to assert that it is *a priori* valid, or *a priori* true. But it seems to me quite certain that they are wrong. . . . *The rationality principle is false. There seems to me to be no way of escaping this conclusion. . . . It should be considered as belonging to empirical theory, and should be submitted to tests*' (italics added).

21 'Euclidean A Priorism', according to Lakatos, is based on the notion that 'there exists a set of trivial first principles from which all truth flows'. Lakatos concluded: 'The fallible sophistication of the empiricist programme has won, the infallible triviality of Euclideans has lost. Euclideans could only survive in those underdeveloped subjects where knowledge is still trivial.' (1978, vol. 2, pp. 6, and 10)

22 Incidentally, Professor Robinson at one time combined her Marxian inclinations with some use of the 'positivist' criteria of Sir Karl Popper

regarding testing and falsifiability. Professors Hollis and Nell, throughout their book, never discuss Popper's arguments and hardly mention his name.

23   Professor Radnitzky has discerningly described how originally, in the 19th century, Marxism was based on dogmatic scientism:

> Of the pseudo-religions of the nineteenth and twentieth centuries, Marxism, in particular, was based on 'scientism'. Classical Marxians regarded science as the source of knowledge which provided certainty. 'Science' was then used by Marxians to legitimise claims to political dictatorship, by referring to the objective laws of development of society for which this 'scientific' certainty was claimed. This kind of scientism, and the use of science as an ideology, culminated in the fiction of Scientific Socialism.

Professor Radnitzky goes on to point out how necessary it was for Marxians (as also, in the same way, Nazis) to denounce the methodological criteria of critical, fallibilist, logical empiricism, which undermined the foundations of dogmatic pseudo-science. See Radnitzky, 1979, p. 92.

Sir Isaiah Berlin reports being addressed as follows when on a visit to Leningrad in 1945: ' "We are a scientifically government society," said a handsome lady who had been Lenin's secretary and was married to a famous Soviet writer, "and if there is no room for free thinking in physics – a man who questions the laws of motion is so obviously ignorant or mad – why should we Marxists, who have discovered laws of history and society, permit free thinking in the social sphere?" ' (1980, p. 170)

24   See Lange, 1945, also Hutchison, 1964. With regard to what Lange calls 'disagreement about facts', he concludes: 'Such disagreement can always be removed by further observation and study of the empirical material. Frequently, however, the empirical data necessary to resolve the disagreement are unavailable. In such cases the issue remains unsettled.' It is then that Lange optimistically puts forward the frequently disregarded prescription that economists should agree to 'withhold judgement'.

25   For example, to take just a few cases from the wide range offered by the history of the subject: surely a challenge in terms of the prescription of testing and testability would have been justified and salutary with regard to the tremendous claims for their scientific 'laws' of value and distribution and for the classical 'law' of markets, made by McCulloch and the Mills; or with regard to the Marxian dogmas of value, exploitation and increasing immiserization; or with regard to Jevons's claim that 'freedom of trade may be regarded as a fundamental axiom of political economy' (1883, p. 182), or more recent assertions that to deny the beneficial effects of devaluation was the epistemological equivalent of asserting that the earth is flat (see Hutchison, 1977, pp. 133–4). Similarly it would appear that the long-drawn-out monetarist *versus* 'Keynesian'

debate has been harmfully protracted by dogmatic attitudes derived from party politics, which would be undermined by prescriptions in favour of testability and testing.

References

Berlin, I. (1980), *Personal Impressions*.

Balogh, T. (1963), *Planning for Growth*.

Bernadelli, H. (1936), 'What has Philosophy to Contribute to the Social Sciences and to Economics in Particular?', *Economica*, N.S., vol. 3, Nov. pp. 443–54.

Cairnes, J. E. (1875), *The Character and Logical Method of Political Economy* 2nd ed.

Caldwell, B. (1980), 'Positive Philosophy of Science and the Methodology of Economics', *Journal of Economic Issues*, vol. 14, no. 1, pp. 53ff.

Friedman, M. (1953), *Essays in Positive Economics*.

(1977), *Inflation and Unemployment* (Nobel Memorial Lecture, 1976).

Grunberg, E. (1978), ' "Complexity" and "Open Systems" in Economic Discourse', *Journal of Economic Issues*, vol. 12, no. 3, pp. 541ff.

Hall, Sir Robert (1959), 'Reflections on the Practical Application of Economics', *Economic Journal*, vol. 69, pp. 659ff.

Hayek, F. A. (1967), *Studies in Philosophy, Politics and Economics*.

Hayek, F. A., ed. (1933), *Collectivist Economic Planning*.

Hicks, Sir John (1979), *Causality in Economics*.

Hollis, M. and Nell, E. J. (1975), *Rational Economic Man*.

Hutchison, T. W. (1938 and 1960), *The Significance and Basic Postulates of Economic Theory*.

(1964), *'Positive' Economics and Policy Objectives*.

(1968), *Economics and Economic Policy in Britain, 1946–1966*.

(1977), *Knowledge and Ignorance in Economics*.

(1978), *Revolutions and Progress in Economic Knowledge*.

Jevons, W. S. (1882), *The State in Relation to Labour*.

(1883) *Essays in Social Reform*.

Kaufmann, F. (1937), 'Do Synthetic Propositions A Priori Exist in Economics?', *Economica*, N.S., vol. 4, Aug. pp. 337ff.

Keynes, Lord (1973), *Collected Writings*, vol. 14, ed. D. Moggridge.

Klappholz, K. and Agassi, J. (1960), 'Methodological Prescriptions: a Rejoinder', *Economica*, vol. 27, pp. 160ff.

(1962), 'Identities in Economic Models', *Economica*, vol. 29, pp. 117ff.

Koertge, N. (1974), 'On Popper's Philosophy of Social Science', in K. F. Schaffner and R. S. Cohen (ed.), *Boston Studies in the Philosophy of Science*, vol. 20, pp. 195ff.

(1979), 'Braucht die Sozialwissenschaft wirklich Metaphysik?', in H.

Albert and K. H. Stapf (ed.), *Theorie und Erfahrung, Beiträge zur Grundlagenproblematik der Sozialwissenschaft*, pp. 55ff.

Kuhn, T. S. (1970), *The Structure of Scientific Revolutions*, 2nd ed.

Lakatos, I. (1970), 'Falsification and the Methodology of Scientific Research Programmes', in I. Lakatos and A. Musgrave (ed.), *Criticism and the Growth of Knowledge*, pp. 91–195.

    (1971), 'History of Science and its Rational Reconstruction', in R. C. Buck and R. S. Cohen (ed.), *Boston Studies in the Philosophy of Science*, vol. 8, pp. 91–136.

    (1978), *Philosophical Papers*, 2 vols, ed. J. Worrall and G. Currie.

Lange, O. (1945), 'The Scope and Method of Economic Science', *Review of Economic Studies*, no. 13; reprinted in H. Feigl and M. Brodbeck (ed.), *Readings in the Philosophy of Science*, 1953, p. 748.

Latsis, S. J. (1976), 'A Research Programme in Economics', in S. J. Latsis (ed.), *Method and Appraisal in Economics*, pp. 1–38.

Lipsey, R. G. (1963–79), *An Introduction to Positive Economics*, 1st–5th eds.

Lucas, R. E. (1980), 'Rules, Discretion, and the Role of the Economic Adviser', in S. Fisher (ed.), *Rational Expectations and Economic Policy*, pp. 199ff.

McCulloch, J. R. (1824), *A Discourse on the Rise, Progress, Peculiar Objects, and Importance of Political Economy*.

Machlup, F. (1955), 'The Problem of Verification in Economics', *Southern Economic Journal*, vol. 22, pp. 1ff.

Marshall, A. (1920), *Principles of Economics*, 8th ed.

Marx, K. (1867), *Capital*, vol. 1.

Mill, J. S. (1884), *System of Logic*.

Moore, Barrington (1958), *Political Power and Social Theory*.

Musgrave, A. (1973), 'Falsification and its Critics', in P. Suppes *et al.* (ed.), *Logic, Methodology and Philosophy of Science*, vol. 4, pp. 393–406.

    (1981), 'Unreal Assumptions in Economic Theory: the F-Twist Untwisted', Kyklos.

Myrdal, G. (1973), *Against the Stream*.

Papineau, D. (1978), *For Science in the Social Sciences*.

Phelps Brown, Sir E. H. (1972), 'The Underdevelopment of Economics', *Economic Journal*, vol. 82, no. 1, pp. 1ff.

    (1980), 'The Radical Reflections of an Applied Economist', *Banca Nazionale del Lavoro Quarterly Review*, no. 132, Mar., pp. 3ff.

Popper, Sir Karl (1959), *The Logic of Scientific Discovery*, 1st ed.

    (1961), *The Poverty of Historicism*, 2nd ed.

    (1979), *Objective Knowledge*, revised ed.

Quine, W. V. (1953), *From a Logical Point of View*.

Radnitzky, G. (1976), 'Popperian Philosophy of Science as an Antidote against Relativism', in R. S. Cohen, P. K. Feyerabend and M. W. Wartofsky (ed.), *Essays in Memory of Imre Lakatos*, pp. 505–46.

    (1979), 'Das Problem der Theorienbewertung', *Zeitschrift für*

Allgemeine Wissenschaftstheorie, vol. 10, no. 1, pp. 67–97.

Ravetz, J. R. (1971), *Scientific Knowledge and its Social Problems*.

Rothbard, M. (1976), 'Praxeology: the Methodology of Austrian Economics', in E. G. Dolan (ed.), *The Foundations of Modern Austrian Economics*, pp. 19ff.

Simon, H. (1962), 'The Architecture of Complexity', *American Philosophical Society, Proceedings*, no. 106, pp. 467–82.

Thomas, D. (1979), *Naturalism and Social Science*.

Times, The, (1980), See June 9th, p. 14, for Dr Scott Armstrong on 'The Fox Phenomenon'.

Worswick, G. D. N. (1972), 'Is Progress in Economic Science Possible?', *Economic Journal*, vol. 82, pp. 73ff.

Index

Acton, Lord 223
Addison, P. 161, 173
Agassi, J. 282, 302, 305
Alpine, R. L. 43–4
Alter, M. 201, 225, 230
Ameche, D. 113
Andersson, G. 22
Aristotle, 178
Armstrong, S. 300
Arrow, K. J. 37
Ashley, W. J. 53
Attlee, C. R. 68
Austin, J. 42
Bagehot, W. 56, 252
Balogh, Lord 133–4, 145, 147, 149, 151, 167–8, 174, 280, 301, 305
Barber, Lord 132
Barro, R. J. 257, 263
Barry, B. 37
Barry, N. 219, 226, 228, 230
Barry, R. 22
Bentham, J. 42
Berthollet, C. L. 4
Beria, L. 85
Berkeley, G. 49
Berlin, I. 304–5
Bernadelli, H. 282, 305
Beveridge, Lord 76, 105, 125–6, 140
Blum, R. 172, 174
Blumenberg-Lampe, C. 172, 174
Böhm-Bawerk, E. 203–5, 224–5, 231, 294
Bombach, G. 173–4, 231, 264
Bostaph, S. 199–201
Boulding, K. 229, 231
Brentano, L. 158, 172, 174, 208
Brittan, S. 263
Bronfenbrenner, M. 109, 141, 151
Brown, A. J. 150
Brüning, H. 243, 261
Buchanan, J. M. 24, 37, 43, 143,

151, 264
Buck, R. C. 306
Burke, E. 186, 191, 223
Burnett, J. 106, 263
Burrows, E. M. 150
Cairnes, J. E. 49, 52–3, 56, 92, 189, 205, 207, 305
Caldwell, B. 302, 305
Callaghan, J. 130
Campbell, R. H. 44, 265
Cantillon, R. 250
Carlton, G. 1, 5, 21
Cartwright, E. 5
Cassel, G. 207
Caute, D. 80, 95, 104–5
Chaloner, W. H. 22
Chamberlain, J. 31, 140, 240
Churchill, W. S. 140, 145
Claassen, E. M. 232
Clark, C. G. 123, 139–40, 149, 151
Clark, J. B. 17, 77
Clark, Kitson 28, 43
Coase, R. H. 53, 66, 105
Cohen, R. S. 306
Cohn, N. 12
Coleridge, S. T. 191
Comte, A. 48
Congdon, T. 135–6, 147, 151
Cournot, A. 47, 89, 200, 207
Cowling, M. 42–3
Cranston, M. 147, 151
Croome, H. M. 231, 264
Crossman, R. H. S. 130, 151
Currie, G. 22
Darwin, C. 48
Davy, H. 4
Deacon, R. 101, 105
Deane, P. 55, 101, 105
Demuth, F. 2, 20
Dicey, A. V. 31, 42–3
Dilthey, W. 200
Dingwall, J. 202
Disraeli, B. 20–1, 30, 42
Dobb, M. H. 47, 55, 65, 78–87,

91, 94–6, 98, 101–3, 105–6, 263
Dolan, E. G. 231, 307
Downs, A. 32, 35, 37, 43
Dräger, H. 147, 151, 173–4
Droysen, J. 225
Eatwell, J. 67, 87, 101, 106–7, 154
Edgeworth, F. Y. 33–5, 63, 92, 213, 228, 231
Einstein, A. 123
Eltis, W. 110–11, 138, 146–50
Engel, E. 181
Engels, F. 1–22, 42–3, 84, 159, 273
Erhard, L. 133, 147, 166
Erlich, R. 103, 106
Eucken, W. 155–74, 185, 201
Eucken-Erdsiek, E. 174
Euclid, 214
Fawcett, H. 110
Feinstein, C. H. 106
Fellner, W. 144, 151, 235, 247, 256, 259, 261, 263
Fetter, F. W. 260, 263
Feyerabend, P. K. 287, 306
Fischer, S. 264–5
Fisher, I. 63, 252
Forster, E. M. 98, 103, 106
Foxwell, H. S. 46–7, 53, 62–3, 101, 106, 240, 263
Freedman, R. 11, 22
Friedman, M. 56, 112, 118, 131, 142–3, 149, 151, 260, 272–3, 275–6, 288–9
Galbraith, J. K. 142, 151, 172, 174
Gash, N. 28, 43
George, D. Lloyd, 43
Gibbon, E. 100, 106
Gladstone, W. E. 30
Glyn, A. 149, 151
Gray, J. 14
Grigg, J. 43
Grunberg, E. 226, 231, 277,

293, 305
Guillebaud, C. W. 244, 263
Haberler, G. 128, 151, 165, 172, 174, 242, 263
Halifax, Lord 123
Hall, R. 281, 295, 302, 305
Hamberger, J. 26, 44
Hanham, H. J. 42, 44
Hansen, R. 199, 201
Harcourt, W. 31
Harney, J. 13
Harris, J. 240, 264
Harris, S. E. 231
Harrod, R. F. 121, 126–8, 133–6, 146–9, 150–1
Hayek, F. A. 15, 29, 35, 37, 44, 69, 88, 107, 111–13, 142, 148, 152, 156–7, 163, 174, 179, 200–1, 209–24, 226–9, 231–2, 234, 242–3, 246, 252–3, 261, 264, 277–8, 305
Heckscher, E. 260, 264
Hegel, G. W. F. 157
Heller, W. 167, 174
Henderson, H. D. 78–9, 113, 150
Henderson, W. O. 3–10, 13, 16–17, 20, 22
Hensel, K. P. 174
Hess, M. 1, 7, 8, 22
Hicks, J. R. 52, 106, 144, 152, 227, 231, 260–1, 264, 266, 278, 305
Hildebrand, B. 6, 193
Hinrichs, A. F. 232
Hitler, A. 69, 88, 137, 157, 168
Hobsbawm, 30–1, 44, 77, 87, 106
Hollis, M. 283, 294–6, 304, 305
Horwitz, M. J. 9, 22, 40, 44, 159, 174
Hoselitz, B. F. 202
Howson, S. 71, 106, 136, 144, 150, 152
Hübner, K. 22
Hughes, T. J. 107
Hume, D. 49, 75, 97–8, 223
Humphrey, D. D. 167, 174
Hunt, E. K. 102, 106
Hutchison, T. W. 14, 22, 36, 44, 48, 106, 114; 134, 142, 145–6, 149, 152, 172, 174, 200–1, 221, 231, 253, 264, 267, 270, 278, 280, 285, 287–8, 300–5
Jacobsson, E. 145, 152
Jacobsson, P. 145–6
Jaffé, W. 202
Jaki, S. 19, 22
Jay, P. 152
Jevons, W. S. 4, 16, 33–4, 39, 44, 77, 92, 99, 108, 192, 207, 239–40, 305
Jewkes, J. 280

Jha, N. 55, 106
Jöhr, W. A. 164, 174
Johnson, E. 152
Johnson, H. G. 111, 142, 152
Juglar, C. 241
Kadish, A. 54
Kahn, Lord 105, 119–22, 124, 126–8, 132–6, 138, 144–9
Kaldor, Lord 105, 124–8, 133, 153, 231, 259, 264
Kalecki, M. 244
Kauder, E. 192, 199, 201
Kaufmann, F. 302, 305
Kearly, J. R. 263–4
Keegan, W. 263–4
Kemeny, J. G. 181, 201
Keynes, J. M. 31; 36, 44, 47, 49, 57, 62, 64, 70–9, 88–9, 91–3, 96, 98–9, 101–2, 104, 106, 108–51, 155–6, 161, 165, 173, 175, 200, 215, 227, 231, 233–4, 238, 240, 242, 244–9, 250, 252–3, 260–2, 264, 268, 277, 305
Keynes, J. N. 47, 51, 53, 56–7, 64–5, 71–2, 76, 80, 93, 98, 100, 106
Kindleberger, C. P. 241–2, 264
Kirzner, I. 220–2, 229–31
Klappholz, K. 282, 302, 305
Knies, K. 193
Knight, F. H. 206, 231, 237, 256, 264, 280
Koertge, N. 277, 297, 303, 305
Korsch, A. 231, 233, 243, 264
Kuhn, T. S. 272–4, 284, 301, 305
Labkowicz, N. 22
Lachmann, L. M. 199–201, 224, 227, 231
Laidler, D. 139–40, 153
Lakatos, I. 21–2, 205, 268–9, 272–4, 284, 294, 299, 301, 303, 306
Lancaster, K. 237, 264
Lange, O. 292, 304, 306
Latsis, S. J. 265, 285, 306
Leavis, F. R. 73, 106
Lenin, V. 304
Leoni, B. 34, 44
Levine, A. L. 101, 106
Lexis, W. 17
Liebig, J. 4
Liebknecht, W. 10
Lindahl, E. 202
Link, R. 260, 264
Lipsey, R. G. 300, 306
List, F. 3, 157
Loasby, B. J. 106, 237, 247, 264
Locke, J. 49, 75, 97, 223
Lowe, R. 29, 42, 110
Luard, D. E. T. 107
Lübbe, H. 22

Lucas, R. E. 264, 300, 306
Lutz, F. A. 165, 172, 175
Macaulay, T. B. 27–8
McCready, H. W. 30, 42, 44
McCulloch, J. R. 3, 44, 301, 304, 306
Mach, E. 204
Machlup, F. 292, 306
McLellan, D. 22
Mallet, C. 117
Malthus, T. R. 5, 92, 240, 261, 264, 268
Mandel, E. 86, 106
Mandeville, B. 223
Mangoldt, H. 193
Mannheim, K. 151
Mao Tse-Tung 98, 100
Marcet, J. 27
Marshall, A. 17, 33–4, 39, 46–8, 51–62, 64–7, 69–72, 74–5, 77, 79, 80–1, 88–9, 92–3, 96–101, 105–7, 164, 192, 237, 240, 252, 268, 301, 306
Martin, K. 165–6, 174
Martineau, H. 27
Marx, G. 113
Marx, K. 1–4, 7, 9–14, 16–18, 20, 22, 24, 30, 42, 44, 47, 62, 77, 80–1, 84, 92–4, 101, 106, 157–9, 200, 204, 273, 300, 306
Mathews, R. C. 138–9, 153
Maurice, F. D. 88, 103
Mayer, G. 22
Mayer, H. 207, 231
Maynard, G. W. 131, 154, 245, 264
Meckling, W. H. 246, 264
Meek, R. L. 102–3, 106
Meltzer, A. 143–5, 153
Mendershausen, H. 166–7, 175
Menger, C. 176–201, 203, 205, 207–9, 212–14, 217, 221, 224, 228, 231, 237, 264
Menger, K. 202, 228, 232
Mill, H. T. 29
Mill, J. 26, 33, 39, 44, 191, 212, 214, 223
Mill, J. S. 4, 29, 33–6, 40, 44, 49, 56, 75, 78, 92, 97–8, 103, 106, 108, 153, 160, 171, 175, 189, 213, 225–6, 228, 232, 236, 239, 262, 264, 268, 274, 306
Miller, R. E. 101, 262
Minford, P. 259, 264
Mitchell, W. C. 241
Mises, L. 15, 148, 158, 189, 199, 204, 208–11, 216, 218–24, 226, 228–9, 232, 283, 294
Moggridge, D. E. 74, 99, 106, 134, 145, 153, 242, 264
Molotov, V. 85
Moore, B. 301, 306
Moore, G. E. 72–4

Morgenstern, O. 227, 232
Müller-Armack, A. 164, 169
Müntzer, T. 12
Mussolini, B. 69
Muth, J. F. 255, 265
Myrdal, G. 47, 64, 106, 135, 246, 269–70, 276, 306
Nasse, E. 158, 172, 175, 208
Nell, E. J. 283, 294–6, 304, 306
Newton, I. 214, 235, 290
Nock, F. J. 202, 231, 264
Nove, A. 20, 22, 83, 106
O'Driscoll, G. P. 226, 230, 232
Olson, M. 37
Opie, R. G. 132, 153
Papineau, D. 300, 306
Pareto, V. 89, 207
Patinkin, D. 238, 253, 265
Payne, R. 13, 22
Pearce, I. 260, 265
Peden, G. C. 150, 153
Pekkarinen, J. 261, 265
Petridis, A. 101, 106
Phelps-Brown, E. H. 299, 300, 306
Phillips, A. W. 249
Pickett, J. 43–4
Pigou, A. C. 35–6, 39, 44, 47, 49, 51–2, 54–6, 59, 60, 62–70, 76, 78, 89, 96–7, 99, 106–7, 112–13, 153, 239, 242, 252, 265
Popper, K. R. 178, 181, 202, 204, 210, 215, 217–19, 223, 226, 229, 230, 232, 267, 270, 272, 276–7, 288, 301, 303–4, 306
Prager, T. 43–4
Price, B. 50
Proudhon, P. J. 14
Quesnay, F. 25
Quine, W. V. O. 281, 301–2, 306
Radcliffe, Lord 128, 132, 146, 153
Raddatz, F. J. 20, 22
Radnitzky, G. 21–2, 288, 304, 306
Ramser, H. J. 257, 265
Ravetz, J. R. 273–4, 284, 306
Rawls, J. 37
Ricardo, D. 3–4, 6, 26–7, 33, 42, 44, 62, 78, 89, 92, 101, 108, 162, 191, 209, 214, 223, 239, 261, 268, 278, 291
Robbins, Lord 28, 44, 102, 107, 127, 136, 145, 148, 154, 189, 226–7, 230, 232, 294, 302
Roberts, C. C. 147, 154, 173, 175

Robertson, D. H. 43, 47, 63–5, 78, 89, 107, 112–13, 127, 135–6, 154
Robinson, E. A. G. 134, 154–5, 175
Robinson, J. 6, 22, 47, 57, 67, 87–96, 98, 100–2, 104–5, 107, 121, 123, 125–7, 129, 133–4, 136, 146, 149–50, 154, 296, 303
Rodbertus, K. J. 14–16
Roscher, W. 177, 190, 193–4, 196, 200
Roskamp, K. W. 164, 175
Rothbard, M. 220, 222, 230, 232, 295, 306
Russell, B. 80
Say, J. B. 3, 6, 88–9, 181, 205, 207, 212, 260, 265, 281
Savigny, F. K. 186, 190, 225
Schäffle, A. 158, 171–2, 175, 208
Schefold, B. 262, 265
Schlick, M. 204, 301
Schmoller, G. 53, 157, 186, 194–5, 200
Schneider, E. 192, 197, 202
Schneider, L. 202, 231
Schumacher, E. F. 275
Schumpeter, J. A. 3, 4, 12, 22, 71, 81, 95, 107, 192, 195, 197, 200, 202, 204–5, 224, 232, 236, 261
Schwartz, A. 142–3, 151
Schwartz, J. 102, 106
Schwartz, P. 260, 265
Seldon, A. 40, 44
Senior, N. W. 6, 7, 44, 49, 54, 56, 155, 189, 205–7, 225, 232
Seymour, C. 28–9, 44
Shackle, G. L. S. 227, 229, 232, 238, 265, 280, 299
Shehab, F. 31, 44
Shove, G. F. 47, 87, 91–3, 100, 107
Sidgwick, A. 107
Sidgwick, H. 39, 47–51, 53–5, 60, 62, 64–7, 72–5, 78–80, 88–90, 92–3, 96–8, 100, 107
Simon, H. 38, 44, 253, 265, 277, 307
Sismondi, S. 241, 243
Skidelsky, R. 103, 107, 114, 138, 140, 146, 154, 240, 265
Skinner, A. S. 44, 265
Smith, A. 3, 8, 25, 33, 35–6, 39–41, 44, 77–8, 98, 122, 159, 163, 184, 190–1, 196, 200, 223, 236, 260, 265, 268
Smyth, R. L. 107
Sohmen, E. 169–70, 173, 175

Solow, R. 265
Sombart, W. 157, 199, 200
Spencer, H. 48
Spengler, O. 200
Sraffa, P. 47, 87, 89, 102, 105
Stalin, J. 82–3, 85–8, 94–5, 98, 100, 103, 218
Stein, H. 154
Stephen, L. 35, 42, 44
Steuart, J. 250
Stewart, M. 130, 154
Stigler, G. J. 42, 44
Stolper, W. F. 164, 175
Stoppard, T. 58
Strachey, J. 44
Strigl, R. 207, 226, 232
Suppes, P. 306
Sutcliffe, R. 149, 151
Sweezy, P. M. 231

Taylor, A. J. P. 145, 154
Thatcher, M. 105
Thirlwall, A. P. 145, 147, 154
Thomas, D. 300, 307
Thünen, J. H. 47, 193
Tocqueville, A. de 223
Todd, W. B. 44, 265
Trevelyan, G. M. 28, 44
Trevithick, J. A. 131, 154, 245, 254, 265
Turgot, A. R. J. 236

Vaizey, Lord 105, 107
Viner, J. 40, 44, 145, 154

Wagner, R. 143, 151
Wallich, H. C. 163, 172, 175
Walras, L. 181, 199, 202, 204, 207, 268
Wartofsky, M. W. 306
Watt, J. 4
Webb, B. 48, 69, 70, 74, 107
Weber, M. 271
Weiss, F. X. 231
Wells, H. G. 80
Whately, R. 49
Williams, P. L. 107
Wilson, H. 167
Wicksell, K. 192, 194, 197, 202, 241, 250
Wieser, F. 188–9, 204–8, 211, 213, 218–21, 223, 225, 232, 283
Wilkinson, F. 146, 154
Winch, D. 71, 106, 144, 150, 152
Wittgenstein, L. 204, 253, 265, 301
Worrall, J. 21–2
Worswick, G. D. N. 267–8, 307

Yeats, W. B. 265

Zis, G. 251, 265